D0982362

LENIN

COLLECTED WORKS

19

THE RUSSIAN EDITION WAS PRINTED
IN ACCORDANCE WITH A DECISION
OF THE NINTH CONGRESS OF THE R.C.P.(B.)
AND THE SECOND CONGRESS OF SOVIETS
OF THE U.S.S.R.

ИНСТИТУТ МАРКСИЗМА-ЛЕНИНИЗМА при ЦК КПСС

В. И. ЛЕНИН

СОЧИНЕНИЯ

Издание четвертое

ГОСУДАРСТВЕННОЕ ИЗДАТЕЛЬСТВО
ПОЛИТИЧЕСКОЙ ЛИТЕРАТУРЫ
МОСКВА

V. I. LENIN

COLLECTED WORKS

VOLUME
19
March-December 1913

PROGRESS PUBLISHERS

MOSCOW 1973

TRANSLATED FROM THE RUSSIAN BY THE LATE GEORGE HANNA
EDITED BY ROBERT DAGLISH

First printing 1963
Second printing 1968
Third printing 1973

Printed in the Union of Soviet Socialist Republics

CONTENTS

ILLUSTRATIONS

PREFACE

Volume Nineteen contains the works of Lenin written between March and December 1913, in the period of the new upsurge of the revolutionary movement in Russia. The greater part of the volume consists of articles published in the Bolshevik legal press—in the newspapers *Pravda* and *Nash Put* and the magazine *Prosveshcheniye*.

In the articles "The Three Sources and Three Component Parts of Marxism", "Twenty-Fifth Anniversary of the Death of Joseph Dietzgen", "Liberal and Marxist Conceptions of the Class Struggle" and "The Marx-Engels Correspondence", Lenin expounded and developed some basic problems of Marxist theory.

The articles "The National Programme of the R.S.D.L.P.", "The Working Class and the National Question" and others elaborate and substantiate the Bolshevik programme on the national question.

An important place in the volume is occupied by articles against the Menshevik liquidators, Trotskyists, Bundists[1] and Socialist-Revolutionaries,[2] all of which deal with questions of the struggle to consolidate the Bolshevik Party and the unity of the working class; among them are "Controversial Issues", "Working-Class Unity", "Has *Pravda* Given Proof of Bundist Separatism?", "There's a Trudovik for You" and the resolutions of the "Summer" Joint Conference of the Central Committee of the R.S.D.L.P. and Party officials held at Poronin.

In "May Day Action by the Revolutionary Proletariat", "The Results of Strikes in 1912 as Compared with Those of the Past", "The Role of Social Estates and Classes in the Liberation Movement", "Liberals as Defenders of the Fourth

Duma," Lenin dealt with the political crisis that was maturing in Russia on a nation-wide scale, showed the leading role of the proletariat in the growing revolutionary movement and exposed the counter-revolutionary liberal bourgeoisie.

The articles "Is the Condition of the Peasants Improving or Worsening?", "The Land Question and the Rural Poor" and "The Agrarian Question and the Present Situation in Russia" expose the impoverishment and ruin of the greater part of the peasantry as a result of Stolypin's agrarian policy and confront the Bolshevik Party and the working class with the task of drawing the peasantry into an active struggle against the autocracy.

The volume includes documents that characterise Lenin's leadership of the Bolshevik group in the Fourth State Duma—the draft speeches "The Question of Ministry of Education Policy", "The Question of the (General) Agrarian Policy of the Present Government", the articles "The Duma 'Seven'", "Material on the Conflict within the Social-Democratic Duma Group", and others.

There is also a group of articles—"Civilised Barbarism", "A Great Technical Achievement", "Armaments and Capitalism", "Who Stands to Gain?" "The Awakening of Asia", "Exposure of the British Opportunists"—devoted to world economics and politics. Lenin cited facts in these articles showing the decay of capitalism, the growth of armaments, the preparations for a world war and the awakening of the colonial peoples and criticised the growing opportunism in the international working-class movement.

Nine of the documents published in this volume appeared for the first time in the fourth Russian edition of the *Collected Works*. In his report on "Contemporary Russia and the Working-Class Movement" and in the articles "Conversation", "For the Attention of *Luch* and *Pravda* Readers", "A Discreditable Role", "The Working-Class Masses and the Working-Class Intelligentsia" and "The Question of Bureau Decisions", Lenin exposed the liquidators, who strove to destroy the illegal Social-Democratic Party, as out-and-out traitors to the working class. The article "The Split in the Russian Social-Democratic Duma Group" was written by Lenin for the international socialist press in

reply to the slander about the Bolshevik Party that was.
being spread by the liquidators and Trotskyists. In the
articles "The 'Oil Hunger'" and "An Incorrect Appraisal (*Luch*
on Maklakov)" Lenin revealed the counter-revolutionary role
of the Russian bourgeoisie and showed that they, in alliance
with the feudal landowners were hampering Russia's economic development.

ПРОСВѢЩЕНІЕ

Ежемѣсячный журналъ.

№ 3.

Мартъ.

СПБ. 1913 годъ.

Title page of the magazine *Prosveshcheniye* No. 3, March 1913; this issue contained Lenin's article "The Three Sources and Three Component Parts of Marxism"

Reduced

THE THREE SOURCES AND THREE COMPONENT PARTS OF MARXISM[3]

Throughout the civilised world the teachings of Marx evoke the utmost hostility and hatred of all bourgeois science (both official and liberal), which regards Marxism as a kind of "pernicious sect". And no other attitude is to be expected, for there can be no "impartial" social science in a society based on class struggle. In one way or another, *all* official and liberal science *defends* wage-slavery, whereas Marxism has declared relentless war on that slavery. To expect science to be impartial in a wage-slave society is as foolishly naïve as to expect impartiality from manufacturers on the question of whether workers' wages ought not to be increased by decreasing the profits of capital.

But this is not all. The history of philosophy and the history of social science show with perfect clarity that there is nothing resembling "sectarianism" in Marxism, in the sense of its being a hidebound, petrified doctrine, a doctrine which arose *away from* the high road of the development of world civilisation. On the contrary, the genius of Marx consists precisely in his having furnished answers to questions already raised by the foremost minds of mankind. His doctrine emerged as the direct and immediate *continuation* of the teachings of the greatest representatives of philosophy, political economy and socialism.

The Marxist doctrine is omnipotent because it is true. It is comprehensive and harmonious, and provides men with an integral world outlook irreconcilable with any form of superstition, reaction, or defence of bourgeois oppression. It is the legitimate successor to the best that man produced in the nineteenth century, as represented by German

philosophy, English political economy and French socialism.

It is these three sources of Marxism, which are also its
component parts that we shall outline in brief.

I

The philosophy of Marxism is *materialism*. Throughout
the modern history of Europe, and especially at the end of
the eighteenth century in France, where a resolute struggle
was conducted against every kind of medieval rubbish,
against serfdom in institutions and ideas, materialism has
proved to be the only philosophy that is consistent, true
to all the teachings of natural science and hostile to superstition, cant and so forth. The enemies of democracy have,
therefore, always exerted all their efforts to "refute", undermine and defame materialism, and have advocated various
forms of philosophical idealism, which always, in one way
or another, amounts to the defence or support of religion.

Marx and Engels defended philosophical materialism in
the most determined manner and repeatedly explained how
profoundly erroneous is every deviation from this basis.
Their views are most clearly and fully expounded in the
works of Engels, *Ludwig Feuerbach* and *Anti-Dühring*, which,
like the *Communist Manifesto*, are handbooks for every
class-conscious worker.

But Marx did not stop at eighteenth-century materialism:
he developed philosophy to a higher level. He enriched it
with the achievements of German classical philosophy, especially of Hegel's system, which in its turn had led to the
materialism of Feuerbach. The main achievement was *dialectics*, i.e., the doctrine of development in its fullest,
deepest and most comprehensive form, the doctrine of the
relativity of the human knowledge that provides us with a
reflection of eternally developing matter. The latest dis-
coveries of natural science—radium, electrons, the trans-
mutation of elements—have been a remarkable confirmation
of Marx's dialectical materialism despite the teachings
of the bourgeois philosophers with their "new" reversions
to old and decadent idealism.

Marx deepened and developed philosophical materialism to the full, and extended the cognition of nature to include the cognition of *human society*. His *historical materialism* was a great achievement in scientific thinking. The chaos and arbitrariness that had previously reigned in views on history and politics were replaced by a strikingly integral and harmonious scientific theory, which shows how, in consequence of the growth of productive forces, out of one system of social life another and higher system develops— how capitalism, for instance, grows out of feudalism.

Just as man's knowledge reflects nature (i.e., developing matter), which exists independently of him, so man's *social knowledge* (i.e., his various views and doctrines—philosophical, religious, political and so forth) reflects the *economic system* of society. Political institutions are a superstructure on the economic foundation. We see, for example, that the various political forms of the modern European states serve to strengthen the domination of the bourgeoisie over the proletariat.

Marx's philosophy is a consummate philosophical materialism which has provided mankind, and especially the working class, with powerful instruments of knowledge.

II

Having recognised that the economic system is the foundation on which the political superstructure is erected, Marx devoted his greatest attention to the study of this economic system. Marx's principal work, *Capital*, is devoted to a study of the economic system of modern, i.e., capitalist, society.

Classical political economy, before Marx, evolved in England, the most developed of the capitalist countries. Adam Smith and David Ricardo, by their investigations of the economic system, laid the foundations of the *labour theory of value*. Marx continued their work; he provided a proof of the theory and developed it consistently. He showed that the value of every commodity is determined by the quantity of socially necessary labour time spent on its production.

Where the bourgeois economists saw a relation between things (the exchange of one commodity for another) Marx revealed a *relation between people*. The exchange of commodities expresses the connection between individual producers through the market. *Money* signifies that the connection is becoming closer and closer, inseparably uniting the entire economic life of the individual producers into one whole. *Capital* signifies a further development of this connection: man's labour-power becomes a commodity. The wage-worker sells his labour-power to the owner of land, factories and instruments of labour. The worker spends one part of the day covering the cost of maintaining himself and his family (wages), while the other part of the day he works without remuneration, creating for the capitalist *surplus-value*, the source of profit, the source of the wealth of the capitalist class.

The doctrine of surplus-value is the corner-stone of Marx's economic theory.

Capital, created by the labour of the worker, crushes the worker, ruining small proprietors and creating an army of unemployed. In industry, the victory of large-scale production is immediately apparent, but the same phenomenon is also to be observed in agriculture, where the superiority of large-scale capitalist agriculture is enhanced, the use of machinery increases and the peasant economy, trapped by money-capital, declines and falls into ruin under the burden of its backward technique. The decline of small-scale production assumes different forms in agriculture, but the decline itself is an indisputable fact.

By destroying small-scale production, capital leads to an increase in productivity of labour and to the creation of a monopoly position for the associations of big capitalists. Production itself becomes more and more social—hundreds of thousands and millions of workers become bound together in a regular economic organism—but the product of this collective labour is appropriated by a handful of capitalists. Anarchy of production, crises, the furious chase after markets and the insecurity of existence of the mass of the population are intensified.

By increasing the dependence of the workers on capital, the capitalist system creates the great power of united labour.

Marx traced the development of capitalism from embryonic commodity economy, from simple exchange, to its highest forms, to large-scale production.

And the experience of all capitalist countries, old and new, year by year demonstrates clearly the truth of this Marxian doctrine to increasing numbers of workers.

Capitalism has triumphed all over the world, but this triumph is only the prelude to the triumph of labour over capital.

III

When feudalism was overthrown and *"free"* capitalist society appeared in the world, it at once became apparent that this freedom meant a new system of oppression and exploitation of the working people. Various socialist doctrines immediately emerged as a reflection of and protest against this oppression. Early socialism, however, was *utopian* socialism. It criticised capitalist society, it condemned and damned it, it dreamed of its destruction, it had visions of a better order and endeavoured to convince the rich of the immorality of exploitation.

But utopian socialism could not indicate the real solution. It could not explain the real nature of wage-slavery under capitalism, it could not reveal the laws of capitalist development, or show what *social force* is capable of becoming the creator of a new society.

Meanwhile, the stormy revolutions which everywhere in Europe, and especially in France, accompanied the fall of feudalism, of serfdom, more and more clearly revealed the *struggle of classes* as the basis and the driving force of all development.

Not a single victory of political freedom over the feudal class was won except against desperate resistance. Not a single capitalist country evolved on a more or less free and democratic basis except by a life-and-death struggle between the various classes of capitalist society.

The genius of Marx lies in his having been the first to deduce from this the lesson world history teaches and to apply that lesson consistently. The deduction he made is the doctrine of the *class struggle.*

People always have been the foolish victims of deception and self-deception in politics, and they always will be until they have learnt to seek out the *interests* of some class or other behind all moral, religious, political and social phrases, declarations and promises. Champions of reforms and improvements will always be fooled by the defenders of the old order until they realise that every old institution, however barbarous and rotten it may appear to be, is kept going by the forces of certain ruling classes. And there is *only one* way of smashing the resistance of those classes, and that is to find, in the very society which surrounds us, the forces which can—and, owing to their social position, *must*—constitute the power capable of sweeping away the old and creating the new, and to enlighten and organise those forces for the struggle.

Marx's philosophical materialism alone has shown the proletariat the way out of the spiritual slavery in which all oppressed classes have hitherto languished. Marx's economic theory alone has explained the true position of the proletariat in the general system of capitalism.

Independent organisations of the proletariat are multiplying all over the world, from America to Japan and from Sweden to South Africa. The proletariat is becoming enlightened and educated by waging its class struggle; it is ridding itself of the prejudices of bourgeois society; it is rallying its ranks ever more closely and is learning to gauge the measure of its successes; it is steeling its forces and is growing irresistibly.

Prosveshcheniye No. 3,   Published according to
     March 1913   the *Prosveshcheniye* text
     Signed: *V. I.*

BIG ACHIEVEMENT OF THE CHINESE REPUBLIC

We know that the great Chinese Republic, established at the cost of such sacrifice by progressive democrats among the Asian masses, recently encountered very grave financial difficulties. The six "Great" Powers, which are considered civilised nations, but which in reality follow the most reactionary policies, formed a financial consortium which suspended the granting of a loan to China.

The point is that the Chinese revolution did not evoke among the European bourgeoisie any enthusiasm for freedom and democracy—only the proletariat can entertain that feeling, which is alien to the knights of profit; it gave rise to the urge to *plunder* China, partition her and take away some of her territories. This "consortium" of the six Powers (Britain, France, Russia, Germany, Japan and the United States) was trying to make China bankrupt in order to weaken and undermine the republic.

The *collapse* of this reactionary consortium is a big success for the young republic, which enjoys the sympathy of the working masses the world over. The President of the United States has announced that his government will no longer support the consortium and will officially *recognise* the Republic of China in the near future. The American banks have now *left* the consortium, and America will give China much-needed financial support, opening the Chinese market to American capital and thereby facilitating the introduction of reforms in China.

Influenced by America, Japan has also changed her policy towards China. At first, Japan would not even allow Sun Yat-sen to enter the country. Now the visit has taken place, and all Japanese democrats enthusiastically welcome an alliance with republican China; the conclusion of that *alliance* is now on the order of the day. The Japanese bourgeoisie, like the American, has come to realise that it stands to profit more from a policy of peace with China than from a policy of plundering and partitioning the Chinese Republic.

The collapse of the robber consortium is, of course, a defeat of no mean importance for Russia's reactionary foreign policy.

Pravda No. 68, March 22, 1913
Signed: *W.*

Published according to
the *Pravda* text

OLD PROBLEMS
AND THE SENILE DECAY OF LIBERALISM

Deputy Shingaryov, one of the most prominent Cadets,[4] recently delivered a lecture in St. Petersburg on "The New Duma and Old Problems", a lively, interesting and topical subject.

As is the custom, our Cadet trounced the Octobrists.[5] "The Octobrists", he exclaimed, "hesitate to associate themselves with the Right wing and dare not associate with the Left" (*Rech*[6] No. 70). Our bold (bold, that is, before a democratic audience) Cadet apparently regards the Progressists as belonging to the "Left". But Mr. Shingaryov remained silent on the fact that three quarters of these closest friends and political comrades-in-arms of the Cadets are themselves Octobrists.

He wants democrats to regard the Cadets as "Lefts" *notwithstanding* the permanent and very close bloc that actually exists between the Cadets and the Progressists, who stand *half way* between the Cadets and the Octobrists! In other words—the Cadets are angling for the democrats although they are themselves actually held in captivity by the Progressists, who are notoriously *anti*-democratic.

"The torpor reminds one of the state of passengers in a train that has been held up at a wayside station," said Mr. Shingaryov, speaking of the Fourth Duma. "To shake off their torpor and get the train going the passengers would have to clear the way themselves. But to get the heavy legislative machine going, the strength of the passengers alone is not enough. There are three padlocks on our reforms—the law of June 3, the upper chamber and the fact that the executive authorities are not responsible. How these three padlocks will be opened, whether in peace and quietness or in some other way, history will show. Our contemporaries cannot remain absolute non-participants; they must all pull together" (*Rech* No. 70).

References to history are convenient! Mr. Shingaryov and the Cadets refer to history *in the same way* as those people about whom Marx said that they defend the whip because it is a historical whip.[7]

"History will," of course, "show *how* the padlocks will be opened"; that is an incontestable and fruitless truism. It is an excuse deriving from senile decay. A politician must be able to say *which* class owns the padlocks and *which* classes must open them and *by what means*.

"History will show" exactly what it showed seven and a half years ago—the fruitlessness of liberal reformism and liberal dreams of living in peace with the class that owns the "padlocks".

Pravda No. 71, March 26, 1913
Signed: *M.*

Published according to
the *Pravda* text

THE "OIL HUNGER"[8]

The question of the "oil hunger", the inordinate increase in the price of oil and the criminal conspiracy of the oil magnates for the purpose of fleecing the consumer, has aroused quite legitimate interest and quite understandable indignation in the Duma, and to a still greater degree outside the Duma.

The duel between the Minister of Commerce and Industry, who in a faintly disguised form *defended* the oil kings of the syndicate, and Mr. Markov the Second, who furiously and ardently expressed the hurt feelings of the noble feudal landowners—this duel (at the State Duma sitting on March 22) deserves the particular attention of the working class and all democrats. The duel throws a bright light on the relations as a whole that exist between the two "ruling" classes of Russia, the two so-called "higher" (but actually very low, despicable, plundering) classes, the class of feudal landowners and the class of financial tycoons.

It would seem at first glance that the question of the oil syndicate is an isolated one. But that is not so. Actually it is only a manifestation of the general and fundamental question of the government of Russia (or rather the plunder of Russia) by the two commanding classes. The speech by Markov the Second was a magnificent reply to the defender of the oil "kings" given from the standpoint of a *diehard*[9] who was cheated when the prey was divided. No wonder Mr. Markov the Second could not "behold himself", could not look at himself (and his landowning friends) in the mirror at the time of his speech. I shall try to do Mr. Markov the Second a service—I will place a mirror in front of him. I will draw him a portrait of himself. I will show that the "quarrel" between Markov the Second and Khvostov, on the one hand and the oil kings, the tycoons of the kerosene syndicate, the millionaires of Baku, on the other, is a *domestic* quarrel, a quarrel between *two* plunderers of the people's property. "The falling-out of lovers is the renewing of love." The Minister and Messrs. Nobel & Co., on the one hand, and Messrs. Khvostov, Markov and their friends in the Senate,[10] the Council of State, etc., on the other, are "*lovers*". But the tens of millions of workers and ruined peasants of Russia get a rough deal from this sweet and loving lot!

What lies at the bottom of the oil question?

First of all it is the shameless inflation of oil prices by the oil kings accompanied by the artificial *curtailment* of oil-well and refinery productivity by these "knights" of capitalist profit.

The chief figures illustrating these points have been quoted in the Duma, but I must repeat them in brief to make my further exposition quite clear. The price of oil was six kopeks a pood* in 1902. By 1904 it had risen to fourteen kopeks. Then the price "race" became all the merrier and, after the Revolution of 1905, the price of a pood of oil rose to twenty-one kopeks in 1908-09 and to *thirty-eight kopeks* in 1912.

Thus the price has increased *more than sixfold* in ten years! In the same period the extraction of oil has *decreased* from 600-700 million poods in 1900-02 to 500-585 million poods in 1908-12.

These figures are worth remembering. They deserve some thought. A reduction of output in a decade of tremendous upward leaps in world production, accompanied by *a more than sixfold* price increase.

The Minister of Commerce and Industry put forward unbelievably weak arguments in defence of these merchants and industrialists who are acting in collusion.

"There is an increased demand for fuel," he said. "There is an increased demand for oil from the automobile and aircraft industry." And he comforted us and the Russian people by saying that it is a "world-wide" phenomenon.

---

* Pood=36.11 lbs.—*Ed.*

"What about America?" we ask. This is a question that arises naturally because everybody knows that America is Russia's only serious competitor in oil production. In 1900 Russia and America together produced over nine-tenths of the world's oil and in 1910 they produced over eight-tenths. If it is a matter of a "world-wide" phenomenon, Mr. Minister, *the same* must also be true of America? In order to create an *impression* on inattentive listeners, the Minister, when defending the conspiring oil plunderers, quoted figures for America ... *but only for two years!* During the two past years the price of oil in America, and in Rumania, too, has doubled.

Very good, Mr. Minister! Why not make your comparison complete? If you want to draw comparisons do so properly. Don't play with figures. You must take the figures for America *for the same period* as that for which the figures for Russia have been given. Surely it must be obvious that this is the most fundamental, the most elementary condition, the very ABC of every conscientious application of statistics!

In Russia in ten years prices have increased *more than sixfold* as compared with the lowest price, that of 1902, quoted by the Minister himself. And in America? Nothing like *such* a rise in prices has occurred. Between 1900 and 1910 the price in America *was reduced.* During recent years it has remained firm.

What, then, is the result? The price has been doubled in America and *increased sixfold* in Russia. In 1900 the output of oil in America was *less* than in Russia and in 1910 it was *three times greater* than in Russia!

This is something the Minister, in his clumsy defence of the oil millionaires' conspiracy, did not want to say. The fact is there, however. Whatever figures you take, there can be no doubt that the rise in prices in America for the past ten years has been *incomparably smaller* than in Russia, while the output has increased *tremendously* at a time of disgraceful stagnation or even a step backward in Russia.

We see immediately how little truth and how much untruth there is in our Minister's reference to the "world-wide" phenomenon of price increase. Yes, there are higher prices everywhere. Yes, there are the causes, common to all capitalism, that give rise to it.

The situation is *intolerable* in Russia, however, because in our country it is on oil that the price increase is immeasurably greater, and because in the oil industry we have stagnation instead of increased output. The situation is *absolutely intolerable* in Russia because we see, instead of a broad, free and rapid development of capitalism, stagnation and decay. High prices are therefore a hundred times more malignant in Russia.

Russia has a population of 170,000,000 and America 90,000,000, i.e., a little more than half. America now extracts *three times* more oil than we do and *eighteen times* more coal. Judging by the wages of the workers, living standards in America are *four times* higher than in Russia.

Is it not clear that the Minister's statement to the effect that the evil is a world-wide phenomenon contains a glaring untruth? The evil bears four times, if not ten times, *more heavily* on Russia.

Written not earlier than
March 26 (April 8), 1913

First published in *Pravda* No. 21,   Published according to
January 21, 1940   the manuscript

THE CADET ASSEMBLY BILL

Among the bills on civil liberties submitted to the Duma by the Cadets there is one on assembly.

The Cadets consider themselves a democratic party. They must realise that an assembly bill submitted to the Fourth Duma has a purely propaganda value, i.e., that the purpose of its submission to the house is the propaganda, dissemination and explanation of the principles of freedom of assembly.

It is from this point of view that the Cadet bill must be appraised—will it help *explain* to the population of Russia the significance of freedom of assembly, the importance of that freedom and the conditions under which it can be achieved?

It will not. The bill has been drawn up by liberal civil servants, *not* by democrats. It contains a mass of absurd, bureaucratic rules, but not what is needed from the standpoint of democracy.

Meetings are forbidden on railway lines (§ 3) or within a distance of one verst* of the building where the State Duma is in session, etc. (§ 4); a preliminary announcement is required in towns but not in villages (§§ 6 and 7), and so on—what is all this? What is the need for all this miserable, ridiculous, pitiful bureaucratic nonsense?

It has all been copied from European *counter-revolutionary* laws, every bit of it reeks of periods when democracy was under suspicion or suppressed, and it is all hopelessly out of date. It is in the towns, for example, that public meetings are announced in the newspapers—so why this idiotic fuss

---

* Verst =0.66 miles.—*Ed.*

about "announcements"? For the sole reason that the Cadets
want to show the powers that be that they, the Cadets, have
a "statesmanly" point of view, that they are "people of law
and order" (i.e., enemies of democracy), and that they are
"also able to appreciate" civil service pettifoggery.

There is nothing important or serious in the bill as far as
present-day democracy is concerned. What the masses need
are premises in which to hold meetings. We need a *law*
to the effect that, on the demand of, say, a definite small
number of citizens, *all* public buildings, schools, etc., *must*
be made available to the people for meetings, free and un-
hindered, in the evenings and, in general, in non-working
hours. This is done in France, and there can be no other
obstacles to this democratic custom than the barbarity of
the Purishkeviches.

The fact of the matter is that the whole spirit of the Cadet
bill on civil liberties, its whole content, is *not* democratic
but liberal bureaucratic.

Pravda No. 72, March 27, 1913   Published according to
                                                         the *Pravda* text

THE BALKAN WAR AND BOURGEOIS CHAUVINISM

The Balkan War is coming to an end. The capture of Adrianople is a conclusive victory for the Bulgarians, and the problem's centre of gravity has shifted from the theatre of operations to that of the squabbles and intrigues of the so-called Great Powers.

The Balkan War is one link in the chain of world events marking the collapse of the medieval state of affairs in Asia and East Europe. To form united national states in the Balkans, shake off the oppression of the local feudal rules and completely liberate the Balkan peasants of all nationalities from the yoke of the landowners—such was the historic task confronting the Balkan peoples.

The Balkan peoples could have carried out this task ten times more easily than they are doing now and with a hundred times fewer sacrifices by forming a Federative Balkan Republic. National oppression, national bickering and incitement on the ground of religious differences would have been impossible under complete and consistent democracy. The Balkan peoples would have been assured of truly rapid, extensive and free development.

What was the real historical reason for settling urgent Balkan problems by means of a war, a war guided by bourgeois and dynastic interests? The chief cause was the weakness of the proletariat in the Balkans, and also the reactionary influence and pressure of the powerful European bourgeoisie. They are afraid of real freedom both in their own countries and in the Balkans; their only aim is profit at other people's expense; they stir up chauvinism and national enmity to facilitate their policy of plunder and to impede the free development of the oppressed classes of the Balkans.

Russian chauvinism over the Balkan events is no less disgusting than that of Europe. And the concealed, prettified chauvinism of the Cadets, coloured with liberal phrases, is more disgusting and more harmful than the crude chauvinism of the Black-Hundred newspapers. Those newspapers openly attack Austria—in that most backward of European countries the peoples (say we in parenthesis) are ensured far greater liberty than in Russia. The Cadet *Rech*, however, said on the occasion of the capture of Adrianople: "The new circumstances give Russian diplomacy every opportunity of showing greater firmness...."

Fine "democrats", who pretend not to understand that the only firmness that can be spoken of here is firmness in the pursuit of chauvinist aims! No wonder Milyukov and Yefremov, Guchkov, Bennigsen, Krupensky and Balashov got on well together at a dinner given by Rodzyanko on March 14. Nationalists, Octobrists, Cadets—these are but different shades of the disgusting bourgeois nationalism and chauvinism that are irrevocably hostile to liberty.

Pravda No. 74, March 29, 1913·   Published according to
Signed: *V. I.*   the *Pravda* text

First page of the manuscript of Lenin's "Conversation".
March-April 1913

Reduced

CONVERSATION

First Bystander. I am following, as closely as 'I can, the struggle among the workers over "the six and the seven".[11] I try to follow both newspapers. I compare, as far as possible, the repercussions in the bourgeois and Black-Hundred newspapers.... And d'you know what I think? It seems to me that the struggle is taking grave forms, that it is degenerating into squabbles and bickerings, and that the result will, in any case, be tremendous demoralisation.

Second Bystander. I don't understand you. Whoever heard of a struggle anywhere that did *not* become grave if it was over something really serious? It is because the struggle is over a serious problem that it cannot stop at "a slight quarrel". Those who are used to denying, and who continue to deny, the principles of party organisation will not surrender without the most desperate resistance. Desperate resistance always and everywhere engenders "grave forms of struggle", engenders *attempts* to shift the dispute from the sphere of principles to that of squabbles. What if it does? Because of that do you want us to reject the struggle for the fundamental principles of party organisation?

First Bystander. You are wandering away a bit from the question I raised and are in too much of a hurry to "go over to the offensive". Every workers' group on both sides is in a hurry to "dash off" a resolution, and there is something almost like competition developing between them to see who can outdo the other in the use of strong language. So much vituperation makes the working-class press repulsive to large numbers of working people who are seeking the light of socialism and who, perhaps, throw down the newspaper with a feeling of confusion, or even a feeling of shame for socialism.... They may even be disappointed in socialism for a long time. A slanging match creates a sort of *"un-natural selection"* that brings the "fist-fight specialists" to the fore.... Prowess in abusing one's opponent is encouraged on both sides. Is *this* the sort of education the socialist party should give the proletariat? Does this not turn out to be approval of, or at least connivance at, opportunism, since opportunism is the sacrifice of the *basic* interests of the working-class movement to momentary success. The basic interests of the working-class movement are being sacrificed to momentary success by both sides.... Instead of experiencing the joy of socialist work, of being inspired by it and showing a serious attitude towards it, the socialists themselves are driving the masses away from socialism. Willy-nilly, those bitter words come to mind—the proletariat will achieve socialism *despite* the socialists.

Second Bystander. We are both outsiders, that is, neither of us is a direct participant in the struggle. But bystanders who are trying to understand what is happening before their eyes may react to the struggle in two ways. Looking on from the outside, one may see only what one might call the outward aspect of the struggle; speaking figuratively, one may see only clenched fists, distorted faces and ugly scenes; one may condemn it all, one may weep and wail on account of it. But one can also, looking on from the outside, understand the *meaning* of the struggle that is going on, which is slightly, if you will excuse my saying so, more interesting and historically more significant than the scenes and pictures of the so-called excesses or extremes of the struggle. There can be no struggle without enthusiasm and no enthusiasm without extremes; and as far as I'm concerned I hate most of all people who focus their attention on "extremes" in the struggle of classes, parties and factions. I always get the impulse—pardon me again—to shout at those people: "I don't care if you drink, as long as you understand what you are doing."[12]

And this is about something big, historically big. A working-class party is being built up. Workers' independence, the influence of the workers on *their own* parliamentary group, decisions by the workers themselves on questions of their own party—such is the great historical significance of what is going on; the mere wish is becoming *fact* before our very eyes. You are afraid of "extremes" and you regret them, but I watch in admiration a struggle that is actually making the working class of Russia more mature and adult, and I am mad about one thing only—that I am a bystander, that I cannot plunge into the midst of that struggle....

First Bystander. And into the midst of the "extremes", eh? And if the "extremes" lead to the fabrication of resolutions will you also proclaim "hatred" for the people who draw attention to it, who are indignant about it and who demand that such things should be stopped at all costs?

Second Bystander. Don't try to frighten me, please! You won't frighten me, anyway! You really are getting like those people who are ready to condemn publicity because of some false information that has been published. I remember once in *Pravda*[13] a report of the political dishonesty of a certain Social-Democrat was published; some time afterwards the report was refuted. I can well imagine what that Social-Democrat's feelings must have been in the period between publication and refutal! But publicity is a sword that itself heals the wounds it makes. There will be fabrication of resolutions, you say? The falsifiers will be exposed and thrown out, that's all. Serious battles are not staged without a field hospital somewhere nearby. But to allow yourself to be scared, or your nerves shattered by "field hospital" scenes is something unpardonable. If you're scared of wolves, keep out of the forest.

As to opportunism, that is, ignoring the basic aims of socialism, you're putting the blame on the wrong side. According to you, those basic aims are some "angelic ideal" that has nothing to do with the "sinful" struggle for the cause of the day, for the urgent matters of the moment. To look on matters that way is simply to turn socialism into a sweet phrase, into saccharine sentimentalising. Every struggle for every matter of the moment must be *intimately connected* with basic aims. It is only this understanding of the historical meaning of the struggle that makes it possible, by deepening and sharpening it, to get rid of that negative side, that "prowess", that "fist-fighting" which is inevitable wherever there is a crowd making a noise, shouting and shoving, but which disappears of itself.

You speak of a socialist party educating the proletariat. In the present struggle *the very* question at issue is that of defending the *basic* principles of party life. The question of *what* policy *it* wants conducted in the Duma, what attitude *it* has to an open party or an underground one, and whether it considers the Duma group to be *above* the party or vice versa, is confronting every workers' study circle starkly, in a form that demands an immediate and direct answer. This, indeed, is the ABC of party existence, it is a question of whether the party is to be or not to be.

Socialism is not a ready-made system that will be mankind's benefactor. Socialism is the class struggle of the present-day proletariat as it advances from one objective today to another objective tomorrow *for the sake* of its basic objective, to which it is *coming nearer* every day. In this country called Russia, socialism is today passing through the stage in which the politically conscious workers are themselves completing the organisation of a working-class party despite the attempts of the liberal intelligentsia and the "Duma Social-Democratic intelligentsia" *to prevent* that work of organisation.

The liquidators are *out to prevent* the workers from building up their own working-class party—that is the meaning and significance of the struggle between "the six and the seven". They cannot, however, prevent it. The struggle is a hard one, but the workers' success is assured. Let the weak and the frightened waver on account of the "extremes" of the struggle—tomorrow they will see for themselves that not a step further could have been taken without going through this struggle.

Written in March-April 1913

First published May 5, 1932
in *Pravda* No. 123
Signed: *K—v*

Published according to
the manuscript

CONTEMPORARY RUSSIA
AND THE WORKING-CLASS MOVEMENT[14]

A NEWSPAPER REPORT

A few days ago in Cracow a report was delivered by Comrade Lenin, one of the most outstanding leaders of the Russian Social-Democrats. Here follows a brief outline of the report; for the information of our Galician readers we must add that Lenin is the leader of the so-called "Bolshevik" trend, that is, the more radical, implacable trend in the Russian Social-Democratic Party.

While describing the working-class movement in Russia, the speaker noted its great importance to the Western countries as well, since there was no doubt that in the period of socialist revolutions events there would resemble those that had taken place in Russia. As an example, the speaker mentioned the sudden transition from relative calm to the emergence of mass movements. In 1895 the number of strikers in Russia had been only 40,000 whereas in 1905 there had been 400,000 striking workers in January alone; in the course of the whole year the figure had increased to three million.

The present political situation in Russia had come about as a result of revolutionary experience, as a result of the class battles that had taken place at that time. A certain Japanese had called the Russian revolution "an impotent revolution under an incompetent government". The government, however, had made full use of the experience of the revolution. It would suffice to mention the attitude of the government to the peasantry. At first, when the law governing the elections to the First Duma had been drawn up, the government had placed great hopes in the peasantry as a quiet, patriarchal element. But when it turned out that the

Russian peasant, fighting for land, is by nature, not a so-cialist indeed, as some Narodnik utopians had thought, but, at any rate, a democrat, the government made a *volte-face* and changed the election law.[15]

The present Duma, he said, was no plaything, but an actual organ of power of the reactionary strata, the tsarist bureaucracy allied to the feudal landowners and the top bourgeoisie.

What had been the role of the Russian liberals? In the First and Second Dumas the liberals had tried to pacify the peasants, to divert them from the revolutionary to the so-called constitutional path. It was obvious, however, that the purchase of part of the landed estates, proposed by the Cadets, was only a fresh attempt to plunder and deceive the Russian peasant. This attempt had failed mainly owing to the tactics of the Social-Democrats in the Duma, who had been persistently urging the peasants leftward.

The October strike had been a turning-point in Russian liberalism. Before the revolution the liberals had said that "the revolution must become the ruling power" (Struve), but they later changed their tone, allegedly in fear of the excesses of the revolution although they knew perfectly well that the only "excesses" were those of the government. The Octobrists departed from liberalism and went over directly to the side of the government, serving the government as its lackeys. It was at that time that Guchkov, leader of the Octobrists, had written to Prince Trubetskoi that further revolutionary explosions menaced the very well-being of the bourgeoisie.

Such was the class basis of contemporary counter-revolu-tion. Acts of lawlessness were committed quite openly and the class character of the government had been exposed. The government handed out praise and medals for lawless acts against revolutionary elements. The speaker gave an exam-ple: during the recent search of Deputy Petrovsky's apart-ment the police, in violation of the law, had locked him in a room, and when a question was asked about it in the Duma, the Minister said that they should be grateful to the police for such zeal.

Stolypin had learned from the experience of class battles during the revolution and had launched his notorious agrarian policy of stratifying the peasants into affluent petty bourgeois and semi-proletarian elements. This new policy was a mockery of the old "patriarchal slogans" of Katkov and Pobedonostsev.[16] The government, however, could not have acted otherwise.

The government, therefore, relied on the landowners and the terrified bourgeoisie in introducing the present counter-revolutionary system. It was true that the "united no-bility"[17] had tried to get the Duma disbanded as far back as 1906, but the government had then waited before making the coup, expecting results from its agrarian policy in respect of the peasants and changes in the psychology of a bourgeoisie terrified by the revolution.

This counter-revolutionary system had now *played itself out*, had exhausted its social forces. Circumstances had arisen that made any social reforms in contemporary Russia impossible. The Duma was concerned with trivialities; if it did adopt any decision, the Council of State and the Court annulled it or changed it beyond all recognition. *There were no possibilities of effecting reforms in contemporary Russia.* This made clear the demagogy of Cadet tactics in submitting to the Duma various "bills of principle" for all kinds of liberties; they introduced them because they knew that the Duma could under no circumstances adopt them. "We have a constitution, thank God!" Milyukov had exclaimed. There could not be any reforms under the existing social system although Russia's internal situation was pitiful and her backwardness, even as compared with Asia, was obvious. Even the Octobrist press had said "it is impossible to go on living like this any longer".

All this made clear the tasks of a proletariat *faced with another revolution*. The mood was rising. In 1910 the number of strikers, according to official statistics, had been only 40,000, but in 1912 it had been 680,000, of which 500,000 had taken part in political strikes.

This made clear the tactics of the Russian Social-Democrats. They would have to strengthen their organisation, their press, etc.; that was the ABC of socialist tactics long since elaborated in the West, especially by the German Social-Democrats. The primary task of the R.S.D.L.P., however, was to train the masses *for democratic revolution.*

This task was no longer on the order of the day in the West; theirs was an altogether different task, that of mobilisation, of mustering the masses and training and organising them for the abolition of the capitalist system.

If attention were concentrated on the question of the approaching revolution in Russia and on the tasks of the Social-Democrats in that revolution, the essence of the dispute with those known as "liquidators" among the Russian Social-Democrats would be understood. Liquidationism was not the invention of a section of the Russian Social-Democrats; the first liquidators were the "Narodniks", who in 1906 published their slogans in the magazine *Russkoye Bogatstvo*[18]—down with the underground movement, down with the republic! The liquidators wanted to abolish the illegal party and organise an open party. That was ridiculous, especially if we bear in mind that even the Progressists (a mixture of Octobrists and Cadets) dared not ask to be legalised. Under such circumstances the liquidators' slogans were downright treachery. It stood to reason that an illegal party should take advantage of all legal opportunities—the press, the Duma, even the insurance law[19]—but only for the purpose of extending agitation and organisation; the substance of the agitation must remain revolutionary. *There must be a struggle against the illusion that there was a constitution in Russia, and reformist slogans should be counterposed by the slogan of revolution, of a republic!*

Such was the content of Comrade Lenin's report. One of those present asked him about his attitude to the national question; the speaker said that the Russian Social-Democratic Party recognised in full the right of every nation to "self-determination", to decide its own fate, even to secede from Russia. The Russian revolution and the cause of democracy were not in any way connected (as was the case in Germany) with the cause of unification, centralisation. The democratisation of Russia depended not on the national but on the agrarian question.

At the same time Comrade Lenin stressed the necessity for full unity throughout the revolutionary army of the proletariat of different nationalities in the struggle for the full democratisation of the country. Only on that basis could the national question be solved, as in America, Belgium and Switzerland. The speaker dealt polemically with Renner's theses on the national question and came out sharply against the slogan of cultural-national autonomy. There were people in Russia who maintained that Russia's further development would follow the Austrian path, a path that was slow and rotten. But, said the speaker, we must beware of any national struggle within Social-Democracy because it would militate against the great task of revolutionary struggle; in that respect the national struggle in Austria should be a warning to us.[20] The Caucasian Social-Democrats should be a model for Russia; they conducted propaganda simultaneously in the Georgian, Armenian Tatar and Russian languages.[21]

Published April 22, 1913
in the newspaper *Naprzód* No. 92

First published in Russian
in the fourth Russian edition
of V. I. Lenin's *Collected Works*

Published according
the *Naprzód* text

EDUCATED DEPUTIES

At the evening sitting on April 2, the Octobrist L. G. Lyuts said, when objecting to the working-class deputies' demand for a discussion of the question asked about the Lena events[22]:

"Two days from now will be the anniversary of the events on the Lena. Apparently the Social-Democrats are trying to *budirovat* the feelings of the workers in order to encourage excesses...."

The French word *bouder*, rendered in Russian by *budirovat* means *to sulk, to pout*. Mr. Lyuts, apparently, derives *budirovat* from *budorazhit* (excite) or, perhaps, *vozbudit* (incite). How the bourgeois deputies and the bourgeois press laughed when a peasant in the First Duma used the foreign word "prerogatives" in the sense of barriers (*"rogatki"* in Russ.—*Ed.*)! The mistake was all the more pardonable since various prerogatives enjoyed by the ruling classes are actually barriers in Russian life. Mr. Lyuts' educational attainments, however, did not *"vozbudirovat"* the laughter of his educated friends or their press.

Pravda No. 83, April 10, 1913
Signed: *B*.

Published according to
the *Pravda* text

"WHO STANDS TO GAIN?"

There is a Latin tag *cui prodest*? meaning "who stands to gain?" When it is not immediately apparent which political or social groups, forces or alignments advocate certain proposals, measures, etc., one should always ask: "Who stands to gain?"

It is not important *who* directly advocates a particular policy, since under the present noble system of capitalism any money-bag can always "hire", buy or enlist any number of lawyers, writers and even parliamentary deputies, professors, parsons and the like to defend any views. We live in an age of commerce, when the bourgeoisie have no scruples about trading in honour or conscience. There are also simpletons who out of stupidity or by force of habit defend views prevalent in certain bourgeois circles.

Yes, indeed! In politics it is not so important *who* directly advocates particular views. What is important is *who stands to gain* from these views, proposals, measures.

For instance, "Europe", the states that call themselves "civilised", are now engaged in a mad armaments hurdle-race. In thousands of ways, in thousands of newspapers, from thousands of pulpits, they shout and clamour about patriotism, culture, native land, peace, and progress—and all in order to justify new expenditures of tens and hundreds of millions of rubles for all manner of weapons of destruction—for guns, dreadnoughts, etc.

"Ladies and gentlemen," one feels like saying about all these phrases mouthed by patriots, so-called. "Put no faith in phrase-mongering, it is better to see *who stands to gain*!"

A short while ago the renowned British firm Armstrong, Whitworth & Co. published its annual balance-sheet. The firm is engaged mainly in the manufacture of armaments of various kinds. A profit was shown of £ 877,000, *about 8 million rubles*, and a dividend of *12.5 per cent* was declared! About 900,000 rubles were set aside as reserve capital, and so on and so forth.

That's where the millions and milliards squeezed out of the workers and peasants for armaments go. Dividends of 12.5 per cent mean that capital is *doubled* in 8 years. And this is in addition to all kinds of fees to directors, etc. Armstrong in Britain, Krupp in Germany, Creusot in France, Cockerill in Belgium—how many of them are there in all the "civilised" countries? And the countless host of contractors?

These are the ones *who stand to gain* from the whipping up of chauvinism, from the chatter about "patriotism" (cannon patriotism), about the defence of culture (with weapons destructive of culture) and so forth!

Pravda No. 84, April 11, 1913   Published according to
       Signed: *V.*   the *Pravda* text

IN BRITAIN

(THE SAD RESULTS OF OPPORTUNISM)

The British Labour Party, which must be distinguished from the *two* socialist parties in Britain, the British Socialist Party and the Independent Labour Party, is the workers' organisation that is most opportunist and soaked in the spirit of liberal-labour policy.

In Britain there is full political liberty and the socialist parties exist quite openly. But the Labour Party is the parliamentary representative of workers' organisations, of which some are non-political, and others liberal, a regular mixture of the kind our liquidators want, those who hurl so much abuse at the "underground".

The opportunism of the British Labour Party is to be explained by the specific historical conditions of the latter half of the nineteenth century in Britain, when the "aristocracy of labour" shared to some extent in the particularly high profits of British capital. Now these conditions are becoming a thing of the past. Even the Independent Labour Party, i.e., the *socialist* opportunists in Britain, realises that the Labour Party has landed in a morass.

In the last issue of *The Labour Leader*, the organ of the Independent Labour Party, we find the following edifying communication. Naval estimates are being discussed in the British Parliament. The socialists introduce a motion to *reduce* them. The bourgeoisie, of course, quash it by voting *for* the government.

And the Labour M.P.s?

Fifteen vote for the reduction, i.e., against the government; 21 *are absent*; 4 vote *for the government*, i.e., against the reduction!

Two of the four try to justify their action on the grounds that the workers in their constituencies earn their living in the armament industries.

There you have a striking example of how opportunism leads to the *betrayal* of socialism, the *betrayal* of the workers' cause. As we have already indicated, condemnation of this treachery is spreading ever wider among British socialists. From the example of other people's mistakes, the Russian workers, too, should learn to understand how fatal are opportunism and liberal-labour policy.

Pravda No. 85, April 12, 1913   Published according to
        Signed: *W*.   the *Pravda* text

CIVILISED EUROPEANS AND SAVAGE ASIANS

The well-known English Social-Democrat, Rothstein, relates in the German labour press an instructive and typical
incident that occurred in British India. This incident reveals better than all arguments why the revolution is growing apace in that country with its more than 300 million
inhabitants.

Arnold, a British journalist, who brings out a newspaper
in Rangoon, a large town (with over 200,000 inhabitants)
in one of the Indian provinces, published an article entitled: "A Mockery of British Justice". It exposed a local
British judge named Andrew. For publishing this article
Arnold was sentenced to twelve months' imprisonment,
but he appealed and, having connections in London, was
able to get the case before the highest court in Britain. The
Government of India hastily "reduced" the sentence to four
months and Arnold was released.

What was all the fuss about?

A British colonel named McCormick had a mistress whose
servant was a little eleven-year-old Indian girl, named Aina.
This gallant representative of a civilised nation had en-
ticed Aina to his room, raped her and locked her up in his
house.

It so happened that Aina's father was dying and he sent
for his daughter. It was then that the village where he lived
learned the whole story. The population seethed with indignation. The police were compelled to order McCormick's
arrest.

But Judge Andrew released him on bail, and later acquitted him, following a disgraceful travesty of justice. The
gallant colonel declared, as gentlemen of noble extraction

usually do under such circumstances, that Aina was a prostitute, in proof of which he brought five witnesses. Eight witnesses, however, brought by Aina's mother were not even examined by Judge Andrew.

When the journalist Arnold was tried for libel, the President of the Court, Sir ("His Worship") Charles Fox, refused to allow him to call witnesses in his defence.

It must be clear to everyone that thousands and millions of such cases occur in India. Only absolutely exceptional circumstances enabled the "libeller" Arnold (the son of an influential London journalist) to get out of prison and secure publicity for the case.

Do not forget that the British Liberals put their "best" people at the head of the Indian administration. Not long ago the Viceroy of India, the chief of the McCormicks, Andrews and Foxes, was John Morley, the well-known radical author, a "luminary of European learning", a "most honourable man" in the eyes of all European and Russian liberals.

The *"European"* spirit has already awakened in Asia, the peoples of Asia have become democratic-minded.

Pravda No. 87, April 14, 1913   Published according to
          Signed: *W.*   the *Pravda* text

MERCHANT ACCOUNTANCY

The biggest millionaires, the tycoons of our big industry, belong to a "council of congresses of industrial and commercial representatives". This council of congresses issues its own periodical, *Promyshlennost i Torgovlya*.[23] The interests of our Kit Kityches[24] are defended by this journal in its ponderous, elaborate and mostly semi-literate articles.

They show particular discontent at the injustice of Zemstvo representation and Zemstvo taxation. Believe it or not, the feudal landowner is unfair to poor Kit Kitych! Here is an instructive table showing the composition of the elected membership at uyezd Zemstvo assemblies[25] (*Promyshlennost i Torgovlya*, 1913, No. 3):

	Number of members	Percentages
From the First Electoral Assembly (landed nobility)	5,508	53.4
From the Second Electoral Assembly (commercial and industrial enterprises, etc.)	1,294	12.6
Jointly from the First and Second Assemblies	290	2.8
From village communes	3,216	31.2
In 34 gubernias with Zemstvos	10,308	100.0

There is indeed a crying injustice in the matter of representation in the Zemstvos. The conclusion to be drawn is obvious and incontestable—the Zemstvos in Russia have been put entirely into the hands of the feudal landowners.

These interesting figures must give any educated person cause to ponder over the conditions that give rise to such unequal representation.

It would, of course, be ridiculous to expect the Kit Kityches and their hack writers to be capable of pondering over
general political questions or to be interested in political
knowledge. The only thing that interests Kit Kitych is that
he pays "a lot" and a member of the nobility pays "little".
The writer hired by Kit Kitych quotes the total amounts
of Zemstvo impositions (as fixed by the official scale)—
First Electoral Assembly (24.5 million rubles in 34 gubernias with Zemstvos), Second Electoral Assembly (49 million rubles) and village communes (45.5 million rubles).
He divides these impositions by the number of members
and in this way determines "the cost of one seat"! Thus it
turns out that a seat for a nobleman "costs" 4,500 rubles, for
a merchant 38,000 rubles and for a peasant 14,000 rubles.

That is how the hired advocates of the merchant class argue—election rights are calmly examined as though they
were an article of commerce. As though those who pay the
impositions fixed by the Zemstvo thereby *purchase* the
right to representation.

Of course, there actually is glaring inequality in Zemstvo
impositions. The full burden of that inequality, however,
is not borne by the industrialists, but by the *peasants* and
workers. If the peasantry pay 45.5 million rubles that they
squeeze out of their poor, exhausted, over-cultivated land
while the landowners pay 24.5 million rubles, that can mean
nothing but the extortion of millions of rubles *tribute* from
the "muzhiks" in the form of Zemstvo impositions in
addition to all their other burdens.

This the Kit Kityches do not see. What they are after
is that privileges, instead of going to the nobility alone,
should be shared "on an equal footing" with the merchants.

Pravda No. 90, April 20, 1913   Published according to
Signed: *V. F.*   the *Pravda* text

A GREAT TECHNICAL ACHIEVEMENT

The world-famous British chemist, William Ramsay, has discovered a method of obtaining gas directly from a coal seam. Ramsay is already negotiating with a colliery owner on the practical application of this method.

A great modern technical problem is thus approaching solution. The revolution that will be effected by this solution will be a tremendous one.

At the present time, to utilise the energy contained in it, coal is transported all over the country and burned in numerous factories and homes.

Ramsay's discovery means a gigantic technical revolution in this, perhaps the most important, branch of production in capitalist countries.

Ramsay has discovered a method of transforming coal into gas right where the coal lies, without hauling it to the surface. A similar but much simpler method is sometimes used in the mining of salt: it is not brought to the surface directly, but is dissolved in water, the solution being pumped to the top.

Ramsay's method is to transform, as it were, the coal mines into enormous distilling apparatuses for the production of gas. Gas is used to drive gas engines which can extract *twice as much* energy from coal as steam-engines can. Gas engines, in their turn, transform the energy into electricity, which modern technology can already transmit over enormous distances.

Such a technical revolution would reduce the cost of electricity to *one-fifth* or even *one-tenth* of its present price. An enormous amount of human labour now spent in extracting and distributing coal would be saved. It would be possible to use even the poorest seams, now not being work-ed. The cost of lighting and heating houses would be greatly reduced.

This discovery will bring about an enormous revolution in industry.

But the consequences this revolution will have for social life as a whole under the present capitalist system will be quite different from those the discovery would yield under socialism.

Under capitalism the "release" of the labour of millions of miners engaged in extracting coal will inevitably cause mass unemployment, an enormous increase in poverty, and a worsening of the workers' conditions. And the profits of this great invention will be pocketed by the Morgans, Rockefellers, Ryabushinskys, Morozovs, and their suites of lawyers, directors, professors, and other flunkeys of capital.

Under socialism the application of Ramsay's method, which will "release" the labour of millions of miners, etc., will make it possible immediately to shorten the working day *for all* from 8 hours to, say, 7 hours and even less. The "elec-trification" of all factories and railways will make working conditions more hygienic, will free millions of workers from smoke, dust and dirt, and accelerate the transformation of dirty, repulsive workshops into clean, bright laboratories worthy of human beings. The electric lighting and heating of every home will relieve millions of "domestic slaves" of the need to spend three-fourths of their lives in smelly kitchens.

Capitalist technology is increasingly, day by day, *out-growing* the social conditions which condemn the working people to wage-slavery.

Pravda No. 91, April 21, 1913
Signed: *I.*

Published according to the *Pravda* text

A FEW WORDS ON RESULTS AND FACTS

The *Pravda* anniversary must turn the thoughts of every politically conscious worker (and, we would add, every politically conscious democrat) to the *results* achieved by the newspaper of consistent democrats and Marxists.

The question of results, of course, is connected with the question of whether the advanced workers of Russia are, in their mass, on the side of *Pravda*. As far as bourgeois subscribers are concerned a newspaper is important if it sells, it does not matter to them where it is sold or whether it serves to rally a certain class and which class; a newspaper is important to the Marxist and consistent democrat as an organ for the *enlightenment* and *consolidation* of truly advanced classes.

We are not indifferent to the question of where and how our newspaper is sold. It is most important for us to *know* whether it really does serve to enlighten and consolidate the advanced class of Russia, i.e., the working class.

To gain this *knowledge* one must look for *facts* that can provide an answer to the question.

By facts, different people understand different things. Bourgeois journalists do not hesitate to lie by omitting to cite a single *precise* and clear fact that can be verified.

Liberal working-class politicians, the liquidators, imitate the bourgeois journalists. One of them, and a leading one at that, F. D.[26] himself, wrote in *Luch*[27] No. 57 (143):

> "It is a fact that cannot be denied and one that we feel [what feeling people they are!] with pride in our day-to-day work, that our newspaper [*Luch*] is truly the organ of a good nine-tenths of the advanced, politically conscious workers of Russia."

It is worth while having a good laugh at this Khlestakov or Nozdryov,[28] and *Pravda* has already had its laugh. Mere ridicule, however, is not enough. Workers must learn to grasp facts and verify them for *themselves* so that the Nozdryovs will not be able to deceive them or their less developed workmates.

How are facts to be sought and verified? Best of all by finding out how *Pravda* and *Luch* circulate among *workers* (and not among the liberal intelligentsia, who are liquidators almost to a man). But no such facts are available.

Let us look for some others.

Let us take the figures for *the workers' groups* that support *Pravda* and *Luch* by voluntary contributions. These figures, *published* in the two papers, are *facts*. Anybody can verify them, anybody can, by studying them, expose the Nozdryovs, of whom there are many in the world of journalism.

Pravda has once already published these facts for a half year (see No. 80 for 1912*)—for the first six months of 1912 —and nobody can refute them. We now give them for *the whole of* 1912 and the beginning of 1913.

Year	Number of collections for newspapers by workers' groups		
	Pravda	*Luch*	Moscow workers' newspaper[29]
1912 1st quarter	108	7	—
" 2nd "	396	8	—
" 3rd "	81	9	—
" 4th "	35	65	5
1913 1st "	309	139	129
" 10 days of April . . .	93	28	43
Totals	1,022	256	177

Any reader can check these figures by taking *Pravda* and *Luch* and can correct the totals if he finds a mistake.

These are real *facts* that it is worth while distinguishing from the boasting and untruths of Messrs. F. D. and other *Luch* gentlemen.

Do not these facts constitute a splendid confirmation of *Luch*'s reference to nine-tenths, made in the Nozdryov manner?

---

* See present edition, Vol. 18, pp. 196-200.—*Ed.*

The "nine-tenths" *Luch* supporters, among whom there are, notoriously, the Bund members and the "upper crust" of the Letts, have not been able, in the *more than six months* of *Luch*'s existence (fourth quarter of 1912 and first quarter of 1913, plus ten days of April), to mobilise even *one half* the number of workers *Pravda* and the future Moscow newspaper have been able to. Is this not a true Nozdryov method, this conversion of an obvious *minority* into "nine-tenths"?

The workers are surrounded on all sides by such a sea of lies in the bourgeois newspapers that they must fight for the truth at all costs, they must learn to recognise falsehoods and reject them. The erroneous· views of the liquidators of the workers' party must be calmly *refuted*. But an impudent Nozdryov lie, this shameless corruption of the workers, must be branded, and the liars chased out of the workers' midst.

The workers want unity in their actions. The workers are right. Without unity of action there is no salvation for the workers.

When you think of it—*how* can there be unity without the submission of the minority to the majority? Everyone realises that without it unity is impossible.

And so, even if the liquidators were not the liquidators of the Party, the workers would have to know what *views* are held by the majority. If they do not know this the workers cannot achieve *unity of action* (because frequently Party and non-Party workers have to act jointly).

The workers cannot build up *their own* party unless they ruthlessly fight every lie that is told about it. In order to expose lies it is necessary to seek *precise* facts, verify them and think about the meaning of what has been verified.

Class-conscious workers, those who oppose liquidationism, have undoubtedly taken first place in creating a working-class press. They have won an incontestable, overwhelming majority for themselves. They will treat every lie that is spread about this serious and very important question with contempt and disdain.

Pravda No. 92, April 23, 1913
Signed: *K. P.*

Published according to the *Pravda* text

SIGNIFICANCE OF THE RESETTLEMENT SCHEME

We know that since 1905, the government, in connection with its "new" agrarian policy in European Russia, has been making particular efforts to promote peasant resettlement to Siberia. The landowners regarded these resettlement schemes as a sort of opening of the safety valve, and as a "blunting" of the agrarian contradictions in the centre of Russia.

What has happened as a result? Has there been a blunting or a sharpening of contradictions following their transfer to a wider arena?

First of all let us cite some general figures on the resettlement of peasants to Siberia.

From 1861 to 1885 about 300,000 peasants migrated, that is, 12,000 a year; from 1886 to 1905 the number was about 1,520,000, that is, about 76,000 a year; from 1906 to 1910 it was about 2,516,075 or about 500,000 a year.

The growth in the number of peasants resettled in the counter-revolutionary period is enormous. Undoubtedly *a temporary* "rarefaction" of the atmosphere in Central Russia was bound to take place as a result.

But for *how long* and at *what cost*?

The answer to this is provided by the figures showing the *drop* in the wave of settlers that began in 1909 and the amazing *growth* in the number of those returning. Here are the figures:

Year	Number of settlers (thousands)	Number returning (percentage)
1905	39	10
1906	141	4
1907	427	6
1908	665	6
1909	619	13
1910	316	36
1911*	183	60

* Eleven months.

Thus the official promoters of resettlement succeeded in rarefying the atmosphere for something like *four* years (1906-09). Then a *new crisis* began, because the huge drop in the number of settlers and the incredible increase in the number of "returnees"—36 per cent and 60 per cent—without any doubt mean a crisis, and an extremely serious one at that, one that covers an immeasurably wider arena.

Thirty-six and 60 per cent of settlers returning means a sharpening of the crisis in Russia and in Siberia. It is the poorest who return to Russia, the most unfortunate, who have lost everything and are bitterly angry. The land question must have become very acute in Siberia for it to have become impossible, despite the efforts of the government, to accommodate hundreds of thousands of settlers.

The figures quoted show without doubt, therefore, that the struggle against the 1905 agrarian crisis in Russia by means of resettlement has brought about a *postponement* of the crisis for only a very short period and at the cost of an incomparably greater sharpening and extension of the crisis, as at present.

An interesting confirmation of this conclusion drawn from dry government statistical data is a book by Mr. A. I. Komarov, a former official of the Forestry Department who was twenty-seven years in the service and took a special interest in the Siberian resettlement scheme. His book is called *The Truth About the Resettlement Scheme* (St. Petersburg, 1913. Price 60 kopeks).

It consists mainly of newspaper articles written by the author under a pseudonym for the newspaper *Novaya Rus*[30] between 1908 and 1910 in which, in a "jovial" manner, he tells a story "of state spoliation or, rather, devastation of Siberian lands and forests that makes the plunder of the Bashkirian lands that once took place seem trivial indeed".

The author's position is that of the well-intentioned official reduced to despair by the "resettlement muddle" (his newspaper articles bore that title), the plunder, ruin and impoverishment of the old inhabitants and the settlers, "the complete disorganisation of all that is called rational forestry", the flight of the settlers back to Russia and the formation of an army, "hundreds of thousands strong", of "vagrant Russia" and, finally, the impenetrable wall of stupidity and officialdom, the system of secret informers, the embezzling and incompetence in the organisation of the whole business.

Despite the fact that the articles are written in a "jovial" manner, or rather *because they are*, their cumulative effect is to produce a very strong impression of the fumes, the fug, the suffocation that surround the old feudal officialdom. Nothing but disaster can come of a new bourgeois agrarian policy that is carried out by such means and methods and under such circumstances and is guided by such social elements.

Here is a picture of the journey to Siberia made in August 1910 by Prime Minister Stolypin and Mr. Krivoshein, the Chief Administrator of Agriculture and Land Settlement. A speech was made from the platform of the minister's railway coach at the Taiga station ... "everything is magnificent and therefore satisfactory".

"This clownish tour," writes the old civil servant, "this journey so similar to that made by Catherine the Great to the south of Russia, with Mr. Schumann, the Resettlement and Land Administrator of Tomsk Gubernia, playing the role of Potyomkin on instructions from St. Petersburg ... was the last straw that made me abandon the service and publish this pamphlet."

Poor, well-intentioned official—it was too much for him! Here is a picture of the resettlement muddle at the time of the greatest wave of settlers.

"The lands allotted were not ready, the roads to them had not been laid, the resettlement centres were only just being built.... Then people began settling of their own accord in surveyed forest areas that took their fancy, and seizing plots leased from the state, reserve plots that had at some earlier date been set aside for the Siberian estates of the nobility, etc.; and then, of course, began the expulsion of these illegal settlers, accompanied by a series of sad and often cruel scenes that it would be superfluous to describe." The resettlement officers were compelled to "tear to pieces areas of state forest that had been surveyed only the day before". "They seized the land piecemeal, took whatever they first laid eyes on, anything so long as they could accommodate, get rid of, the scores of emaciated exhausted people hanging around the resettlement centre and standing for long hours outside the resettlement office, people who for some unknown reason invade the gubernia municipal offices in crowds and, in general, do not leave a single government office in peace."

"Many millions of rubles" are being embezzled and wasted. "One conclusion that suggests itself", writes the author, "is the need to transfer the resettlement scheme to the future Siberian Zemstvo." This naïve, "honest-minded" Russian official believes that this threadbare cloak can be patched up ... with a Zemstvo.

Here is a picture of the way the forests are being looked after. Settlers "upon whom fortune had smiled" were permitted to sell timber; they sold 300 dessiatines of mature building timber at 17 rubles per dessiatine. Even by Siberian standards a dessiatine of mature building timber is worth, at the very least, about 200 rubles. Another picture: settlers sold the contractor Zhogolyov 25,000 railway sleepers at four kopeks each. He paid 5 kopeks for felling, 25 kopeks for removal from the forest and 10 kopeks each for transport by steamer, and received *80 kopeks a sleeper* from the treasury.... There you have Octobrist capitalism in the epoch of primitive accumulation, and it lives comfortably side by side with the Purishkeviches and the Purishkevichism of Russian life!

Here is a series of pictures of land settlement. Minusinsk Uyezd, the "Siberian Italy". The old inhabitants of Minusinsk received four dessiatines each and "came to know the sacred rights of property". At the same time they were banned from using tens of thousands of dessiatines of the best land.

"In recent times, this Italy, because of the general organisation of state economy, has been very regularly visited by, to use the official expression, 'crop failures' ...."

"... In Yeniseisk Uyezd there is the famous Ob-Yenisei Canal, that has for a number of years duly devoured a good many millions from the treasury, but has not thereby got itself into a decent condition fitting it for the transport of goods, since it was dug in a place where it should not have been dug...."

"Kurinsky resettlement area ... is made up of lands that belonged to non-Russians around the Altai Salt Refinery. The non-Russians had a tough time of it after their land had been taken away from them, but the settlers had a worse time—the local water was quite unsuitable for drinking. Nor did well-digging produce any results. Then the resettlement administration started drilling and drilled down to water that was saltier still. The settlers now drive seven or eight versts to the Yenisei from the village for water, so 'everything is satisfactory'...."

... A very valuable stand of pine had been completely eaten away by the pine moth. When the trouble began the forest warden had to *send a written application*   asking for credit. While the correspondence and negotiations with St. Petersburg proceeded, the timber was ruined.... "Everything that is usually called forestry," writes the old warden, "has been totally abandoned."

People of any integrity are squeezed out of the civil service world by informers (p. 118) and the "higher authorities" cut short foresters who have thirty-five years' service behind them with roars of "Silence!" if they dare to tell the truth (p. 121). "A base and sordid period," says the good Mr. Komarov, indignantly, who suggests this "period" began when a "good" boss was changed for a bad one.

The author summarises his illustrations as follows:

"If all I have said sounds like so many anecdotes, then they are anecdotes from a reality that Russian constitutional—save the mark! —life has accustomed us to; and is not the whole of our present-day Russian life one long and rather unpleasant anecdote?"

With regard to the settlers that are returning, Mr. Komarov ridicules the assertion of some "bold" medical man that they constitute no more than 6 per cent. We have quoted exact figures on this question above.

"The Russian landowners, more than anybody, are very, very interested in this [in the number of settlers returning]," writes Mr. Komarov. "This is understandable: those returning are the sort that are destined to play a terrible role in the future. The man who is returning is not the one who all his life has been a farm labourer and is no longer accustomed to that which gave him, like Antaeus of old, gigantic, incredible strength. The man who is returning is the one who, until recently, was a property-owner, a man who never dreamed that he and the land could exist apart. This man is justifiably indignant, to him it is a mortal offence that he has not been provided for, but, on the contrary, that he and his family have been ruined and transformed from farmers and growers of corn into people of no consequence; this man is a menace to any political system, no matter what it be. And the best minds, those that have seen the light since 1905, are paying due consideration to this."

In the spring of 1910, the author visited a Marshal of the Nobility[31] in European Russia; he was a man of conservative convictions who enjoyed the author's trust and esteem.

"'We are considering it, indeed we are,' he told me. 'It is not for nothing that we have fled from the country into the town. The muzhik glowers at us like a wild beast. The young people are almost all hooligans, and now there are these people coming back from you in Siberia who have nothing to lose.'

"I understood dear Pyotr Fyodorovich best of all," continues kindly Mr. Komarov, "when among others who came to me for information 'about the lands in Siberia' was one of the forgotten friends of my childhood, one with whom I had played tip-cat and other games and with whom I had later taken part in fist-fights. Alas, he was no longer my former companion in the village fist-fights but a respectable-looking muzhik with a big beard with silver threads in it and a bald patch exposing half his pate. We had a talk, recalled old times and I mentioned 1905. I must mention that our uyezd was one of those that had been particularly brightly·illuminated by the ruddy glow of burning landowners' mansions and ruined estates, and I for my part made a quite natural reproach to my friend, as far as I remember in the following terms:

"'The devil alone knows what you people got up to in 1905! You could have got much better conditions....'

"When I said this, I did not have in mind the theory of the agrarian question as propounded by the Social-Democrats and Socialist-Revolutionaries which, to anybody in any degree acquainted with political economy, somehow sounds completely inacceptable; I was given this answer:

"'How true your words are.... You're quite right.... That was not what we should have done....'

"'There you are,' I said soothingly, glad that we had understood each other.

"'Yes, it's true enough.... We made a fine blunder.... We shouldn't have let anyone go....'

"'What do you mean by that?'

"'I mean we should have gone through with it, ... given all of them short shrift....'

"And as he spoke his face was smiling and kindly, there were attractive wrinkles around his bright, gentle, childishly naïve and smiling eyes....

"But I admit quite frankly that a cold shiver ran down my back and the hair on my head must have stood on end; if that was how the gentle ones felt about it, what could we expect from those who were coming back, those who had sold their land and were ruined for ever?

"Yes, indeed, the 'banking on the strong' that was presented to Russia by the late Prime Minister and the Octobrists, may, as time goes on and the full effect of the resettlement muddle is felt, bring many horrors into our lives" (p. 75).

We will stop here, at this conversation between a kindly, peaceable intellectual and a gentle, mild, naïve, respectable-looking, bald-headed muzhik.

Pravda Nos. 96 and 99,
April 27 and May 1, 1913
Signed: V. I.

Published according to
the *Pravda* text

VEKHI CONTRIBUTORS AND NATIONALISM

(BIBLIOGRAPHICAL NOTE)

A boring magazine, that *Russkaya Mysl*.[32] There is only one interesting thing about it. Among its writers there are liberals who contribute to and support *Vekhi*,[33] the notorious renegade book in which yesterday's champions of liberty poured mud and filth on *the struggle of the masses for liberty*, a book in which, furthermore, the democratic masses of workers and peasants were depicted as a herd led by "intellectuals"—an old trick used by all Black-Hundred supporters.

It was not mere chance that Russian liberal "educated society" turned against the revolution and against democracy; this was inevitable after 1905. The bourgeoisie was frightened by the independent action of the workers and the awakening of the peasants. The bourgeoisie, especially its richer section, anxious to preserve its position as exploiter, decided that reaction was better than revolution.

It was these selfish class interests of the money-bags that gave rise to the extensive and deep-going *counter-revolutionary* trend among the liberals, a trend against democracy, in defence of any kind of imperialism, nationalism and chauvinism, in defence of all obscurantism.

Class-conscious workers are not surprised at this apostasy, this defection, because the workers never did have a very high opinion of the liberals. It is, however, worth while examining what the liberal renegades are preaching, *with what ideas* they hope to fight democracy in general and Social-Democracy in particular.

"Russian intellectual society," writes Mr. Izgoyev in *Russkaya Mysl*, "was, and, in the mass, still is convinced that the fundamental question of European life is the proletariat's struggle for socialism against the bourgeoisie...."

Mr. Izgoyev says that this idea is "preconceived and erroneous"; he points out that among the Poles in Germany struggling to maintain their nationality, a new middle stratum has been created and is growing up—"a democratic middle class".

When Izgoyev speaks of "intellectuals" he actually means socialists and democrats. The liberal *is not pleased* that the struggle of the proletariat against the bourgeoisie is regarded as the fundamental question. The liberal strives to ignite and fan the flames of national struggle in order *to divert attention from the serious questions* of democracy and socialism.

Socialism actually does take first place among the "questions of European life" and the national struggle takes ninth place and becomes, furthermore, the weaker and less harmful the more consistently democracy functions. It is ridiculous even to compare the struggle of the proletariat for socialism, a world phenomenon, with the struggle of one of the oppressed nations of Eastern Europe against the reactionary bourgeoisie that oppresses it (and the *Polish* bourgeoisie willingly joins forces with the *German* bourgeoisie against the proletariat on every convenient occasion).

Prosveshcheniye No. 4, April 1913
Signed: *V.*

Published according to
the *Prosveshcheniye* text

THE LIBERALS AND FREEDOM FOR THE UNIONS

The Mining Congress has declared itself in favour of the freedom for the unions. One of the biggest liberal bourgeois newspapers, *Kievskaya Mysl*,[34] has this to say about it:

"One of the greatest services rendered by the Congress is this declaration of the right of workers to organise, this support for the demand for freedom of workers' association.

"Since the working-class movement in Russia re-emerged after the interval of 1908-09 and greater and more frequent repressions have been showered upon it, the demand for freedom of association is increasingly becoming a demand put forward by *the masses* of the working-class. Until now, however, the demand for the right of asso-ciation has been regarded as the slogan of the day only in working-class circles. Liberal society showed complete indifference towards it. The Congress, which included quite a number of industrialists, has now been compelled to afford moral support to the demand of the working class."

Here we can clearly see how the liberals are employing their widely circulated, profit-making press *to curtail* the demands and slogans of the working class. The liberals know full well that the workers have quite different "*slogans of the day*", uncurtailed slogans. The liberals *are foisting* on the workers their own liberal narrowness which they claim to be the opinion of "masses" of workers; this is the old, worn-out method of making the supposedly undeveloped masses responsible for the unwillingness of the liberal bourgeoisie to face up to the real source of political privileges and lack of political rights! This was the method employed by the "liberal" serf-owners who, half a century ago, said that the abolition of *all* landowner privileges was *not* "a slogan of the day" for "the masses".

Characteristically, the liberals give themselves away. The Congress demand is incomplete, they say. Why? Listen to this:

"The Congress favoured the right of association but could not hide from itself the fact that the realisation of this right inevitably presupposes a whole series of legal conditions. It is impossible to grant freedom to trade unions where general freedom for unions and societies does not exist. Freedom for the working-class press can only be established where there is freedom for the liberal and democratic press. Freedom of association cannot exist where administrative control is the rule and where the masses of the population are kept from participation in elections to legislative bodies. The Congress should have indicated the need to bring about these conditions if it wished to be consistent."

So the Congress was not consistent. In what way was it not consistent? In its not having listed *certain* reforms, answers the liberal.

But did you list *everything*, gentlemen?

Of course not! You got as far as the *"conditions"* that are "presupposed" before certain liberties can be *"brought about"*, but you did not say what these conditions were. You stopped there. You are today afraid of the slogan of the "working-class masses"—not *reforms* but *"reform"*. In substance you adopt the viewpoint of Struve. Struve took up this slogan in the spring *preceding* October 17, but he does not accept it today because the entire bourgeoisie, even the most liberal, has turned to the right.

There was a similar situation at the time of the abolition of serfdom. The consistent democrats, Dobrolyubov and Chernyshevsky, justly ridiculed the liberals for their *reformism*, underlying which there was always a striving to curtail the activities of the masses and defend a little bit of privilege for the landowners, such as redemption payments for the land, etc.

The liberals are wasting their time trying to blame the poverty of their reformism on the "masses of the working class"!

Pravda No. 101, May 4, 1913   Published according to
                                                    the *Pravda* text

FOR THE ATTENTION *OF LUCH* AND *PRAVDA* READERS

Both *Luch* and *Pravda* have on a number of occasions published letters from workers demanding that the editors of these newspapers give them a calm and clear exposition of the substance of their differences. This is a legitimate and natural demand, and it is worth while seeing how the two editorial boards have complied with it.

Under the heading "Controversial Issues"* *Pravda* published the explanatory articles that had been asked for. What were they about? Those articles outlined and explained *Party decisions* on disputed questions. Through the author of those articles *Pravda* stated that to decide who is right in the dispute, where the truth lies, one must examine the facts and documents of Party history, try to put aside everything personal, everything extraneous and understand the social roots of the dispute. The dispute with the liquidators, said *Pravda*, "is not a matter of the evil will of certain individuals, but of the historical situation of the working-class movement".** Those who seriously want to get at the bottom of the dispute must take the trouble to understand that historical situation.

"It is necessary to understand," says *Pravda*, "the *class* origin of the discord and disintegration, to understand what *class* interests emanating from a non-proletarian environment foster confusion among the friends of the proletariat."**

This is a serious presentation of the question. It is a direct response to the workers' demand that they be helped to

---

* See pp. 147-56 of this volume.—*Ed.*
** See p. 154 of this volume.—*Ed.*

understand the serious dispute between *Pravda* and *Luch*. In this way the workers will get to know the *facts* of Party life and will learn to distinguish what in this dispute is true and a matter of principle, and what is shallow and fortuitous; they will seek the *class* roots of the discord.

It is possible that a worker, having learned the facts, having read through the documents, etc., will in the end not agree with *Pravda*—that is a matter of his own convictions and his experience. But in any case, if he follows *Pravda*'s advice he will learn a lot and will realise what the whole dispute is about.

Such is *Pravda*'s reply to the workers' demand to make them familiar with the existing differences. How did *Luch* act?

At the same time as *Pravda* published its articles on "controversial issues", *Luch* printed a lengthy article on the same subject. Not a single *fact* is cited in the article, the author does not attach any social significance at all to the dispute and does not call the reader's attention to a single document.

This enormous article, spread over two issues of the paper, is packed with gossip and allusions to personalities. The working-class reader is informed of the "touchiness" and "charming witticisms" of one Marxist, the "superman" pretensions of a second and the "cynicism" of a third. All disputes are attributed to "the settling of personal accounts", to "discontent over matters of seniority" and to the "struggle for power" in the Party. And an underhand rumour, worthy of the official press, is slipped in to suggest that certain "master-hands at revolution" are to blame for it all because they are afraid of losing their influence if the broad masses of the workers enter into the dispute.

What the author and the newspaper that published his article are aiming at is to pack people's heads with gossip, squabbles and personalities, and thus avoid the necessity of explaining their point of view. It would not be half as bad if it were merely gossip. But this is the gossip of an embittered renegade, that is the trouble. Read what he writes at the beginning of the second part of his article about "provoked and provoking acts", about "the dictatorship in the Party of supermen with a cynical attitude to the masses"; read how he abuses the devoted people of 1905 by

calling them "master-hands at revolution" who have behaved in a way that would be quite "impermissible in an environment with any degree of culture". All that, of course,
is lifted straight from *Zemshchina*,[35] or from *Vekhi*!

This appeared not in *Novoye Vremya*[36] but in a paper
that calls itself a workers' newspaper, it is offered as a reply
to working men's demands for a serious explanation of
the paper's point of view! And even after that *Luch* dares
protest against sharper forms of polemic and set itself up
as a model of decorum that wants to put *Pravda* to shame.

We most insistently advise those workers who still believe
that *Luch*, unlike *Pravda*, is a newspaper that stands for
unification and the cessation of internal squabbles, to read
the above-mentioned article and compare it with the way
Pravda discusses the same questions.

Pravda No. 102, May 5, 1913   Published according to
  Signed: Reader of *Pravda*   the *Pravda* text
        and *Luch*

TWENTY-FIFTH ANNIVERSARY OF THE DEATH
OF JOSEPH DIETZGEN

Joseph Dietzgen, a tannery worker and one of the most eminent German Social-Democratic philosophical writers, died twenty-five years ago, in 1888.

Joseph Dietzgen was the author of a number of works (most of them translated into Russian) that include *The Nature of the Workings of the Human Mind* (published in 1869), *A Socialist's Excursions into the Theory of Knowledge, Acquisition of Philosophy*, etc. It was Karl Marx, in a letter to Kugelmann on December 5, 1868, who made the best appraisal of Dietzgen and his place in the history of philosophy and of the working-class movement:

"A fairly long time ago he sent me a fragment of a manuscript on the 'faculty of thought' which, in spite of a certain confusion and of too frequent repetition, contains much that is excellent and—as the independent product of a working man—admirable."

Such is the importance of Dietzgen—a worker who arrived at dialectical materialism, i.e., Marx's philosophy, independently. In forming an assessment of the worker Dietzgen it is of great value to remember that he never considered himself the founder of a school.

Dietzgen spoke of Marx as the *leader of a trend* as early as 1873, when few people understood Marx. Dietzgen emphasised that Marx and Engels "possessed the necessary philosophical training". And in 1886, a long time after the publication of Engels's *Anti-Dühring*, one of the chief Marxist philosophical works, Dietzgen wrote of Marx and Engels as the "recognised founders" of a trend.

This must be borne in mind when judging the many supporters of bourgeois philosophy, i.e., idealism and agnosticism (including Machism), who attempt to take advantage of "*a certain confusion*" in Dietzgen's writing. Dietzgen himself would have ridiculed such admirers and would have repulsed them.

To become politically conscious, workers should read Dietzgen but should *never* for a moment *forget* that he *does. not always give a true* picture of the doctrine of Marx and Engels, who are the only writers from whom philosophy can *be learned.*

Dietzgen wrote at a time when simplified, vulgarised *materialism* was most widespread. Dietzgen, therefore, laid his greatest stress on the historical changes that had taken place in materialism, on the *dialectical* character of materialism, that is, on the need to support the point of view of development, to understand that all human knowledge is relative, to understand the multilateral connections between, and interdependence of, all phenomena in the universe, and to develop the materialism of natural history to a materialist conception of history.

Because he lays so much stress on the relativity of human knowledge, Dietzgen often becomes confused and makes incorrect concessions to idealism and agnosticism. Idealism in philosophy is a defence, sometimes extremely elaborate, sometimes less so, of clericalism, of a doctrine that places faith above science, or side by side with science, or in some way or another gives faith a place. Agnosticism (from the Greek words "a" *no* and "gnosis" *knowledge*) is vacillation between materialism and idealism, i.e., in practice it is vacillation between materialist science and clericalism. Among the agnostics are the followers of Kant (the Kantians), Hume (the positivists, realists and others) and the present-day Machists. This is why some of the most reactionary bourgeois philosophers, the most thorough-placed obscurantists and direct defenders of clericalism, try to "use" Dietzgen's mistakes.

By and large, however, Dietzgen was a materialist. He was an enemy of clericalism and agnosticism. "The only thing we have in common with earlier materialists," wrote Dietzgen, "is that we accept matter as the prerequisite to, or foundation of, the idea." That "only thing" is precisely the *essence* of philosophical materialism.

"The materialist theory of knowledge," wrote Dietzgen, "may be reduced to a recognition of the fact that the human organ of knowledge does not irradiate any metaphysical light but is a bit of nature that reflects other bits of nature." That is the materialist theory of the *reflection* in human knowledge of eternally moving and changing matter, a theory that evokes hatred and horror, calumny and distortion on the part of all official, professorial philosophy. And how Dietzgen berated and branded the "certificated lackeys of clericalism", the idealist professors, the realists and others —how he lambasted them with the deep passion of a true revolutionary! "Of all parties," Dietzgen rightly said, speaking of the philosophical "parties", i.e., materialism and idealism, "the vilest is the party of the centre".

To this "vile party" belong the *Luch* editorial board and Mr. S. Semkovsky (*Luch* No. 92). The editors made a tiny reservation. "We do not share the general philosophical point of view", they say, but the exposition of Dietzgen's views is "correct and clear".

That is an appalling untruth. Mr. Semkovsky unconscionably misquoted and distorted Dietzgen, seizing upon the *"confusion"* and ignoring *Marx's appraisal of Dietzgen.* Incidentally, both Plekhanov, a socialist who possesses the greatest knowledge of the philosophy of Marxism, and the best Marxists of Europe *have recognised that appraisal in full.*

Mr. Semkovsky distorts both philosophical materialism and Dietzgen, talking nonsense on the question of "one or two worlds" (this, supposedly, is the "key question"! Learn a little, my friend, at least read Engels's *Ludwig Feuerbach*) and on the question of the universe and phenomena (Dietzgen is supposed to have reduced the real world to nothing but phenomena; this is clerical and professorial slander of Dietzgen).

It is impossible to list all Mr. Semkovsky's distortions. Let workers interested in Marxism know that the *Luch* editors are *a union of liquidators* of Marxism. Some want to liquidate the underground, i.e., the Party of the proletariat (Mayevsky, Sedov, F. D., etc.), others, the idea of the hegemony of the proletariat (Potresov, Koltsov, etc.), the third, the philosophical materialism of Marx (Mr. Semkovsky & Co.), the fourth, the internationalism of proletarian socialism (the Bund members Kosovsky, Medem and other supporters of "cultural-national autonomy"), the fifth, the economic theory of Marx (Mr. Maslov with his theory of rent and the "new" sociology) and so on and so forth.

This blatant distortion of Marxism by Mr. Semkovsky and the editors who defend him is only one of the more obvious examples of the "activities" of this literary "union of liquidators".

Pravda No. 102, May 5, 1913   Published according to
Signed: *V. Ilyin*   the *Pravda* text

THE BOURGEOISIE AND PEACE

The conference of French and German parliamentarians held in Berne last Sunday, May 11 (April 28 O.S.), reminds us once more of the attitude of the European bourgeoisie to war and peace.

The initiative in calling the conference was taken by representatives from Alsace-Lorraine and Switzerland. Socialist deputies from France and Germany turned up in full force. Of the bourgeois deputies quite a number of French Radicals and Radical-Socialists (petty-bourgeois democrats who are, in fact, alien and, for the greater part, hostile to socialism). An insignificant number of bourgeois deputies from Germany attended. The National-Liberals (midway between the Cadets and the Octobrists, something like our "Progressists") confined themselves to sending greetings. From the party of the "Centre" (the Catholic petty-bourgeois party in Germany that loves playing at democracy) *two* promised to come but—decided not to turn up!

Among the prominent socialists who spoke at the conference were Greulich, a veteran Swiss Social-Democrat, and August Bebel.

A resolution condemning chauvinism and declaring that the overwhelming majority of the two nations, French and German, want peace and demand the settlement of international conflicts by courts of arbitration, was adopted unanimously.

There is no doubt that the conference was an impressive demonstration in favour of peace. But it would be a huge mistake to trust the tender-hearted speeches of those few bourgeois deputies who attended the conference and voted for the resolution. If they seriously wanted peace those

bourgeois deputies should have *condemned* outright the increase in Germany's armaments (the German army is to be
increased by 140,000 officers and men; this new government
proposal will no doubt be adopted by the bourgeois parties
of Germany despite the vigorous protests of the socialists);
they should also have condemned in exactly the same way
the French government proposal to increase army service to
three years.

That was something the bourgeois deputies would not
venture to do. Still less were they capable of making a resolute demand for a militia, that is, for the replacement of
the standing army by arming the entire people. This measure, which does not go beyond the bounds of bourgeois
society, is the only one that can democratise the army and
advance the question of peace even one step forward in a
manner at all *serious*.

But no, the European bourgeoisie clings frantically to the
militarists and reactionaries out of fear of the working-class
movement. The insignificant number of petty-bourgeois
democrats is not capable of a strong desire for peace and
still less capable of bringing it about. Power is in the hands
of the banks, the trusts and big capital in general. The one
guarantee of peace is the organised, conscious movement of
the working class.

Pravda No. 103, May 7, 1913   Published according to
                                                     the *Pravda* text

THE AWAKENING OF ASIA

Was it so long ago that China was considered typical of the lands that had been standing still for centuries? Today China is a land of seething political activity, the scene of a virile social movement and of a democratic upsurge. Following the 1905 movement in Russia, the democratic revolution spread to the whole of Asia—to Turkey, Persia, China. Ferment is growing in British India.

A significant development is the spread of the revolutionary democratic movement to the Dutch East Indies, to Java and the other Dutch colonies, with a population of some forty million.

First, the democratic movement is developing among the masses of Java, where a nationalist movement has arisen under the banner of Islam. Secondly, capitalism has created a local intelligentsia consisting of acclimatised Europeans who demand independence for the Dutch East Indies. Thirdly, the fairy large Chinese population of Java and the other islands have brought the revolutionary movement from their native land.

Describing this awakening of the Dutch East Indies, van Ravesteyn, a Dutch Marxist, points out that the age-old despotism and tyranny of the Dutch Government now meet with resolute resistance and protest from the masses of the native population.

The usual events of a pre-revolutionary period have begun. Parties and unions are being founded at amazing speed. The government is banning them, thereby only fanning the resentment and accelerating the growth of the movement. Recently, for example, it dissolved the "Indian Party" because its programme and rules spoke of the striving for

independence. The Dutch *Derzhimordas*[37] (with the approval,
incidentally, of the clericals and liberals—European liberalism is rotten to the core!) regarded this clause as a criminal
attempt at separation from the Netherlands! The dissolved
party was, of course, revived under a different name.

A National Union of the native population has been
formed in Java. It already has a membership of 80,000 and
is holding mass meetings. There is no stopping the growth
of the democratic movement.

World capitalism and the 1905 movement in Russia have
finally aroused Asia. Hundreds of millions of the downtrodden and benighted have awakened from medieval stagnation to a new life and are rising to fight for elementary
human rights and democracy.

The workers of the advanced countries follow with interest
and inspiration this powerful growth of the liberation movement, in all its various forms, in every part of the world.
The bourgeoisie of Europe, scared by the might of the working-class movement, is embracing reaction, militarism,
clericalism and obscurantism. But the proletariat of the
European countries and the young democracy of Asia,
fully confident of its strength and with abiding faith in the
masses, are advancing to take the place of this decadent and
moribund bourgeoisie.

The awakening of Asia and the beginning of the struggle
for power by the advanced proletariat of Europe are a symbol
of the new phase in world history that began early this
century.

Pravda No. 103, May 7, 1913   Published according to
         Signed: *F.*   the *Pravda* text

SEPARATISTS IN RUSSIA AND SEPARATISTS IN AUSTRIA

Among the various representatives of Marxism in Russia the Jewish Marxists, or, to be more exact, some of them—those known as the Bundists—are carrying out a policy of *separatism*. From the history of the working-class movement it is known that the Bundists *left the Party* in 1903, when the majority of the party of the working class refused to accept their demand to be recognised as the "sole" representatives of the Jewish proletariat.

This exit from the Party was a manifestation of separatism deeply harmful to the working-class movement. But, in fact, the Jewish workers have entered and continue to enter the Party everywhere in spite of the Bund. Side by side with the *separate* (isolated) organisations of the Bundists, there have *always* existed *general* organisations of the workers—Jewish, Russian, Polish, Lithuanian, Latvian, etc.

From the history of Marxism in Russia we know, furthermore, that when the Bund in 1906 again returned to the Party, the Party stipulated the condition that separatism should cease, i.e., that there should be local unity of *all* the Marxist workers of *whatever* nationality. But this condition *was not* fulfilled by the Bundists, despite its *special* confirmation by a special decision of the Party in December 1908.[38]

That, shortly, is the history of Bundist separatism in Russia. Unfortunately, it is little known to the workers, and little thought is given to it. Those having the closest practical acquaintance with this history are the Polish, the Lithuanian (especially in Vilna in 1907) and the Latvian Marxists (at the same time, in Riga), and the Marxists of South and Western Russia. It is well known, incidentally, that the Caucasian Marxists, including *all* the Caucasian Mensheviks, have until quite recently maintained local *unity* and even fusion of the workers of all nationalities, and have condemned the separatism of the Bundists.

We should also note that the prominent Bundist, Medem, in the well-known book, *Forms of the National Movement* (St. Petersburg, 1910), admits that the Bundists have never implemented unity in the localities, i.e., they have always been separatists.

In the international working-class movement, the question of separatism came to the front most urgently in 1910, at the Copenhagen Congress. The *Czechs* came forward as separatists in Austria, and destroyed the unity that had existed previously between the Czech and German workers. The International Congress at Copenhagen *unanimously* condemned separatism, but the Czechs have unfortunately remained separatists right up to the present.

Feeling themselves isolated in the proletarian International, the Czech separatists spent a long time searching unsuccessfully for supporters. Only now have they found some—in the *Bundists and liquidators*. The *čechoslavische Sozialdemokrat*, the bit of a journal published by the separatists in German, printed an article in its issue No. 3 (Prague, April 15, 1913) under the title "A Turn for the Better". This "turn" that is supposed to be for the "better" (actually, towards separatism) the Czech separatists saw—where do you think, reader? In *Nasha Zarya*,[39] the liquidators' journal, in an article by the *Bundist* V. Kosovsky!

At last the Czech separatists are not alone in the proletarian International! Naturally they are glad to be able to rope in even liquidators, even Bundists. But all class-conscious workers in Russia should give this fact some thought: the Czech separatists, unanimously condemned by the International, are clinging to the coat-tails of liquidators and Bundists.

Only that complete unity (in every locality, and from top to bottom) of the workers of all nations, which has existed so long and so successfully in the Caucasus, corresponds to the interests and tasks of the workers' movement.

Pravda No. 104, May 8, 1913   Published according to
                                                    the *Pravda* text

THE RESETTLEMENT SCHEME AGAIN

In *Pravda* No. 96 (300)* I quoted the chief resettlement data for Russia. Those data were up to 1911, and that year was incomplete (11 months). In *Rech*, Mr. Kaufmann has now quoted data from official, recently published records for the whole of 1911 and 1912.

It appears that the number of settlers has increased, albeit very slightly—from 190,000 in 1911 to 196,500 in 1912. The number of returning settlers, however, has greatly increased—from 36,000 (1911) to 58,000 (1912).

The explanation of this phenomenon discloses to us still more profoundly the collapse of the new agrarian policy. Until now between three quarters and four-fifths of all settlers have come from the Ukrainian and Central Black-Earth gubernias. That is the centre of Russia where the survivals of serfdom are strongest, where wages are lowest and where the mass of the peasantry live under particularly difficult conditions.

The ruined, impoverished, hungry masses of this centre—the "heart" of Russia—rushed for resettlement (1907-09) and provided, in the end, 60 per cent of those returning, that is, of those who were ruined and still more embittered.

A wave of settlers has now come from another area, this time from the Volgaside gubernias, which until recently produced very few settlers.

What is the reason?

The "harvest failure", the famine of 1911!... The famine embraced a new part of Russia. A new wave of fugitives has left for Siberia. We already know that Siberia will

---

* See p. 66 of this volume.—*Ed.*

ruin and embitter the Volgaside peasants still further, as it did the peasants of Central Russia.

In other words, resettlement to Siberia has shown first the peasants of Central Russia and now those of the Volga-side that salvation cannot be achieved in this way.

The "new" agrarian policy, ruining one area of Russia after another, the peasants of one district after another, is gradually making it clear to all peasants that their real salvation is not to be found there.

Pravda No. 105, May 9, 1913   Published according to
         Signed: *V. I.*   the *Pravda* text

THE WORKING CLASS AND THE NATIONAL QUESTION

Russia is a motley country as far as her nationalities are concerned. Government policy, which is the policy of the landowners supported by the bourgeoisie, is steeped in Black-Hundred nationalism.

This policy is spearheaded against the *majority* of the peoples of Russia who constitute the *majority* of her population. And alongside this we have the bourgeois nationalism of other nations (Polish, Jewish, Ukrainian, Georgian, etc.), raising its head and trying *to divert* the working class from its great world-wide tasks by a national struggle or a struggle for national culture.

The national question must be clearly considered and solved by all class-conscious workers.

When the bourgeoisie was fighting for freedom together with the people, together with all those who labour, it stood for full freedom and equal rights for the nations. Advanced countries, Switzerland, Belgium, Norway and others, provide us with an example of how free nations under a really democratic system live together in peace or separate peacefully from each other.

Today the bourgeoisie fears the workers and is seeking an alliance with the Purishkeviches, with the reactionaries, and is betraying democracy, advocating oppression or unequal rights among nations and corrupting the workers with *nationalist* slogans.

In our times the proletariat alone upholds the real freedom of nations and the unity of workers of all nations.

For different nations to live together in peace and freedom or to separate and form different states (if that is more convenient for them), a full democracy, upheld by the working class, is essential. No privileges for any nation or any one language! Not even the slightest degree of oppression or the slightest injustice in respect of a national minority—such are the principles of working-class democracy.

The capitalists and landowners want, at all costs, to keep the workers of different nations apart while the powers that be live splendidly together as shareholders in profitable concerns involving millions (such as the Lena Goldfields); Orthodox Christians and Jews, Russians and Germans, Poles and Ukrainians, everyone who possesses *capital*, exploit the workers of all nations in company.

Class-conscious workers stand for *full unity* among the workers of all nations in every educational, trade union, political, etc., workers' organisation. Let the Cadet gentlemen disgrace themselves by denying or belittling the importance of equal rights for Ukrainians. Let the bourgeoisie of all nations find comfort in lying phrases about national culture, national tasks, etc., etc.

The workers will not allow themselves to be disunited by sugary speeches about national culture, or "national-cultural autonomy". The workers of all nations together, concertedly, uphold full freedom and complete equality of rights in organisations common to all—and that is the guarantee of genuine culture.

The workers of the whole world are building up their own internationalist culture, which the champions of freedom and the enemies of oppression have for long been preparing. To the old world, the world of national oppression, national bickering, and national isolation the workers counterpose a new world, a world of the unity of the working people of all nations, a world in which there is no place for any privileges or for the slightest degree of oppression of man by man.

Pravda No. 106, May 10, 1913
Published according to
the *Pravda* text

BRITISH SOCIALIST PARTY CONFERENCE

The British Socialist Party was founded in Manchester in 1911. It included the former Socialist Party, which had earlier been known as the Social Democratic Federation, and several isolated groups and individuals, among them Victor Grayson, a very fiery socialist but one not strong in principles and given to phrase-mongering.

The Second Conference of the British Socialist Party was held in the seaside town Blackpool from May 10 to May 12 (N S.). Only 100 delegates were present, less than one-third of the full number, and this circumstance, coupled with the bitter struggle of the majority of the delegates against the old party executive, produced a very bad impression on outside observers. The British bourgeois press (exactly like that of Russia) does its best to pick out, colour up and make a splash of episodes from any particularly acute struggle between the party and its executive.

The bourgeois press is not concerned with the *ideological* content of the struggle inside the socialist movement. All it needs is sensation, and a spicy bit of scandal....

The ideological content of the struggle in the B.S.P., however, was very serious. The old executive was headed by Hyndman, one of the founders of the party. He has been acting for a number of years without any attention to the party, and even against the party, on the important question of armaments and war. Hyndman has got it into his head that Germany is threatening to crush and enslave Britain and that socialists should, therefore, support the demand

for a "proper" (i.e., strong) navy for the defence of
Britain!

Socialists in the role of supporters of a "strong" navy—
and this in a country whose navy helps enslave and plunder
in the most shameless, feudal manner the *three hundred
millions* of India's population, tens of millions of people in
Egypt and other colonies.

Understandably, this fancy idea of Hyndman's pleased the
British bourgeoisie (the Conservatives and Liberals). It can
also be understood that British Social-Democrats—be it
said to their credit—would not tolerate this disgrace and
shame and heatedly opposed it.

The struggle was a long and stubborn one; attempts at
a compromise were made, but Hyndman was incorrigible.
It is greatly to the advantage of British socialism that Hyndman was forced to leave the executive at this Conference and
the composition of the executive was, in general, changed by
75 per cent (of its eight members only two were re-elected—
Quelch and Irving).

The Conference adopted a resolution against the old executive which reads as follows:

"This Conference congratulates our French and German comrades on their vigorous opposition to the increase of armaments in their
respective countries, and pledges the British Socialist Party, as an
integral part of the International Socialist Party, bound by the resolutions on war passed at Stuttgart and Basle, 1912, to pursue the
same policy in Great Britain, with the object of checking the growth
of all forms of militarism and of reducing the existing abominably
high expenditure on armaments."

The resolution is sharply worded. But the truth has to
be told, even if sharply. The British Social-Democrats
would have forfeited their right to struggle against the
opportunists of the so-called Independent (independent of
socialism, but dependent on the Liberals) Labour Party if
they had not sharply opposed the nationalist sins of their
executive.

Let the bourgeois press display their wrath and their
buffoonery over the internal struggle among Social-Democrats. The Social-Democrats do not regard themselves as
saints; they know that now and again the proletariat be-

comes infected by some dirty disease from the bourgeoisie in its environment—this is inevitable in filthy, disgusting capitalist society But the Social-Democrats are able to heal their party with direct and fearless criticism. In Britain, too, they will certainly cure the disease.

Pravda No. 109, May 14, 1913
Signed: *V.*

Published according to
the *Pravda* text

IS THE CONDITION
OF THE PEASANTS IMPROVING OR WORSENING?

Under this heading some official ink-slinger, a Mr. Y.
P—v, published an article in the official *Torgovo-Promysh-lennaya Gazeta*[40] (No. 100), to prove, of course, that the
peasants' condition is improving and "undoubtedly ... is
steadily progressing year by year".

It is extraordinarily instructive to note that the figures
quoted by the author show *the exact opposite*! This is typical
proof of the shameless lying of official writers and official
newspapers!

What are the author's figures? First, be it noted that
he does not give an exact source. We should not for a moment
conclude, therefore, that the official ink-slinger is quoting
this unknown source at first hand, or that he is quoting correctly.

Let us, however, for a minute suppose that he is quoting
correctly.

"Some Zemstvos," writes the author, "for instance, the Moscow
Zemstvo, resort to questionnaires to determine whether the condition of the peasants is worsening or improving. The Zemstvo's local
correspondents provide general answers that are then summarised.

"The result of these lengthy investigations (taking six years),"
writes Mr. Y. P—v, "was a rather interesting numerical summary
for the central zone. To each hundred answers of all types we get"

Answers indicating the economic condition of the peasants:

Year	Improved	Worsened	Unchanged	Total
1907	15	44	41	100
1908	8	53	39	100
1909	8	64	28	100
1910	21	34	45	100
1911	32	16	52	100
1912	38	15	47	100

And so the writer in an official newspaper draws the conclusion—"in the last three years ... we have seen a continuous improvement in the economic level of the peasantry, with a corresponding reduction in the percentage under the headings 'worsened' and 'unchanged'."

Examine the figures carefully. For the first three years there was an obvious and considerable *worsening*. For the last three years there was an *improvement*, but to a far lesser degree than the worsening of the first three years!

Mr. Y. P—v himself admits that these fluctuations "are coincident with the fluctuations in harvests".

Why does he take the three years with good harvests for his *general* conclusions and *ignore* the three years with bad harvests? What would we think of a merchant who summed up the results of his trading by showing his profit and *concealing his losses*? We should call him a swindler, should we not, Mr. Official Writer in an official newspaper?

Now let us make the simple calculation of profit and loss that is obligatory for everyone except swindlers, taking into consideration the "minuses" as well as the "pluses", the "bad" as well as the "good" harvests. To do this we must add up the figures for the six years and divide by six (amazingly clever, Mr. Official Journalist, isn't it?). We then get the *average* for all the six counter-revolutionary years.

The figures are these. From 100 answers:

Favourable ("improved")—20
Unfavourable ("worsened")—38
Average ("unchanged")—42.

That is the result. What does it mean?

It means that the *peasants are growing poorer and being ruined*. For the six years of the counter-revolution the number of *un*favourable answers is, on the average, *almost twice as great* as the number of favourable answers!

This conclusion can be demonstrated clearly by applying the figures to the whole of Russia, to 20,000,000 peasant families, as follows:

In six years 4,000,000 peasant families have impoved their condition, 7,600,000 have grown poorer and 8,400,000 families have remained at the former (i.e., impoverished) level!

And this is in a period of high prices when the landowners and bourgeoisie are raking in gold by the shovelful.

In all probability the peasants will thank and bless the landowners' Duma and the government of the landowners.

Pravda No. 111, May 16, 1913   Published according to
          Signed: *F.*   the *Pravda* text

BACKWARD EUROPE AND ADVANCED ASIA

The comparison sounds like a paradox. Who does not know that Europe is advanced and Asia backward? But the words taken for this title contain a bitter truth.

In civilised and advanced Europe, with its highly developed machine industry, its rich, multiform culture and its constitutions, a point in history has been reached when the commanding bourgeoisie, fearing the growth and increasing strength of the proletariat, comes out in support of everything backward, moribund and medieval. The bourgeoisie is living out its last days, and is joining with all obsolete and obsolescent forces in an attempt to preserve tottering wage-slavery.

Advanced Europe is commanded by a bourgeoisie which supports everything that is backward. The Europe of our day is advanced not *thanks to*, but *in spite of*, the bourgeoisie, for it is only the proletariat that is adding to the million-strong army of fighters for a better future. It alone preserves and spreads implacable enmity towards backwardness, savagery, privilege, slavery and the humiliation of man by man.

In "advanced" Europe, the *sole advanced* class is the proletariat. As for the living bourgeoisie, it is prepared to go to any length of savagery, brutality and crime in order to uphold dying capitalist slavery.

And a more striking example of this decay of the *entire* European bourgeoisie can scarcely be cited than the support it is lending to *reaction* in Asia in furtherance of the selfish aims of the financial manipulators and capitalist swindlers.

Everywhere in Asia a mighty democratic movement is growing, spreading and gaining in strength. The bourgeoisie there is *as yet* siding with the people against reaction. *Hundreds* of millions of people are awakening to life, light and freedom. What delight this world movement is arousing in the hearts of all class-conscious workers, who know that the path to collectivism lies through democracy! What sympathy for young Asia imbues all honest democrats!

And "advanced" Europe? It is plundering China and helping the foes of democracy, the foes of freedom in China!

Here is a simple but instructive little calculation. A new Chinese loan has been concluded *against* Chinese democracy: "Europe" is *for* Yüan Shih-kai, who is preparing a military dictatorship. Why does it support him? Because it is good business. The loan has been concluded for about 250,000,000 rubles, at the rate of 84 to a 100. That means that the bourgeois of "Europe" will *pay* the Chinese 210,000,000 rubles, but will take from the public 225,000,000 rubles. There you have at one stroke—a clear profit of *fifteen million rubles* in a few weeks! It really is a *"clear"* profit, isn't it?

What if the Chinese people do not recognise the loan? China, after all, is a republic, and the majority in parliament are *against* the loan.

Oh, then "advanced" Europe will raise a cry about "civilisation", "order", "culture" and "fatherland"! It will set the *guns* in motion and, in alliance with Yüan Shih-kai, that adventurer, traitor and friend of reaction, crush a republic in "backward" Asia.

All the commanders of Europe, all the European bourgeoisie are *in alliance* with all the forces of reaction and medievalism in China.

But all young Asia, that is, the hundreds of millions of Asian working people, has a reliable ally in the proletariat of all civilised countries. No force on earth can prevent its victory, which will liberate both the peoples of Europe and the peoples of Asia.

Pravda No. 113, May 18, 1913   Published according to
                                                    the *Pravda* text

A DISCREDITABLE ROLE!

(ONCE MORE FOR THE ATTENTION OF *LUCH* AND *PRAVDA* READERS)

In *Pravda* No. 102* I called the attention of reader comrades to an article in *Luch* Nos. 93 and 94.

I compared that article with those published *simultaneously* in *Pravda* under the heading "Controversial Issues".** I said that *Pravda* in its articles gives the reader facts and documents with which to decide disputed questions of organisation and tactics while *Luch* in its article gives him gossip and personal insults that do not help the workers to understand the dispute and only serve to clutter up their heads.

I said that the *Luch* article speaks of the active people of 1905 in the same terms as the organs of terrified landowners and of liberals embittered against the workers.

Luch has sent the worker Herman against me. The worker Herman is a man of determination and possesses a ready tongue. He has berated me in no uncertain terms. I, he says, "want to mislead our reader comrades" and am telling "obvious untruths" and nothing of what I said has ever actually happened. Having thus accused me of a number of crimes, the worker Herman then rounds off his article with a list of titles of articles printed in *Luch*.

Very good! But what about the article in *Luch* that I actually spoke about, and which I quoted? The worker Herman *does not say a single word* about that article, makes no attempt to dispute the correctness of the words I quoted from it, and offers nothing to contest my characterisation of the article as impermissible in the working-class press. What reason is there for that? You cursed me uphill and down dale, my dear man, but not only could you not dis-

---

* See pp. 76-78 of this volume.—*Ed.*
** See pp. 147-56 of this volume.—*Ed.*

prove a single word of what I said about the *Luch* article, you did not even try to.

Did the article I wrote about appear in issues 93 and 94? It did. And so what right have you to state that "nothing of the sort has actually happened"?

Is that article full of gossip and bickering instead of a calm analysis of the disagreements? You did not dare say a word against that! What right have you to suspect me of a desire to "mislead the comrades"?

Did you understand what you were writing? Did you realise that you, in accusing a contributor to a working-class newspaper of "obvious untruths" and a desire to "mislead readers", have to be ready to answer for it, not to me, but to all those who stand behind *Pravda*, that is, to its working-class readers?

You undertook to defend *Luch* against my accusation that the article in issues 93 and 94 does not explain disputed questions but clutters up the heads of its readers with gossip and "personalities". For that purpose you published in the columns of the same *Luch* a number of unfounded accusations and obvious libels ("Reader" [referring to me] wants to mislead our reader comrades), i.e., you did exactly what I accused *Luch* of doing in its article in issue 94. *Your article was a confirmation of my accusation against Luch* and not a refutation of it.

Perhaps you will now say—it was all due to your inexperience. Very good. But your article was read by the editors. Why did they not warn you? Why did they not tell you that when accusing me you would first of all have to refute what I had said about the facts I mentioned, and not evade them by further silence? Why? Apparently because the editors knew that everything I had said about the article in issues 93 and 94 was true, they knew that what I said could not be refuted. That is why they allowed you to indulge in plain vituperation, that is, they repeated the very method I had accused them of in my first article.

Was this a creditable role that you, who signed yourself "worker", played in the hands of the *Luch* editors?

Pravda No. 114, May 19, 1913   Published according to
Signed: *Reader*   the *Pravda* text

THE LAND QUESTION SETTLED—LANDOWNER FASHION

As usual there was an immoderate amount of rubbish in the budget debate in the Fourth State Duma. The vain efforts of Markov the Second to trip up Kokovtsov, and the vain efforts of Kokovtsov "to charm away" with words the feudal character of "our" policy and our budget, and the vain efforts of the Cadets to assure a gullible public that Kokovtsov "admitted it was *the Cadets* who had to be taken into consideration" in the Fourth Duma—this was just a lot of tedious, overworked and hypocritical rubbish.

There are, however, a few grains of truth in this rubbish heap. The Markovs, Kokovtsovs and Shingaryovs tried to hide them deeper in it. But it is worth while pulling them out.

"I have dealt at such length with the settlement of the land question," Kokovtsov exclaimed on May 13, "because in that question is contained the whole solution of Russia's future...."

It was not the "whole" solution and the "future" in general that needed to be discussed, but the future of the June Third system,[41] which gives all power to the "bureaucracy" and the feudal landowners. Under the *old* rural organisation *we* cannot retain power—that was what the landowners, taught by bitter experience, had decided. In order to retain power they had to arrange in their own way for the reorganisation of the old countryside on bourgeois lines. That is the basis and the essence of "the land question".

"... Whether the government will be able to do this, whether it [the settlement of the land question] will bring the benefit the government and the legislative institutions expect," continued the Minister, "the future will show...."

Of course, the future will reveal *everything* and show *everything*. It will show the *outcome* of the efforts of the feudals and the efforts of the proletariat that marches at the head of the democrats. But the figures given by the "serious" (by Cadet standards) Mr. Kokovtsov show absolutely nothing. The number of applications for land is rapidly increasing—and Mr. Kokovtsov is enraptured, the Rights in the Duma are enraptured. The number of applications was: in 1907—221,000; in 1908—385,000; in 1909—711,000; in 1910 —651,000; in 1911—683,000; in 1912—1,183,000; total 3,834,000.

Arrangements have been made for only 1,592,000 peasant households.

Such are the Minister's "proofs" and his material for judging the future.

On that very same May 13 the *government* newspaper *Novoye Vremya* published data for the house-to-house Zemstvo census taken in 1911 in Samara Uyezd. The number of households obtaining titles to land amounted in that uyezd to forty per cent, that is, higher than the average for Russia. This uyezd, therefore, is most "favourable" for the government.

And how did it turn out? Of the total number obtaining titles to land *less than three out of a hundred* (2.9 per cent) own real, separate farmsteads; only one-sixteenth (6.5 per cent) own their land in one piece and *more than nine-tenths* (90.6 per cent) have land in strips in different places!

Nine-tenths of the title-holding peasants farm strips that are isolated from each other, just as they did before. Farming conditions are even *worse* than before because *formerly* the commune could "correct" the strip system to some extent by frequent redistributions.

In a mere four years *a third* of the land transferred to the title-holders has already passed into other hands. Loss of land is increasing, impoverishment is increasing still more rapidly and there is growing confusion because of the strips of land. Unbelievable poverty is increasing in the villages, as is the number of famines. The number of landless peasants, pure proletarians, is increasing. The number of impoverished "would-be proprietors" is increasing; they are *trapped* both by the old bondage and by the system of allotting scattered strips of land that has resulted from the notorious landowners' solution to the land problem.

Apparently this bondage will not be abolished by the *landowners*' solution to the *peasant* land problem. It can only be cured if the land question is settled on broad democratic lines.

Pravda No. 115, May 21, 1913   Published according to
                                        the *Pravda* text

ARMAMENTS AND CAPITALISM

Britain is one of the richest, freest and most advanced countries in the world. The armaments fever has long afflicted British "society" and the British Government, in exactly the same way as it has the French, German and other governments.

And now the British press, particularly the labour press, is publishing very interesting data, which reveal the ingenious capitalist "mechanics" of arms manufacture. Britain's naval armaments are particularly great. Britain's shipyards (Vickers, Armstrong, Brown and others) are world-famous. Hundreds and thousands of millions of rubles are being spent by Britain and other countries on war preparations, and of course it is all being done exclusively in the interests of peace, for the preservation of culture, in the interests of the country, civilisation, etc.

And we find that admirals and prominent statesmen of both parties, Conservative and Liberal, are shareholders and directors of shipyards, and of gunpowder, dynamite, ordnance and other factories. A shower of gold is pouring straight into the pockets of bourgeois politicians, who have got together in an exclusive international gang engaged in instigating an armaments race among the peoples and *fleecing* these trustful, stupid, dull and submissive peoples like sheep.

Armaments are considered a national matter, a matter of patriotism; it is presumed that everyone maintains strict secrecy. But the shipyards, the ordnance, dynamite and small-arms factories are *international enterprises*, in which the capitalists of the various countries work together in duping and fleecing the public of the various countries, and making ships and guns alike for Britain against Italy, and for Italy against Britain.

An ingenious capitalist set-up! Civilisation, law and order, culture, peace—and hundreds of millions of rubles being plundered by capitalist businessmen and swindlers in shipbuilding, dynamite manufacture, etc.!

Britain is a member of the Triple Entente, which is hostile to the Triple Alliance. Italy is a member of the Triple Alliance. The well-known firm of Vickers (Britain) has *branches* in Italy. The shareholders and directors of this firm (through the venal press and through venal parliamentary "figures", Conservative and Liberal alike) incite Britain against Italy, and vice versa. And profit is taken both from the workers of Britain and those of Italy; the people are fleeced in both countries.

Conservative and Liberal Cabinet Ministers and Members of Parliament are almost all shareholders in these firms. They work hand in glove. The son of the "great" Liberal Minister, Gladstone, is a director of the Armstrong concern. Rear-Admiral Bacon, the celebrated naval specialist and a high official at the Admiralty, has been appointed to a post at an ordnance works in Coventry at a salary of £7,000 (over 60,000 rubles). The salary of the British Prime Minister is £5,000 (about 45,000 rubles).

The same thing, of course, takes place in all capitalist countries. Governments manage the affairs of the capitalist class, and the managers are well paid. The managers are shareholders themselves. And they shear the sheep together, under cover of speeches about "patriotism...."

Pravda No. 115, May 21, 1913
Signed: *Fr.*

Published according to
the *Pravda* text

HELPLESSNESS AND CONFUSION

(NOTE)

The reasons for the chaos and confusion among modern Social-Democrats and "near Social-Democrats" are not only external (persecutions, etc.), but also *internal*. A huge number of old "prominent Party people" are completely confused, they have understood absolutely nothing about the new state of affairs (the counter-revolution of the June Third system), and their helpless "dithering"—today to the left, tomorrow to the right—has caused hopeless confusion in everything they undertake.

A perfect example of this embarrassment, helplessness and confusion is to be found in the article by A. Vlasov in *Luch* No. 109 (195).

There is not a single idea, a single sound word in the whole of Vlasov's article. It is all confusion and helpless limping after the liquidators combined with futile efforts to disassociate himself from them. It is not true that "formerly" our Party was sometimes built up "without the workers themselves", or that "the activities of the underground amounted largely (!!?) to abstract (!?) propaganda of the ideas of socialism". The history of the old *Iskra* (1900-03), which created the Party programme and the fundamentals of Party tactics, fully refutes this. It is not true that the Party's task today is "open *work* (!!?), but the secret organisation of it". A. Vlasov has completely failed to understand the liquidationist content of the slogan "struggle for an open party", although it was explained in *Pravda* No. 108 (312), popularly and not for the first time.

It is not true that *Pravda* advises "adopting the work of the old Party organisation as an example". "It is essential

to outline, even if briefly, the nature of the activity of this
(new) underground, i.e., its tactics," says A. Vlasov with
amusing pomposity ("we, the practical workers"). *As far
back as* December 1908[42] the Party "outlined" *its* tactics
(and in 1912[43] and 1913[44] confirmed and explained them)
and its organisation, giving a clear *"example"* of old tasks
and *new* forms of preparation. If A. Vlasov has not yet understood this he has only himself to blame: it is his fate to
repeat fragments of liquidationism, the dispute with which,
incidentally, has nothing to do with the "organisation question".

Pravda No. 115, May 21, 1913
    Signed: *V. Ilyin*

Published according to
    the *Pravda* text

DRAFT PLATFORM FOR THE FOURTH CONGRESS OF SOCIAL-DEMOCRATS OF THE LATVIAN AREA[45]

The revolutionary upsurge of the working-class movement in Russia, the sharpening of the political crisis in the country, the economic crisis that will begin in the near or not far distant future, the wavering and confusion among the many groups and circles of Social-Democrats—all this compels class-conscious Latvian workers to appeal to their comrades to make intensive preparations for the convocation of the Fourth Congress of Social-Democrats of the Latvian Area and to engage in a thorough discussion of the tasks now confronting revolutionary Social-Democracy.

A group consisting of members of various Latvian Social-Democratic organisations proposes to all Social-Democratic organisations, as material for discussion, the following *platform* of views on the most important questions of principle, questions that concern the very existence of our Social-Democratic Labour Party, and the whole direction its activities should take—in particular those questions which the present Central Committee of the Latvian Social-Democratic Party stubbornly ignores or, we are convinced, decides incorrectly.

APPRAISAL OF THE POLITICAL SITUATION AND THE GENERAL TACTICAL TASKS OF THE SOCIAL-DEMOCRATS

It is an open secret that the prevalence of counter-revolution has brought about a deep-going ideological disintegration and a confusion of mind among Social-Democrats. Everywhere there are Social-Democrats who, as Comrade An[46] so aptly put it (*Luch* No. 95), are wandering about like lost sheep. Views are expressed in the Social-Democratic press to the effect that workers should not prepare for a revolution, that they should not expect a revolution, that the democratic revolution is over, etc. The so-called liquidators (*Nasha Zarya* and *Luch*), supported by the present Central Committee of the Social-Democratic Party of the Latvian Area, regularly base their tactical arguments on such views, although no responsible group or organisation of the R.S.D.L.P. has expounded them in a manner that is in any way definite, precise and formal.

In the press of this trend we meet at every turn with references to the fundamental difference between Russia's present state system and the pre-October system (as though we no longer needed a revolution to win for ourselves the elements of political liberty), or comparisons of the present tactics of the Russian Social-Democrats with those of European Social-Democrats living under a constitution, the tactics, for example, of the Austrians and Germans in the seventies of the nineteenth century (as though a constitution already existed in Russia, as Milyukov thinks it does), or the promulgation of the slogan of an open workers' party and freedom to form associations (a slogan that could be understood only if there existed the general foundation and the pillars of political liberty and a bourgeois constitution in the country), and so on and so forth.

Under such circumstances, to refuse to give a precise definition of the tactical tasks of Social-Democrats or an appraisal of the political situation, or to postpone this appraisal or definition, would mean not only not fighting against ideological confusion, disintegration, despondency and lack of faith, it would mean directly assisting that disintegration and giving indirect support to views that nullify the old revolutionary Party decisions adopted by the Social-Democrats.

The R.S.D.L.P., however, has an accurate Party answer to these urgent and fundamental questions. The answer was given in the resolution of December 1908, which is a resolution binding on Party members and has not been annulled by anyone.

The years that have passed since the resolution was adopted have fully confirmed its correctness—its statements on the change in the nature of the autocracy, on the counter-revolutionary nature of liberalism, etc., and its conclusion that the autocracy continues to exist, although in a partly renovated form, that the conditions that gave rise to the 1905 Revolution are still there, that the Social-Democratic Party is confronted with the *old tasks* that demand a revolutionary solution and revolutionary tactics. The employment of the Duma as a tribune, and of *all* legal opportunities, which is categorically demanded in the decisions of the same conference of the R.S.D.L.P. (December 1908), must be effected *entirely* in the spirit of these revolutionary tactics and *in the name of* the old revolutionary tasks of the R.S.D.L.P.

We therefore suggest that all Social-Democratic organisations once more hold a thorough discussion of the resolution, which was, incidentally, confirmed by the January 1912 Conference of the R.S.D.L.P., and *propose to the Congress of Social-Democrats of the Latvian Area that it definitely confirm this resolution.*

We call the serious attention of all comrades to the anti-Party method of the August 1912 (liquidators') Conference of "Social-Democratic organisations", which removed from the agenda the appraisal of the current situation and the definition of general tactical tasks, thus throwing open the door to every possible *renunciation of revolutionary tasks* (on the excuse that "the forecast" concerning the revolution had not been proved, etc.).

We protest in particular against the Bund, which played such an important role at the August Conference, and which at its own Ninth Conference went so far in renouncing revolutionary tasks as to withdraw the slogan of a democratic republic and confiscation of landed estates!

THE QUESTION OF THE UNITY OF THE R.S.D.L.P.

The more widespread the economic and political struggle of the workers, the more urgently they feel the need for unity. Unless the working class is united, its struggle cannot be successful.

What is this unity? Obviously, *the unity of the Social-Democratic Party.* All Latvian Social-Democratic workers belong to the Social-Democratic Party and know full well that the Party is illegal, underground, and cannot be anything else.

There cannot, therefore, be *any other way* in which unity *in deed* (not merely in word) can be achieved except from below, by the workers themselves, in their underground organisations.

It is this demand for unity that the Congress of Social-Democrats of the Latvian Area must definitely recognise. It was, incidentally, put forward by the February 1913 meeting held at the Central Committee of the R.S.D.L.P.

If *Luch* answered *such an* appeal for unity by ridiculing "Lenin's party", and if the Bund (in the shape of "active Jewish members of the working-class movement") rejected the appeal, both of them, the "Luchists" and Bund members, thereby *proved* their allegiance to the liquidators.

Latvian Social-Democratic workers, who recognise the illegal Party not merely in word but in deed, will not allow themselves to be deceived by legal orations in favour of unity. Let him who wants unity join the illegal Party!

ATTITUDE TO THE LIQUIDATORS

The question of liquidationism, which was first brought up by Party decisions and by the press abroad, has now been offered for the judgemel t of all class-conscious workers in Russia. Latvian Social-Democratic workers must also endeavour to ensure that there are no evasions or reservations on this question, that it is presented clearly, discussed from all angles and given a definite solution.

We have had enough fairy-tales about the liquidators being the champions of an open movement. These tales have been refuted by *facts* proving that Party members who are against the liquidators, those who are unmistakably supporters of the underground movement, are *incomparably stronger* than the liquidators in *all* spheres of the open movement.

Liquidationism is the rejection or the belittling of the underground, that is, the illegal (and only existing) Party. It is only the underground that works out *revolutionary* tactics and takes those tactics to the masses through both the illegal *and the legal* press.

The decisions adopted by the R.S.D.L.P. in December 1908 and January 1910, which no one has annulled, and which are obligatory for all Party members, clearly and precisely recognise the content of liquidationism as described above, and roundly condemn it.

Nevertheless, *Nasha Zarya* and *Luch* continue preaching liquidationism. In *Luch* No. 15 (101) the growth of sympathy for the underground on the part of the workers was declared *deplorable*. In *Nasha Zarya* No. 3 (March 1913) the author of that article (L. Sedov) emphasised his liquidationism *more than ever*. This was admitted *even by An* in *Luch* (No. 95)! And the *Luch* editors, replying to An, *defend the liquidator Sedov*.

Latvian Social-Democratic workers must at all costs ensure that the Congress of Social-Democrats of the Latvian Area *resolutely condemns the liquidationism of "Nasha Zarya" and "Luch"*. The conduct of these periodicals has fully confirmed and is daily continuing to confirm the correctness of the resolution on liquidationism adopted at the meeting in February 1913 at the Central Committee of the R.S.D.L.P.

THE QUESTION OF SUPPORT FOR THE LIQUIDATORS' CONFERENCE AND ORGANISING COMMITTEE BY THE CENTRAL COMMITTEE OF THE SOCIAL-DEMOCRATIC PARTY OF THE LATVIAN AREA

The present Central Committee of the Social-Democratic Party of the Latvian Area maintains that it supports the August Conference and the Organising Committee *not* because they are liquidator institutions but *for the sake of unity* in the R.S.D.L.P.

Such an answer could satisfy only children, and the Latvian Social-Democratic workers are not children.

Those who organised the August Conference *themselves* invited Plekhanov and the *Vperyod*[47] group to it. Neither of them had taken part in the January Conference, that is, they *showed* not merely in word but in deed that they are *neutral* in the struggle between the trends.

And what did these neutral Social-Democrats say? Plekhanov and Alexinsky forthrightly recognised the August

Conference to be a liquidators' conference. The resolutions of that conference show its liquidationist character to the full. *Luch*, by announcing that it supports the decisions of the August Conference, is preaching liquidationism.

Whom are the worker Social-Democrats of Russia following?

This was demonstrated by the elections to the Duma in the worker curia and by the data on the working-class press.

In the Second Duma the Bolsheviks gained 47 per cent of the votes of the workers' curia (11 deputies out of 23); in the Third Duma they had 50 per cent (4 out of 8) and in the Fourth Duma they had 67 per cent (6 out of 9). The working-class press of the anti-liquidators (*Pravda* and the Moscow newspaper) is supported by 1,199 groups of workers as compared with 256 groups supporting *Luch*.

And so, the present Central Committee of the Social-Democratic Party of the Latvian Area, in the name of Latvian revolutionary worker Social-Democrats, supports the liquidators *against* the obvious majority of worker Social-Democrats in Russia!

An end must be put to this. We all recognise the underground and revolutionary tactics. We must support the Central Committee of the R.S.D.L.P., which implements these tactics and which has behind it the overwhelming majority of worker Social-Democrats in Russia *both* in the underground *and* in the open movement.

THE NATIONAL QUESTION

This question, both in its general theoretical, socialist presentation, and from the practical, organisational point of view (the organisation of our own Party) is in urgent need of discussion and solution by all Social-Democratic organisations.

The liquidators' conference in August 1912—as was admitted even by the neutral Menshevik Plekhanov—*contravened* the Programme of the R.S.D.L.P. in the spirit of *"adaptation of socialism to nationalism"*.

In fact, this conference recognised, on the proposal of the Bund, the permissibility of the slogan of "cultural-national autonomy", which was contrary to the decision taken by the Second Party Congress.

This slogan (defended in Russia by *all the bourgeois* Jewish nationalist parties) contradicts the *internationalism* of Social-Democracy. As democrats, we are irreconcilably hostile to any, however slight, oppression of any nationality and to any privileges for any nationality. As democrats, we demand the right of nations to self-determination *in the political sense* of that term (see the Programme of the R.S.D.L.P.), i.e., the right to secede. We demand unconditional *equality* for all nations in the state and the unconditional protection of the rights of every national minority. We demand broad self-government and autonomy for regions, which must be demarcated, among other terms of reference, in respect of nationality too.

All these demands are obligatory for every consistent democrat, to say nothing of a socialist.

Socialists, however, do not limit themselves to general-democratic demands. They *fight* all possible manifestations of *bourgeois nationalism*, crude or refined. "National-cultural autonomy" is a manifestation precisely of this type—it *joins* the proletarians and bourgeoisie of *one* nation and *keeps* the proletarians of *different* nations *apart.*

Social-Democrats have always stood and still stand for the *internationalist* point of view. While protecting the equality of all nationalities against the serf-owners and the police state we do not support *"national culture"* but *international* culture, which includes only part of each national culture—only the consistently democratic and socialist content of each national culture.

The slogan of "national-cultural autonomy" deceives the workers with the phantom of a cultural unity of nations, whereas in every nation today a landowners', bourgeois or petty-bourgeois "culture" predominates.

We are against national culture as one of the slogans of bourgeois nationalism. *We are in favour of the international culture of a fully democratic and socialist proletariat.*

The unity of the workers of *all* nationalities coupled with the fullest equality for the nationalities and the most consistently democratic state system—that is our slogan, and it is the slogan of international revolutionary Social-Democracy. This truly proletarian slogan will not create the false phantom and illusion of "national" unity of the proletariat and the bourgeoisie, while the slogan of "national-cultural autonomy" undoubtedly does create that phantom and does sow that illusion among the working people.

We, Latvian Social-Democrats, living in an area with a population that is very mixed nationally, we, who are in an environment consisting of representatives of the bourgeois nationalism of the Letts, Russians, Estonians, Germans, etc., see with particular clarity the bourgeois falsity of the slogan of "cultural-national autonomy". The slogan of the *unity* of all and every organisation of workers of *all* nationalities, tested in practice in our own Social-Democratic organisation, is particularly dear to us.

Reference is frequently made to Austria in justification of the slogan of "national-cultural autonomy". As far as this reference is concerned it must be remembered that: first, the point of view of the chief Austrian theoretician on the national question, Otto Bauer (in his book *The National Question and Social-Democracy*) has been recognised as an *exaggeration* of the national factor and a *terrible underestimation* of the international factor even by such a cautious writer as Karl Kautsky (see: K. Kautsky, *Nationalität und Internationalität*; it has been translated into Russian); secondly, in Russia *only* the Bund members, together with all Jewish bourgeois parties, have so far defended "cultural-national autonomy", whereas *neither* Bauer *nor* Kautsky *recognise* national autonomy for the Jews, and Kautsky (*op. cit.*) declares outright that the Jews of Eastern Europe (Galicia and Russia) are *a caste* and not a nation; thirdly, the Brünn* national programme of the Austrian Social-Democratic Party (1899)[48] *does not* fully recognise extra-territorial (personal) national autonomy and goes only as far as to demand the union of all national regions of one nationality throughout the state (Sec. 3 of the Brünn Programme); fourthly, even this programme, obviously a compromise (and unsatisfactory from the standpoint of internationalism), was *a complete fiasco* in Austria itself, because the compromise did not bring peace but led, instead,

---

* Now Brno in Czechoslovakia.—*Ed.*

to the secession of the Czech separatists; fifthly, these Czech separatists, unanimously condemned at the Copenhagen Congress by the entire International, declare the Bund type of separatism to be close to them (see: *Der čechoslavische Sozial-demokrat* No. 3, organ of the separatists, which may be obtained gratis from *Prague*: Praha, Hybernska 7); sixthly, Bauer himself demands the unity of Social-Democratic political organisations of various nationalities *in each locality*. Bauer himself considers the "national system" of the Austrian party, which has now led to a *complete* schism, to be unstable and contradictory.

In short, references to Austria speak *against* the Bund and not *in its favour*.

Unity from below, the complete unity and consolidation in each locality of Social-Democratic workers of all nationalities in all working-class organisations—that is our slogan. Down with the deceptive bourgeois, compromise slogan of "cultural-national autonomy"!

We are *against* federation in the structure of our Party, too; we are for the *unity* of local (and not only central) organisations of Social-Democrats of all nations.

The Congress must reject both the slogan of cultural-national autonomy and the principle of federation in the structure of the Party. The Latvian Social-Democrats, like the Polish Social-Democrats, like the Social-Democrats of the Caucasus throughout the period from 1898 to 1912 (for *14* whole years of Party history) must remain true to Social-Democratic internationalism.

Written in May,
before June 25 (7), 1913
First published in Lettish
in the newspaper *Cinas Biedrs*
No. 4 in August 1913

First published in Russian
in 1929 in the second
and third editions of V. I. Lenin's
Collected Works, Vol. XVII

Published according to
the manuscript

LIBERAL AND MARXIST CONCEPTIONS
OF THE CLASS STRUGGLE

NOTE

A. Yermansky, a liquidator, poured down an amazing abundance of angry words in *Nasha Zarya* on my criticism of his (and Gushka's) point of view on the question of the political role of the big commercial and industrial bourgeoisie (*Prosveshcheniye* Nos. 5-7).*

Mr. Yermansky, with his vituperation and recollections of old "insults" (including the "insult" to Mr. Dan & Co., who tried, unsuccessfully, to split the St. Petersburg Social-Democratic organisation in 1907), tries *to conceal* the real substance of the issue.

We shall, however, not permit Mr. Yermansky to conceal the substance of the present dispute by recalling undeserved insults to and defeats of the liquidators. For the present dispute concerns a very important question of principle that comes up again and again for a thousand different reasons.

To be precise, it is the question of the liberal falsification of Marxism, the substitution of a Marxist, revolutionary conception of the class struggle by a liberal conception. We shall never tire of explaining this ideological basis of all the disputes between the Marxists and the liquidators.

Mr. A. Yermansky writes:

"The 'Marxist' Ilyin refuses to recognise, in the activities of industrial organisations, the class struggle 'on a nation-wide (and partly even international) scale' as I [Yermansky] described them in my article. Why? Because of the 'absence' here 'of the fundamental feature of the nation-*wide* or state-*wide*—the organisation of state power'"... (*Nasha Zarya*, p. 55).

---

* See present edition Vol. 18 pp. 56-72.—*Ed.*

Here is an exposition of *the substance* of the question given by Mr. Yermansky himself, who does everything possible and impossible to evade that substance! No matter how he may accuse me of distorting his views and of all the mortal sins, no matter how he twists and turns, even seeking refuge in recollections of the 1907 split, the truth will out.

My thesis, therefore, is clear—the basic feature of the nation-wide is the organisation of state power.

You do not share that view, my angry opponent? You do not think this the only Marxist view?

Then why not say so straight out? Why not counterpose a correct view to an incorrect one? If the view that the fundamental feature of the nation-wide is the organisation of state power is, in your opinion, only Marxism in inverted commas, why do you not refute my error and expound *your* understanding of Marxism clearly, precisely and without evasion?

The answer to these questions will be clear to the reader if we quote the passage from Mr. A. Yermansky which folowed *immediately after* the one quoted above:

"Ilyin wants the big Russian bourgeoisie to carry on their class struggle in a different way, he wants them to try to bring about a change in the entire state system. Ilyin wants, the bourgeoisie do not want—and the one at fault, of course, is Yermansky the 'liquidator', who 'substitutes the *liberal* conception of the class struggle for the conception of the class struggle in the Marxist sense'."

Here you have Mr. Yermansky's tirade in full and it will enable you to get a picture of the evasive liquidator *caught in the act.*

The evasion is obvious.

Have I or have I not indicated correctly the "fundamental feature" of the nation-wide?

Mr. A. Yermansky himself was forced to admit that I indicated precisely the substance of the matter.

And Mr. Yermansky evades an answer, realising that he has been caught!

And having been caught in the act, Mr. Yermansky evades the question of the correctness or incorrectness of the fundamental feature I indicated and jumps over this question to the question of what Ilyin and the bourgeoisie "want".

But no matter how bold, how daring Mr. Yermansky's leaps, they do not disguise the fact that he has been caught.

What have "wants" got to do with it, my dear opponent, when the dispute concerns the *concept* of the class struggle?! You had to admit that I accused you of substituting a liberal for a Marxist *conception*, and that I indicated the "fundamental feature" of the *Marxist* conception as including the organisation of state power in the idea of a nation-wide class struggle.

Mr. A. Yermansky is such a clumsy polemicist, even if an angry one, that he gave a clear explanation, *by his own example*, of the connection between liquidationism in general and his own, Yermansky's, mistakes in particular and the liberal conception of the class struggle!

The question of the class struggle is one of the fundamental questions of Marxism. It is, therefore, worth while dealing with the *concept* of class struggle in greater detail.

Every class struggle is a political struggle.[49] We know that the opportunists, slaves to the ideas of liberalism, understood these profound words of Marx incorrectly and tried to put a distorted interpretation on them. Among the opportunists there were, for instance, the Economists, the elder brothers of the liquidators. The Economists believed that any clash between classes was a political struggle. The Economists therefore recognised as "class struggle" the struggle for a wage increase of five kopeks on the ruble, and refused to recognise a higher, more developed, nation-wide *class* struggle, the struggle for *political aims*. The Economists, therefore, recognised the embryonic class struggle but did not recognise it in its developed form. The Economists recognised, in other words, only that part of the class struggle that was more tolerable to the liberal bourgeoisie, they refused to go farther than the liberals, they refused to recognise the higher form of class struggle that is unacceptable to the liberals. By so doing, the Economists became liberal workers' politicians. By so doing, the Economists rejected the Marxist, revolutionary conception of the class struggle.

To continue. It is not enough that the class struggle becomes real, consistent and developed only when it embraces the sphere of politics. In politics, too, it is possible to restrict oneself to minor matters, and it is possible to go deeper, to the very foundations. Marxism recognises a class struggle as fully developed, "nation-wide", *only* if it does not merely embrace politics but takes in the most significant thing in politics—the organisation of state power.

On the other hand, the liberals, when the working-class movement has grown a little stronger, dare not deny the class struggle but attempt to narrow down, to curtail and emasculate the concept of class struggle. Liberals are prepared to recognise the class struggle in the sphere of politics, too, but on one condition—that the organisation of state power should *not* enter into that sphere. It is not hard to understand which of the bourgeoisie's class interests give rise to the liberal distortion of the concept of class struggle.

Now, when Mr. Yermansky rehashed the work of the moderate and punctilious civil servant Gushka, when he expressed solidarity with him, *not noticing* (or not wishing to see?) the liberal emasculation of the concept of class struggle, I pointed out to Mr. Yermansky his chief sin against theory and general principles. Mr. Yermansky grew angry and began to use bad language and to twist and turn, being unable to refute what I had said.

In doing so, Mr. A. Yermansky proved such a clumsy polemicist that he exposed himself with particular clarity! "Ilyin wants, the bourgeoisie do not want," he writes. We now know what particular features of the point of view of the proletariat (Marxism) and of the bourgeoisie (liberalism) give rise to these different "wants".

The bourgeoisie "want" to curtail the class struggle, to distort and narrow the conception and *blunt* its sharp edge. The proletariat "wants" this deception exposed. The Marxist wants whoever undertakes to speak of the class struggle of the bourgeoisie in the name of Marxism *to expose* the narrowness, the *selfish* narrowness, indeed, of the bourgeois conception of the class struggle, and not merely to quote figures, not merely to go into ecstasies over "big" figures. The liberal "wants" to appraise the bourgeoisie and its class struggle in such a way as *to conceal* its narrowness, *to conceal* the failure to include in the struggle that which is "basic" and most important.

Mr. A. Yermansky was caught out in discussing in *liberal fashion* the interesting, but ideologically empty or slavishly compiled figures of Mr. Gushka. Obviously, when this was revealed, there was nothing left for Mr. A. Yermansky to do but curse and wriggle.

Let us continue the passage from Mr. A. Yermansky's article where we left off:

"It is clear that, in fact, Ilyin is the only person who is replacing a study of the real state of affairs by his own qualifications, and also [!!] by a stereotyped pattern based on schoolboy models drawn from the history of the great French Revolution."

Mr. A. Yermansky has got into such a tangle that he becomes ever more ruthless in "destroying" himself! He does not notice the extent to which his liberalism is revealed by this angry sally against the "stereotypes" of the great French Revolution!

My dear Mr. Yermansky, you must understand (no matter how difficult it may be for a liquidator to understand) that it is impossible "to study the real state of affairs" *without qualifying* it, without appraising it from the Marxist, or the liberal, or the reactionary, etc., point of view!

You, Mr. Yermansky, qualified and still qualify the "study" of the good civil servant Gushka in liberal fashion and I qualify it in Marxist fashion. That is what is at the bottom of it all. By leaving your critical analysis *on the threshold* of the question of *the organisation* of state power, you thereby *proved* the liberal limitations of *your* conception of the class struggle.

Which was to be shown!

Your sally against the "stereotype" of the great French Revolution gives you away completely. Anybody can understand that a stereotype or a French model has nothing to do with the matter—for instance, there were not and could not have been strikes, especially political strikes *at that time*, under "stereotype and model" conditions.

The fact of the matter is that when you became a liquidator you forgot how to apply the *revolutionary* point of view to an appraisal of social events. That is where the trouble lies. Marx certainly did not limit his thinking to "stereotypes and models" taken from the end of the eighteenth century, but the point of view he adopted was always revolutionary, he always *appraised* ("qualified" if you prefer that "learned" word, my dear Mr. Yermansky!) the class struggle most *profoundly*, always revealing whether it affected "fundamentals", always mercilessly berating any timidity of thought, any concealment of underdeveloped, emasculated, selfishly distorted class struggle.

The class struggle at the end of the eighteenth century showed us how it can become political, how it can develop to really "nation-wide" forms. Since then capitalism and the proletariat have developed to a gigantic extent. The "models" of the old do not prevent, for instance, the study of the new *forms* of struggle that I have, in part, outlined above.

The point of view of the Marxist, however, will *always* require a profound and not a superficial "appraisal", will always expose the poverty of *liberal* distortions, understatements and cowardly concealment.

Let us congratulate Mr. Yermansky on his devoted and splendid explanation of the way in which the liquidators substitute a liberal conception of the class struggle for the Marxist conception, forgetting how to examine social events from the revolutionary point of view.

Prosveshcheniye No. 5, May 1913   Published according
         Signed: *V. Ilyin*   to the *Prosveshcheniye* text

FACTORY OWNERS ON WORKERS' STRIKES

I

P. P. Ryabushinsky's press in Moscow has published an interesting book entitled *The Association of Factory Owners in the Moscow Industrial Area in 1912* (Moscow, 1913). The price is not given. The factory owners do not wish their publications to be put on sale.

Yuli Petrovich Guzhon, the president of the association, when opening this year's annual meeting on March 30, congratulated the industrialists "on the beginning of. the seventh operative year" of :their organisation and declared that the industrialists had "by their unity created for themselves a conception of the might of the .industrial corporation that could not be ignored". "The present main task of new members of the association must be the strengthening of the prestige of that might," said Mr. Guzhon.

As you see, the speech was not what one might call literate, it was reminiscent of the speech of some army clerk; nevertheless it was full of arrogance.

Let us look at the sections of the book dealing with facts. More than one-third of it (pp. 19-69) is taken up by the section devoted to *strikes*. The industrialists give us the following picture of the total number of workers taking part in strikes in.1912.

Category of strike	Number of striking workers	
	1912	1911
Economic	*207,720*	*96,730*
Metal goods industry	64.200	17,920
Textiles ” ”	90,930	51,670
Other branches	52,590	27,140
Political	*855,000*	*8,380*
Over Lena events	215,000	
May Day celebrations	300,000	
Autumn political strikes	340,000	
Totals	*1,062,720*	*105,110*

It is easy to see that the industrialists' figures are an *understatement*. But for the time being we shall not deal with that (the Lena strike of 6,000 workers has been omitted because the Lena Goldfields do not come under the Factory Inspectorate), but we shall examine the factory owners' statistics.

The number of workers who took part in strikes in 1912 was *more than a half* of the total number of industrial workers in Russia, to be exact, 51.7 per cent. Economic strikes, furthermore, accounted for only *one-tenth* of the workers (10.1 per cent) and political strikes for more than *four-tenths* (41.6 per cent).

"Typical of the past year," write the factory owners, "was the extraordinary growth in the number of political strikes that time and again interrupted the normal course of work and kept the entire industry in a state of tension." This is followed by a list of the most important strikes in the second half of the year—August, in Riga, against the disenfranchisement of workers; September, in Warsaw, over the events at the Kutomary Penal Colony; October, in St. Petersburg, over the annulment of the elections of representatives, in Revel, in memory of the events of 1905, and in St. Petersburg, over the well-known verdict in the case of naval ratings; November, in St. Petersburg, over the Sevastopol verdict and on the day of the opening of the Duma, and then a strike on the occasion of the second anniversary of Leo Tolstoy's death; December, in St. Petersburg, over the appointment of workers in insurance institutions. From this the factory owners draw the conclusion:

'The frequency of the demonstration strikes, which occur one after another, and the unusual variety and difference in the importance of the motives for which the workers considered it necessary to interrupt work, are evidence, not only of a considerable thickening of the political atmosphere, but also of the decline of factory discipline." Then follow the usual threats of "severe measures"—fines, stopping of bonuses, lock-outs. "The interests of the country's production," declare the factory owners, "urgently demand the raising of factory discipline to the high level at which it stands in the West-European countries."

The factory owners wish to raise "discipline" to the "Western" level but do not think of raising the "political atmosphere" to the same level....

We shall leave for subsequent articles the data concerning strike distribution over various areas, and in various branches of industry and according to the degree of success achieved.

II

The 1912 data of the Moscow Factory Owners Association on the incidence of strikes in various areas and branches of industry are very badly compiled. It would do no harm if our millionaires were to hire, say, some high-school boy to help them compile their books and check the tables. Mistakes and absurdities leap to the eye when we compare, for example, the data given on pages 23, 26 and 48. Oh yes, we love talking about culture and "the prestige of the might" of the merchants, but we can't do even the simplest job half-way decently.

Below we give the factory owners' strike statistics—*for economic strikes only*—by areas for 1912 as a whole and for the last seven months of that year:

| | For all 1912 | | For the last 7 months of 1912 | |
Areas	Number of strikers	Number of days lost (000)	Number of strikers	Number of days lost (000)
Moscow	60,070	799.2	48,140	730.6
St. Petersburg	56,890	704.8	35,390	545.7
Baltic	18,950	193.5	13,210	153.6
South	23,350	430.3	22,195	427.6
Kingdom of Poland . .	21,120	295.7	12,690	249.9
Totals	180,380	2,423.5	131,625	2,107.4

A glance at the figures for the South is enough to show how useless, i.e., extremely incomplete, the factory owners' statistics are. The figures for the last seven months of 1912 seem to be more reliable, because here, and only here, the distribution of strikers is given in detail according to areas, major industries and the results achieved.

The area data show us that the St. Petersburg workers are in advance of all the workers of Russia in the economic struggle as well (to say nothing of the political struggle). The number of strikers in the St. Petersburg area (35,000 for the last seven months of 1912) is about three-quarters of the number of strikers in the Moscow area (48,000) although the number of factory workers there is *about four times* that of the number in the St. Petersburg area. In the Kingdom of Poland there are slightly more workers than in the St. Petersburg area but the number of strikers there was little more than a third of the St. Petersburg figure.

As far as Moscow is concerned, there is, of course, the need to consider the worsening marketing conditions in the textile industry, although in Poland two-thirds of those participating in economic strikes were textile workers and we shall see later that these textile strikes in Poland were particularly successful.

In 1912, therefore, the St. Petersburg workers to a certain extent drew the workers of other parts of Russia into the economic strike movement.

In respect of *determination*, on the other hand, the strikes in the South and in Poland take first place; in these areas nineteen days per striker were lost, whereas in St. Petersburg and Moscow the figure was fifteen days (in the Baltic area 12 days per striker). The average for all Russia was sixteen days on strike per striker. The gentlemen who compile the factory owners' statistics give the figure for the whole of 1912 as 13.4 days. It follows from this that the persistence of the workers and their determination in struggle were greater in the second half of the year.

Statistics show, furthermore, the *increased persistence* of the workers in the strike struggle. From 1895 to 1904 the average number of days lost per striker was 4.8, in 1909 it was 6.5 days, in 1911 it was 7.5 days (8.2 days if political strikes are excluded) and in 1912, 13.4 days.

The year 1912, therefore, showed that there is a *growing persistence* among workers in the economic struggle and that the number of strikers—compared with the number of workers—is greatest in St. Petersburg.

In our next article we shall examine data on the degree of success achieved by strikes.

III

The factory owners' statistics give the following figures for strikers (in economic strikes) for 1912 according to branches of industry:

Branch of industry	For all 1912		For the last 7 months of 1912	
	Number of strikers	Number of days lost (000)	Number of strikers	Number of days lost (000)
Metalworkers	57,000	807.2	40,475	763.3
Textile workers	85,550	1,025.8	66,590	930.6
Others	37,830	590.5	24,560	413.5
Totals	180,380	2,423.5	131,625	2,107.4

Here the extreme insufficiency of the factory owners' statistics and the extreme carelessness with which they have been compiled are still more apparent—the number of strikers for the first five months (which was 79,970) added to that for the last seven months gives a total of 211,595, and not 180,000, and not 207,000!

The factory owners themselves prove that they *underestimate* the number of strikers.

The metalworkers are in the lead both in the ratio of number of strikers to the total number of workers and in the duration of the strikes; 18 days were lost per metalworker on strike, 14 days per textile worker and 16 days per worker in other industries. The better marketing conditions in the iron and steel industry do not, as we see, relieve the workers of the necessity of striking for a tiny wage increase!

As far as the results of the strikes are concerned, the factory owners' statistics declare that 1912 was a *less favour-*

able year for the workers than 1911 had been. In 1911, they say, 49 per cent of the strikers suffered a defeat and in 1912, 52 per cent were defeated. These data, however, are not convincing, because the figures compared are for *the whole* of 1911 and for *seven months* of 1912.

The strikes of 1912 were offensive and not defensive in character. The workers were fighting *for improved* working conditions and not *against worse conditions*. This means that 52 per cent of the workers did not gain any improvement, 36 per cent were fully or partially *successful* and for 12 per cent the results are unclear. It is very likely that the factory owners concealed their defeat in this 12 per cent of all cases because every success of capital over labour arouses their special attention and jubilation.

If we compare the outcome of strikes for the last seven months of 1912 by areas and by branches of industry, we get the following picture.

The least successful of all were the strikes in the Moscow area—75 per cent of the strikers failed (i.e., did not gain any improvement); then follow the St. Petersburg area with 63 per cent, the South with 33 per cent, the Baltic area with 20 per cent and Poland with 11 per cent of failures. In the last-named *three* areas, therefore, the workers achieved *tremendous* victories. Out of the 48,000 strikers in these three areas, *27,000* achieved improvements, *they were victorious*; 11,000 suffered defeats; the results achieved by 10,000 are uncertain.

In the first two areas (Moscow and St. Petersburg), on the contrary, out of the 83,000 strikers only *20,000* were successful; 59,000 were defeated (i.e., did not achieve any improvement) and the results achieved by 4,000 are uncertain.

Taken by branches of industry, the number of strikers who were defeated was: textile workers, 66 per cent, metalworkers, 47 per cent, and others, 30 per cent.

Marketing conditions were worst of all for the textile workers. In the Moscow area only *6,000* of the 38,000 strikers in the textile industry were successful, 32,000 were defeated; in St. Petersburg there were 4,000 successful and 9,000 defeated. Textile workers in Poland, however, had *8,000* successful strikers and 400 defeated.

The financial results of the strikes (economic strikes) for the last two years are shown as follows by the factory owners' statistics:

	Industrialists' direct losses	Losses of wages	Losses in output for the country
	(thousand rubles)		
Iron and steel industry . .	558	1,145	4,959
Textile industry	479	807	6,010
Other branches	328	529	3,818
Totals for 1912 . . .	1,365	2,481	14,787
Totals for 1911 . . .	402	716	4,563

Thus the factory owners' total losses for two years amount to 1,800,000, workers' losses in wages to *3,000,000 rubles*, and losses in output to 19,000,000 rubles.

Here the factory owners place a period. How wise they are! What did the workers *gain*?

In two years *125,000 workers* gained a victory. Their wages for the year amount to 30,000,000 rubles. They demanded pay increases of 10 per cent, 25 per cent and even 40 per cent, as the factory owners themselves admit. Ten per cent of 30,000,000 rubles is *3,000,000 rubles*. And the reduction in the working day?

And what of the *"new"* (the factory owners' expression) demands, such as the demand *"not* to discharge workers without the consent of their fellow-workers"?

You are wrong, you gentlemen who own factories! Even in the economic sense (to say nothing of political strikes) the workers' gains are *terrifying*. The bourgeoisie does not understand either workers' solidarity or the conditions of proletarian struggle.

About 300,000 workers have sacrificed 3,000,000 rubles to the economic struggle in two years. A direct gain was *immediately* achieved by 125,000 workers. And the whole working class made a step forward.

Pravda Nos. 123, 126, 127 and 131;
May 30, June 2, 5 and 9, 1913
Signed: *V. I.*

Published according to
the *Pravda* text

AN INCORRECT APPRAISAL
(*LUCH* ON MAKLAKOV)[50]

...programmes and resolutions of the liberals.*

In the *Luch* (No. 122) editorial we come across a profoundly incorrect appraisal of this important speech. "Cadet doctrinairism" is what *Luch* saw in it. Deputy Maklakov is likened to an animal that brushes out its tracks with its tail. "The numerous parentheses in his speech completely destroyed its oppositional character"—and *Luch* quotes the words of Mr. V. Maklakov to the effect that "reaction is an historical law", that one should (according to Bismarck's theory) be able to distinguish moments when it is necessary to rule in liberal fashion and moments when despotic rule is essential.

"Such speeches could be made by a professor," concludes *Luch*, "but not by a politician upholding the right of democracy to self-determination" [?].

No, Mr. V. Maklakov is by no means a doctrinaire and his speech is not that of a professor. And it is nothing less than ridiculous to expect V. Maklakov to uphold the rights of democracy. He is a liberal-bourgeois businessman who has fearlessly exposed the very "guts" of the policy of his class. Mr. V. Maklakov made the accusation that the government "could have comprehended [when the revolution had died down] *how to stamp out the revolution entirely*" but failed to comprehend:

"When a government fights against a revolution it is right, that is its duty," exclaimed Mr. V. Maklakov, and added, "the same will be true of the revolution, when it is victorious, it will fight against counter-revolution" (here this

---

* The first page of the manuscript has not been found.—*Ed.*

"experienced" orator made an amusing slip, using, for some unknown reason, only the future tense.) Mr. V. Maklakov repeated several times that he blamed the government "not for fighting disorder and revolution, but for fighting against law and order itself".

. Mr. V. Maklakov compared Stolypin to a fireman who breaks the windows of a burning house.

From this it can be seen that the predominant tone and substance of this noteworthy speech are not a professorial stunt or doctrinairism but whole-hearted, persistent counter-revolution. It is all the more important to deal at length with this since the newspaper hubbub over petty details of the "conflict" so zealously hides the substance of it. The policy of liberalism and its class roots cannot be *understood* unless this, its typical and fundamental feature, is mastered.

Luch displays an amazing and amusing lack of understanding of this matter when it exclaims: "Is it not the worst form of doctrinairism to worship the statesmanship of Bismarck who, whatever is said about him, always remained a man of blood and iron?"

What has this to do with doctrinairism, gentlemen? You are right off the mark. V. Maklakov said as clearly as it could be said that he approves "fighting disorder and revolution", approves of "the fireman", and, it goes without saying, V. Maklakov knows very well what that means—blood and iron. V. Maklakov said as clearly as it could be said that *this* was the very policy he favoured—*provided* it succeeded! You have to break windows, he preaches, don't be afraid of breaking windows, we are not sentimental people, we are not professors, not doctrinaires, but when you break windows, do it as Bismarck did, i.e., successfully, *strengthening* the alliance of the bourgeoisie and the landowners.

And you, says V. Maklakov to the government, you break windows *for no reason*, like a street lout, not like a fireman.

Bismarck represented the counter-revolutionary landowners of Germany. He realised he could save them (for a few decades) *only* by a sound alliance with the counter-revolutionary liberal bourgeoisie. He succeeded in forming this alliance because the resistance of the proletariat was weak and lucky wars helped solve the *current* problem—that of the national unification of Germany.

We have our counter-revolutionary landowners. And we have our counter-revolutionary liberal bourgeoisie. V. Maklakov is their foremost representative. He showed by his speech that he is prepared to do any amount of bowing and scraping before Purishkevich & Co. This, however, is not enough for the "marriage" to be a success. The current historical task must be fulfilled, and ours is not national unification (of which we have more than enough...) but *the agrarian problem* ... at a time when the resistance of the proletariat is stronger.

About this, the pitiful liberal, V. Maklakov, who pines for a Russian Bismarck, was unable to say a single articulate word.

Written at the beginning of June 1913

First published in 1937
in *Lenin Miscellany XXX*
Signed: *W*.

Published according to
the manuscript

FRANK SPEECHES BY A LIBERAL

V. M. Sobolevsky, editor of *Russkiye Vedomosti*,[51] recently passed away. The liberals honoured him as a "staunch progressive figure". They spoke and wrote of his personal qualities. They avoided the question of the political trend followed by *Russkiye Vedomosti*.

There is nothing more convenient for our liberals than that ancient, colourless, general haziness—"oppositionism", "progressism". What is hidden behind those words, *what sort* of oppositional activity was displayed by an individual, *which* class he served, are things they prefer not to discuss. These things are distasteful to liberals.

Democracy, however, should try to establish the truth. Honour V. M. Sobolevsky as a progressive, that is your right. But if you really want to teach politics to the people do not forget the *trend* followed by *Russkiye Vedomosti*, that provides a unique combination of *Right* Cadetism and Narodnik overtones.

Mr. L. Panteleyev, who published in *Rech* an article to the memory of V. M. Sobolevsky, wrote that he was a "great sceptic in respect of the availability of the forces possessed by our progressive society".

Nothing here is definite. What sort of scepticism was it? What society is he talking about? The curtain is drawn back slightly by the words of V. M. Sobolevsky that Mr. Panteleyev quotes: "What has a society to offer that in the mass is saturated to the marrow of its bones with the traditions and habits of serfdom? What support for a new system is to be expected from millions of semi-slaves, beggars, starving people, drunkards and ignoramuses?"

Mr. Panteleyev, who deemed it proper to publish these frank statements, did not notice the light they cast on the attitude of Russian liberals to democracy.

In the summer of 1905, *Russkiye Vedomosti* published an article by Mr. Vinogradov, the star of liberal scholarship, arguing that these semi-slaves should not go too far, that they should be more modest and calm. *Russkiye Vedomosti* was probably a little ahead of other liberal newspapers in declaring quite definitely its counter-revolutionary attitude to events.

There is scepticism and scepticism. As far as a public figure is concerned, one should ask: in respect of *which* class is he a sceptic? Sobolevsky (and his *Russkiye Vedomosti*) was a sceptic and even a pessimist in respect of the peasantry. He was an optimist in respect of the landowners; he pictured them as being capable of "reforms", as "sincerely sympathising with the new social system" as "cultured people", etc. The mixture of this landowner liberalism (not semi-slavish but utterly slavish) and Narodism, was a sign of the rottenness of the "enlightened", well-to-do, satiated liberal society that *taught* slave morality and slave politics to the "millions of semi-slaves" who were awakening. This liberal society was, "to the marrow of its bones", slavish towards the landowners, and the Narodism of *Russkiye Vedomosti* reflects more than anything else the patriarchal Russia of the humble muzhik and the landowner flirting with liberalism.

Pravda No. 125, June 1, 1913   Published according to
                                                  the *Pravda* text

THE QUESTION OF MINISTRY OF EDUCATION POLICY[52]

(SUPPLEMENT TO THE DISCUSSION ON PUBLIC EDUCATION)

Our Ministry of Public (forgive the expression) "Education" boasts inordinately of the particularly rapid growth of its expenditure. In the explanatory note to the 1913 budget by the Prime Minister and the Minister of Finance we find a summary of the estimates of the Ministry of Public (so-called) Education for the post-revolutionary years. These estimates have increased from 46,000,000 rubles in 1907 to 137,000,000 in 1913. A tremendous growth—almost trebled in something like six years!

But our official praise-mongers who laud the police "law and order" or *disorder* in Russia ought not to have forgotten that ridiculously small figures always do grow with *"tremendous"* rapidity when increases in them are given as percentages. If you give five kopeks to a beggar who owns only three his "property" will immediately show a "tremendous" growth—it will be 167 per cent greater!

Would it not have been more fitting for the Ministry, if it did not aim at *befogging* the minds of the people and *concealing* the beggarly position of public education in Russia, to cite *other data*? Would it not have been more fitting to cite figures that do not compare today's five kopeks with yesterday's three, but compare what we have with what *is essential to* a civilised state? He who does not wish to deceive either himself or the people should admit that the Ministry was *in duty bound* to produce these figures, and that by not producing *such* figures the Ministry was not doing its duty. Instead of *making clear* to the people, and the people's representatives, what the needs of the state are, the

Ministry *conceals* these needs and engages in a foolish governmental game of figures, a governmental rehash of old figures that explain nothing.

I do not have at my disposal, of course, even a hundredth part of the means and sources for studying public education that' are available to the Ministry. But I have made an attempt to obtain *at least a little* source material. And I assert boldly that I can cite *indisputable* official figures that really *do make clear* the situation in our official public "miseducation".

I take the official government *Russian Yearbook* for 1910, published by the Ministry of the Interior (St. Petersburg, 1911).

On page 211, I read that the *total* number attending schools in the Russian Empire, lumping together primary, secondary and higher schools and educational establishments of all kinds, was 6,200,172 in 1904 and 7,095,351 in 1908. An obvious increase. The *year 1905*, the year of the great awakening of the masses of the people in Russia, the year of the great struggle of the people for freedom under the leadership of the proletariat, was a year that *forced* even our hidebound Ministry to make a move.

But just look at the *poverty* we are doomed to, thanks to the retention of officialdom, thanks to the almighty power of the feudal landowners, *even* under conditions of the most rapid "departmental" progress.

The same *Russian Yearbook* relates in the same place that there were 46.7 people attending school to every 1,000 inhabitants in 1908 (in 1904 the figure was 44.3 to every 1,000 inhabitants).

What do we learn from these figures from a Ministry of the Interior publication that the Ministry of Public Education did not feel inclined to report to the Duma? What does that proportion mean—*less than 50 people* out of a 1,000 *attending school*?

It tells us, you gentlemen who uphold our hidebound public miseducation, of the *unbelievable* backwardness and barbarity of Russia thanks to the omnipotence of the feudal landowners in our state. The number of children and adolescents of school age in Russia amounts to over 20 per cent of the population, that is, to more than *one-fifth*. *Even*

Messrs. Kasso and Kokovtsov could without difficulty have learned these figures from their departmental clerks. And so, we have 22 per cent of the population of school age and 4.7 per cent attending school, which is only a *little more than one-fifth!* This means that about *four-fifths* of the children and adolescents of Russia are *deprived* of public education!

There is no other country so barbarous and in which the masses of the people are *robbed* to such an extent of education, light and knowledge—no other such country has remained in Europe; Russia is the exception. This reversion of the masses of the people, especially the peasantry, to savagery, is not fortuitous, it is *inevitable* under the yoke of the landowners, who have seized tens and more tens of millions of dessiatines of land, who have seized state power both in the Duma and in the Council of State, and not only in these institutions, which are relatively *low-ranking* institutions....

Four-fifths of the rising generation are doomed to illiteracy by the feudal state system of Russia. This stultifying of the people by the feudal authorities has its correlative in the country's illiteracy. The same government *Russian Yearbook* estimates (on page 88) that only 21 per cent of the population of Russia are literate, and even if children of *pre-school* age (i.e., children under nine) are deducted from the total population, the number will still be only 27 per cent.

In civilised countries there are no illiterates at all (as in Sweden or Denmark), or a mere one or two per cent (as in Switzerland or Germany). Even backward Austria-Hungary has provided her Slav population with conditions *incomparably* more civilised than feudal Russia has; in Austria there are 39 per cent of illiterates and in Hungary 50 per cent. It would be as well for our chauvinists, Rights, nationalists and Octobrists *to think about* these figures, if they have not set themselves the "statesmanlike" aim of forgetting how to think, and of teaching the same to the people. But even if they have forgotten, the people of Russia *are learning* more and more to think, and to think, furthermore about which class it is that by its dominance in the state condemns the Russian peasants to material and spiritual poverty.

America is *not* among the advanced countries as far as the number of literates is concerned. There are about 11 per

cent illiterates and among the Negroes the figure is as high
as 44 per cent. But the American Negroes are *more than twice*
as well off in respect of public education as the Russian peasantry. The American Negroes, no matter how much they
may be, to the shame of the American Republic, oppressed,
are better off than the Russian peasants—and they are better
off because exactly half a century ago the people routed
the American slave-owners, crushed that serpent and completely swept away slavery and the slave-owning state
system, and the political privileges of the slave-owners in
America.

The Kassos, Kokovtsovs and Maklakovs will teach the
Russian people to copy the American example.

In 1908 there were *17,000,000* attending school in America,
that is, *192 per 1,000 inhabitants—more than four times*
the number in Russia. Forty-three years ago, in 1870, when
America had only just *begun* to build her free way of life
after *purging* the country of the diehards of slavery—forty-
three years ago there were in America 6,871,522 people attending school, i.e., more than in Russia in 1904 and
almost as many as in 1908. But even as far back as 1870 there
were 178 *(one hundred and seventy-eight)* people enrolled in
schools to every 1,000 inhabitants, little short of four times
the number enrolled in Russia *today*.

And there, gentlemen, you have further proof that Russia
still has to win for herself in persistent revolutionary struggle by the people *that freedom* the Americans won for themselves half a century ago.

The estimate for the Russian Ministry of Public Miseducation is fixed at 136,700,000 rubles for 1913. This amounts
to only 80 kopeks per head of the population (170,000,000
in 1913). Even if we accept the "sum-total of state expenditure on education" that the Minister of Finance gives us
on page 109 of his explanatory text to the budget, that is,
204,900,000 rubles, we still have only 1 ruble 20 kopeks
per head. In Belgium, Britain and Germany the amount
expended on education is two to three rubles and even
three rubles fifty kopeks per head of the population. In
1910, America expended 426,000,000 dollars, i.e.,
852,000,000 rubles or 9 rubles 24 kopeks per head of the
population, on public education. Forty-three years ago,

in 1870, the American Republic was spending 126,000,000 rubles a year on education, i.e., *3 rubles 30 kopeks* per head.

The official pens of government officials and the officials themselves will object and tell us that Russia is poor, that she has no money. That is true, Russia is not only poor, she is a beggar when it comes to public education. To make up for it, Russia is very "rich" when it comes to expenditure on the feudal state, ruled by landowners, or expenditure on the police, the army, on rents and on salaries of ten thousand rubles for landowners who have reached "high" government posts, expenditure on risky adventures and plunder, yesterday in Korea or on the River Yalu, today in Mongolia or in Turkish Armenia. Russia will *always* remain poor and beggarly in respect of expenditure on public education *until* the public educates itself sufficiently to cast off the yoke of feudal landowners.

Russia is poor when it comes to the salaries of school-teachers. They are paid a miserable pittance. School-teachers starve and freeze in unheated huts that are scarcely fit for human habitation. School-teachers live together with the cattle that the peasants take into their huts in winter. School-teachers are persecuted by every police sergeant, by every village adherent of the Black Hundreds, by volunteer spies or detectives, to say nothing of the hole-picking and persecution by higher officials. Russia is too poor to pay a decent salary to honest workers in the field of public education, but Russia is rich enough to waste millions and tens of millions on aristocratic parasites, on military adventures and on hand-outs to owners of sugar refineries, oil kings and so on.

There is one other figure, the last one taken from American life, gentlemen, that will show the peoples oppressed by the Russian landowners and *their* government, *how* the people live who have been able to achieve freedom through a revolutionary struggle. In 1870, in America there were 200,515 school-teachers with a total salary of 37,800,000 dollars, i.e., an average of 189 dollars or *377 rubles* per teacher per annum. And that was *forty years* ago! In America today there are *523,210* school-teachers and their total salaries come to 253,900,000 dollars, i.e., 483 dollars or *966 rubles* per teacher per annum. And in Russia, even at the present level of the productive forces, it would be quite possible at this very moment to guarantee a no less satisfactory salary to an army of school-teachers who are helping to lift the people out of their ignorance, darkness and oppression, if ... if the whole state system of Russia, from top to bottom, were reorganised on lines as democratic as the American system.

Either poverty and barbarism arising out of the full power of the feudal landowners, arising out of the law and order or disorder of the June Third law, or freedom and civilisation arising out of *the ability and determination* to win freedom—such is *the object-lesson* Russian citizens are taught by the estimates put forward by the Ministry of Public Education.

So far I have touched upon the purely material, or even financial, aspect of the matter. Incomparably more melancholy or, rather, more disgusting, is the picture of spiritual bondage, humiliation, suppression and lack of rights of the teachers and those they teach in Russia. The whole activity of the Ministry of Public Education in this field is pure mockery of the rights of citizens, mockery of the people. Police surveillance, police violence, police *interference* with the education of the people in general and of workers in particular, police *destruction* of whatever the people themselves do for their own enlightenment—this is what the *entire* activity of the Ministry amounts to, the Ministry whose estimate will be approved by the landowning gentry, from Rights to Octobrists inclusive.

And in order to *prove* the correctness of my words, gentlemen of the Fourth Duma, I will call a witness that *even* you, the landowners, cannot object to. My witness is the Octobrist Mr. *Klyuzhev*, member of the Third and Fourth Dumas, member of the supervisory council of the Second and Third Women's Gymnasia in Samara, member of the school committee of the Samara City Council, member of the auditing board of the Samara Gubernia Zemstvo, former inspector of public schools. I have given you a list of the offices and titles (using the official reference book of the Third Duma) of this Octobrist *to prove* to you that the government *itself*, the landowners *themselves* in our landowners' Zemstvo, have given Mr. Klyuzhev most important posts in the "work" (the work of spies and butchers) of our Ministry of Public Stultification.

Mr. Klyuzhev, if anybody, has, of course, made his entire career as a law-abiding, God-fearing civil servant. And, of course, Mr. Klyuzhev, if anybody, has by his faithful service in the district earned the confidence of the nobility and the landowners.

And now here are some passages from a speech by this most thoroughly reliable (from the feudal point of view) witness; the speech was made in the *Third* Duma in respect of the estimate submitted by the Ministry of Public Education.

The Samara Zemstvo, Mr. Klyuzhev told the Third Duma, *unanimously* adopted the proposal of Mr. Klyuzhev to make application for the conversion of some village two-year schools into four-year schools. The regional supervisor, so the law-abiding and God-fearing Mr. Klyuzhev reports, *refused* this. Why? The official explanation was: *"in view of the insignificant number of children of school age."*

And so Mr. Klyuzhev made the following comparison: *we* (he says of landowner-oppressed Russia) have *not a single* four-year school for the 6,000 inhabitants of the Samara villages. In the town of Serdobol (Finland) with *2,800* inhabitants there are *four* secondary (and higher than secondary) schools.

This comparison was made by the Octobrist, the most worthy Peredonov* ... excuse the slip, the most worthy Mr. Klyuzhev in the Third Duma. Ponder over that comparison, Messrs. Duma representatives, if not of the people, then at least of the landowners. Who made application to open schools? Could it be the Lefts? The muzhiks? The workers? God forbid! It was the Samara Zemstvo that made the application *unanimously*, that is, it was the Samara *landowners*, the most ardent Black-Hundred adherents among them. And the government, through its supervisor, refused the request on the excuse that there was an *"insignificant"* number of children of school age! Was I not in every way right when I said that the government *hinders* public education in Russia, that the government is the biggest enemy of public education in Russia?

---

* Peredonov—a type of teacher-spy and dull lout from Sologub's novel *The Petty Imp.*

The culture, civilisation, freedom, literacy, educated women and so on that we see in Finland derive *exclusively* from *there being no* such "social evil" as the Russian Government in Finland. Now you want to foist this evil on Finland and make her, too, an enslaved country. You will not succeed in that, gentlemen! By your attempts to impose political slavery on Finland you will only accelerate the awakening of the peoples of Russia from political slavery!

I will quote another passage from the Octobrist witness, Mr. Klyuzhev. "How are teachers recruited?" Mr. Klyuzhev asked in his speech and himself provided the following answer:

"One prominent Samara man, by the name of Popov, bequeathed the necessary sum to endow a Teachers' Seminary for Women." And who do you think was appointed head of the Seminary? This is what the executor of the late Popov writes: "*The widow of a General of the Guards* was appointed head of the Seminary and she herself admitted that this was the first time in her life she had heard of the existence of an educational establishment called a Teachers' Seminary for Women"!

Don't imagine that I took this from a collection of Demyan Bedny's fables, from the sort of fable for which the magazine *Prosveshcheniye* was fined and its editor imprisoned. Nothing of the sort. This fact was taken from the speech of the Octobrist Klyuzhev, who fears (as a God-fearing and police-fearing man) even *to ponder* the significance of this fact. For this fact, once again, shows beyond all doubt that there is no more vicious, no more implacable enemy of the education of the people in Russia than the Russian Government. And gentlemen who bequeath money for public education should realise that they are throwing it away, worse than throwing it away. They desire to bequeath their money to provide education for the people, but *actually* it turns out that they are giving it to *Generals of the Guards* and their *widows*. If such philanthropists do not wish to throw their money away they must understand that they should bequeath it to the Social-Democrats, who *alone* are able to use that money to provide the people with *real* education that is really independent of "Generals of the Guards"—and of timorous and law-abiding Klyuzhevs.

Still another passage from the speech of the same Mr. Klyuzhev.

"It was in vain that we of the Third Duma desired free access to higher educational establishments for seminar pupils. The Ministry did not deem it possible to accede to our wishes." "Incidentally the government bars the way to higher education, not to seminar pupils alone, but to the children of the peasant and urban petty-bourgeois social estates in general. This is no elegant phrase but the truth," exclaimed the Octobrist official of the Ministry of Public Education. "Out of the 119,000 Gymnasium students only 18,000 are peasants. Peasants constitute only 15 per cent of those studying in all the establishments of the Ministry of Public Education. In the Theological Seminaries only 1,300 of the 20,500 pupils are peasants. Peasants are not admitted at all to the Cadet Corps and similar institutions." (These passages from Klyuzhev's speech were, incidentally, cited in an article by K. Dobroserdov in *Nevskaya Zvezda* No. 6, for 1912, dated May 22, 1912.)

That is how Mr. Klyuzhev spoke in the Third Duma. The depositions of that witness will not be refuted by those who rule the roost in the Fourth Duma. The witness, *against* his own will and *despite* his wishes, fully corroborates the *revolutionary* appraisal of the present situation in Russia in general, and of public education in particular. And what, indeed, does a government deserve that, in the words of a prominent government official and member of the ruling party of Octobrists, *bars the way* to education for the peasants and urban petty bourgeois?

Imagine, gentlemen, what such a government deserves from the point of view of the urban petty bourgeoisie and the peasants!

And do not forget that in Russia the peasants and the urban petty bourgeoisie constitute 88 per cent of the population, that is, a little less than *nine-tenths* of the people. The nobility constitute only *one and a half per cent.* And so the government is taking money from nine-tenths of the people for schools and educational establishments of all kinds *and using that money* to teach the nobility, *barring the way* to the peasant and urban petty bourgeois! Is it not clear what this government of the nobility deserves? This government that oppresses nine-tenths of the population in order to preserve the privileges of *one-hundredth* of the population—what does it deserve?

And now, finally, for the last quotation from my witness, the Octobrist official of the Ministry of Public Education, and member of the Third (and Fourth) Dumas, Mr. Klyuzhev:

"In the five years from 1906 to 1910," said Mr. Klyuzhev, "in the Kazan area, the following have been removed from their posts: 21 head masters of secondary and primary schools, 32 inspectors of public schools and *1,054* urban school-teachers; *870* people of these categories have been transferred. Imagine it," exclaimed Mr. Klyuzhev, "how can our school-teacher sleep peacefully? He may go to bed in Astrakhan and not be sure that he will not be in Vyatka the next day. Try to understand the psychology of the pedagogue who is driven about like a hunted rabbit!"

This is not the exclamation of some "Left" school-teacher, but of an Octobrist. These figures were cited by a diligent civil servant. He is *your* witness, gentlemen of the Right, nationalists and Octobrists! This witness of "yours" is compelled to admit the most scandalous, most shameless and most disgusting arbitrariness on the part of the government in its attitude to teachers! This witness of *yours*, gentlemen who rule the roost in the Fourth Duma and the Council of State, has been forced to admit the fact that teachers in Russia are *"driven"* like rabbits by the Russian Government!

On the basis provided by this fact, one of thousands and thousands of similar facts in Russian life, we ask the Russian people and all the peoples of Russia: do we need a government to protect the privileges of the nobility and to *"drive"* the people's teachers "like rabbits"? Does not this government deserve to be *driven out* by the people?

Yes, the Russian people's teachers are driven like rabbits. Yes, the government bars the way to education to nine-tenths of the population of Russia. Yes, our Ministry of Public Education is a ministry of police espionage, a ministry that derides youth, and jeers at the people's thirst for knowledge. But far from all the Russian peasants, not to mention the Russian workers, resemble *rabbits*, honourable members of the Fourth Duma. The working class were able to prove this in 1905, and they will be able to prove again, and to prove more impressively, and much more seriously, that they are capable of a revolutionary struggle for real freedom and for *real public* education and not that of Kasso or of the nobility.

Written April 27 (May 10), 1913
First published in 1930
in the second and third editions
of V. I. Lenin's *Collected Works,*
Vol. XVI

Published according to
the manuscript

CONTROVERSIAL ISSUES

AN OPEN PARTY AND THE MARXISTS

Pravda Nos. 85, 95, 110, 122, 124
and 126; April 12, 26,
May 15, 29, 31, and June 2, 1913
Signed: *V. I.*

Published according to
the *Pravda* text,
collated with that of the
pamphlet *Marxism and
Liquidationism*, Part II,
St. Petersburg, 1914

10*

I. THE DECISION OF 1908

To many workers the struggle that is now going on between *Pravda* and *Luch* appears unnecessary and not very intelligible. Naturally, polemical articles in separate issues of the newspaper on separate, sometimes very special questions, do not give a complete idea of the subject and content of the struggle. Hence the legitimate dissatisfaction of the workers.

Yet the question of liquidationism, over which the struggle is now being waged, is at the present time one of the most important and most urgent questions of the working-class movement. One cannot be a class-conscious worker unless one studies the question in detail and forms a definite opinion on it. A worker who wishes to participate independently in deciding the destiny of *his* Party will not waive aside polemics, even if they are not quite intelligible at first sight, but will earnestly seek until he finds the truth.

How is the truth to be sought? How can one find one's way through the tangle of contradictory opinions and assertions?

Every sensible person understands that if a bitter struggle is raging on any subject, in order to ascertain the truth, he must not confine himself to the statements made by the disputants, but must examine the *facts* and *documents* for himself, see for himself whether there is any evidence to be had from *witnesses* and whether this evidence is reliable.

This, of course, is not always easy to do. It is much "easier" to take for granted what comes to hand, what you *happen* to hear, what is more "openly" shouted about, and so on. But people who are satisfied with this are dubbed "shallow", feather-brained people, and no one takes them seriously. The truth about any important question cannot be found unless a certain amount of *independent* work is done, and anyone who is afraid of work cannot possibly arrive at the truth.

Therefore, we address ourselves only to those workers who are not afraid of this work, who have decided to get to the bottom of the matter *themselves,* and try to *discover facts, documents, the evidence of witnesses.*

The first question that arises is—what is liquidationism? Where did this word come from, what does it mean?

Luch says that the liquidation of the Party, i.e., the dissolution, the break-up of the Party, the renunciation of the Party, is merely a wicked invention. The "factionalist" Bolsheviks, it alleges, invented this charge against the Mensheviks!

Pravda says that the whole Party has been condemning and fighting liquidationism for over four years.

Who is right? How to discover the truth?

Obviously, the only way is to seek for facts and documents of the Party's *history* in the last four years, from 1908 to 1912, when the liquidators *finally split away* from the Party.

These four years, during which the present liquidators *were still* in the Party, constitute the most important period for *discovering* where the term liquidationism came from and how it arose.

Hence, the first and basic conclusion: whoever talks of liquidationism, but *avoids* the facts and *Party* documents of the 1908-11 period, is hiding the truth from the workers.

What are these facts and Party documents?

First of all there is the *Party decision* adopted in December 1908. If the workers do not wish to be treated like children who are stuffed with fairy-tales and fables, they must ask their advisers, leaders or representatives, whether a *Party decision* was adopted on the question of liquidationism in December 1908 and what that decision was.

The decision contains a *condemnation* of liquidationism and an *explanation* of what it is.

Liquidationism is "an attempt on the part of a group of Party intellectuals to *liquidate* [i.e, dissolve, destroy, abolish, close down] the existing organisation of the Party and to replace it at all costs, even at the price of *downright re-*

nunciation of the programme, tactics, and traditions of the Party [i.e., past experience], by a loose association functioning legally [i.e., in conformity with the law, existing "openly"]".

Such was the Party's *decision* on liquidationism, adopted more than four years ago.

It is obvious from this decision what the essence of liquidationism is and why it is condemned. Its essence is the *renunciation* of the "underground", its liquidation and *replacement* at all costs by an amorphous association functioning legally. Therefore, it is *not* legal work, not insistence on the need for it that the Party condemns. The Party condemns—and unreservedly condemns—the *replacement* of the old Party by something amorphous, "open", something which cannot be called a party.

The Party cannot exist unless it defends its existence, unless it unreservedly fights those who want to liquidate it, destroy it, who do not recognise it, who renounce it. This is self-evident.

Anyone who renounces the existing Party in the name of some new party must be told: try, build up a new party, but you cannot remain a member of the old, the present, the existing Party. Such is the meaning of the Party decision adopted in December 1908, and it is obvious that no other decision could have been taken on the question of the Party's existence.

Of course, liquidationism is ideologically *connected* with *renegacy,* with *the renunciation of the programme and tactics,* with *opportunism.* This is exactly what is indicated in the concluding part of the above-quoted decision. But liquidationism is not *only* opportunism. The opportunists are leading the Party on to a wrong, bourgeois path, the path of a liberal-labour policy, but they *do not renounce* the Party itself, they do not liquidate it. Liquidationism is *that brand* of opportunism which goes to the length of *renouncing* the Party. It is self-evident that the Party cannot exist if its members *include* those who do not recognise its existence. It is equally evident that the renunciation of the underground under existing conditions is renunciation of the old Party.

The question is, what is the attitude of the liquidators towards this Party decision adopted in 1908?

This is the crux of the matter, this puts the sincerity and political honesty of the liquidators to the test.

Not one of them, unless he has taken leave of his senses, will deny that such a decision was adopted by the Party and has not been rescinded.

And so the liquidators resort to evasions; they either avoid the question and *withhold* from the workers the Party's decision of 1908, or exclaim (often adding abuse) that this was a decision carried by the Bolsheviks.

But abuse only betrays the weakness of the liquidators. There are *Party decisions* that have been carried by the *Mensheviks*, for example, the decision concerning municipalisation, adopted in Stockholm in 1906.[53] This is common knowledge. Many Bolsheviks do not agree with that decision. But not one of them denies that it is a *Party decision*. In exactly the same way the decision of 1908 concerning liquidationism is a *Party decision*. All attempts to sidestep this question only signify a desire to mislead the workers.

Whoever wants to recognise the Party, not merely in words, will not permit any sidestepping, and will insist on getting at the truth concerning the *Party's decision* on the question of liquidationism. This decision has been supported ever since 1909 by *all the pro-Party Mensheviks*,[54] headed by Plekhanov who, in his *Dnevnik* and in a whole series of other Marxist publications, has repeatedly and quite definitely explained that nobody who wants to liquidate the Party can be a member of the Party.

Plekhanov was and will remain a Menshevik. Therefore, the liquidators' usual references to the "Bolshevik" nature of the Party's 1908 decision are doubly wrong.

The more abuse the liquidators hurl at Plekhanov in *Luch* and *Nasha Zarya*, the clearer is the proof that the liquidators are in the wrong and that they are trying to obscure the truth by noise, shouting and squabbling. Sometimes a novice can be stunned at once by such methods, but for all that the workers will find their bearings and will soon come to ignore this abuse.

Is the unity of the workers necessary? It is.

Is the unity of the workers possible without the unity of the workers' organisation? Obviously not.

What prevents the unity of the workers' party? Disputes over liquidationism.

Therefore, the workers must understand what these disputes are about in order that they *themselves* may decide the destiny of their Party and *defend it*.

The first step in this direction is to acquaint themselves with the *Party's first* decision on liquidationism. The workers must know this decision thoroughly and study it carefully, putting aside all attempts to evade the question or to side-track it. Having studied this decision, every worker will begin to understand the essence of liquidationism, why it is such an important and such a "vexed" question, why the Party has been faced with it during the four years and more of the period of reaction.

In the next article we shall consider another important Party decision on liquidationism which was adopted about three and a half years ago, and then pass on to facts and documents that show how the question stands at present.

II. THE DECISION OF 1910

In our first article (*Pravda* No. 289) we quoted the first and basic document with which those workers who wish to discover the truth in the present disputes must make themselves familiar, namely, the Party decision of December 1908 on liquidationism.

Now we shall quote and examine another, no less important Party decision on the same question adopted three and a half years ago, in January 1910. This decision is especially important because it was carried *unanimously*: all the Bolsheviks, without exception, all the *Vperyod* group, and finally (this is most important) *all* the Mensheviks and the present liquidators without exception, and also all the "national" (i.e., Jewish, Polish and Latvian) Marxists accepted this decision.

We quote here in full the most important passage in this decision:

"The historical situation of the Social-Democratic movement in the period of bourgeois counter-revolution inevitably gives rise, as a manifestation of bourgeois influence over the proletariat, on the one hand, to the renunciation of the illegal Social-Democratic Party,

the belittling of its role and importance, attempts to curtail the programmatic and tactical tasks and slogans of consistent Social-Democracy, etc.; on the other hand, it gives rise to the renunciation of Social-Democratic activities in the Duma and of the utilisation of legal possibilities, to failure to understand the importance of both,
to inability to adapt consistent Social-Democratic tactics to the
peculiar historical conditions of the given moment, etc.

"It is an integral part of Social-Democratic tactics under such
conditions to overcome both deviations by broadening and deepening Social-Democratic work in all spheres of proletarian class struggle and to explain the danger of such deviations."[55]

This decision clearly shows that three and a half years ago
all the Marxists, as represented by all the trends without
exception, were obliged *unanimously* to recognise two *devi-*
ations from Marxist tactics. Both deviations were recognised
as *dangerous.* Both deviations were explained as being
due, not to accident, not to the evil will of certain individuals, but to the *"historical situation"* of the working-
class movement in the present period.

Moreover, this unanimous Party decision points to the
class origin and significance of these deviations. For Marxists do not confine themselves to bare and hollow references
to disruption and disintegration. That sense of confusion,
lack of faith, despondency and perplexity reign in the minds
of many adherents of democracy and socialism is obvious to
all. It is not enough to admit this. It is necessary to understand the *class* origin of the discord and disintegration, to
understand what *class* interests emanating from a non-proletarian environment foster "confusion" among the friends
of the proletariat.

And the Party decision adopted three and a half years
ago gave an answer to this important question: *the devi-*
ations from Marxism are generated by "bourgeois counter-
revolution", by *"bourgeois influence over the proletariat".*

What are these deviations that threaten to surrender
the proletariat to the influence of the bourgeoisie? One of
these deviations, connected with the *Vperyod* line and renouncing Social-Democratic activities in the Duma and the
utilisation of legal possibilities, *has almost completely dis-*
appeared. None of the Social-Democrats in Russia now
preach these erroneous non-Marxian views. The *Vperyod*

group (including Alexinsky and others) have begun to work in *Pravda* alongside the pro-Party Mensheviks.

The other *deviation* indicated in the Party decision is *liquidationism*. This is obvious from the reference to the "renunciation" of the underground and to the "belittling" of its role and importance. Finally, we have a very precise document, published *three years* ago and refuted by no one, a document emanating from *all* the "national" Marxists and from Trotsky (better witnesses the liquidators could not wish for). This document states directly that "in essence it would be desirable to call the trend indicated in the resolution *liquidationism*, a trend which *must be combated...*".

Thus, the fundamental and most important fact that must be known by everyone who wants to understand what the present controversy is about is the following—three and a half years ago the Party *unanimously* recognised *liquidationism* to be a "dangerous" deviation from Marxism, a deviation which must be combated and which expresses "*bourgeois influence over the proletariat*".

The interests of the bourgeoisie, whose attitude is against democracy, and, generally speaking, counter-revolutionary, demand the *liquidation*, the dissolution of the old Party of the proletariat. The bourgeoisie are doing everything they can to spread and foster all ideas aimed at *liquidating* the party of the working class. The bourgeoisie are trying to encourage renunciation of the old tasks, to "dock" them, cut them back, prune them, sap them of meaning, to substitute conciliation or an agreement with the Purishkeviches and Co. for the determined destruction of the foundations of their power.

Liquidationism is, in fact, the spreading of these bourgeois ideas of renunciation and renegacy among the proletariat.

Such is the *class* significance of liquidationism as indicated in the Party decision *unanimously* adopted three and a half years ago. It is in this that the entire Party sees the greatest harm and the danger of liquidationism, its pernicious effect on the working-class movement, on the consolidation of an independent (not merely in word but in deed) party of the working class.

Liquidationism means not only the liquidation (i.e., the dissolution, the destruction) of the old party of the working class, it also means the destruction of the *class independence* of the proletariat, the corruption of its class-consciousness by *bourgeois* ideas.

We shall give an illustration of this appraisal of liquidationism in the next article, which will set forth in full the most important arguments of the liquidationist *Luch*. Now let us sum up briefly what we have stated. The attempts of the *Luch* people in general, and of Messrs. F. Dan and Potresov in particular, to make it appear that "liquidationism" is an invention, are astonishingly mendacious subterfuges based on the assumption that the readers of *Luch* are completely uninformed. Actually, apart from the Party decision of 1908, there is the *unanimous* Party decision of 1910, which gives a complete appraisal of liquidationism as a bourgeois deviation from the proletarian path, a deviation that is dangerous and disastrous to the working class. Only the enemies of the working class can conceal or evade this Party appraisal.

III. THE ATTITUDE OF THE LIQUIDATORS TO THE DECISIONS OF 1908 AND 1910

In the preceding article [*Pravda* No. 95 (299)], we quoted the exact words of the unanimous Party decision on liquidationism, which define it as a manifestation of bourgeois influence over the proletariat.

As we have pointed out, this decision was adopted in *January 1910*. Let us now examine the behaviour of those liquidators who are brazenly assuring us that there is not, and never has been, any such thing as liquidationism.

In February 1910, in No. 2 of the magazine *Nasha Zarya*, which had only just begun to appear at that time, Mr. Potresov wrote bluntly that "*there is no Party* in the shape of an integral and organised hierarchy" (i.e., ladder, or system of "institutions") and that it was impossible to liquidate "*what in reality no longer exists* as an organised body". (See *Nasha Zarya*, 1910, No. 2, 61.)

This was stated a month or even less *after* the unanimous decision of the Party!

And in March 1910, another liquidationist journal, namely *Vozrozhdeniye*,[56] having the same set of contributors—

Potresov, Dan, Martynov, Yezhov, Martov, Levitsky and Co.—stressed and gave a popular explanation of Mr. Potresov's words: .

"There is nothing to liquidate and—we for our part [i.e., the editors of *Vozrozhdeniye*] would add—the dream of re-establishing this hierarchy in its old, underground form is simply a harmful, reactionary utopia indicating a loss of political intuition by members of a party which at one time was the most realistic of all." (*Vozrozhdeniye*, 1910, No. 5, p. 51.)

There is no party, and the idea of re-establishing it is a harmful utopia—these are clear and definite words. Here we have a plain and direct renunciation of the Party.The renunciation (and the invitation to the workers to renounce) came from people who had deserted the underground and were "longing for" an open party.

This desertion from the underground was, moreover, quite definitely and openly supported by P. B. Axelrod in 1912, both in *Nevsky Golos*[57] (1912, No. 6) and in *Nasha Zarya* (1912, No. 6).

"To talk about non-factionalism in the conditions now obtaining," wrote P. B. Axelrod, "means behaving like an ostrich, means deceiving oneself and others." "Factional organisation and consolidation is the manifest responsibility and urgent duty of the supporters of Party reform, or to be more exact, of a revolution in the Party."

Thus P. B. Axelrod is openly in favour of a *Party revolution*, i.e., the destruction of the old Party and the formation of a new one.

In 1913, *Luch* No. 101, in an unsigned editorial stated plainly that "among the workers in some places there is even a revival and growth of sympathy for the underground" and that this was "*a regrettable fact*". L. Sedov, the author of that article, admitted himself (*Nasha Zarya*, 1913, No. 3, p. 49) that the article had "caused dissatisfaction", even among the supporters of *Luch* tactics. L. Sedov's explanations, furthermore, were such as to cause renewed dissatisfaction on the part of a *Luch* supporter, namely An, who has an item in No. 181 of *Luch*, opposing Sedov. He protests against Sedov's assumption that the "underground is an obstacle to the political organisation of our movement, to the building up of a workers' Social-Democratic Party. An ridicules L. Sedov for his "vagueness" as to whether the underground is desirable or not.

In their long comment on the article the editors of *Luch* came out *in favour of Sedov* and stated An to be "mistaken in his criticism of L. Sedov".

We will examine the arguments of the *Luch* editors and the liquidationist mistakes of An himself in their proper place. That is not the point we are discussing here. What we must go into carefully at the moment is the fundamental and principal conclusion to be drawn from the documents quoted above.*

The entire Party, both in 1908 and in 1910, condemned and rejected liquidationism, and explained the class origin and the danger of this trend clearly and in detail. *All* the liquidationist newspapers and journals — *Vozrozhdeniye* (1909-10), *Nasha Zarya* (1910-13), *Nevsky Golos* (1912), and *Luch* (1912-13)** *all of them, after* the most definite and even unanimous decisions of the Party, reiterate thoughts and arguments of an *obvious* liquidationist nature.

---

* In the symposium *Marxism and Liquidationism* Lenin substituted for this paragraph, up to the word "fundamental", the following text (reproduced from the manuscript):

"In No. 8 of *Zhivaya Zhizn* (July 19, 1913) Vera Zasulich repeating dozens of liquidationist arguments wrote: 'It is difficult to say whether the new organisation [the Social-Democratic Party]... helped or hindered the work.' Clearly these words are tantamount to renunciation of the Party. Vera Zasulich justifies desertion from the Party by saying: the organisations lost their members 'because at that time there was nothing to do in them'. Vera Zasulich is creating a purely anarchist theory about 'a broad section' *instead of* a party. See the detailed analysis of this theory in *Prosveshcheniye* No. 9, 1913. (See pp. 394-416 of this volume.—*Ed.*)

"What then constitutes the ..."—*Ed.*)

** The symposium *Marxism and Liquidationism* adds "and *Novaya Rabochaya Gazeta* (1913-14)" with the following footnote:

"See, for example, *Novaya Rabochaya Gazeta* No. 1, 1914, the New Year's leading article: 'The road to an open political party of action is also the road to party unity' [to the unity of the builders of an open party?]. Or No. 5, 1914: 'surmounting [all the obstacles that are placed in the way of organising workers' congresses] is nothing more nor less than a most genuine struggle for the right of association, i.e., for the legality of the working-class movement, closely connected with the struggle for the open existence of the Social-Democratic Labour Party.'"—*Ed.*

Even "Luch" supporters are forced to declare that they disagree with these arguments, with this preaching. That is a fact. Therefore, to shout about the "baiting" of liquidators, as Trotsky, Semkovsky and many other patrons of liquidationism do, is downright dishonesty, for it is an absolute distortion of the truth.

The truth proved by the documents I have quoted, which cover a period of more than *five* years (1908-13), is that the liquidators, flouting all Party decisions, continue to abuse and bait the Party, i.e., the "underground".

Every worker who *himself* wants to examine seriously the controversial and vexed questions of the Party, who wants to decide these questions *for himself*, must first of all assimilate this truth, making an independent study and verification of these Party decisions and of the liquidator arguments. Only those who carefully study, ponder over and reach an independent decision on the problems and the *fate* of their Party deserve to be called Party members and builders of the workers' party. One must not be indifferent to the question of whether it is the Party that is "guilty" of "baiting" (i.e., of too trenchant and mistaken attacks on) the liquidators *or* whether it is the liquidators who are guilty of *flagrantly violating* Party decisions, of *persistently advocating the liquidation*, i.e., *the destruction* of the Party.

Clearly, the Party cannot exist unless it fights with might and main against those who seek to destroy it.

Having quoted the documents on this fundamental question, we shall, in the next article, pass on to an appraisal of the *ideological* content of the plea for an *"open party"*.

IV. THE CLASS SIGNIFICANCE OF LIQUIDATIONISM

In the preceding articles (*Pravda* Nos. 289, 299 and 314) we showed that all the Marxists, both in 1908 and in 1910, irrevocably condemned liquidationism as renunciation of the past. The Marxists explained to the working class that liquidationism is the spreading of bourgeois influence among the proletariat. And *all* the liquidationist publications, from 1909 up to 1913, have flagrantly violated the decisions of the Marxists.

Let us consider the slogan, an "open workers' party", or "a struggle for an open party", which the liquidators are still advocating in *Luch* and *Nasha Zarya*.

Is this a Marxist, proletarian slogan, or a liberal, bourgeois slogan?

The answer must be sought not in the attitude or plans of the liquidators or of other groups, but in an analysis of the relation of social forces in Russia in the present period. The significance of slogans is determined not by the intentions of their authors, but by the relation of forces of *all* the classes in the country.

The feudal-minded landowners and *their* "bureaucracy" are hostile to all changes making for political liberty. This is understandable. The bourgeoisie, because of its economic position in a backward and semi-feudal country, *must* strive for freedom. But the bourgeoisie fears the activity of the people *more* than it fears reaction. This truth was demonstrated with particular clarity in 1905; it is fully understood by the working class, but not by opportunist and semi-liberal intellectuals.

The bourgeoisie are both liberal and counter-revolutionary. Hence their ridiculously impotent and wretched *reformism*. They dream of reforms and fear to settle accounts in real earnest with the feudal-minded landowners who not only refuse to grant reforms, but even withdraw those already granted. They preach reforms and fear the popular movement. They strive to oust the landowners, but fear to lose *their* support and fear to lose *their own* privileges. It is upon this relation of classes that the June Third system has been built up, which gives unlimited power to the feudal landowners and privileges to the bourgeoisie.

The class position of the proletariat makes it altogether impossible for it to "share" privileges or *be afraid* of anyone losing them. That is why selfishly narrow, miserable and dull-witted reformism is quite foreign to the proletariat. As to the peasant masses—on the one hand they are immeasurably oppressed, and instead of enjoying privileges suffer from starvation; on the other hand, they are undoubtedly petty bourgeois—hence, they inevitably vacillate between the liberals and the workers.

Such is the objective situation.

From this situation it clearly follows that the slogan of an open working-class party is, in its class origin, a slogan of the counter-revolutionary liberals. It contains nothing save reformism; it does not contain even a hint that the proletariat, the only thoroughly democratic class, is conscious that its task is one of fighting the liberals for influence over democrats as a whole; there is not even a suggestion of removing the foundation of all the privileges of the feudal-minded landowners, of the "bureaucracy", etc.; there is not a thought of the general basis of political liberty or of a democratic constitution; instead, this slogan implies the tacit renunciation of the old, and consequently, renegacy and the dissolution (liquidation) of the workers' party.

In brief. In a period of counter-revolution this slogan spreads among the workers the *advocacy of the very thing* the liberal bourgeoisie are themselves *practising*. Therefore, had there been no liquidators, the clever bourgeois Progressists would have *had* to find, or hire, intellectuals to advocate this to the working class!

Only the foolish people will seek to compare the *words* of the liquidators with their *motives*. Their *words* must be compared with the *deeds* and the objective position of the liberal bourgeoisie.

Look at these *deeds*. In 1902, the bourgeoisie was *in favour* of the underground. It commissioned Struve to publish the underground *Osvobozhdeniye*. When the working-class movement led to October 17, the liberals and the Cadets abandoned the underground, then repudiated it, and declared it to be useless, mad, sinful and godless (*Vekhi*).* *Instead of* the underground, the liberal bourgeoisie favoured *a struggle for an open party*. This is an historical fact, confirmed by the incessant attempts at legalisation made by the Cadets (1905-07) and the Progressists (1913).

Among the Cadets we see "open work and its secret organisation"; the kind-hearted, i.e., unwitting, liquidator,

---

* In the symposium *Marxism and Liquidationism* the word *Vekhi* is omitted and the following footnote is given:

"There is a fine book *Vekhi* which has gone through numerous editions and contains an excellent compilation of these ideas of counter-revolutionary liberalism".—*Ed.*

A. Vlasov, has only retold the deeds of the Cadets "in his own words".

Why did the liberals renounce the underground and adopt the slogan of "a struggle for an open party"? Was it because Struve is a traitor? No, just the opposite. Struve went over to the other side because the entire bourgeoisie took a turn. And the bourgeoisie turned (1) because it obtained privileges on December 11, 1905,[58] and even on June 3, 1907 obtained the status of a *tolerated* opposition; (2) because it was itself mortally afraid of the popular movement. The slogan of "a struggle for an open party", translated from the language of "high politics" into plain and intelligible language, means the following:

"Landowners! Don't imagine that we want to make life impossible for you. No, just move up a little and make room for us bourgeois [an open party], we shall then defend you five times more 'intelligently', ingenuously, 'scientifically' than the Timoshkins and Sabler's parsons did."[59]

The petty-bourgeois Narodniks,[60] in imitation of the Cadets, took up the slogan of "a struggle for an open party". In August 1906, Messrs. Peshekhonov and Co. of *Russkoye. Bogatstvo* renounced the underground, proclaimed the "struggle for an open party", and cut the consistently democratic "underground" slogans out of their programme.

Thanks to their reformist chatter about a "broad and open party", these philistines have been left, as all can see, *without any* party, *without any* contact with the masses, while the Cadets have even stopped thinking of such contacts.

Only in this way, only by analysing the position of the classes, by analysing the general history of the counter-revolution, is it possible to *understand* the nature of liquidationism. The liquidators are petty-bourgeois intellectuals, sent by the bourgeoisie to sow liberal corruption among the workers. The liquidators are traitors to Marxism and traitors to democracy. The slogan of "a struggle for an open party" in their case (as in the case of the liberals and the Narodniks) only serves to camouflage their renunciation of the past and their *rupture with the working class*. This is a fact that has been proved both by the elections in the worker curia for the Fourth Duma and by the history of the founding of the workers' paper *Pravda*. It is obvious to all that contact with the masses has been maintained only by those who have not renounced the past and who know how to make use of "open work" and of all and sundry "possibilities" exclusively in the spirit of *that* past, and for the purpose of strengthening, consolidating and developing it.

In the period of the June Third system it could not be otherwise.

"Curtailment" of the programme and tactics by the liquidators (i.e., liberals) will be discussed in our next article.

V. THE SLOGAN OF "STRUGGLE FOR AN OPEN PARTY"

In the preceding article (*Pravda* No. 122) we examined the objective significance (i.e., the significance that is determined by the relations of classes) of the slogan "an open party" or "a struggle for an open party". This slogan is a slavish repetition of the tactics of the bourgeoisie, for whom it correctly expresses their renunciation of the revolution, or their counter-revolutionary attitude.

Let us consider some of the attempts most frequently made by liquidators to defend the slogan of "a struggle for an open party". Mayevsky, Sedov, Dan and all the *Luch* writers try to confuse the open *party* with open work or *activity*. Such confusion is downright sophistry, a trick, a deception of the reader.

In the first place, open Social-Democratic activity in the period 1904-13 is a *fact*. An open party is a *phrase* used by intellectuals to cover up renunciation of the Party. Secondly, the Party has repeatedly condemned liquidationism i.e., the slogan of an open party. But the Party, far from condemning open activities, has, on the contrary, condemned those who neglected or renounced them. In the third place, from 1904 to 1907, open activities were *especially* developed among *all* the Social-Democrats. But *not a single* trend, *not a single* faction of Social-Democracy at that time advanced the slogan of "a struggle for an open party"!

This is an historical fact. Those who wish to *understand* liquidationism must give thought to this fact.

Did the absence of the slogan "a struggle for an open party" hamper open activities in the 1904-07 period? Not in the least.

11*

Why did no such slogan arise among the Social-Democrats *at that time*? Precisely because at that time there was no raging counter-revolution to draw a section of the Social-Democrats into extreme opportunism. It would have been only *too clear* at the time that the slogan "a struggle for an open party" was an opportunist phrase, a renunciation of the "underground".

Gentlemen, try to grasp the meaning of this historical change. During the 1905 period, when open activities were splendidly developed, there was *no* slogan of "a struggle for an open party"; during the period of counter-revolution, when open activities are less developed, a section of the Social-Democrats (following the bourgeoisie) has taken up the slogan of renunciation of the "underground" and "a struggle for an open party".

Are the meaning and the class significance of this change still not clear?

Finally, the fourth and most important circumstance. *Two kinds* of open activity, in two diametrically opposite directions, are possible (and are to be seen)—one in defence of the old and entirely *in the spirit* of the old, *on behalf* of its slogans and tactics; and another *against* the old, on behalf of its renunciation, of belittling its role, its slogans, etc.

The existence of these two kinds of open activity, hostile and irreconcilable in principle, is a most indisputable historical fact of the period from 1906 (the Cadets and Messrs. Peshekhonov and Co.) to 1913 (*Luch, Nasha Zarya*). Can one restrain a smile when one hears a simpleton (or one who for a while plays the simpleton) asking: what is there to argue about if both sides carry on open activities. What the argument, my dear sir, is about is whether these activities should be carried on in defence of the "underground" and in its spirit, or in belittlement of it, against it and not in its spirit! The dispute is only—*only!*—about whether this particular open work is conducted in the liberal or in the consistently democratic spirit. The dispute is "only" about whether it is possible to *confine* oneself to open work—recall Mr. Liberal Struve who did not confine himself to it in 1902, but has wholly "confined himself" to it in the years 1906-13!

Our *Luch* liquidators just cannot understand that the slogan "a struggle for an open party" means carrying into the midst of the workers liberal (Struve) ideas, decked out in the rags of "near-Marxist" catchwords.

Or take, for instance, the arguments of the *Luch* editors themselves, in their reply to An (No. 181):

"The Social-Democratic Party is not limited to those few comrades whom the realities of life force to work underground. If the entire *Party* were limited to the underground, how many members would it have? Two to three hundred? And where would those thousands if not tens of thousands of workers be, who are actually bearing the brunt of all Social-Democratic work?"

For any man who thinks, this argument alone is enough to identify its authors as liberals. First, they are telling a deliberate untruth about the "underground". It numbers far more than "hundreds". Secondly, all over the world the number of Party members is *"limited"*, as compared with the number of workers who carry on Social-Democratic work. For example, in Germany there are only one million members in the Social-Democratic Party, yet the number of votes cast for the Social-Democrats is about five million, and the proletariat numbers about fifteen million. The proportion of Party members to the number of Social-Democrats is determined in various countries by the differences in their historical conditions. Thirdly, we have *nothing* that could be a substitute for our "underground". Thus, in *opposing* the Party, *Luch* refers to the *non-Party* workers, or those who are *outside the Party*. This is the usual method of the liberal who tries to separate the masses from their *class-conscious* vanguard. *Luch* does not understand the relation between *Party* and *class*, just as the Economists of 1895-1901 failed to understand it. Fourthly, so far our "Social-Democratic work" is genuine *Social-Democratic* work only when it is conducted *in the spirit* of the old, under its slogans.

The arguments of *Luch* are the arguments of liberal intellectuals, who, unwilling to join the actually existing Party organisation, try to *destroy* that organisation by inciting the non-Party, scattered, unenlightened mass against it. The German liberals do the same when they say that the Social-Democrats do not represent the proletariat since their "Party" comprises "only" one-fifteenth of the proletariat!

Take the even more common argument advanced by *Luch*: "we" are for an open party, "just as in Europe". The liberals and the liquidators want a constitution and an open party "as in Europe" *today*, but they do not want the path by which Europe reached that today.

Kosovsky, a liquidator and Bundist, teaches us in *Luch* to follow the example of the Austrians. But he forgets that the Austrians have had a constitution *since 1867*, and that they could not have had it without (1) the movement of 1848; (2) the profound political crisis of 1859-66, when the *weakness* of the working class allowed Bismarck and Co. to *extricate* themselves by means of the famous "revolution from above". What then follows from the precepts of Kosovsky, Dan, Larin and all the *Luch* writers? Only that they are helping to solve our crisis in the spirit of "revolution from above" and *in no other* spirit! But such work of theirs *is precisely* the "work" of a Stolypin workers' party.[61]

No matter where we look—we see the liquidators renouncing both Marxism and democracy.

In the next article we shall examine in detail their arguments on the need to tone down our Social-Democratic slogans.

VI

We must now consider the toning down of Marxist slogans by the liquidators. For this purpose it would be best to take the decisions of their August Conference, but for obvious reasons these decisions can be analysed only in the press published abroad. Here we are obliged to quote *Luch*, Issue No. 108 (194), which, in the article by L. S.[62] gave a remarkably precise exposition of the whole essence, the whole spirit of liquidationism.

Mr. L. S. writes as follows:

"Deputy Muranov so far recognises only three partial demands, which, as is known, were the three pillars of the election platform of the Leninists: the complete democratisation of the state system, an eight-hour day and the transfer of the land to the peasants. *Pravda*, too, continues to maintain this point of view. Yet we, as well as the whole of European Social-Democracy [read—"we, and also Milyukov, who assures us that, thank God, we have a constitution"], see in partial demands a method of agitation which may be crowned with success only if it takes into account the everyday struggle of the working masses. We think that only things that, on the one hand, are of fundamental importance to the further development of the working-class movement, and on the other hand, may acquire urgency for the masses, should be advanced as the partial demand upon which the Social-Democrats should concentrate their attention at the present moment. Of the three demands advanced by *Pravda*, only one—the eight-hour day—plays and can play a part in the everyday struggle of the workers. The other two demands may at the present moment serve as subjects for propaganda, but not for agitation. Concerning the difference between propaganda and agitation, see the brilliant pages of G. V. Plekhanov's pamphlet *The Struggle Against Famine.* [L. S. is knocking at the wrong door; it is "painful" for him to recall Plekhanov's controversy in 1899-1902 with the Economists whom he is copying!]

"Apart from the eight-hour day, the demand for the right of association, the right to form any kind of organisation, with the corresponding freedom of assembly and freedom of speech, both the oral and the printed word, is a partial demand advanced both by the requirements of the working-class movement and by the entire course of Russian life."

Here you have the tactics of the liquidators. What L. S. describes by the words "complete democratisation, etc.", and what he calls the "transfer of the land to the peasants" are *not*, you see, of "urgency for the masses", they are *not* "advanced by the requirements of the working-class movement" and "the entire course of Russian life"! How old these arguments are and how familiar they are to those who remember the *history* of Russian Marxist practice, its many years of struggle against the Economists, who renounced the tasks of democracy! With what talent *Luch* copies the views of Prokopovich and Kuskova, who *in those days* tried to entice the workers on to the liberal path!

But let us examine the *Luch* arguments more closely. From the standpoint of common sense they are sheer madness. Can anyone in his right mind really affirm that the above-mentioned "peasant" demand (i.e., one designed to benefit the peasants) is *not* "urgent for the masses", is *not* "advanced both by the requirements of the working-class movement and by the entire course of Russian life?" This is not only an untruth, it is an obvious absurdity. The entire history of nineteenth-century Russia, the entire "course of Russian life" *produced* that question, *made* it urgent, even most urgent; this has been reflected in the *whole* of the legislation of Russia. How could *Luch* arrive at such a monstrous untruth?

It had to arrive at it, because *Luch* is in bondage to *liberal* policy, and the liberals are true to themselves when they reject (or, like *Luch*, put aside) the peasant demand. The liberal bourgeoisie does so, because its *class* position forces it to humour the landowners and to oppose the people's movement. *Luch* brings to the workers the ideas of the liberal landowners and is guilty of treachery to the democratic peasantry.

Further. Can it be that only the right of association is of "urgency"? What about inviolability of person? or the abolition of despotism and tyranny, or universal, etc., suffrage, or a single chamber, etc.? Every literate worker, everyone who remembers the recent past, knows perfectly well that all this is urgent. In thousands of articles and speeches all the liberals acknowledge that all this is urgent. Why then did *Luch* declare urgent only one of these *liberties*, albeit one of the most important, while the fundamental conditions of political liberty, of democracy and of a constitutional system were struck out, put aside, relegated to the archives of "propaganda", and excluded from agitation?

The reason, and the only reason is, that *Luch* does not accept what is *unacceptable to the liberals*.

From the standpoint of urgency for the masses, the requirements of the working-class movement and the course of Russian life, there is *no* difference between the three demands of Muranov and of *Pravda* (or, to put it briefly, the demands of consistent Marxists). Working-class, peasant and general political demands are all of *equal* urgency for the masses, are *equally* brought to the forefront both by the requirements of the working-class movement and by "the entire course of Russian life". All three demands are also alike because they are the partial demands dear to our worshipper of moderation and precision; they are "partial" compared with the final aims, but they are of a very high level compared, for example, with "Europe" in general.

Why then does *Luch* accept the eight-hour day and reject the rest? Why did it decide *on behalf of* the workers that the eight-hour day does "play a part" in their everyday struggle, whereas the general political and peasant demands *do not* play such a part? The facts show, on the one hand, that the workers in their daily struggle advance both the general political and the peasant demands—and, on the other hand, that they often *fight* for more moderate reductions of the working day.

What is the trouble, then?

The trouble lies in the reformism of *Luch*, which, as usual, *attributes* its own liberal narrow-mindedness to the "masses", to the "course of history", etc.

Reformism, in general, means that people confine themselves to agitating for changes which do not require the removal of the main foundations of the old ruling class, changes that are *compatible* with the *preservation* of these foundations. The eight-hour day is compatible with the preservation of the power of capital. The Russian liberals, in order to attract the workers, are themselves prepared to endorse this demand ("as far as possible"). Those demands for which *Luch* does not want to "agitate" are *incompatible* with the preservation of the foundations of the pre-capitalist period, the period of serfdom.

Luch eliminates from agitation precisely what is not acceptable to the liberals, who do not want to abolish the power of the landlords, but want only to share their power and privileges. *Luch* eliminates precisely what is incompatible with the point of view of reformism.

That's where the trouble lies!

Neither Muranov, nor *Pravda*, nor any Marxist rejects partial demands. That is nonsense. Take insurance, for example. We reject the *deception* of the people by idle talk about partial demands, by *reformism*. We reject *liberal reformism* in present-day Russia as being utopian, self-seeking and false, as based on constitutional illusions and full of the spirit of servility to the landlords. That is the point which *Luch* tries to confuse and hide by phrases about "partial demands" in general, although it admits itself that neither Muranov nor *Pravda* rejects certain "partial demands".

Luch tones down the Marxist slogans, tries to fit them to the narrow, reformist, liberal yardstick, and thus spreads bourgeois ideas among the workers.

The struggle the Marxists are waging against the liquidators is nothing but an expression of the struggle the advanced workers are waging against the liberal bourgeoisie for influence over the masses of the people, for their political enlightenment and education.

LETTER TO M. S. OLMINSKY (VITIMSKY)

Dear Colleague,

First let me congratulate you on your two articles that, in my opinion, were *particularly* well done—one about the liberals and the conference of *Pravda* and *Luch* with liberal editors, and the other in No. 123, about *Pravda*.[63]

In respect of the question of An and Vlasov that you have raised, I cannot agree with you. I think you have taken the *superficial*, external aspect that is immediately visible, and are prepared to forget what is more important, what is basic. And that is dangerous in the highest degree.

You say that An and Vlasov "attack the *Luch* editors" and that "this has not been used".

You are wrong. An and Vlasov *accept what is basic* in *Luch*, i.e., the slogan of "the struggle for an open party", or the slogan of peace (or unity) with the liquidators. *That is basic*. That is what *Luch* wants. The very thing *Luch* wants is to represent itself, *not* as an organ of the liquidators, but as an organ of *both* liquidators *and* Party people. This is a deception that cannot be allowed, it is more dangerous than anything. And it is the deception Trotsky and Semkovsky are gambling on.

To continue—it is not quite true to say "this has not been used". *How* should it be used? To say that An and Vlasov "attack the *Luch* editors and vindicate the *Pravda* line"? That would be untrue. An and Vlasov do not vindicate the *fundamental* line of *Pravda*, they either reject it (An) or do not understand it (Vlasov).

Or should it be used in this way—the *fact* of Sedov's liquidationism is admitted *not only by the enemies* but also by the supporters of *Luch*? That would be true. And that is what has been done, incidentally, in my article ("Controversial Issues" No. 3, in *Pravda* No. 110).*

"You should divide and not unite your enemies", you write reproachfully to the tactless V. I., who, you say, "unites" them.

Permit me a few words in my defence.

One should divide and not unite one's enemies—that is indisputable. Suppose, however, it is to the *advantage* of one's enemies *to pretend* that they are "divided", that they have on their side not only liquidators but "also" the Letts, "and" Trotsky, "and" the Bund, "and" An? It is this *essence* of liquidationist tactics that you have not noticed— perhaps because you have not read or have not heard everything about the August Conference. This, indeed, is the *essence* and the *substance* of the entire tactics of "saving" the liquidators, i.e., saving the *freedom* of liquidationist lies and liberalism to operate *from inside* the Party.

This is the only way a further attempt at saving the liquidators can be made. And that adroit diplomat An (with the year-old babe Vlasov toddling after him) is engaged in *a very subtle* game. You don't know An! I have studied his diplomacy for years and know how he hoodwinks the *whole of the Caucasus* with it! An has a real talent for diplomacy (I have known him since 1903)—it is, unfortunately, badly employed. He wants to pretend he is against *Luch* and *in this way save Luch*! This is quite obvious to anyone who has a good knowledge of the history of the Party, especially during *January* 1910 and *August* 1912! An chided Dan over petty issues and gave in to him on the main thing (*the slogan* of the struggle for an open party), because he wanted to show "his side" that *he too* is against the liquidators. *No* mistake could be more disastrous than to take An's bait. You *do not know* (and that is understandable) all the ins and outs of the relations between Trotsky, An, the Bund, Braun, etc., and *Luch*—but I do. There is nothing that could *help* the liquidators more than to recognise *An* as an anti-liquidator. This is a fact. An is their one "reliable" *support*. That

---

* See pp. 156-59 of this volume.—*Ed.*

is also a fact. Warmest regards. My best wishes for your health, keep in good spirits. Write to me, I shall always be glad to chew things over with you.

Yours,

V. I.

P.S. I hear there are many rumours in St. Petersburg to the effect that An (Chkheidze as well) "wanted to take" *Luch* away from Dan ... but did not. I believe this "wanting to take" was *for show* and it ended in an *apparent compromise* that was actually surrender to Dan! Dan is an enemy battery poorly masked. An is another battery of the same enemy, but skilfully masked. I assure you that I know this from my own experience in the matter.

Written June 3 (16), 1913

First published in 1930
in the second and third
editions of V. I. Lenin's
Collected Works, Vol. XVI

Published according to
the manuscript

THE QUESTION OF MR. BOGDANOV
AND THE *VPERYOD* GROUP[64]

(FOR THE EDITORS OF *PRAVDA*)

The action of the editors in respect of Mr. Bogdanov's distortion of Party history is so scandalous that, to tell the truth, one does not know whether it is possible after this to remain a contributor.

What actually happened?

In my article there was *not a word* against Mr. Bogdanov (who is not a member of the *Vperyod* group); there was not a word of *censure* in general.

As cautiously as possible I stated a *fact*—that the trend condemned *unanimously by the entire Party was "connected with the Vperyod line"*.*

Not a word more. *Nor could* Mr. Bogdanov quote anything more himself!

The question arises—can this fact be evaded? It cannot, for the Party *simultaneously* condemned both liquidationism and otzovism.[65] Anyone who tried to avoid this fact when speaking of Party history in respect of liquidationism would be *swindling*. I dare say the editors do not demand that I should engage in swindling. I have to believe this, especially in view of the editorial board's having announced its agreement with No. 95!

Is the fact true? The editors agree that it is. It would be difficult *not to agree* since the *Vperyod* group itself declared that otzovism was a "legitimate tendency"!

If the fact is true, then how could they possibly allow ("for the sake of impartiality") Mr. Bogdanov *to lie* about it? The only explanation I can think of is that the editors lack

---

* See p. 154 of this volume.—*Ed.*

knowledge of the *Vperyod* group's history (unless someone
has been affected by an absolutely blinding enthusiasm for
the reactionary trash that philosopher Bogdanov teaches
the workers).

The editors probably do not know that the *Vperyod* group
is disintegrating completely. Mr. Bogdanov left them a
long time ago—his "philosophy" was *condemned* in the press
by Alexinsky of the *Vperyod* group. That same Alexinsky
condemned "proletarian culture" (from the *Vperyod* platform)
in the press. Does the editorial board not know this?

Bogdanov, Domov,[66] Lyadov, Volsky[67] and Stepinsky[68]
have now *left* the *Vperyod* group (and Lunacharsky is on the
point of leaving—see the *new leaflets in Paris*). Does the editorial board not know this?

The editors are supporting the worst (hopeless) elements
among the bourgeois liars from the *Vperyod* group *against*
the best (like Alexinsky) who have *broken* with Mr. Bogdanov!

The devil alone knows what this all means! This is a
mockery of the truth, *of the Party.*

I demand categorically that the enclosed article be printed *in full*. I have always permitted the editors to make
changes in a comradely manner, but after Mr. Bogdanov's
letter, *I do not grant* any right to alter or do anything else
of that kind with this article. If you do not print it, pass it
on to *Prosveshcheniye*; I insist on having *complete freedom*
to fight against the distortion of Party history. We are struggling against liquidationism and *concealing* otzovism—this
is such a despicable position that I can only assume that
the blunder was due to *lack of knowledge in the matter.*

The editorial board must state that it has convinced itself
that Mr. Bogdanov expounded the *Vperyod* platform *incorrectly* and gave the *facts* incorrectly.

I insist on an immediate reply. I cannot continue to contribute articles in face of Mr. Bogdanov's despicable lying.

　　　　　　　　　　　　　　At your service, *V. Ilyin*

Written June 3 (16), 1913

First published in 1930
in the second and third
editions of V. I. Lenin's
Collected Works, Vol. XVI

　　　　　　　　　　Published according to
　　　　　　　　　　the manuscript

HAS *PRAVDA* GIVEN PROOF OF BUNDIST SEPARATISM?

Pravda No. 104 (308) published an article "Separatists in Russia and Separatists in Austria".* Now Mr. V. Kosovsky has published an article in *Luch* No. 119 (205) refuting it, or, to be more exact, containing a mass of vituperation against *Pravda* for that article. All we can do is draw the attention of the workers, who are interested in the fate of *their own* organisation, to these slanging attacks by the *Luch* gentlemen, who *evade* the controversial questions.

What proof did *Pravda* offer of Bundist separatism?

1) The Bund *left the Party* in 1903. Mr. Kosovsky's invective did nothing to disprove this fact. The Kosovskys scold because they are *powerless* to disprove the facts.

2) Jewish workers have joined and are still joining the Party everywhere *in spite of the Bund*.

This poor defender of the Bund cannot say a word against that either!

3) The Bund has deliberately *contravened* the Party decision on the unity of workers of *all nationalities* in local organisations, a decision that was taken in 1906 and given special confirmation in 1908.

Mr. Kosovsky *could not* say a word against that!

4) The Bundist Medem admitted that Bund members had never put into effect this unity in local organisations, that is, had always been separatists.

Again not a single objection from Mr. Kosovsky!

Just think of it, reader; what is the gentleman to do but scold and rage when he *cannot* say *a single word* against the *four* chief points in *Pravda*?

---

* See pp. 87-88 of this volume.—*Ed.*

Pravda, furthermore, gave an exact quotation from the organ of the Czech separatists in Austria, who have been unanimously condemned for their separatism *by the entire* International. That organ *praises* Mr. Kosovsky (his article in the liquidators' *Nasha Zarya*) for his "turn for the better" in respect of the separatists.

Now what, Mr. Kosovsky? Is our quotation not correct? Mr. Kosovsky knows that it is, and is malicious in his impotence: "a review in some Czech news-sheet".

Don't lie, Mr. separatist and Jewish liberal! Lies will not help you, for you will be exposed.

Not "a review" and not in "some Czech news-sheet", but a *special* article in the German *organ* of the Czech separatists.[69] This is a fact, and you have not refuted it.

I do not defend the separatists, says Mr. Kosovsky to justify himself, summarising his article in *Nasha Zarya*.

Is that so? Then the *Czech separatists* have *misunderstood* you? The poor liberal leaders of the Bund! Not only their enemies, even their *friends* "*misunderstood*" them!

Any worker, however, will understand well enough that a petty liar who has been caught red-handed is seeking salvation in evasion and imprecation. You will not scare the workers that way, gentlemen.

Pravda has proved that the Bundists are separatists. Mr. V. Kosovsky has failed to refute it.

Messrs. Kosovsky, Medem & Co., are a group of liberal intellectuals that is corrupting the Jewish workers with bourgeois nationalism and separatism. For this reason *Pravda* has fought against and will continue to fight against the Bund.

Jewish Social-Democratic workers are joining the working-class party in spite of the Bund and against the Bund.

Pravda No. 127, June 5, 1913   Published according to
Signed: *V. I.*   the *Pravda* text

LIBERALS AS DEFENDERS OF THE FOURTH DUMA

From the very inception of the Third Duma, the Marxists pointed out—not in an article here and an article there, but in a formal decision—that the June Third system had deliberately created *two* possible Duma majorities—Right-Octobrist and Octobrist-Cadet.* Both are reactionary in nature, both are *necessary* to the government in the same way as the support of the bourgeoisie is necessary to the landowners.

And now we have lived long enough to see the liberals systematically defending the Fourth Duma and demanding *"popular and public support"* for it.

Improbable as it is, it is a fact. The quoted words are in the leading article of *Rech* No. 139. This leading article is more deserving of the title "historical" than is the voting in the Fourth Duma on the budget estimate of the Ministry of the Interior. This leading article is truly programmatic. The question of the attitude of the Duma to the country and of the country to the Duma—presented broadly and splendidly explained—is an object-lesson to democrats.

"We will leave it to the Social-Democrats to assert," writes the chief liberal newspaper, "that the Duma is only a decoration, that the work of the Duma is deception and hypocrisy, and that the ideologists of the Duma only deceive the people and feed them constitutional illusions."

Our congratulations to the new *ideologists* of the Duma, of the *Fourth* Duma! It is only a pity that they are such ignoramuses. The Social-Democratic Party has never asserted that the Third and Fourth Dumas are only a decoration,

---

* See present edition, Vol. 13, p. 144.—*Ed.*

but has always pointed to the mistake made by the Left
Narodniks in thinking and saying so; the Party has always
given proof that the Third and Fourth Dumas signify the
foundation of a serious and business-like alliance of the counter-revolutionary forces.

"While awaiting [?] the social forces that are still conspicuous
only by their absence in the arena of social struggle," writes *Rech*,
"the Duma *is* a social force."

It is indisputable that the Duma, liberal gentlemen, is
a force. But what kind of force? It is a landowners' and
bourgeois counter-revolutionary force. And if the Cadets "notice" only the "absence" of democratic forces in the arena,
there is nothing left for us to do but remind them of that wise
saying: there are none so blind as those who *will not* see.

Let us cite here a little historical parallel; eighteen years
ago, in 1895 and 1896, a movement of tens of thousands of
workers was noticed, noticed *very much* indeed, by liberal
society. At the present moment that same "society" notices
only the "absence" of a quantity ten times greater. There
are none so blind as those who *will not* see.

This unwillingness to see is to be explained by the class
interests of the Octobrist and Cadet bourgeoisie, who have
turned away from democracy.

"We call upon public opinion," says *Rech*, "to see in the Duma
its own force ... the direct manifestation of the social will to create
interest in the Duma on the part of society," etc., etc.

To what disgraceful depths, into what baseness and filth
did the liberals and Cadets have to fall in order to laud the
Octobrists and the Octobrist Duma in this manner! Here
you have for the hundredth and thousandth time proof that
the Cadets are those same Octobrists painted pink to deceive
simpletons.

Let us conclude with another historical parallel. Half
a century ago the Prussian Octobrists and Cadets[70] "fought"
against Bismarck, not only with formulations demanding
reforms, but also by refusing him credits. And what happened? In Prussia, the "Third Duma" election law predominates
to this day. To this day Prussia stands as an example of a
country in which the amazing economic might of the bour-

geoisie is combined with its amazing servility towards the landowners.

Not support for the Cadet-Octobrist bloc in the Duma, but an explanation of its internal rottenness and of the independent tasks of democracy—that is what the interests of the working class and of all democracy demand.

Pravda No. 128, June 6, 1913

Published according to
the *Pravda* text

THE QUESTION OF THE (GENERAL) AGRARIAN POLICY OF THE PRESENT GOVERNMENT[71]

The agrarian policy of the government has radically changed in character since the Revolution of 1905. Formerly, the autocracy followed the line of Katkov and Pobedonostsev and tried to appear in the eyes of the masses of the people as standing "above classes", safeguarding the interests of the peasant masses, safeguarding them from loss of land and from ruin. Needless to say, this hypocritical "concern" for the muzhik in reality masked a purely feudal policy which the above-mentioned "public men" of old pre-revolutionary Russia were conducting with pig-headed directness in all spheres of public and state life. Autocracy in those days relied entirely on the backwardness, ignorance and lack of class-consciousness on the part of the peasant masses. By posing as a champion of the "inalienability" of the peasants' allotments, as an advocate of the "village commune",[72] the autocracy, in the pre-revolutionary period, tried to find support in the economic immobility of Russia, in the deep political slumber of the masses of the peasant population. At that time the land policy was through and through that of the feudal aristocracy.

The Revolution of 1905 caused a change in the entire land policy of the autocracy. Stolypin, punctiliously carrying out the dictates of the Council of the United Nobility, decided, as he himself expressed it, to "bank on the strong". This means that our government was no longer able to *pose* as a champion of the *weak* after the mighty awakening of the proletariat and the broad strata of the democratic peasantry which the Revolution of *1905* brought about in Russia. The people, having succeeded in making the first (though

First page of the manuscript of Lenin's "The Question of the (General) Agrarian Policy of the Present Government". 1913

Reduced

as yet inadequate) breach in the old feudal state system of Russia, proved thereby that they had so far awakened from their political slumber, that the tale of the government protecting the "village commune" and the "inalienability of allotments", of the defence of the weak by a government standing above classes—that this tale had finally lost credence among the peasants.

Up to 1905 the government had been able to entertain the hope that the downtrodden state and inertness of the peasants in the mass, of people incapable of ridding themselves of the age-long political prejudices of slavery, patience and obedience, would serve as a prop for it. As long as the peasants remained obedient and downtrodden, the government *could* pretend that it "banked on the weak", i.e., was taking care of the weak, although, in fact, it was concerned exclusively with the feudal landowners and the preservation of its own absolute power.

After 1905, the collapse of the old political prejudices was so profound and widespread that the government and the "Council of the United Feudalists" that controlled it saw that they could no longer gamble on the ignorance and the sheep-like obedience of the muzhik. The government saw that there *could be no peace* between it and the *masses* of the peasant population it had ruined and reduced to complete destitution and starvation. It was this consciousness of the impossibility of "peace" with the peasants that caused the "Council of the United Feudalists" to change its policy. The Council decided to try at all costs to split the peasantry and to create out of it a stratum of "new landowners", well-to-do peasant proprietors, who would *"conscientiously"* protect *from the masses* the peace and security of the huge landed estates, which, after all, had suffered somewhat from the onslaught of the revolutionary masses in 1905.

Therefore, the change in the entire agrarian policy of the government after the revolution was by no means accidental. On the contrary, from the *class* point of view, this change was a *necessity* for the government and for the "Council of the United Feudalists". The government could find no other way out. The government saw that there could be no "peace" with the masses of the peasants, that the peasantry had awakened from its age-long slumber of serfdom. The government had no alternative but *to try* by frantic efforts *to split* the peasantry, no matter how much this might ruin the villages, to surrender the countryside to "plunder and exploitation" by the kulaks and the well-to-do muzhiks, and to seek support in an *alliance* between the feudal nobles and the "new landowners", i.e., an alliance with the rich peasant proprietors, with the peasant bourgeoisie.

Stolypin himself, who served the "Council of the United Feudalists" faithfully and well and carried out their policy, said "Give me twenty years of quiet and I shall reform Russia." By "quiet" he meant the *quiet of a graveyard*, the quiet suffering of the countryside silently enduring like sheep the unprecedented ruin and destitution that had overtaken it. By "quiet" he meant the quiet of the *landowners* who would like to see the peasants utterly inert, downtrodden, offering no protest, ready to starve peacefully and amiably, to give up their land, to abandon their villages, to be ruined, as long as it were convenient and pleasing to the landed gentry. By the reform of Russia, Stolypin meant a change that would leave in the villages only contented landowners, contented kulaks and bloodsuckers, and scattered, downtrodden, weak and helpless farm labourers.

Quite naturally and understandably Stolypin, as a landowner, wanted twenty years of this graveyard quiet in Russia, wanted it with all his heart. But we now know, we now all see and feel, that the result of it has been famine affecting thirty million peasants and neither "reform" nor "quiet", that there has been an unparalleled (unparalleled even in long-suffering Russia) intensification of destitution and ruin, and extremely great bitterness and ferment among the peasantry.

To make clear the causes of the *failure* of the government's so-called "Stolypin" agrarian policy, the policy which the State Duma is invited once more to approve by sanctioning the budget (and which undoubtedly will be approved by the landowners' parties in the Duma), I shall dwell at somewhat greater length on the *two* principal, so to say, *trump cards* of our "new" agrarian policy:

First, on the resettlement of the peasants, and, secondly, on the notorious *farmsteads*.

As far as resettlement is concerned, the Revolution of 1905 revealed to the landowners the political awakening of the peasantry and forced them to "open" the safety valve a little and, instead of hampering migration as they had done before, to try to *pack off* as many *restless* peasants as possible to Siberia in an attempt to render the atmosphere less "tense" in Russia.

Did the government achieve success? Did it achieve any *pacification* of the peasantry, any improvement in the peasants' conditions in Russia and in Siberia? Just the opposite. The government only brought about a new sharpening and worsening of the conditions of the peasants *both in Russia and in Siberia*.

I shall prove this to you in a moment.

In the explanatory memorandum of the Minister of Finance on the budget for 1913 we find the usual official optimism and applause for the "successes" of the government's policy.

The settlers, we are told, transform the unsettled regions into "civilised localities", the settlers are growing rich, improving their farms, and so on and so forth. The usual official panegyric. The old, old *"everything is all right"*, *"all quiet on Shipka"*.[73]

The only pity is that the explanatory memorandum *completely ignored* the statistics of returned settlers! A strange and significant silence!

Yes, gentlemen, the number of settlers increased after *1905* to an average of half a million a year. Yes, by 1908, the migration wave reached its highest point—665,000 settlers in one year. But later the wave began *rapidly to recede*, and in 1911 dropped to *189,000*. Is it not clear that the highly praised government "arrangements" for the settlers have turned out to be *bluff*? Is it not clear that only six years after the revolution the government is *back where it started*?

And the statistics of the number of returned settlers—so prudently ignored by the Minister of Finance in his "explanatory" (or rather, confusing) memorandum—these statistics reveal a *monstrous* increase in the number of returned settlers—up to *30 or 40 per cent in 1910, and up to 60 per cent in 1911*. This gigantic wave of returning settlers reveals the desperate suffering, ruin and destitution of the peasants who sold everything at home in order to go to Siberia, and who are now forced to come back from Siberia completely ruined and pauperised.

This enormous stream of destitute returned settlers reveals with irrefutable clarity the *complete failure* of the government's resettlement policy. To produce tables of figures showing the improvement in the farms of the settlers who remained in Siberia for a long time (as was done in the explanatory memorandum on the estimates of the resettlement administration) and to *hush up* the complete and utter ruin of *tens of thousands* of returned settlers simply means distorting the facts! This means presenting the Duma deputies with castles in Spain and fairy-tales about general well-being, whereas in fact we observe ruin and destitution.

Gentlemen, the fact that the Minister of Finance's explanatory memorandum *conceals* the figures of the returned settlers, their desperate, destitute condition, their utter ruin, signifies *frantic* attempts on the part of the government to *conceal the truth*. The attempts are in vain. The truth will out! The truth will have to be admitted. The destitution of the ruined peasants who *returned* to Russia, the destitution of the ruined old inhabitants of Siberia, will *have* to be spoken about.

In order to explain graphically the conclusion I have drawn concerning the complete failure of the government's resettlement policy, I shall quote another opinion, that of a civil servant, who for twenty-seven years—*twenty-seven years*, gentlemen!—served in the Forestry Department in Siberia, an official who has studied resettlement conditions, an official who *was unable to bear* all the abominations that are committed in our resettlement administration.

This civil servant is State Councillor *A. I. Komarov*, who, after serving for twenty-seven years, was compelled to acknowledge that the notorious journey made to Siberia in 1910 by Stolypin and Krivoshein, the Prime Minister and the Chief Administrator of Agriculture and Land Settlement respectively, was a *"clownish tour"*—such is literally the expression used by a State Councillor, a civil servant of twenty-seven years' standing! This official *resigned the service*, he could not tolerate the deception of all Russia that was being practised by means of such *"clownish tours"*, and he published a special pamphlet containing a truthful account of all the thefts and embezzlement of government funds, the utter absurdity, brutality and wastefulness of our resettlement policy.

The pamphlet is entitled *The Truth About the Resettlement Scheme* and was published in St. Petersburg in the present year, 1913, price sixty kopeks—not expensive, considering the wealth of revealing material it contains. As usual our government, in resettlement, as in all other "affairs" and "branches of administration", is exerting every effort to conceal the truth, and fears lest "its dirty linen be washed in public". Komarov had to *lie low* as long as he was in the service, he had to write his letters of exposure to the newspapers under an *assumed name*, and the authorities tried to *"catch"* the correspondent. Not all civil servants are able to leave the service and publish pamphlets that reveal the truth! But one such pamphlet enables us to judge what rottenness, what an abomination of desolation reigns in general in this "dark realm".

The civil servant A. I. Komarov is not a revolutionary, nothing like one. He himself tells us about his loyal hostility to the theories of both the Social-Democrats and the Socialist-Revolutionaries. He is just an ordinary, very loyal, Russian civil servant, who would be quite satisfied with elementary, rudimentary honesty and decency. He is a man who is hostile to the Revolution of 1905 and ready to serve the counter-revolutionary government.

It is all the more significant, therefore, that even such a man has left, has abandoned the service, shaking its dust from his feet. He could not stand *"the complete disruption of all that is called rational forestry"* (p. 138) by our resettlement policy. He could not stand the *"expropriation of the arable land of the old inhabitants"* which leads to the *"gradual impoverishment of the old inhabitants"* (pp. 137 and 138). He could not stand "state *spoliation* or, rather, *devastation* of Siberian lands and forests that makes the *plunder of the Bashkirian lands* that once took place seem *trivial indeed*" (p. 3).

The following are Komarov's conclusions:

"*Absolute unpreparedness* of the Chief Resettlement Administration for work on a large scale ... absolute lack of planning in the work and its bad quality ... allotment of plots with soil unsuitable for agriculture, where there is no water at all, or with no *drinking water*" (p. 137).

When the tide of migration rose, the officials were caught napping. They "tore to pieces areas of state forest that had been surveyed only the day before ... took whatever they first laid eyes on, anything so long as they could accommodate, get rid of, *the scores of emaciated exhausted people* hanging around the resettlement centre and standing for long hours outside the resettlement office..." (p. 11).

Here are a few examples. The *Kurinsky* area is set apart for settlers. This area consists of land that had been taken from the native population near the Altai salt works. The natives have been robbed. The new settlers get salt water unfit for drinking purposes! The government wastes money endlessly on digging wells—but without success. The new settlers have to drive *7 or 8* (seven or eight!) versts for water! (p. 101).

The Vyezdnoi area in the upper reaches of the River Mana, where thirty families were settled. After seven hard years the new settlers finally became convinced that farming was impossible there. *Nearly all of them fled.* The few who remained engage in hunting and fishing (p. 27).

The Chuna-Angara region: *hundreds* of plots are mapped out—900 plots, 460 plots, etc. There are no settlers. Impossible to live there. Mountain ridges, marshes, undrinkable water.

And now the civil servant, A. I. Komarov, tells about those returned settlers whom the Minister of Finance did not mention the *truth* the government finds *unpleasant.*

"*There are hundreds of thousands of them,*" writes civil servant Komarov, referring to the ruined and destitute returning settlers. "Those returning are the sort who, in the future revolution, if it takes place, are destined to play a terrible role.... The man who is returning is not the one who all his life has been a farm labourer ... but the one who until recently was a property-owner, a man who never dreamed that he and the land could exist apart. This man is justifiably exasperated, to him it is a mortal offence that he has not been provided for, but, on the contrary, has been ruined—this man is a menace to any political system" (p. 74).

Thus writes Mr. Komarov, a civil servant who is terrified of the revolution. Komarov is mistaken in thinking that only *landowner* "political systems" are possible. In the best and most civilised states they manage to get along *even without* the landowners. Russia could also manage without them to the advantage of the people.

Komarov exposes the *ruin* of the old inhabitants. "Crop failures"—what he really means is *famine*—arising from the plunder of the old inhabitants, began to visit even the "Siberian Italy"—Minusinsk Uyezd. Mr. Komarov exposes the way in which the contractors rob the Treasury, the absolute fiction, the falsity of the reports and plans drawn up by the officials, the worthlessness of their work which swallowed up millions, such as the Ob-Yenisei Canal, the waste of *hundreds of millions of rubles.*

All our resettlement schemes, states this God-fearing modest official, are *"nothing but one long and unpleasant anecdote"* (p. 134).

Such is the *truth* concerning the *returned* settlers that has been hushed up by the Minister of Finance! Such in *reality* is the complete *failure* of our resettlement policy! Ruin and destitution *both* in Russia and in Siberia. Plunder of lands, the *destruction* of forests, false reports and official mendacity and hypocrisy.

Let us pass on to the question of the farmsteads.

On this question, too, the explanatory memorandum of the Minister of Finance gives us the same, general, meaningless, official, hypocritical data (or rather *alleged* data) as on the question of migration.

We are informed that by 1912 over one and a half million families had definitely abandoned the village commune; that over a million of these families have been established on farmsteads.

There is *not a single* truthful word *anywhere* in the government reports about the real state of the farmsteads!

Yet we know already, from the descriptions given of the new land settlements by honest observers (like the late Ivan Andreyevich Konovalov) and from our own observations of the countryside and of peasant life, that there are *farmstead peasants* of two altogether different categories. The government, by confusing these categories, by giving data of a general kind, is only deceiving the people.

One category, an insignificant minority, are the well-to-do

peasants, the kulaks, who even before the new land settlement schemes were introduced, lived very well. Such peasants, by leaving the village commune and buying up the
allotments of the poor, are undoubtedly enriching themselves at other people's expense, and still further ruining
and enslaving the masses of the population. But, I repeat,
there are *very few* farmstead peasants of this type.

The other category predominates, and predominates to an
overwhelming degree—that of the ruined destitute peasants,
who set up farmsteads out of sheer need, because they had
nowhere else to go. These peasants say: "Nowhere to go,
then let us set up a farmstead." Starving and toiling on their
beggarly farms, they clutch at anything for the sake of the
resettlement grant, for the sake of the loan they can obtain
by settling on a farmstead. On these farmsteads they suffer
untold hardships; they sell all their grain in order to pay the
bank the instalment on the loan; they are always in debt;
they live like beggars in a state of dire distress; they are
driven from the farmsteads for *defaulting with their instalments* and they are finally transformed into vagabonds.

Now, if instead of handing us meaningless pictures of
fictitious prosperity, official statistics had truthfully informed us of the number of these *destitute farmsteaders* who
are living in dug-outs, who keep cattle in their own miserable quarters, who never have enough to eat, whose children are sick and in rags—then we would hear the *"truth
about the farmsteads"*.

But the point is that the government does its utmost
to conceal this truth. Independent, detached observers of
peasant life are persecuted and sent out of the villages.
Peasants writing to the newspapers come up against tyranny, oppression and persecution by the authorities and the
police, of a nature unparalleled even in Russia.

A handful of rich farmsteaders are represented as masses
of thriving peasants! The official lie about the kulaks is
represented as the truth about the countryside! But the
government will not succeed in concealing the truth. The
attempts of the government to conceal the truth about the
ruined and starving countryside only call forth legitimate
anger and *indignation* among the peasants. The fact that
tens of millions of peasants are starving, as was the case

last year and the year before, reveals better than any lengthy argumentation the mendacity and hypocrisy of the tales about the beneficial influence of the farmsteads. This fact shows most clearly that *even after* the change in the government's agrarian policy, *and after* the notorious Stolypin reforms,[74] the Russian countryside is just as much overwhelmed by oppression, exploitation, destitution, lack of human rights as it was under serfdom. The *"new"* agrarian policy of the Council of the United Nobility left untouched the *old* serf-owners and the oppression on their estates of thousands and tens of thousands of dessiatines. The *"new"* agrarian policy enriched the *old* landowners and a handful of the peasant bourgeoisie, and ruined the masses of the peasants to a still greater extent.

"We bank on the strong," exclaimed the late Stolypin in explanation and justification of his agrarian policy. These words are well worth noting and remembering as extraordinarily truthful, exceptionally truthful words for a minister. The peasants have fully understood and learned through their own bitter experience the truthfulness of these words, which mean that the *new* laws and the *new* agrarian policy are laws *for the rich* and made by the *rich*, a policy for the *rich* and carried out by the *rich*. The peasants have understood the *"simple"* game, that the Duma of the master class makes laws for the master class—that the government is the instrument of the will of the feudal landowners and of their rule over Russia.

If Stolypin wanted to teach *this* to the peasants by means of his "famous" (shamefully famous) dictum, "we bank on the strong", we are sure he has found and will find apt pupils among the masses of the ruined and embittered who, having learned *on whom* the government banks, will understand so much the better *on whom they themselves* should bank— on the working class and on its struggle for freedom.

In order not to make unsupported statements, I shall quote a few examples drawn from real life by so able an observer, one so boundlessly devoted to his work, as Ivan Andreyevich Konovalov. (Ivan Konovalov, *Sketches of the Modern Village*, St. Petersburg, 1913. Price 1 ruble 50 kopeks. In the quotations the pages are indicated.)

In Livny Uyezd, Orel Gubernia, four estates have been

divided into farmsteads: that of Grand Duke Andrei Vladimirovich—5,000 dessiatines, of Polyakov—900 dessiatines, of Nabokov—400 dessiatines, of Korf—600 dessiatines. The total is about 7,000 dessiatines. The size of the farmsteads is fixed at 9 dessiatines each and only in exceptional cases at 12 dessiatines. Thus, there are in all a little over *600* farmsteads.

In order to explain the significance of these figures more graphically, I shall quote the official statistics of 1905 for Orel Gubernia. *Five* nobles in this gubernia owned *143,446* dessiatines, i.e., an average of *28,000 dessiatines* each. It is obvious that such monstrously big estates are not wholly cultivated by the owners; they only serve for oppression and enslavement of the peasants. The number of former serfs of landowners in Orel Gubernia in 1905 with holdings not exceeding 5 dessiatines per farm was 44,500, owning a total of 173,000 dessiatines of land. The landowner has *28,000 dessiatines* and the "*landowner's*" muzhik of the poorer class—*4 dessiatines*.

In 1905, the number of nobles in Orel Gubernia owning 500 dessiatines of land and over was *378*, the total amount of land in their possession being *592,000* dessiatines, i.e., an average of over *1,500 dessiatines* each; while the number of "*former serfs of landowners*" in Orel Gubernia having up to 7 dessiatines per household was 124,000, giving them a total of *647,000* dessiatines, i.e., an average of *5 dessiatines* per household.

One may judge by this to what extent the Orel peasants are oppressed by the feudal estates and what a drop in the ocean of misery and destitution were the *four* estates in Livny Uyezd that were divided into farmsteads. But how do the farmstead peasants live on their 9 dessiatine plots?

The land has been valued at 220 rubles per dessiatine. They have to pay 118 rubles and 80 kopeks per annum (i.e., about 20 rubles per dessiatine of sown area). A poor peasant is incapable of paying so much. He lets a part of the land cheaply just to get some ready cash. He sells all his grain to pay the instalment due to the bank. He has nothing left, either for seed or for food. He borrows, enslaves himself again. He has only one horse, he has sold his cow. His implements are old. Improving the farm is out of the question.

"The kids have simply forgotten the colour, let alone the taste, of milk" (p. 198). This sort of farmer falls into arrears with his instalments and is driven off his plot; his ruin is then complete.

In his explanatory memorandum, the Minister of Finance complacently tried to gloss over this ruin of the peasants by the new land settlement, or rather land unsettlement.

On page 57 of the second part of the explanatory memorandum the Minister gives official figures for the number of peasants who had sold their land by the end of 1911. The number is *385,407 families*.

And the Minister *"consoles"* us by saying: the number of buyers (362,840) *"is very close to the number of sellers"* (385,407). For each seller we get on an average 3.9 dessiatines, for each buyer—4.2 dessiatines (p. 58 of the explanatory memorandum).

What is consoling in this? In the first place, even these official figures show that the number of buyers is *less* than the number of sellers. This means that the ruin and destitution of the countryside is increasing. And secondly, who does not know that the buyers of allotments evade the law, which forbids the purchase of land above a small number of dessiatines, by buying in the name of wife, relations, or of some other person? Who does not know that the selling of land under the guise of various other transactions, such as a lease, etc., is very widely practised by the peasants out of sheer necessity? Read, for instance, the works of the semi-Cadet, semi-Octobrist Prince Obolensky in *Russkaya Mysl*, and you will see that even this landowner, who is thoroughly imbued with the views of his class, admits the fact that the allotments are bought up to an *enormous* extent by the rich, and that these purchases are *masked* by means of evasions of the law in thousands of different ways!

And so, gentlemen, the "new" agrarian policy of the government and the nobles was *all* the honourable nobles could produce, leaving their property and their revenues intact (often they even *increased* their revenues by *inflating* the price of the land for sale and by means of the thousands of favours the Peasant Bank extends to the nobility).

And the *"all"* of these nobles proved to be *nothing*. The countryside is even more destitute, even more *angered*.

Terrible anger reigns in the villages. What is called hooliganism is due mainly to the incredible anger of the peasants, and is their *primitive* form of *protest*. No persecution, no increasing of punishments will allay this anger and stop this protest by millions of hungry peasants who are now being ruined by the "redistribution" of the land with unprecedented rapidity, roughness and brutality.

No, the nobles' or Stolypin's agrarian policy is not the way out; it is only a very painful *approach* towards a new *solution* of the agrarian problem in Russia. What this solution should be is shown indirectly even by the fate of Ireland where, in spite of a thousand delays, hindrances and obstacles placed in the way by the landowners, the land has after all passed into the hands of the farmers.

The essence of the agrarian problem in Russia is most strikingly revealed by the figures for the big landed estates. These figures are given in the official government statistics of 1905, and anyone who is seriously concerned about the fate of the Russian peasantry and the state of affairs in the entire field of politics of our country should study them with great attention.

Let us consider the big landed estates in European Russia: *27,833* landowners own over 500 dessiatines each, giving them a total of *62,000,000 dessiatines of land*! Adding to these the land owned by the imperial family and the enormous estates of the manufacturers in the Urals, we get *70,000,000 dessiatines* owned by less than *30,000* landowners. This gives on an average over *2,000* dessiatines to each big landed proprietor. The size the biggest estates attain in Russia is seen from the fact that *699* proprietors own more than *10,000 dessiatines* each, giving them a total of 20,798,504 dessiatines. On an average these magnates possess almost *30,000* (29,754) *dessiatines* each!

It is not easy to find in Europe, or even in the entire world, another country where big feudal landownership has been preserved on such a monstrous scale.

And the most important point is that capitalist farming, i.e., the cultivation of the soil by hired labourers with the implements and tools of the owners, is being conducted only on a part of these lands. For the most part, farming is being conducted on *feudal* lines, i.e., the landowners enslave the peasants as they did one hundred, three hundred, and five hundred years ago, forcing the peasants to cultivate the estate land with *their own* horses, with *their own implements.* This is not capitalism. This is not the European method of farming, gentlemen of the Right and Octobrists; take note of this, you who are boasting of your desire to "Europeanise" (i.e., refashion in the European way) agriculture in Russia! No, this is not European at all. This is the *old Chinese way*. This is the *Turkish way*. This is the *feudal way.*

This is not up-to-date farming, it is land usury. It is the old, old enslavement. The poor peasant, who even in the best year remains a pauper and is half-starved, who owns a weak, scrawny nag and old, miserable, wretched implements, is becoming the slave of the landowner, of the *"master"*, because he, the muzhik, has no alternative.

The "master" will neither lease his land, nor give right of way, nor watering-places for animals, nor meadows, nor timber, unless the peasant enslaves himself. If a peasant is caught "illegally" felling wood in the forests, what happens? He is beaten up by the foresters, Circassians, etc., and then the *"master"*, who in the Duma delivers fervent speeches on the progress of our agriculture and on the necessity of copying Europe—this same master offers the following alternative to the beaten muzhik: either go to prison or cultivate, plough, sow and harvest two or three dessiatines! The same thing happens when the peasants' cattle trespass on the landowners' estates. The same for the winter loan of grain. The same for the use of meadows and pastures, and so on without end.

This is not big landowner farming. It is the *enslavement* of the muzhik. It is *feudal* exploitation of millions of impoverished peasants by means of estates of thousands of dessiatines, the estates of the landowners who have been squeezing and stifling the muzhik in all directions.

The farmsteads are helping out a handful of rich peasants. But the masses continue to starve as before. Why is it, you landowning gentlemen, that Europe has not known famine for a long time? Why is it that terrible famines, such as that which raged in our country in 1910-11, occurred in Europe only under serfdom?

Because in Europe there is no serf bondage. There are rich and middle peasants and there are labourers in Europe, but not millions of ruined, destitute peasants, driven to despair by perennial suffering and hard labour, disfranchised, downtrodden, dependent on the "master".

What is to be done? What is the way out?

There is only one way out: the liberation of the countryside from the oppression of these feudal latifundia, the transfer of these *seventy million* dessiatines of land from the landed proprietors to the peasants, a transfer that must be effected without any compensation.

Only such a solution can make Russia really resemble a European country. Only such a solution will enable the millions of Russian peasants to breathe freely and recover. Only such a solution will make it possible to transform Russia from a country of perennially starving, destitute peasants, crushed by bondage to the landowner, into a country of "European progress", from a country of illiterate people into a literate country, from a country of backwardness and hopeless stagnation into a country capable of developing and going forward, from a disfranchised country, a country of slaves, into a free country.

And the party of the working class, knowing that without free, democratic institutions there is not and cannot be a road to socialism, points, as a way out of the blind alley into which the government with its agrarian policy has again led Russia, to the free transfer of all the landed estates to the peasants, to the winning of full political liberty by a new revolution.

Written not later than
June 7 (20), 1913

First published in 1930   Published according to
in the second   the manuscript
and third editions of V. I. Lenin's
Collected Works, Vol. XVI

CAPITALISM AND TAXATION

Novy Ekonomist (No. 21 for 1913), a journal published by Mr. P. Migulin, with the Octobrists and Cadets jointly collaborating, carries an interesting note about income tax in the United States.

The bill exempts from taxation all incomes up to 4,000 dollars (8,000 rubles). Taxation is envisaged at the rate of one per cent on all incomes exceeding 4,000 dollars, two per cent on all incomes exceeding 20,000 dollars and so on, with slight increases in the percentage as incomes increase. Thus the plan is for a progressive income tax, but with an exceedingly slow rate of progression, so that the owner of a million dollar income generally pays less than three per cent.

The plan estimates that the 425,000 people whose incomes exceed 4,000 dollars will pay 70 million dollars in taxes (about 140 million rubles) and the Octobrist-Cadet editors of *Novy Ekonomist* note with reference to this:

"Compared with the 700 million rubles import duty and the 500 million rubles excise duty, the expected revenue of 140 million rubles from income tax is negligible and will not change the significance of indirect taxation."

It is a pity that our bourgeois liberal economists who are in words prepared to accept a progressive income tax and have even recorded it in their programme, have evinced no desire to make a definite and precise statement on *what* rates of income tax *they* consider to be obligatory.

Such rates that the significance of indirect taxation would merely be changed, and if so to what extent? Or such rates that indirect taxation would be completely abolished?

The American statistics that *Novy Ekonomist* touches upon provide an instructive illustration to this question.

It can be seen from the bill that the total income of 425,000 capitalists (if the tax provides 70 million dollars) is estimated at 5,413,000,000 dollars. This is an obvious understatement; a *hundred persons* are shown as having an income of over a million dollars and their income is shown as 150,000,000 dollars. We know that *a dozen* American multimillionaires have incomes incomparably greater. The Secretary of the Treasury in America wants to be "polite" to the multimillionaires....

But even these figures, excessively "polite" to the capitalists, show a noteworthy picture. Statistics in America record only 16,000,000 families. Of these, therefore, *less than half a million* are counted as capitalists. The remaining mass of people are wage-slaves or petty farmers oppressed by capital, etc.

The statistics fix the size of the income enjoyed by the working masses in America quite accurately for a number of categories. For instance, 6,615,046 industrial workers received (in 1910) 3,427,000,000 dollars, i.e., 518 dollars (1,035 rubles) per worker. Then, 1,699,420 railway workers received 1,144,000,000 dollars (673 dollars per worker). Further, 523,210 public school-teachers received 254,000,000 dollars (483 dollars per teacher).

Combining this mass of working people and rounding off the figures we get: workers—8,800,000 with a total income of 4,800,000,000 dollars or 550 dollars each; capitalists—500,000 with a total income of 5,500,000,000 dollars or 11,000 dollars each.

Half a million capitalist families receive an income that is *greater* than that of almost 9,000,000 workers' families. What, might we ask, is the role of indirect taxation and of the planned income tax?

Indirect taxation brings in 1,200,000,000 rubles, i.e., 600,000,000 dollars. The amount of indirect taxation is 75 rubles (37.50 dollars) per family in America. Let us compare the way in which the incomes of capitalists and workers are taxed:

	Million families	Total income	Total indirect taxes	% of income paid as taxes
		(million dollars)		
Workers . . .	8.8	4,800	330	7
Capitalists . .	0.5	5,500	19	0.36

We see that the workers pay seven kopeks to the ruble in indirect taxes while the capitalists pay *one-third* of a kopek. The workers pay, proportionally, *twenty times* more than the capitalists. A system of indirect taxes inevitably creates such an "order" (a very disorderly order) in *all* capitalist countries.

If the capitalists were to pay the same percentage in taxes as the workers, the tax imposed would be *385,000,000* and not 19,000,000 *dollars*.

Does a progressive income tax *of the sort* planned in America change much? Very little. From the capitalists 19,000,000 dollars indirect taxes plus 70,000,000 dollars income tax would be obtained, that is, altogether 89,000,000 dollars *or only one and a half per cent of income!*

Let us divide the capitalists into middle (income 4,000 to 10,000 dollars, i.e., 8,000-20,000 rubles) and wealthy (with an income over 20,000 rubles). We get the following: middle capitalists—304,000 families with a total income of 1,813,000,000 dollars, and wealthy capitalists—121,000 families with a total income of 3,600,000,000 dollars.

If the middle capitalists paid as much as the workers pay, i.e., 7 per cent of income, the revenue would be about 130,000,000 dollars. Fifteen per cent from the income of wealthy capitalists would produce 540,000,000 dollars. The total *would more than cover all indirect taxes.* After the deduction of this tax the middle capitalists would still have an income of 11,000 rubles each and the wealthy an income of 50,000 rubles each.

We see that the demand put forward by the Social-Democrats—the *complete* abolition of all indirect taxes and their replacement by a real progressive income tax and not one that merely plays at it—is *fully* realisable. Such a measure would, without affecting the foundations of capitalism, give tremendous immediate relief to nine-tenths of the population; and, secondly, it would serve as a gigantic impetus to the development of the productive forces of society by expanding the home market and liberating the state from the nonsensical hindrances to economic life that have been introduced for the purpose of levying indirect taxes.

The capitalists' advocates usually point to the difficulty of assessing big incomes. Actually, with banks, savings societies, etc., at their present level of development, this is a purely imaginary difficulty. The *one* difficulty is the class-avarice of the capitalists and the existence of undemocratic institutions in the political structure of bourgeois states.

Pravda No. 129, June 7, 1913   Published according to
          Signed: *V. Ilyin*   the *Pravda* text

ECONOMIC STRIKES IN 1912 AND IN 1905

The statistics on economic strikes compiled by the Association of Factory Owners in the Moscow Area enable us
to draw some parallels between 1912 and 1905. In doing so
we shall have to limit ourselves to three groups of industries—metalworking, textile and "others", because the factory owners' association does not give a more detailed clas-
sification in its statistics.

Here are the parallel figures:

	Number of strikers participating in economic strikes		
	1905	1911	1912
Metalworkers	230,216	17,920	78,195
Textile workers	559,699	59,950	89,540
Others	230,527	18,880	43,860
Totals	1,020,442	96,750	211,595

The figures for 1905 include only *purely* economic strikes;
those with mixed motives, both economic and political,
have been omitted. The figures for 1911 and 1912 seem to be
far from complete.

If we take the 1905 figures as the starting-point, a comparison of these figures shows us that in 1911 the strike effort
of the textile workers was *greater* than that of the metalworkers and "others". In 1911 more than half the total number of strikers were textile workers; their number was more
than three times that of the metalworkers. In 1905 the number of textile workers on strike was only two and a half
times the number of metalworkers.

As far as the "others" are concerned, the number of strikers in these branches was about the same as the number of striking metalworkers in both 1905 and 1911.

In 1912, however, the metalworkers made an astounding advance, leaving the "others" far behind and almost catching up with the textile workers.

The number of metalworkers who took part in strikes in 1912 was more than *four times* the number for 1911. In the same period the number of strikers among the textile workers increased by only 50 per cent (60,000 and 89,000), while that of the "others" increased by just 150 per cent.

It follows, therefore, that the metalworkers made good use of the favourable market conditions of 1912. Encouraged by the victories of 1911, they went over to a more extensive and more determined offensive.

Workers in the "other" branches of industry were also in a favourable position in 1912. Their economic struggle was still more successful than that of the metalworkers, but they did not make such good use of their favourable position as the metalworkers did.

The position of the textile workers in 1912 was worse than that of workers in any other branch of industry; their economic struggle was the least successful. In view of this the number of strikers among them increased more slowly than in other branches.

The factory owners of the Moscow area hope that the wave of strikes will be weaker in 1913. We read in their report for 1912: "The situation in the textile industry is clear enough; until the state of the new harvest is known the mills will work at a slower rate and for the workers to strike under these conditions would be very imprudent."

We shall see to what extent this assumption is justified. In any case both the year of 1912 and the beginning of 1913 have shown that *economic* strikes constitute only a small part of the *entire* "strike wave".

Pravda No. 130, June 8, 1913
Signed: *V. I.*

Published according to
the *Pravda* text

THE GROWTH OF CAPITALIST WEALTH

Capitalists are not inclined to be frank about their incomes. "Commercial secrets" are strictly guarded and it is very difficult for the uninitiated to penetrate the "mysteries" of how riches are piled up. Private property is sacred—nobody is permitted to meddle in the affairs of its owner. Such is the principle of capitalism.

Capital, however, has long since overstepped the bounds of private property and introduced joint-stock companies. Hundreds and thousands of shareholders who do not know each other make up a single enterprise; and these property-owners are quite often diddled by smart businessmen who empty the pockets of their business partners using "commercial secrets" as a cover.

Sacred private property has been forced to sacrifice a bit of its sacredness; laws have had to be made compelling joint-stock companies to keep proper books and publish the chief results of their accountancy. This, of course, has not prevented the public being swindled; the swindling has merely taken new forms and become more subtle than before. Big capital, gathering around itself small sums of shareholders' capital from all over the world, has become more powerful still. Through the joint-stock company, the millionaire now has at his disposal not only his own million, but additional capital of, say, 800,000 rubles that may have been gathered from 8,000 petty proprietors.

This makes the absurdity of capitalism much clearer to the masses of the population.

Take, for example, the published reports of insurance companies in Russia over a period of ten years, from 1902 to 1911.

In 1902 share capital amounted to 31.3 million rubles (in 21 joint-stock companies), and in 1911 (in the same 21 companies) it was 34.8 million rubles. The greater part of the capital usually belongs to a handful of millionaires. Ten or twenty magnates perhaps hold shares for eighteen million rubles, which gives them a majority vote, and they can, without any control, dispose of the other thirteen or sixteen million rubles belonging to "small" shareholders.

The professors who defend capitalism chatter about the increase in the number of property-owners when they see a growth in the number of small shareholders. What actually happens is that the power (and the income) of the millionaire magnates *over* the capital of the "small fry" is increased.

Just see how our insurance kings have expanded in the course of this ten years. The *average* dividend on share capital for the ten years was *more* than 10 per cent! Not a bad profit, eh? In the worst year of the decade they "earned" six kopeks in the ruble, and in the best year twelve kopeks!

Reserve capital was doubled—in 1902 it amounted to 152,000,000 rubles and in 1911 to 327,000,000 rubles. Property was almost doubled as well—in 1902 it was valued at 44,000,000 rubles and in 1911 at 76,000,000 rubles.

The result—in ten years in twenty-one companies, 32,000,000 rubles' worth of *new* property!

Who "earned" this property?

Those who did not work, the shareholders, and first and foremost the millionaire magnates who hold most of the shares.

The work was done by hundreds of employees, who canvassed insurance clients, inspected their property and laboured over the accounts. These employees remained employees. They do not receive anything more than their salaries (which, as we know, are in the majority of cases insufficient even to maintain a family decently). They cannot accumulate any property.

If any of the magnates did a bit of "work" *as a director*, he received *special* remuneration in the form of a ministerial salary and bonuses.

The gentlemen holding the shares grew rich *for not* work-ing. During the decade they received on the average three millions a year net profit for the "toil" of clipping coupons, and accumulated additional capital to the tune of thirty-two million rubles.

Pravda No. 131, June 9, 1913
Signed: *V. I.*

Published according to
the *Pravda* text

THE PEASANTRY AND THE WORKING CLASS

In the Narodnik newspapers and magazines we often meet with the assertion that the workers and the "working" peasantry belong to the same class.

The absolute incorrectness of this view is obvious to anyone who understands that more or less developed capitalist production predominates in all modern states—i.e., capital rules the market and transforms the masses of working people into wage-workers. The so-called "working" peasant is in fact a *small proprietor*, or a petty bourgeois, who nearly always either hires himself out to work for somebody else or hires workers himself. Being a small proprietor, the "working" peasant also vacillates in politics between the masters and the workers, between the bourgeoisie and the proletariat.

Statistics on *wage-labour* in agriculture provide one of the most striking proofs of this property-owning, or bourgeois, nature of the "working" peasant. Bourgeois economists (including the Narodniks) usually praise the "vitality" of small production in agriculture, by which they mean farming without wage-labour. But they are not at all fond of precise figures on wage-labour among the peasantry!

Let us examine data on this question gathered by the most recent agricultural censuses—the Austrian census of 1902 and the German of 1907.

The more developed a country, the more extensively is wage-labour employed in agriculture. In Germany, out of a total of 15,000,000 wage-workers, it is estimated that 4,500,000, or 30 per cent, are employed in agriculture; and in Austria, the figure is 1,250,000, or 14 per cent, out of a total of 9,000,000. But even in Austria, if we take farms usually regarded as peasant (or "working" peasant) farms, i.e., those from 2 to 20 hectares (one hectare equals nine-tenths of a dessiatine), we will find that wage-labour plays an important part. Farms from 5 to 10 hectares number 383,000; of these 126,000 employ wage-workers. Farms from 10 to 20 hectares number 242,000; of these 142,000, or nearly three-fifths, employ wage-workers.

Thus, small ("working") peasant farming exploits *hundreds of thousands* of wage-workers. The larger the peasant farm, the larger the number of wage-workers employed, together with a larger contingent of family workers. For example, in Germany, for every 10 peasant farms, there are:

Size of farm	Family workers	Wage-workers	Total
2 to 5 hectares	25	4	29
5 to 10 "	31	7	38
10 to 20 "	34	17	51

The more affluent peasantry, who have more land and a larger number of "their own" workers in the family, employ *in addition* a larger number of *wage-workers.*

In capitalist society, which is entirely dependent on the market, small (peasant) production on a mass scale is *impossible* in agriculture without the mass employment of wage-labour. The sentimental catchword, "working" peasant, merely deceives the workers by *concealing* this exploitation of wage-labour.

In Austria, about one and a half million peasant farms (from 2 to 20 hectares) employ *half a million* wage-workers. In Germany, two million peasant farms employ *more than one and a half million* wage-workers.

And what about the smaller farmers? They hire themselves out! They are wage-workers with a plot of land. For example, in Germany there are over three and a third million (3,378,509) farms of less than two hectares. Of these *less than half a million* (474,915) are *independent* farmers, and only a little less than *two million* (1,822, 792) are *wage-workers!*

The very position of the small farmers in modern society, therefore, inevitably transforms them into petty bourgeois. They are eternally hovering between the wage-workers and the capitalists. The majority of the peasants live in poverty, are ruined and become proletarians, while the minority trail after the capitalists and help keep the masses of the rural population dependent upon the capitalists. That is why the peasants in all capitalist countries have so far mostly kept aloof from the workers' socialist movement and have joined various reactionary and bourgeois parties. Only an independent organisation of wage-workers which conducts a consistent class struggle can wrest the peasantry from the influence of the bourgeoisie and explain to them the absolute hopelessness of the small producers' position in capitalist society.

In Russia the position of the peasants in relation to capitalism is just the same as in Austria, Germany, etc. Our "specific feature" is our backwardness: the peasant is still confronted, not with the capitalist, but with the big *feudal* landowner, who is the principal bulwark of the economic and political backwardness of Russia.

Pravda No. 132, June 11, 1913
Signed: *V. I.*

Published according to
the *Pravda* text

CHILD LABOUR IN PEASANT FARMING

In making a proper appraisal of the conditions in which capitalism places small agricultural production the most important things to study are the conditions of the worker, his earnings, the amount of labour he expends, his conditions of life; then the way the livestock is kept and tended, and, finally, the methods of cultivating and fertilising the soil, the waste of its fertility, etc.

It is not difficult to understand that if these questions are ignored (as they often are in bourgeois political economy) a totally distorted picture of peasant farming is obtained, for the *real* "viability" of the latter depends precisely on the conditions of the worker, on the condition of his livestock, and on the way he tends his land. To assume without proof that in this respect small production is in the same position as large-scale production is merely begging the question. It means at once adopting the bourgeois point of view.

The bourgeoisie wants to prove that the peasant is a sound and viable "proprietor", and not the slave of capital, crushed in the same way as the wage-worker, but more tied up, more entangled than the latter. If one seriously and conscientiously wants the *data* required to solve this controversial problem, he must look for the regular and objective indicators of the *conditions of life and labour* in small and large-scale production.

One of these indicators, and a particularly important one, is the extent to which *child* labour is employed. The more child labour is exploited the worse, undoubtedly, is the position of the worker, and the harder his life.

The Austrian and German agricultural censuses give the number of children and adolescents employed in agriculture in relation to the total number of persons employed in agriculture. The Austrian census gives separate figures for all workers, male and female, *under* 16 years of age. Of these, there were 1,200,000 out of a total of 9,000,000, i.e., 13 per cent. The German census gives figures only for those *of 14 years of age and under*; of these there were six hundred thousand (601,637) out of fifteen million (15,169,549), or 3.9 per cent.

Clearly, the Austrian and German figures are not comparable. Nevertheless, the *relative numbers* of proletarian, peasant and capitalist farms they reveal are quite comparable.

By proletarian farms we mean the tiny plots of land (up to two hectares or almost two dessiatines per farm) which provide the wage-worker with supplementary earnings. By peasant farms we mean those from 2 to 20 hectares; in these, family labour predominates over wage-labour. Finally, there are the capitalist farms; these are big farms, in which wage-labour predominates over family labour.

The following are the figures on child labour in the three types of farms.

Type of farm	Group according to size of farm	Children employed (% of total number of workers)	
		Austria (under 16)	Germany (under 14)
Proletarian	Less than half a hectare . . .	8.8	2.2
	½ to 2 hectares	12.2	3.9
Peasant	2 " 5 "	15.3	4.6
	5 " 10 "	15.6	4.8
	10 " 20 "	12.8	4.5
Capitalist	20 " 100 "	11.1	3.4
	100 hectares and over	4.2	3.6
Total		13.0	3.9

We see from the above that in both countries the exploitation of child labour is *greatest* in *peasant* farms in general, and among the *middle peasant* farms (5 to 10 hectares, i.e., 4.5 to 9 dessiatines) in particular.

Thus, not only is small production worse-off than large-scale production, we also see that the peasant farms, in particular, are worse-off than the capitalist farms and even than the proletarian farms.

How is this to be explained?

On the proletarian farm, farming is conducted on such an insignificant plot of land that, strictly speaking, it cannot seriously be called a "farm". Here farming is a *secondary* occupation; the principal occupation is wage-labour in agriculture and in industry. In general, the influence of industry raises the standard of life of the worker, and in particular, it reduces the exploitation of child labour. For example, the German census shows the number of persons under the age of 14 employed in industry to be only 0.3 per cent of the total (i.e., one-tenth of that in agriculture) and those under 16 years of age only 18 per cent.

In peasant farming, however, the influence of industry is felt least of all, while the competition of capitalist agriculture is felt most of all. The peasant is unable to keep going without almost working himself to death and compelling his children to work as hard. Want compels the peasant to make up for his lack of capital and technical equipment with his own muscles. The fact that the peasant's children work hardest also indicates that the peasant's cattle work hard and are fed worse: the necessity of exerting the utmost effort and of "economising" in everything inevitably affects every side of the farm.

German statistics show that among wage-workers the largest percentage of children (3.7 or nearly 4 per cent) is to be found in the big capitalist farms (of 100 dessiatines and over). But among family workers, the largest percentage of children is to be found among the peasants—about five per cent (4.9 per cent to 5.2 per cent). As many as 9 per cent of *temporary* wage-workers employed in big capitalist enterprises are children; but among the peasants as many as 16.5 to 24.4 per cent of the temporary *family* workers are children!

In the busy season the peasant suffers from a shortage of workers; he can hire workers only to a small extent; he is compelled to employ the labour of his own children to the greatest extent. The result is that in German agriculture, in general, the percentage of children among family workers is *nearly half as big again* as that among wage-workers—

children among family workers—4.4 per cent; among wage-workers—3 per cent.

The peasant has to work *harder* than the wage-worker. This fact, confirmed by thousands of independent observations, is now fully proved by statistics for whole countries. Capitalism condemns the peasant to extreme degradation and ruin. There is no other salvation for him than through joining the class struggle of the wage-workers. But before the peasant can arrive at this conclusion he will have to experience many years of being disillusioned by deceptive bourgeois slogans.

Pravda No. 133, June 12, 1913
Signed: *V. I.*

Published according to
the *Pravda* text

THE RESULTS OF STRIKES IN 1912 AS COMPARED WITH THOSE OF THE PAST

The Association of Factory Owners in the Moscow Area has issued statistics on the results of strikes during the last seven months of 1912. These statistics embraced 131,625 workers out of a total of 211,595 who participated (according to the factory owners' figures, undoubtedly reduced) in economic strikes over the whole year of 1912.

We have the figures for the results of strikes in previous years in the official publications of the Ministry of Commerce and Industry covering the decade preceding the revolution (1895-1904) and the three revolutionary years (1905-07).

The data, unfortunately, are not similar weights, and those gathered by the factory owners' association are not so well processed. Official statistics on the results of strikes divide them into three categories: (1) ending to the advantage of the workers, (2) to the advantage of the owners and (3) in a compromise. The statistics of the factory owners divide them into: (1) ending in the defeat of the workers, (2) the complete or partial satisfaction of the workers and (3) strikes whose results are unspecified.

The two sets of data may be compared (even relatively) only in the following way. The workers taking part in strikes that ended in a compromise or whose results are unspecified, are divided into two equal parts between the strikes *won* and *lost*, obtaining as a result only these two headings (approximate, of course). Here are the results of the comparison:

		Number of strikers	Number of strikers in strikes won (thousands)	Percentage won
For ten years before the revolution	1895-1904	424	159	37.5
Three revolutionary years	1905	1,439	705	48.9
	1906	458	233	50.9
	1907	200	59	29.5
For all	1911	96	49	51.0
For last 7 months of . .	1912	132	55	41.6

All these figures refer only to economic strikes, and the data for 1911 and 1912, furthermore, are incomplete. The number of workers for the whole of 1912 who took part in economic strikes (212,000) *exceeded* the number for 1907.

As can be seen, the year 1911 was a record year for the success of economic strikes, even surpassing the most successful revolutionary year of 1906. In 1906 the percentage of strikers who won their strikes was 50.9 per cent and in 1911 it was 51 per cent.

Strikes in 1912 were less successful than they were in *1905* (1905—48.9 per cent won, 1912—41.6 per cent won), but they were more successful than were, on the average, those of the *decade* 1895-1904 (37.5 per cent), to say nothing of 1907 (29.5 per cent won).

It is interesting to compare these figures with those of Western Europe. In Germany, during the entire first decade of the twentieth century (1900-09) there were 1,607,000 strikers (in Russia the *two years* of the revolution *alone*, counting only economic strikes, yielded as many). Of these, 698,000 or 36.8 per cent won their strikes, i.e., somewhat less than in Russia in the decade preceding the revolution. In Britain for the ten years, 1900-09, the number of strikers was 1,884,000. Out of 1,234,000 strikers, 588,000, or 47.5 per cent, won their strikes, i.e., many more than in Russia in the pre-revolutionary decade, but fewer than in 1905 1906 and 1911. (The number of strikers winning their strikes was calculated for Germany and Britain on the same basis as for Russia.)

The number of strikers in Russia who won their strikes in 1905 *alone*, was *greater* than the number *for ten years* in Germany or Britain. One may judge from this how much of the proletariat's latent strength is still untapped.

Pravda No. 133, June 12, 1913
Signed: *N.*

Published according to
the *Pravda* text

IN AUSTRALIA

A general election recently took place in Australia. The Labour Party, which had a majority in the Lower House—44 seats out of 75—was defeated. It now has only 36 seats out of 75. The majority has passed to the Liberals, but this majority is a very unstable one, because 30 of the 36 seats in the Upper House are held by Labour.

What sort of peculiar capitalist country is this, in which the workers' representatives predominate in the *Upper* House and, till recently, did so in the Lower House as well, and yet the capitalist system is in no danger?

An English correspondent of the German labour press recently explained the situation, which is very often misrepresented by bourgeois writers.

The Australian Labour Party does not even call itself a socialist party. Actually it is a liberal-bourgeois party, while the so-called Liberals in Australia are really Conservatives.

This strange and incorrect use of terms in naming parties is not unique. In America, for example, the slave-owners of yesterday are called Democrats, and in France, enemies of socialism, petty bourgeois, are called Radical Socialists! In order to understand the real significance of parties, one must examine not their signboards but their class character and the historical conditions of each individual country.

Australia is a young British colony.

Capitalism in Australia is still quite youthful. The country is only just taking shape as an independent state. The workers are for the most part emigrants from Britain. They left the country at the time when the liberal-labour policy held almost undivided sway there, when the masses of the British workers were *Liberals*. Even now the majority of the skilled factory workers in Britain are Liberals or semi-

Liberals. This is the results of the exceptionally favourable, monopolist position enjoyed by Britain in the second half of the last century. Only now are the masses of the workers in Britain turning (but turning slowly) towards socialism.

And while in Britain the so-called Labour Party is an *alliance* between the non-socialist trade unions and the extremely opportunist Independent Labour Party, in Australia the Labour Party is the *unalloyed* representative of the *non*-socialist workers' trade unions.

The leaders of the Australian Labour Party are trade union officials, everywhere the most moderate and "capital-serving" element, and in Australia, altogether peaceable, purely liberal.

The ties binding the separate states into a united Australia are still very weak. The Labour Party has had to concern itself with developing and strengthening these ties, and with establishing central government.

In Australia the Labour Party has done what in other countries was done by the Liberals, namely, introduced a uniform tariff for the whole country, a uniform educational law, a uniform land tax and uniform factory legislation.

Naturally, when Australia is finally developed and consolidated as an independent capitalist state, the condition of the workers will change, as also will the *liberal* Labour Party, which will make way for a *socialist* workers' party. Australia is an illustration of the conditions under which *exceptions* to the rule are possible. The rule is: a socialist workers' party in a capitalist country. The exception is: a liberal Labour Party which arises only for a short time by virtue of specific conditions that are abnormal for capitalism in general.

Those Liberals in Europe and in Russia who try to "teach" the people that class struggle is unnecessary by citing the example of Australia, only deceive themselves and others. It is ridiculous to think of transplanting Australian conditions (an undeveloped, young colony, populated by liberal British workers) to countries where the state is long established and capitalism well developed.

Pravda No. 134, June 13, 1913
Signed: *W.*

Published according to the *Pravda* text

MAY DAY ACTION
BY THE REVOLUTIONARY PROLETARIAT

A year has passed since the Lena events and the first, decisive upsurgence in the revolutionary working-class movement since the June Third coup. The tsar's Black Hundreds and the landowners, the mob of officials and the bourgeoisie have celebrated the 300th anniversary of plunder, Tatar incursions, and the disgracing of Russia by the Romanovs. The Fourth Duma has convened and begun its "work", though it has no faith in that work and has quite lost its former counter-revolutionary vigour. Confusion and tedium have beset liberal society, which is listlessly making appeals *for reforms* while admitting the impracticability of anything even approximating reform.

And now comes a May Day action by Russia's working class, who first held a rehearsal in Riga, then went into resolute action in St. Petersburg on May 1 (O.S.); this action has rent the dim and dreary atmosphere like a thunderbolt. The tasks of the approaching revolution have come to the fore again in all their grandeur, and the forces of the advanced class leading it stand out in bold relief before hundreds of old revolutionaries, whom persecution by hangmen and desertion by friends have not defeated or broken, and before millions of people of the new generation of democrats and socialists.

Weeks before May Day, the government appeared to have lost its wits, while the gentlemen who own factories behaved as if they had never had any wits at all. The arrests and searches seemed to have turned all the workers' districts in the capital upside down. The provinces did not lag behind the centre. The harassed factory owners called

conferences and adopted contradictory slogans, now threatening the workers with punishment and lock-outs, now making concessions in advance and consenting to stop work,
now inciting the government to commit atrocities, now
reproaching the government and calling on it to include May
Day in the number of official holidays.

But even though the gendarmes showed the utmost zeal,
even though they "purged" the industrial suburbs, even
though they made arrests right and left according to their
latest "lists of suspects", it was no use. The workers laughed
at the impotent rage of the tsar's gang and the capitalist
class and derided the governor's menacing and pitiful "announcements"; they wrote satirical verses and circulated
them by hand or passed them on by word of mouth; they
produced, as if from nowhere fresh batches of small, poorly
printed "leaflets", short and plain, but very instructive,
calling for strikes and demonstrations, and reminding the
people of the old, uncurtailed, revolutionary slogans of the
Social-Democrats, who in 1905 led the first onslaught of the
masses against the autocracy and against monarchy.

A hundred thousand on strike on May Day, said the government press the next day. Bourgeois newspapers, using the
first telegraphed information, reported a hundred and twenty-five thousand (*Kievskaya Mysl*). A correspondent of the
central organ of the German Social-Democrats wired from
St. Petersburg that it was a hundred and fifty thousand.
And the day after the whole bourgeois press quoted a figure
of 200,000-220,000. Actually the number of strikers reached
250,000!

But, apart from the number of May Day strikers, much
more impressive—and much more significant—were the revolutionary street demonstrations held by the workers.
Everywhere in and around the capital crowds of workers
singing revolutionary songs, calling loudly for revolution
and carrying red flags fought for several hours against police
and security forces frantically mobilised by the government.
And those workers made the keenest of the tsar's henchmen
feel that the struggle was in earnest, that the police were
not faced with a handful of individuals engaged in a trivial
Slavophil affair,[75] that it was actually the *masses* of the
capital's working class who had risen.

This was a really brilliant, open demonstration of the
proletariat's revolutionary aspirations, of its revolutionary
forces steeled and reinforced by new generations, of revolutionary appeals to the people and the peoples of Russia.
Last year the government and the manufacturers were able
to take comfort from the fact that the Lena explosion could
not have been foreseen, that they could not have made immediate preparations to combat its consequences; this time,
however, the monarchy had displayed acute foresight,
there had been ample time for preparation and the "measures" taken were most "vigorous"; the result was that the
tsarist monarchy revealed its complete *impotence* when faced
with a revolutionary awakening of the proletarian masses.

Indeed, one year of strike struggle since Lena has shown,
despite the pitiful outcries of the liberals and their yes-men
against the "craze for striking", against "syndicalist" strikes,
against combining economic with political strikes and
vice versa—this year has shown what a great and irreplace-
able weapon for agitation among the masses, for rousing
them, for drawing them into the struggle the Social-Democratic proletariat had forged for itself in the revolutionary
epoch. The revolutionary mass-scale strike allowed the
enemy neither rest nor respite. It also hit the enemy's
purse, and in full view of the whole world it trampled into
the mud the political prestige of the allegedly "strong"
tsarist government. It enabled more and more sections of
the workers to regain at least a small part of what had been
achieved in 1905 and drew fresh sections of the working
people, even the most backward, into the struggle. It did
not exhaust the capacity of the workers, it was frequently
demonstrative action of short duration, and at the same
time it paved the way for further, still more impressive
and more revolutionary open action by the masses in the
shape of street demonstrations.

During the last year, no country in the world has seen
so many people on strike for political ends as Russia, or
such perseverance, such variety, such vigour in strikes.
This circumstance alone shows to the full the pettiness,
the contemptible stupidity of those liberal and liquidationist sages who tried to "adjust" the tactics of the Russian
workers in 1912-13, using the yardstick of "European" con-

stitutional periods, periods that were mainly devoted to the preparatory work of bringing socialist education and enlightenment to the masses.

The colossal superiority of the Russian strikes over those in the European countries, the most advanced countries, demonstrates, not the special qualities or special abilities of Russia's workers, but the *special* conditions in present-day Russia, the existence of a revolutionary situation, the growth of a directly revolutionary crisis. When the moment of a similar growth of revolution approaches in Europe (there it will be a socialist and not a bourgeois-democratic revolution, as in our country), the proletariat of the most developed capitalist countries will launch far more vigorous revolutionary strikes, demonstrations, and armed struggle against the defenders of wage-slavery.

This year's May Day strike, like the series of strikes in Russia during the last eighteen months, was revolutionary in character as distinguished not only from the usual economic strikes but from demonstration strikes and from political strikes demanding constitutional reforms, like, for instance, the last Belgian strike.[76] Those who are in bondage to a liberal world outlook and no longer able to consider things from the revolutionary standpoint, cannot possibly understand this distinctive character of the Russian strikes, a character that is due entirely to the revolutionary state of Russia. The epoch of counter-revolution and of free play for renegade sentiment has left behind it too many people of this kind even among those who would like to be called Social-Democrats.

Russia is experiencing a revolutionary situation because the oppression of the vast majority of the population—not only of the proletariat but of nine-tenths of the small producers, particularly the peasants—has intensified to the maximum, and this intensified oppression, starvation, poverty, lack of rights, humiliation of the people is, furthermore, glaringly inconsistent with the state of Russia's productive forces, inconsistent with the level of the class-consciousness and the demands of the masses roused by the year 1905, and inconsistent with the state of affairs in all neighbouring—not only European but Asian—countries.

But that is not all. Oppression alone, no matter how

great, does not always give rise to a revolutionary situation
in a country. In most cases it is not enough for revolution
that *the lower classes should not want* to live in the old way.
It is also necessary that *the upper classes should be unable*
to rule and govern in the old way. This is what we see in
Russia today. A political crisis is maturing before our very
eyes. The bourgeoisie has done *everything* in its power to
back counter-revolution and ensure "peaceful development"
on this counter-revolutionary basis. The bourgeoisie gave
hangmen and feudal lords as much money as they wanted,
the bourgeoisie reviled the revolution and renounced it,
the bourgeoisie licked the boots of Purishkevich and the
knout of Markov the Second and became their lackey, the
bourgeoisie evolved theories based on "European" arguments, theories that revile the Revolution of 1905 as an
"intellectualist" revolution and describe it as wicked, criminal, treasonous, and so on and so forth.

And yet, despite all this sacrificing of its purse, its honour and its conscience, the bourgeoisie—from the Cadets
to the Octobrists—*itself* admits that the autocracy and landowners *were unable* to ensure "peaceful *development*", were
unable to provide the basic conditions for "law" and "order",
without which a capitalist country cannot, in the twentieth
century, live side by side with Germany and the new China.

A nation-wide political crisis is in evidence in Russia,
a crisis which affects the very *foundation* of the state system
and not just parts of it, which affects the *foundation* of the
edifice and not an outbuilding, not merely one of its storeys.
No matter how many glib phrases our liberals and liquidators trot out to the effect that "we have, thank God, a constitution" and that political *reforms* are on the order of the
day (only very limited people do not see the close connection
between these two propositions), no matter how much of
this reformist verbiage is poured out, the fact remains that
not a single liquidator or liberal can point to any reformist
way out of the situation.

The condition of the mass of the population in Russia,
the aggravation of their position owing to the new agrarian
policy (to which the feudal landowners had to snatch at as
their last means of salvation), the international situation,
and the nature of the general political crisis that has taken

shape in our country—such is the sum-total of the objective conditions making Russia's situation a revolutionary one because of the impossibility of carrying out the tasks of a bourgeois revolution by following the present course and by the means available to the government and the exploiting classes.

Such is the social, economic, and political situation, such is the class relationship in Russia that has given rise to a specific type of strike impossible in modern Europe, from which all sorts of renegades would like to borrow the example, not of yesterday's bourgeois revolutions (through which shine gleams of tomorrow's proletarian revolution), but of today's "constitutional" situation. Neither the oppression of the lower classes nor a crisis among the upper classes can cause a revolution; they can only cause the decay of a country, unless that country has a revolutionary class capable of transforming the passive state of oppression into an active state of revolt and insurrection.

The role of a truly advanced class, a class really able to rouse the masses to revolution, really capable of saving Russia from decay, is played by the industrial proletariat. This is the task it fulfils by means of its revolutionary strikes. These strikes, which the liberals hate and the liquidators cannot understand, are (as the February resolution of the R.S.D.L.P. puts it) "one of the most effective means of overcoming the apathy, despair, and disunion of the agricultural proletariat and the peasantry, ... and *drawing them* into the most concerted, simultaneous, and extensive *revolutionary actions*".*

The working class draws into revolutionary action the masses of the working and exploited people, who are deprived of basic rights and driven to despair. The working class teaches them revolutionary struggle, trains them for revolutionary action, and explains to them where to find the way out and how to attain salvation. The working class teaches them, not merely by words, but by deeds, by example, and the example is provided not by the adventures of solitary heroes but by *mass* revolutionary action combining political and economic demands.

---

* See present edition, Vol. 18, p. 457.—*Ed.*

How plain, how clear, how close these thoughts are to every honest worker who grasps even the rudiments of the theory of socialism and democracy! And how alien they are to those traitors to socialism and betrayers of democracy from among the intelligentsia, who revile or deride the "underground" in liquidationist newspapers, assuring naïve simpletons that they are "also Social-Democrats".

The May Day action of the proletariat of St. Petersburg, supported by that of the proletariat of all Russia, clearly showed once again to those who have eyes to see and ears to hear the great historic importance of the revolutionary underground in present-day Russia. The only R.S.D.L.P. Party organisation in St. Petersburg, the St. Petersburg Committee, compelled even the bourgeois press, before the May Day action as well as on the eve of January 9, and on the eve of the Tercentenary of the Romanovs as well as on April 4,[77] to note that St. Petersburg Committee leaflets had appeared again and again in the factories.

Those leaflets cost colossal sacrifices. Sometimes they are quite unattractive in appearance. Some of them, the appeals for demonstration on April 4, for instance, merely announce the hour and place of the demonstration, in six lines evidently set in secret and with extreme haste in different printing shops and in different types. We have people ("also Social-Democrats") who, when alluding to these conditions of "underground" work, snigger maliciously or curl a contemptuous lip and ask: "If the entire Party were limited to the underground, how many members would it have? Two or three hundred?" [See No. 95 (181) of *Luch*, a renegade organ, in its *editorial* defence of Mr. Sedov, who has the sad courage to be an outspoken liquidator. This issue of *Luch* appeared five days before the May Day action, i.e., *at the very time* the underground was preparing the leaflets!]

Messrs. Dan, Potresov and Co., who make these disgraceful statements, must know that there were thousands of proletarians in the Party ranks as early as 1903, and 150 thousand in 1907, that even now thousands and tens of thousands of workers print and circulate *underground* leaflets, as members of *underground* R.S.D.L.P. cells. But the liquidationist gentlemen know that they are protected by Stolypin "legality" from a legal refutation of their foul lies and their "grimaces", which are fouler still, at the expense of the underground.

See to what extent these despicable people have lost touch with the mass working-class movement and with revolutionary work in general! Use even their own yardstick, deliberately falsified to suit the liberals. You may assume for a moment that "two or three hundred" workers in St. Petersburg took part in printing and distributing those underground leaflets.

What is the result? "Two or three hundred" workers, the flower of the St. Petersburg proletariat, people who not only call themselves Social-Democrats but work as Social-Democrats, people who are esteemed and appreciated for it by the *entire* working class of Russia, people who do not prate about a "broad party" but make up in actual fact the only underground Social-Democratic Party existing in Russia, these people print and circulate underground leaflets. The *Luch* liquidators (protected by Stolypin censors) laugh contemptuously at the "two or three hundred", the "underground" and its "exaggerated" importance, etc.

And suddenly, a miracle occurs! In accordance with a decision drawn up by *half a dozen* members of the Executive Commission of the St. Petersburg Committee—a leaflet printed and circulated by "two or three hundred"—*two hundred and fifty thousand* people rise as one man in St. Petersburg.

The leaflets and the revolutionary speeches by workers at meetings and demonstrations do not speak of an "open working-class party", "freedom of association" or reforms of that kind, with the phantoms of which the liberals are fooling the people. They speak of revolution as the only way out. They speak of the republic as the only slogan which, in contrast to liberal lies about reforms, indicates the change needed to ensure freedom, indicates the forces capable of rising consciously to defend it.

The two million inhabitants of St. Petersburg see and hear these appeals for revolution which go to the hearts of all toiling and oppressed sections of the people. All St. Petersburg sees from a real, mass-scale example what is the real way out and what is lying liberal talk about reforms. Thou-

sands of workers' contacts—and hundreds of bourgeois newspapers, which are compelled to report the St. Petersburg
mass action at least in snatches—spread throughout Russia the news of the stubborn strike campaign of the capital's proletariat. Both the mass of the peasantry and the
peasants serving in the army hear this news of strikes, of
the revolutionary demands of the workers, of their struggle
for a republic and for the confiscation of the landed estates
for the benefit of the peasants. Slowly but surely, the revolutionary strikes are stirring, rousing, enlightening, and
organising the masses of the people *for revolution*.

The "two or three hundred" "underground people" express
the interests and needs of *millions and tens of millions*,
they tell them the truth about their hopeless position,
open their eyes to the necessity of revolutionary struggle,
imbue them with faith in it, provide them with the correct
slogans, and win these masses away from the influence of
the high-sounding and thoroughly spurious, reformist slogans of the bourgeoisie. And "two or three" dozen liquidators
from among the intelligentsia, using money collected abroad
and among liberal merchants to fool unenlightened workers,
are carrying the slogans of that bourgeoisie into the workers' midst.

The May Day strike, like all the revolutionary strikes of
1912-13, has made clear the three political camps into which
present-day Russia is divided. The camp of hangmen and
feudal lords, of monarchy and the secret police. It has done
its utmost in the way of atrocities and is already impotent
against the masses of the workers. The camp of the bourgeoisie, all of whom, from the Cadets to the Octobrists, are
shouting and moaning, calling for reforms and making
fools of themselves by thinking that reforms are possible in
Russia. The camp of the revolution, the only camp expressing the interests of the oppressed masses.

All the ideological work, all the political work in this
camp is carried out by underground Social-Democrats alone,
by those who know how to use every legal opportunity in
the spirit of Social-Democracy and who are inseparably
bound up with the advanced class, the proletariat. No one
can tell beforehand whether this advanced class will succeed
in leading the masses all the way to a victorious revolution.

But this class is fulfilling its duty—*leading* the masses to that solution—despite all the vacillations and betrayals on the part of the liberals and those who are "also Social-Democrats". All the living and vital elements of Russian socialism and Russian democracy are being educated solely by the example of the revolutionary struggle of the proletariat, and under its guidance.

This year's May Day action has shown to the whole world that the Russian proletariat is steadfastly following its revolutionary course, apart from which there is no salvation for a Russia that is suffocating and decaying alive.

Sotsial-Demokrat No. 31,
June 15 (28), 1913

Published according to
the *Sotsial-Demokrat* text

NOTES OF A PUBLICIST

The political ignorance of the people of Russia is to be seen, in part, in their inability to look for exact proofs concerning controversial and important historical questions, and in the naïve credence they give to shouting and expostulation, and to the assurances and vows made by people with interests at stake.

The question of liquidationism is confused precisely because the people with interests at stake (i.e., the liquidators themselves) are not too lazy to make assurances and vows, while the "public" are too lazy to look for exact proofs.

What is the substance of the matter? It is the attitude to the revolution and to the underground, the effort to create a mass working-class movement.

Well, are there no exact proofs to offer on the factual aspect of these issues?

Of course, there are. One has only to get out of the habit of taking on trust what the loud-mouthed and the liberals say.

The "issue" of the underground. Should not those who are interested in this question ask: *"Who* works in the underground? *Who* belongs to the underground organisations?" Is it not clear that underground organisations that do not make their presence felt are nothing, are a deception?

In St. Petersburg there are two newspapers—one is anti-liquidationist, the other is the liquidationist *Luch*, "also Social-Democratic". In other cities there are not yet any working-class newspapers.

Should it not be assumed that the liquidators are stronger in St. Petersburg than elsewhere? But who works *in the Party* in St. Petersburg?

Take the evidence of the bourgeois press. You will find there the news that *leaflets were distributed by the St. Petersburg Committee* before January 9, and on the occasion of the Tercentenary of the Romanovs, and on the eve of April 4 and on the eve of May Day.

Have you any reason to doubt the bourgeois press on such a question of fact?

No sensible person would risk expressing such doubt. And anyone who is at all close to the Social-Democratic movement will have *seen* the St. Petersburg Committee's leaflets.

Not a single newspaper mentioned any leaflets issued by the liquidators' "initiative group" in St. Petersburg in connection with these dates that are famous for the great revolutionary acts of the proletarian masses in St. Petersburg.

And no matter how the *Luch* people may "vow" that they are "also Social-Democrats", "also for the underground", and that the "Leninists" and Plekhanov are wrong in "harassing" them, etc., we shall not stop pointing to *facts* that disprove the fables and lies told by *Luch*.

Find us a bourgeois newspaper that reported the appearance of leaflets issued by the liquidators in St. Petersburg on the eve of January 9, on the eve of April 4, or on the eve of May Day. There is none. *There were no leaflets.* The liquidators are not working in the underground. It is *not* the liquidators who constitute the underground organisations of the Party. There are no liquidators on the St. Petersburg Committee. The liquidators are *outside the Party* because *there is no* other Party but that of the underground, and no other organisation in St. Petersburg except the one led by the St. Petersburg Committee.

We have deliberately avoided mentioning the leaflets of the Central Committee and the Organising Committee,[78] because it is difficult to prove that *they* are distributed locally, while from the Organising Committee for almost a whole year we have seen only the *Vienna* May Day leaflet, which has nothing to do with work in St. Petersburg or in Russia.

The liquidators evade direct answers to the question of "the underground" because *they are not there*. Oath-taking and vows, shouts and curses will not disprove that fact.

Trotsky, doing faithful service to liquidators, assured himself and the naïve "Europeans" (lovers of Asiatic scandal-mongering) that the liquidators are "stronger" in the legal movement. And this lie, too, is refuted by the *facts*.

Take the Duma elections. In the Second Duma the Bolsheviks had 47 per cent of the worker curia; in the Third they had 50 per cent and in the Fourth, 67 per cent. Should these facts be believed, or should one believe Trotsky and the liquidators?

Take the working-class press. In 1912 the anti-liquidationist newspaper comes into being at a much earlier date and is supported by a considerably greater number of workers' groups (according to the published data on collections). There were 620 workers' groups for *Pravda* and 89 for *Luch*.

1913. Party people are already collecting funds for two newspapers, the liquidators have a deficit and their *one* newspaper lives on foreign and undefined (bourgeois) support. *Pravda* is supported by 402 workers' groups, a Moscow workers' paper of the same trend by 172 workers' groups, and *Luch* by 167 workers' groups.

Should one believe these facts or the vows made by *Luch*, Trotsky, F. D. & Co.?

The Metalworkers' Union in St. Petersburg. At the first *open* election where platforms[79] were put forward, ten out of the fourteen were *Pravda* supporters. In the same way as a thief, caught red-handed, shouts "Stop thief!" so the liquidators are shouting "Beware of a split!"

In May 1910 the liquidators were told publicly and clearly (*Diskussionny Listok* No. 2[80]) that they were legalist-independents who had seceded from the Party.* Since then *three years* have passed and only people who are completely wrapped up in their own lies, or who are absolutely ignorant, could deny the *facts* that fully confirm those words.

The liquidators are parasites on the Social-Democratic organism. To "Europe" (the Organising Committee's German pamphlet and Mr. Semkovsky in *Kampf*[81]) they boast of strikes, but in Russia they write disgusting articles in *Luch*

---

* See present edition, Vol. 16, pp. 238-51.—*Ed.*

against strikes, about the "strike craze" and about the "syndicalism" of revolutionary strikes. To Europe (and to naïve An, also) they claim to be *in favour of* the underground. *Actually*, there are none of them in the underground. Powerless in the working class, they are strong in the moral (and, of course, *not only* moral) support they receive from the bourgeoisie. One has to be as naïve as An, whom the *Luch* editors laugh at as they would at a little child (No. 95), to recognise the slogan of an "open party" while defending the underground! That means surrendering the *content* to the liquidators and fighting them over the *form*! Let An ponder over whether the complete acceptance of the "open party" slogan by a bourgeoisie hostile to the underground is fortuitous!

The "open party" slogan is the slogan of *reformism*, a slogan that means—given the present alignment of class and political forces in Russia—*rejection* of the revolution. The slogan of the underground is the slogan of revolution.

The bourgeoisie cannot influence the workers *directly* in contemporary Russia. As a result of 1905 the workers jeer at the bourgeoisie and its liberalism. The word "Cadet" has become an expletive. And so the role of the bourgeoisie among the workers is played by the liquidators. Their objective significance is that they are the vehicle of bourgeois influence, bourgeois reformism and bourgeois opportunism.

All F.D.'s articles in *Luch*, all the tactical premises of the liquidators are based on reformism, on rejection of the revolution. You have not proved the inevitability of revolution—such is the liquidator's usual answer. Your "forecast" of the revolution is one-sided—trills Mr. Semkovsky, playing up to the liquidators.

That can be answered in a few words. The onset of the revolution, Messrs. Liberals, can be demonstrated *only* by the onset of the revolution. And when the revolution begins, both cowardly liberals and even purely casual people and adventurists are capable of becoming "revolutionaries". October and November 1905 proved this to the hilt.

A revolutionary is not one who becomes revolutionary with the onset of the revolution, but one who defends the principles and slogans of the revolution when reaction is most violent and when liberals and democrats vacillate to the greatest degree. A revolutionary is one who *teaches the masses* to struggle in a revolutionary manner and nobody can possibly foresee (make a "forecast" of) the results of that "teaching".

The situation in Russia is a revolutionary one. The proletariat, with whom *only* anti-liquidators co-operate and march in step, is training the masses for revolution, *is preparing the revolution*, and is using any and every legal possibility *for it*. In the matter of preparing the revolution, or, which is the same thing, in the matter of the consistent democratic education of the masses, in the matter of fulfilment of our *socialist* duty (since outside of democracy there is no socialism), the revolutionary Social-Democrats are making a *positive* contribution, while the liquidators' contribution is *negative*.

True Social-Democratic work is possible in Russia only when conducted against reformism, against the liquidators.

Sotsial-Demokrat No. 31,   Published according to
June 15 (28), 1913   the *Sotsial-Demokrat* text

APROPOS OF ONE UNTRUTH

(LETTER TO THE EDITORS)

We should have welcomed, from all points of view, the appearance of L. Martov's articles in *Luch*, promising an analysis of the question of "the tactical essence of the present dispute", if the very first article had not contained a blatant untruth. My words to the effect that the dispute with the liquidators had nothing to do with the organisational question* were declared to be "unexpected" by L. Martov. "Just look at this!" he exclaimed. "All of a sudden, with the help of God, we have a change", and so on.

Yet L. Martov knows full well that there has been no change at all, that nothing whatever unexpected has happened. In May 1910, over three years ago, I wrote in a Paris publication, which Martov knows quite well, "*about a group of legalist-independents*" (the ideas of *Nasha Zarya* and *Vozrozhdeniye*) and said that it had "definitely rallied together and definitely broken with the Party".** It is obvious that here, too, the dispute does not concern the organisational question (*how* to organise the Party?) but the question *of the existence* of the Party, of the secession of the liquidators from the Party, of their complete breakaway from the Party. Martov must realise that this is not a dispute on the question of organisation.

In October 1911, in a publication equally well known to Martov, signed also by me, it was said: "In reality, it is by no means the organisational question that is now in the forefront", but of the "*existence*" of the Party.***

---

* See p. 109 of this volume.—*Ed.*
** See present edition, Vol. 16, p. 244.—*Ed.*
*** See present edition, Vol. 17, p. 260.—*Ed.*

The affairs of the liquidators must be in a bad way if Martov, to evade an examination of the Party's precise decisions, is telling fairy-tales and publishing a blatant untruth.

Pravda No. 136, June 15, 1913
Signed: *V. Ilyin*

Published according to
the *Pravda* text

THE WORKING CLASS AND NEOMALTHUSIANISM

At the Pirogov Doctors' Congress much interest was aroused and a long debate was held on the question of abortions. The report was made by Lichkus, who quoted figures on the exceedingly widespread practice of destroying the foetus in present-day so-called civilised states.

In New York, 80,000 abortions were performed in one year and there are 36,000 every month in France. In St. Petersburg the percentage of abortions has more than doubled in five years.

The Pirogov Doctors' Congress adopted a resolution saying that there should never be any criminal prosecution of a mother for performing an artificial abortion and that doctors should only be prosecuted if the operation is performed for "purposes of gain".

In the discussion the majority agreed that abortions should not be punishable, and the question of the so-called neomalthusianism (the use of contraceptives) was naturally touched upon, as was also the social side of the matter. Mr. Vigdorchik, for instance, said, according to the report in *Russkoye Slovo*,[82] that "contraceptive measures should be welcomed" and Mr. Astrakhan exclaimed, amidst thunderous applause:

"We have to convince mothers to bear children so that they can be maimed in educational establishments, so that lots can be drawn for them, so that they can be driven to suicide!"

If the report is true that this exclamation of Mr. Astrakhan's was greeted with thunderous applause, it is a fact that does not surprise me. The audience was made up of bourgeois, middle and petty bourgeois, who have the psychology of the philistine. What can you expect from them but the most banal liberalism?

From the point of view of the working class, however, it would hardly be possible to find a more apposite expression of the completely reactionary nature and the ugliness of "social neomalthusianism" than Mr. Astrakhan's phrase cited above.

... "Bear children so that they can be maimed" ... For that alone? Why not that they should *fight* better, more unitedly, consciously and resolutely than we are fighting against the present-day conditions of life that are maiming and ruining our generation?

This is the radical difference that distinguishes the psychology of the peasant, handicraftsman, intellectual, the petty bourgeois in general, from that of the proletarian. The petty bourgeois sees and feels that he is heading for ruin, that life is becoming more difficult, that the struggle for existence is ever more ruthless, and that his position and that of his family are becoming more and more hopeless. It is an indisputable fact, and the petty bourgeois protests against it.

But *how* does he protest?

He protests as the representative of a class that is hopelessly perishing, that despairs of its future, that is depressed and cowardly. There is nothing to be done ... if only there were fewer children to suffer our torments and hard toil, our poverty and our humiliation—such is the cry of the petty bourgeois.

The class-conscious worker is far from holding this point of view. He will not allow his consciousness to be dulled by such cries no matter how sincere and heartfelt they may be. Yes, we workers and the mass of small proprietors lead a life that is filled with unbearable oppression and suffering. Things are harder for our generation than they were for our fathers. But in one respect we are luckier than our fathers. *We have begun to learn and are rapidly learning to fight*—and to fight not as individuals, as the best of our fathers fought, not for the slogans of bourgeois speechifiers that are alien to us in spirit, but for our slogans, the slogans of our class. We are fighting better than our fathers did. Our children will fight better than we do, and *they will be victorious.*

The working class is not perishing, it is growing, becoming stronger, gaining courage, consolidating itself, educating itself and becoming steeled in battle. We are pessimists as far as serfdom, capitalism and petty production are concerned, but we are ardent optimists in what concerns the working-class movement and its aims. We are already laying the foundation of a new edifice and our children will complete its construction.

That is the reason—the only reason—why we are unconditionally the enemies of neomalthusianism, suited only to unfeeling and egotistic petty-bourgeois couples, who whisper in scared voices: "God grant we manage somehow by ourselves. So much the better if we have no children."

It goes without saying that this does not by any means prevent us from demanding the unconditional annulment of all laws against abortions or against the distribution of medical literature on contraceptive measures, etc. Such laws are nothing but the hypocrisy of the ruling classes. These laws do not heal the ulcers of capitalism, they merely turn them into malignant ulcers that are especially painful for the oppressed masses. Freedom for medical propaganda and the protection of the elementary democratic rights of citizens, men and women, are one thing. The social theory of neomalthusianism is quite another. Class-conscious workers will always conduct the most ruthless struggle against attempts to impose that reactionary and cowardly theory on the most progressive and strongest class in modern society, the class that is the best prepared for great changes.

Pravda No. 137, June 16, 1913
Signed: *V. I.*

Published according to
the *Pravda* text

LIBERAL APPEALS TO SUPPORT
THE FOURTH DUMA

The question of the State Duma's attitude to the government and the country is becoming an ever more frequent subject for discussion in the press and is arousing quite a lot of interest. The June Third election law created two possible majorities—Right-Octobrist and Octobrist-Cadet. This latter, the "liberal" majority if you will, was also formed on a number of occasions in the Third Duma.

In the present Fourth Duma the Octobrist-Cadet majority occurs still more frequently. It must not be forgotten, however, that this is not only due to an Octobrist shift to the left but also to a Cadet *shift to the right*, which is expressed by the secession of part of the Cadets to the Progressists, on the one hand, and the constant deals between the Octobrists and the Cadets with the Progressists as intermediaries, on the other.

There is no doubt that the more frequent oppositionist decisions carried in the Fourth Duma by the Octobrist-Cadet majority are evidence of the growing political crisis in Russia, are evidence that the June Third system has entered a blind alley and has not satisfied even the bourgeoisie, who were prepared to sacrifice, for the benefit of that system, for the strengthening of the counter-revolution, their money, their honour and their conscience.

It is typical that even such an out-and-out, implacable reactionary as the German historian Schiemann, who knows Russian and writes for the organ of the German Purishkeviches, comes to the conclusion that the crisis in Russia is growing—either in the form of a system that is purely Plehve[83] in spirit (surely we have already entered that "system"?) or in the form of what this German historian calls upheavals.

What conclusions in practical politics, may we ask, emerge from these increasingly frequent liberal Duma decisions?

The Cadets have already drawn their conclusion on the Octobrists' condemnation of the policy pursued by the Ministry of the Interior. Their conclusion is to demand "the support of the people and society" for the Fourth Duma, to call upon "public opinion" to "see in the Duma one's own strength, the direct manifestation of the public will", etc. (See *Pravda* No. 128.)

We have already spoken of the complete ineffectiveness of such a conclusion.* The voting on the Ministry of Public Education estimates was an exceedingly clear confirmation of our appraisal.

The Duma adopted three formulations: (1) a nationalistic, arch-reactionary formulation passed by the votes of the Rights and the Octobrists, (2) an Octobrist formulation passed by the Cadet vote (it expresses the wish, disgusting in its hypocrisy and absolutely impermissible for democrats or even honest liberals, that the Ministry of Public Education will "not be distracted by irrelevant political considerations"); lastly, (3) the wish of the peasant group, which was most likely passed not only with the help of the Constitutional-Democrats but of all democrats, including the Social-Democrats. The wish expressed by the peasants received 137 votes for and 134 against with 4 abstaining.

There can scarcely be any doubt that the error of the Social-Democrats, if they voted for the peasant formulation, was in not presenting their own statement or declaration. It was right to vote in favour, but they should also have added a proviso expressing their disagreement with, for instance, point five of the peasant formulation. That point speaks of the native language in *elementary* schools. Democracy cannot confine itself to elementary schools. And in general, it cannot be admitted that the wishes of the peasants are *consistently* democratic.

It was right to vote in favour, because in the peasant formulation there are no points in support of the government, and no hypocrisy, but it was essential to express disagree-

---

* See pp. 177-79 of this volume.—*Ed.*

ment with the inconsistency and timidity of peasant democracy. Silence on the relationship between the school and the church, for instance, is absolutely impermissible for Social-Democrats, etc.

That, however, is *en passant*.

The main thing is that the Fourth Duma, *after* the Cadets' appeals to support it, adopted the formulation of the nationalists!

Only a blind man could fail to see that support for the Fourth Duma is support for *the wavering Octobrists*.

The Cadets boast that they are pushing the Octobrists into opposition by their support. Let us suppose for a moment that that is so. On what basis is this Octobrist opposition founded? At best, *when* they are in opposition they undoubtedly support the point of view of counter-revolutionary liberalism. That they continue *to depend* on the ministers and to *gratify* them, was demonstrated even by the "progressist" N. Lvov, who was surely pursuing a policy of *gratification* when he banned Shchepkin from two sittings because of an expression a hundred times milder than the usual expressions of the Rights.

When they call on the people to support the wavering Octobrists, the Cadets are trying to make democrats follow in the wake of the worst of the liberals.

The democrats, however, have seen from hundreds of more impressive examples just what our liberals are worth. Democracy would be enfeebled and deprived of leadership if it were again to follow the liberals.

The clash between the bourgeoisie and the government is not an accident, it is an indication of the profound crisis that is maturing on all sides. It is, therefore, imperative to keep a close watch on these clashes. But democracy will be able to achieve something better for Russia only if it does not for one moment forget its duty—to do everything to develop in the population a consciousness of the independent nature of the tasks of democracy as distinct from liberalism, in contrast to liberalism and regardless of liberalism's vacillations.

Pravda No. 139, June 20, 1913   Published according to
Signed: *V. I.*   the *Pravda* text

BOURGEOIS FINANCIAL MAGNATES
AND POLITICIANS

The British Labour press is continuing its exposure of the connection between financial "operations" and high politics. These revelations deserve the attention of the workers of all countries because they expose the very basis of state administration in capitalist society. The words of Karl Marx that the government is a committee for managing the affairs of the capitalist class[84] are confirmed to the full.

The Labour Leader No. 24 (June 12, N.S.) devotes a whole page to listing the names of British Ministers (7 names), ex-Ministers (3 names), Bishops and Archdeacons (12 names), Peers (47 names), Members of Parliament (18 names), big newspaper owners, financiers and bankers, who are shareholders or directors in joint-stock companies dealing mainly in munitions.

The author of the article, Walton Newbold, collected all this information from official banking, commercial and industrial, financial and other sources, from the reports of patriotic organisations (like the *Navy League*), etc.

We get a picture quite similar to that once drawn from Russian data by Rubakin, who showed how many big landowners in Russia were members of the Council of State, high dignitaries—now we may add, members of the State Duma, shareholders or directors of joint-stock companies, etc. It is high time to bring Rubakin's facts up to date by using the latest reference books, particularly adding data on participation in financial, commercial and industrial undertakings.

Our liberals (especially the Cadets) have a strong aversion for the "theory" of the class struggle, and particularly insist on their view that the governments of modern states *can* stand *outside* classes or *above* classes. But what can you do, gentlemen, if the "theory" which is so distasteful to you corresponds exactly to reality? If all the *fundamentals* of contemporary legislation and contemporary politics clearly show us the class character of the structure and administration of all contemporary states? If even information about the personalities of prominent politicians, members of parliament, high officials, etc., reveals the inseparable connection existing between economic rule and political rule?

The denial or concealment of the class struggle is the worst form of hypocrisy in politics; is banking on the ignorance and prejudices of the least developed strata of the people, the small proprietors (peasants, handicraftsmen, etc.), who are furthest removed from the most acute and direct struggle of classes, and cling as before, as of old, to their patriarchal views. But what is ignorance and backwardness in the peasant is a subtle method of corrupting the people and keeping them in slavery on the part of the liberal intellectuals.

Pravda No. 142, June 23, 1913
Signed: *M*.

Published according to
the *Pravda* text

THESES ON THE NATIONAL QUESTION[85]

1. The article of our programme (on the self-determination of nations) cannot be interpreted to mean anything but *political* self-determination, i.e., the right to secede and form a separate state.

2. This article in the Social-Democratic programme is *absolutely* essential to the Social-Democrats of Russia

a) for the sake of the basic principles of democracy in general;

b) also because there are, within the frontiers of Russia and, *what is more, in her frontier areas*, a number of nations with sharply distinctive economic, social and other conditions; furthermore, these nations (like all the nations of Russia except the Great Russians) are unbelievably oppressed by the tsarist monarchy;

c) lastly, also in view of the fact that throughout Eastern Europe (Austria and the Balkans) and in Asia—i.e., in countries bordering on Russia—the bourgeois-democratic reform of the state that has everywhere else in the world led, in varying degree, to the creation of independent national states or states with the closest, interrelated national composition, has either not been consummated or has only just begun;

d) at the present moment Russia is a country whose state system is more backward and reactionary than that of *any* of the contiguous countries, beginning—in the West—with Austria where the fundamentals of political liberty and a constitutional regime were consolidated in 1867, and where universal franchise has now been introduced, and ending—in the East—with republican China. In all their propaganda, therefore, the Social-Democrats of Russia must insist on the right of all nationalities to form separate states or to choose freely the state of which they wish to form part.

3. The Social-Democratic Party's recognition of the right of all nationalities to self-determination requires of Social-Democrats that they should

a) be unconditionally hostile to the use of force in any form whatsoever by the dominant nation (or the nation which constitutes the majority of the population) in respect of a nation that wishes to secede politically;

b) demand the settlement of the question of such secession only on the basis of a universal, direct and equal vote of the population of the given territory by secret ballot;

c) conduct an implacable struggle against both the Black-Hundred-Octobrist and the liberal-bourgeois (Progressist, Cadet, etc.) parties on every occasion when they defend or sanction national oppression in general or the denial of the right of nations to self-determination in particular.

4. The Social-Democratic Party's recognition of the right of all nationalities to self-determination most certainly does not mean that Social-Democrats reject an independent appraisal of the advisability of the state secession of any nation in each separate case. Social-Democracy should, on the contrary, give its independent appraisal, taking into consideration the conditions of capitalist development and the oppression of the proletarians of various nations by the united bourgeoisie of all nationalities, as well as the general tasks of democracy, first of all and most of all the interests of the proletarian class struggle for socialism.

From this point of view the following circumstance must be given special attention. There are two nations in Russia that are more civilised and more isolated by virtue of a number of historical and social conditions and that could most easily and most "naturally" put into effect their right to secession. They are the peoples of Finland and Poland. The experience of the Revolution of 1905 has shown that even in these two nations the ruling classes, the landowners and bourgeoisie, reject the revolutionary struggle for liberty and seek a *rapprochement* with the ruling classes of Russia and with the tsarist monarchy *because of their fear* of the **revolutionary proletariat of Finland and Poland.**

Social-Democracy, therefore, must give most emphatic warning to the proletariat and other working people of all nationalities against direct deception by the nationalistic slogans of "their own" bourgeoisie, who with their saccharine or fiery speeches about "our native land" try to *divide* the proletariat and *divert its attention* from their bourgeois intrigues while they enter into an economic and political alliance with the bourgeoisie of other nations and with the tsarist monarchy.

The proletariat cannot pursue its struggle for socialism and defend its everyday economic interests without the closest and fullest alliance of the workers of all nations in all working-class organisations without exception.

The proletariat cannot achieve freedom other than by revolutionary struggle for the overthrow of the tsarist monarchy and its replacement by a democratic republic. The tsarist monarchy *precludes* liberty and equal rights for nationalities, and is, furthermore, the bulwark of barbarity, brutality and reaction in both Europe and Asia. This monarchy can be overthrown only by the united proletariat of all the nations of Russia, which is giving the lead to consistently democratic elements capable of revolutionary struggle from among the working masses of all nations.

It follows, therefore, that workers who place political unity with "their own" bourgeoisie above complete unity with the proletariat of all nations, are acting against their own interests, against the interests of socialism and against the interests of democracy.

5. Social-Democrats, in upholding a consistently democratic state system, demand unconditional equality for all nationalities and struggle against absolutely all privileges for one or several nationalities.

In particular, Social-Democrats reject a "state" language. It is particularly superfluous in Russia because more than seven-tenths of the population of Russia belong to related Slav nationalities who, given a free school and a free state, could easily achieve intercourse by virtue of the demands of the economic turnover without any "state" privileges for any one language.

Social-Democrats demand the abolition of the old administrative divisions of Russia established by the feudal

landowners and the civil servants of the autocratic feudal
state and their replacement by divisions based on the requirements of present-day economic life and in accordance, as
far as possible, with the national composition of the population.

All areas of the state that are distinguished by social
peculiarities or by the national composition of the population, must enjoy wide self-government and autonomy, with
institutions organised on the basis of universal, equal and
secret voting.

6. Social-Democrats demand the promulgation of a law,
operative throughout the state, protecting the rights of every
national minority in no matter what part of the state. This
law should declare inoperative any measure by means of
which the national majority might attempt to establish
privileges for itself or restrict the rights of a national minority (in the sphere of education, in the use of any specific
language, in budget affairs, etc.), and forbid the implementation of any such measure by making it a punishable
offence.

7. The Social-Democratic attitude to the slogan of "cultural-national" (or simply "national") "autonomy" or to
plans for its implementation is a negative one, since this
slogan (1) undoubtedly contradicts the internationalism of
the class struggle of the proletariat, (2) makes it easier for
the proletariat and the masses of working people to be drawn
into the sphere of influence of bourgeois nationalism, and
(3) is capable of distracting attention from the task of the
consistent democratic transformation of the state as a whole,
which transformation alone can ensure (to the extent that
this can, in general, be ensured under capitalism) peace
between nationalities.

In view of the special acuteness of the question of cultural-national autonomy among Social-Democrats, we give some
explanation of the situation.

a) It is impermissible, from the standpoint of Social-
Democracy, to issue the slogan of *national* culture either
directly or indirectly. The slogan is incorrect because already under capitalism, all economic, political and spiritual
life is becoming more and more international. Socialism
will make it completely international. International culture,

which is now already being systematically created by the proletariat of all countries, does not absorb "national culture" (no matter of what national group) as a whole, but accepts from *each* national culture *exclusively* those of its elements that are consistently democratic and socialist.

b) Probably the one example of an approximation, even though it is a timid one, to the slogan of national culture in Social-Democratic programmes is Article 3 of the Brünn Programme of the Austrian Social-Democrats. This Article 3 reads: "All self-governing regions of one and the same nation form a single-national alliance that has complete autonomy in deciding its national affairs."

This is a compromise slogan since it does not contain a shadow of extra-territorial (personal) national autonomy. But this slogan, too, is erroneous and harmful, for it is no business of the Social-Democrats of Russia to unite into one nation the Germans in Lodz, Riga, St. Petersburg and Saratov. Our business is to struggle for full democracy and the annulment of *all* national privileges and to unite the German workers in Russia with the workers of all other nations in upholding and developing the international culture of socialism.

Still more erroneous is the slogan of extra-territorial (personal) national autonomy with the setting up (according to a plan drawn up by the consistent supporters of this slogan) of national parliaments and national state secretaries (Otto Bauer and Karl Renner). Such institutions contradict the economic conditions of the capitalist countries, they have not been tested in any of the world's democratic states and are the opportunist dream of people who despair of setting up consistent democratic institutions and are seeking salvation from the national squabbles of the bourgeoisie in the artificial isolation of the proletariat and the bourgeoisie of each nation on a number of ("cultural") questions.

Circumstances occasionally compel Social-Democrats to submit for a time to some sort of compromise decisions, but from other countries we must borrow not compromise decisions, but consistently Social-Democratic decisions. It would be particularly unwise to adopt the unhappy Austrian compromise decision today, when it has been a complete failure in Austria and has led to the separatism and secession of the Czech Social-Democrats.

c) The history of the "cultural-national autonomy" slogan in Russia shows that it has been adopted by *all* Jewish bourgeois parties and *only* by Jewish bourgeois parties; and that they have been uncritically followed by the Bund, which has inconsistently rejected the national-Jewish parliament (sejm) and national-Jewish state secretaries. Incidentally, even those European Social-Democrats who accede to or defend the compromise slogan of cultural-national autonomy, admit that the slogan is quite unrealisable for the Jews (Otto Bauer and Karl Kautsky). "The Jews in Galicia and Russia are more of a caste than a nation, and attempts to constitute Jewry as a nation are attempts at preserving a caste" (Karl Kautsky).

d) In civilised countries we observe a fairly full (relatively) approximation to national peace under capitalism *only* in conditions of the *maximum* implementation of democracy throughout the state system and administration (Switzerland). The slogans of consistent democracy (the republic, a militia, civil servants elected by the people, etc.) unite the proletariat and the working people, and, in general, all progressive elements in each nation in the name of the struggle for conditions that preclude even the slightest national privilege—while the slogan of "cultural-national autonomy" preaches the isolation of nations in educational affairs (or "cultural" affairs, in general), an isolation that is quite compatible with the retention of the grounds for all (including national) privileges.

The slogans of consistent democracy *unite* in a single whole the proletariat and the advanced democrats of all nations (elements that demand not isolation but the uniting of democratic elements of the nations in all matters, including educational affairs), while the slogan of cultural-national autonomy *divides* the proletariat of the different nations and links it up with the reactionary and bourgeois elements of the separate nations.

The slogans of consistent democracy are implacably hostile to the reactionaries and to the counter-revolutionary bourgeoisie of all nations, while the slogan of cultural-national autonomy is quite acceptable to the reactionaries and counter-revolutionary bourgeoisie of some nations.

8. The sum-total of economic and political conditions in Russia therefore demands that Social-Democracy should *unite* unconditionally workers of all nationalities in *all* proletarian organisations without exception (political, trade union, co-operative, educational, etc., etc.). The Party should not be federative in structure and should not form national Social-Democratic groups but should unite the proletarians of all nations in the given locality, conduct propaganda and agitation in *all* the languages of the local proletariat, promote the common struggle of the workers of all nations against every kind of national privilege and should recognise the autonomy of local and regional Party organisations.

9. More than ten years' experience gained by the R.S.D.L.P. confirms the correctness of the above thesis. The Party was founded in 1898 as a party of all Russia, that is, a party of the proletariat of all the nationalities of Russia. The Party remained "Russian" when the Bund seceded in 1903, after the Party Congress had rejected the demand to consider the Bund the *only* representative of the Jewish proletariat. In 1906 and 1907 events showed convincingly that there were no grounds for this demand, a large number of Jewish proletarians continued to co-operate in the common Social-Democratic work in many local organisations, and the Bund re-entered the Party. The Stockholm Congress (1906) brought into the Party the Polish and Latvian Social-Democrats, who favoured *territorial* autonomy, and the Congress, furthermore, did *not* accept the principle of federation and demanded unity of Social-Democrats of all nationalities in each locality. This principle has been in operation in the Caucasus for many years, it is in operation in Warsaw (Polish workers and Russian soldiers), in Vilna (Polish, Lettish, Jewish and Lithuanian workers) and in Riga, and in the three last-named places it has been implemented *against* the separatist Bund. In December 1908, the R.S.D.L.P., through its conference, adopted a special resolution confirming the demand for the *unity* of workers of all nationalities, *on a principle other than* federation. The splitting activities of the Bund separatists in not fulfill-

ing the Party decision led to the collapse of all that "federation of the worst type"[86] and brought about the *rapprochement* of the Bund and the Czech separatists and vice versa (see Kosovsky in *Nasha Zarya* and the organ of the Czech separatists, *Der čechoslavische Sozialdemokrat* No. 3, 1913, on Kosovsky), and, lastly, at the August (1912) Conference of the liquidators it led to an *undercover* attempt by the Bund separatists and liquidators and some of the Caucasian liquidators to insert "cultural-national autonomy" into the Party programme *without any defence of its substance!*

Revolutionary worker Social-Democrats in Poland, in the Latvian Area and in the Caucasus still stand for territorial autonomy and the *unity* of worker Social-Democrats of *all* nations. The Bund-liquidator secession and the alliance of the Bund with *non*-Social-Democrats in Warsaw place the *entire* national question, both in its theoretical aspect and in the matter of Party structure, *on the order of the day* for all Social-Democrats.

Compromise decisions have been broken by the very people who introduced them against the will of the Party, and the demand for the unity of worker Social-Democrats of all nationalities is being made more loudly than ever.

10. The crudely militant and Black-Hundred-type nationalism of the tsarist monarchy, and also the revival of *bourgeois* nationalism—Great-Russian (Mr. Struve, *Russkaya Molva*,[87] the Progressists, etc.), the Ukrainian, and Polish (the anti-Semitism of Narodowa "Demokracja"[88]), and Georgian and Armenian, etc.—all this makes it particularly urgent for Social-Democratic organisations in all parts of Russia to devote greater attention than before to the national question and to work out consistently Marxist decisions on this subject in the spirit of consistent internationalism and unity of proletarians of all nations.

———

α) The slogan of national culture is incorrect and expresses only the limited bourgeois understanding of the national question. International culture.

β) The perpetuating of national divisions and the promoting of refined nationalism—unification, *rapprochement*, the mingling of nations and the expression of the principles of a *different*, international culture.

γ) The despair of the petty bourgeois (hopeless struggle against national bickering) and the fear of radical-democratic reforms and the socialist movement—only radical-democratic reforms can establish national peace in capitalist states and only socialism is able to terminate national bickering.

δ) National curias in educational affairs.[89]

ε) The Jews.

Written in June 1913

First published in 1925 in the *Lenin Miscellany III*

Published according to the manuscript

INSTRUCTIVE SPEECHES

Mr. Izgoyev, the well-known renegade, who was a Social-Democrat until 1905, but rapidly "grew wiser" ... until he reached a Right-liberal position after October 17, frequently turns his benevolent attention to Social-Democracy in *Russkaya Mysl*, the chief organ of "Octobrist" or counter-revolutionary liberalism.

We can only recommend workers who wish to gain a full understanding of the serious problems of working-class politics to read Mr. Izgoyev's article in the last issue of *Russkaya Mysl* for June of this year.

It is worth while thinking again and again over the exuberant praises of liquidationist *ideology* and *tactics* (i.e., the basic principles of liquidationism) that Mr. Izgoyev so generously dispenses. The liberals are bound to praise the principles and tactics of liberal working-class politicians!

It is worth while thinking again and again over the independent tactical considerations of Mr. Izgoyev, who sympathises whole-heartedly with the liquidators, and who has, after all, been through "the Marxist elementary school" and understands the necessity of seeking the serious roots of the serious struggle of Party members against the liquidators.

Unfortunately we must confine ourselves here to quoting very brief passages from Mr. Izgoyev's instructive article and to giving them the briefest and most incomplete explanation.

In Mr. Izgoyev's opinion, the success of Bolshevism depends on "what hopes there are for the peaceful development of Russia on constitutional lines, even if it is only of the German type. Was it not found possible in Germany to have a monarchist constitution with civil liberties, without additional security measures and with a widely developed Social-Democratic workers' party? Is this possible in Russia or not? As the scales turn to one side or the other, so the chances of the liquidators and the Bolsheviks rise and fall....

"If no limit is set to the pressure of reaction, and if the constitutional forces in Russia do not prove sufficient for peaceful state reforms, Bolshevism will undoubtedly be victorious and will drive the liquidators into the background." Mr. Izgoyev himself considers the Bolsheviks to be anarchists and the liquidators "true Social-Democrats", who quite reasonably discarded the first two points of the Bolshevik platform and replaced them by freedom of association!

"The storm will pass," writes Mr. Izgoyev, "the time for positive work will come and the liquidators will again (!!?) stand at the head of the working class." Such are the dreams of Mr. Izgoyev. The tactics of the liquidators will, he says, be magnificent when "the storm passes".... And here are his "ideas on tactics":

"If we think deeply over Bolshevik tactics we have to admit that they are based on the conviction that the struggle for the monarchist constitution in Russia ... [Mr. Izgoyev's dots] ended on June 3. The struggle may, perhaps, go on for direct or consistent democracy, but, given the cardinal Russian historical basis, there cannot be any other constitution than that of June 3. Russian constitutionalists can only count on a constitution without civil liberties, but containing exceptional conditions. We consider the Bolshevik point of view, although at the opposite pole, to be related to that of the Black Hundreds, and to be erroneous and politically harmful. It cannot be denied, however, that it has some content. The continuing inability of the Russian constitutionalists to give the country a guarantee of a system based on law may, in the future, even justify the pessimism of the Bolsheviks. But so far, as *Luch* correctly notes ... [of course!] ... it leads only to mingling with semi-anarchist elements..." (here Mr. Izgoyev, gasping with admiration for *Luch*, follows up with quotations from liquidationist articles).

Mr. Izgoyev calls pessimism *in respect of* the landowners and the bourgeoisie pessimism in general. Is not *such* pessimism inseparably connected with *optimism* in respect of, first and foremost, the proletariat, and secondly, of the petty-bourgeois working masses—this is something Mr. Izgoyev is afraid to consider. Of course, he has good reason to be afraid!

The strangest thing about the kisses this renegade bestows on the liquidators, the most instructive thing in the speeches of this liberal, is that while he sympathises whole-heartedly with the liquidators he *will not risk* denying *the content* of Bolshevik tactics! He, a supporter of "peaceful" development and liquidationist opportunism, is *quite unable* to promise that such a development will be victorious! He, a rabid enemy of Bolshevism, who showers invective upon us (anarchists, Blanquists, indulging in self-praise, etc., etc.), he, the bosom friend of the liquidators, *is compelled* to admit that Bolshevism will be victorious if "the constitutional forces in Russia do not prove sufficient" (i.e., if they prove to be just what they are today...)!

The very angry Mr. Izgoyev, who has a good knowledge of Social-Democratic affairs, is not very bright and did not notice that all these considerations*. . . . . removed the fig-leaf from Messrs. F. D., L. S., Yezhov, Larin, Martov, Potresov & Co.

Thank you, thank you very much, Mr. Izgoyev, you who are so angry with the Bolsheviks! The truth hurts. And you have *accidentally* hurt your liquidator friends with the truth. You have embraced them so "gently" that they are being strangled in your embrace.

Just a few words on a purely historical question. Why is it that the constitution which was "found possible" in Germany is more to the liking of counter-revolutionary liberalism than the French constitution? Only because, my angry but not very bright Mr. Izgoyev, that constitution turned out to be the *mathematical resultant* of the efforts of Bismarck and the liberals, who feared civil liberties for the workers, and of the efforts of the workers who were struggling for the *full* democratisation of Germany in the forties, in the fifties and in the sixties. The German workers proved weak *at that time.* Therefore Bismarck and the Prussian liberals were *one-half* victorious. If the German workers had been stronger, Bismarck would have been one-quarter victorious. If they had been still stronger, Bismarck would not have been victorious at all. Germany obtained civil liberties despite Bismarck, *despite* the Prussian liberals and

---

* The next page of the manuscript has not been found.—*Ed.*

only because of the persistent and stubborn efforts of the working class (partly, also, of the petty-bourgeois democrats, but only to a very small extent) to achieve the fullest possible democratisation.

Don't you understand anything, Mr. Izgoyev? Don't you understand that history justified "Bolshevik" tactics in Germany, too? Be less angry with the Bolsheviks, be less "kind" to the liquidators, and perhaps you will come to understand.

V. I.
(or unsigned)

P. S. If this is not suitable please pass it on to *Prosveshcheniye*. I think it would be better printed as a satirical piece in *Pravda*.

Written at the beginning
of July 1913
First published in 1925
in the magazine *Krasnaya Nov* No 1.

Published according to
the manuscript

PICTURES FROM LIFE

Any mention of serfdom in Russian life in general, and in the Russian countryside in particular, calls forth a protest from our liberals, especially from those liberals who love to picture themselves as almost Marxists. What sort of serfdom, they say, is there in twentieth-century Russia! It is simply nothing but "agitation"....

Nevertheless amazingly clear pictures of serfdom are to be met with in the contemporary Russian countryside at every step, and only the accursed inertness of the Russian man in the street, who has "got used to it", makes him pass these pictures by indifferently.

Here is one of them that we have borrowed from the official register of decisions passed by Chernigov Gubernia Zemstvo Assembly for the ten years 1900-09.

"Leaving intact *until the present time* the archaic method of maintaining rural roads by compulsory service is a dark stain on our Zemstvo..." writes Mr. Khizhnyakov on this subject (*Russkoye Bogatstvo*). "To say nothing of the great injustice of this being a service performed exclusively by the peasants ... the very way in which it is done is shameful. After the snow has melted and after torrential rains, the village elders, usually under a threatening order from the police sergeant, 'drive out the people', as we put it, to mend the road. The work is done without any sort of organisation, with no levelling or any technical instructions. I happened to see such work being done with unusual energy, to the accompaniment of menacing shouts from the police sergeants and *with blows of a whip to urge on the slower workers*. It was at the end of summer, just before the governor was due to pass that way.... About five hundred men and women with spades were driven out to work on a stretch of about three versts. On the orders of the police they dug ditches that were absolutely unnecessary and that later had to be filled in again.... And our Zemstvo, in the course of its almost fifty years' existence, has not only failed to remove this burden from the peasant population *but has even increased it....*"

That Zemstvo, like all Russian Zemstvos, is a landowners' Zemstvo.

And so the landowners are continuing to increase the old "service" performed by the peasants. When so instructed by the landowners, the police and the elders "drive out the people", compelling hundreds of peasants to leave the work on their farms and "dig absolutely unnecessary ditches", "without any sort of organisation" and *with blows of a whip to urge on the slower workers*".

That is where the roots of the power of the Purishkeviches, Markovs & Co., lie. And how disgustingly hypocritical are our smooth, sedate, well-intentioned reformist liberal programmes when compared with such roots!

Pravda No. 149, July 2, 1913
· Signed: *T—in*

Published according to
the *Pravda* text

THE ADJOURNED DUMA
AND THE EMBARRASSED LIBERALS

More than a week has passed since the Fourth Duma[90] adjourned, but reviews and appraisals of its work still continue to appear in the newspapers. Everybody admits that there is general dissatisfaction with the Fourth Duma. It is not only the liberals, not only the "responsible" (to the landowners) opposition that are dissatisfied. The Octobrists, too, are dissatisfied. And the Rights are dissatisfied.

Undoubtedly, this dissatisfaction with the reactionary Duma on the part of the reactionary landowners and the bourgeoisie is extremely typical and portentous. These classes have done *everything* possible to guarantee what they call "peaceful, constitutional" development.

They did *everything*—and now they have realised that *nothing* has come of it! Hence the general dissatisfaction in the camp of the landowners and the bourgeoisie themselves. Neither the Rights nor the Octobrists show that rapture and enthusiasm for the June Third system that was typical of the Third Duma epoch.

Our so-called "upper" classes, the social and political "summit" *cannot* rule Russia in the old way, despite the fact that all the fundamentals of the state system and of the government of Russia have been determined exclusively *by them* and arranged in *their* interests. But the "lower" classes are full of the desire to change this form of government

The coincidence of this inability of the "upper" classes to administer the state in the old way, and this increased reluctance on the part of the "lower" classes to put up with such administration of the state, makes up precisely wha is called (admittedly somewhat inaccurately) a political crisis on a nation-wide scale.

The growth of this crisis before our eyes is a fact, and a fact that can scarcely be open to doubt.

It would seem that from this it should be clear to democrats and even to intelligent liberals that the centre of gravity of this desire for improvement is not in the Duma, and that the Duma is in this respect only an inaccurate indicator.

But our liberals have for a long time been letting themselves slide. "Both the Third and the Fourth Dumas are a parody of popular representation," said a *Rech* leading article, "*but they do* exist and *hic Rhodus, hic salta*" (a Latin expression that means literally "Here is Rhodes, here jump", i.e., here is the main thing, here is the essence, here prove what you've got to prove, here fight).

You are mistaken, gentlemen! *Rhodes* is *not* here and you will *not* "jump" from here since the beginning was *not* here.

Only the lackeys of the landowners and the money-bags could take the Fourth Duma as a *Rhodes* for democracy, could forget that in addition to the Duma there "*exists*", for example, a working-class movement of nation-wide significance, no matter how the liberals may keep quiet about that significance and no matter how the liberal working-class politicians, the liquidators, may try to curtail and belittle that significance.

"Have we done everything in our power," asks *Rech*, "to bring influence to bear on the Duma to compel it to follow and fulfil our demands?"

That is not particularly literate but it is clear enough. "We"—refers to the landowners and the bourgeoisie. That is the *only* "society", the *only* "public" opinion, that *Rech* sees and only that society interests it.

Are the more reactionary landowners to be compelled "to fulfil the demands" of the liberal landowners and liberal bourgeoisie who do not themselves know what to "demand" or what they want—a change for the better or a weakening of the working-class movement with its nation-wide scope that is bringing about that change?

Poor liberals!

Pravda No. 151, July 5, 1913

Published according to
the *Pravda* text

17*

FIFTH INTERNATIONAL CONGRESS
AGAINST PROSTITUTION

The *fifth* international congress for the suppression of the white slave traffic recently ended in London.

Duchesses, countesses, bishops, priests, rabbis, police officials and all sorts of bourgeois philanthropists were well to the fore! How many festive luncheons and magnificent official receptions were given! And how many solemn speeches on the harm and infamy of prostitution!

What means of struggle were proposed by the elegant bourgeois delegates to the congress? Mainly two methods—religion and police. They are, it appears, the valid and reliable methods of combating prostitution. One English delegate boasted, according to the London correspondent of the *Leipziger Volkszeitung*,[91] that he had introduced a bill into parliament providing for *corporal punishment* for pimps. See the sort he is, this modern "civilised" hero of the struggle against prostitution!

One lady from Canada waxed enthusiastic over the police and the supervision of "fallen" women by policewomen, but as far as raising wages was concerned, she said that women workers did not deserve better pay.

One German pastor reviled present-day materialism, which, he said, is taking hold among the people and promoting the spread of free love.

When the Austrian delegate Gärtner tried to raise the question of the social causes of prostitution, of the need and poverty experienced by working-class families, of the exploitation of child labour, of unbearable housing conditions, etc., he was forced to silence by hostile shouts!

But the things that were said about highly-placed personages—among groups of delegates—were instructive and sublime. When, for example, the German Empress visits a maternity hospital in Berlin, *rings are placed on the fingers* of mothers of "illegitimate" children in order that this august individual may not be shocked by the sight of unmarried mothers!

We may judge from this the disgusting bourgeois hypocrisy that reigns at these aristocratic-bourgeois congresses. Acrobats in the field of philanthropy and police defenders of this system which makes mockery of poverty and need gather "to struggle against prostitution", which is supported precisely by the aristocracy and the bourgeoisie....

Rabochaya Pravda No. 1,
July 13, 1913
Signed: *W*.

Published according to
the *Rabochaya Pravda* text

WORD AND DEED

We are constantly making the mistake in Russia of judging the slogans and tactics of a certain party or group, of judging its general trend, by the intentions or motives that the group claims for itself. Such judgement is worthless. The road to hell—as was said long ago—is paved with good intentions.

It is not a matter of intentions, motives or words but of the objective situation, independent of them, that determines the fate and significance of slogans, of tactics or, in general, of the trend of a given party or group.

Let us approach the analysis of the most important questions of the contemporary working-class movement from that point of view. The strike in St. Petersburg on July 1-3 involved over 62,000 workers even according to the estimates of the bourgeois papers *Rech* and *Russkoye Slovo*, which always give reduced figures in these cases.

We are, therefore, faced with the fact that a mass, over 60,000 strong, went into action. As we know, the direct reason for the strike was to protest against the persecution of the working-class press, the daily confiscation of newspapers, etc., etc. We also know from reports even in such newspapers as *Novoye Vremya*, *Rech*, *Sovremenka*[92] and *Russkoye Slovo* that workers stressed, in their speeches and in other ways, the nation-wide significance of the protest.

How did the various classes of Russian society react to the event? What position did they adopt?

We know that *Rossiya*,[93] *Zemshchina* and similar papers printed the usual sharply condemnatory statements—often accompanied by the crudest invective, threats, etc. There is nothing new in that. It is understandable. It is inevitable.

First page of the newspaper *Rabochaya Pravda* No. 3, July 16, 1913, which contained Lenin's articles "Word and Deed", "Cadets on the Question of the Ukraine", "Fresh Data on German Political Parties" and "Exposure of the British Opportunists"

Reduced

Much "newer" is the amazing indifference of the bourgeoisie, as reflected in the indifference of the liberal newspapers; furthermore, in many cases this indifference changes to a negative attitude, whereas working-class actions that were less important, numerically less significant (17 or 18 years ago), met with the obvious sympathy of liberal-bourgeois society. Here we undoubtedly have a decisive liberal turn to the right, away from democracy and against democracy.

With reference to the events of July 1-3 in St. Petersburg, one of the most widely circulated, if not the most widely circulated, newspapers in Russia (the liberal *Russkoye Slovo*) said:

"It is interesting to note the attitude to this strike on the part of the Social-Democratic newspapers published in St. Petersburg. The Social-Democratic *Pravda* devotes considerable space to yesterday's [written on July 3] strike, but the organ of the so-called liquidators' group, the newspaper *Luch*, confines itself to a small note on the strike and devotes a leading article to political strikes [*Luch*, July 2], in which the newspaper protests against such actions by the workers." (*Russkoye Slovo*, July 3, 1913.)

Such are the facts. Hostility on the part of the reactionaries. Indifference and denial by the liberals and liquidators. Unity of liberalism and liquidationism in deed. Unity of mass working-class action, possible only in the struggle against the liquidators.

The proletariat cannot do its democratic duty, serve as the advanced contingent, give service to, educate and consolidate the masses of the people other than by a decisive struggle against the liquidators, who, in fact, are completely dependent on liberalism.

The liberals, too, frequently play at being radicals from the Duma rostrum and do it as well as the various near-Marxist or wavering elements, but that does not prevent the liberals from fighting (with the aid of the liquidators) the democratic aspirations of the masses outside the Duma.

Rabochaya Pravda No. 3,   Published according to
     July 16, 1913   the *Rabochaya Pravda* text

CADETS ON THE QUESTION OF THE UKRAINE

For a long time mention has been made in the press and from the Duma rostrum (in the speech of the Social-Democrat Petrovsky, for instance[94]) of the absolute indecency, the reactionary character and the impudence of statements made by certain influential Cadets (headed by Mr. Struve) on the Ukrainian question.

A few days ago we came across an article in *Rech*, the official organ of the Constitutional-Democratic Party, written by one of its regular contributors, Mr. Mikhail Mogilyansky, an article that *must not* be ignored.

This article is real chauvinist badgering of the Ukrainians for "separatism". "Reckless adventurism", "political delirium", "a political adventure"—are some of the expressions which fill the article of Mr. Mikhail Mogilyansky, a *Novoye Vremya adherent* of the purest water who hides under a mantle of "democracy"! Yet the Constitutional-"Democratic" Party shamelessly provides cover for this article, publishes it with sympathy and by its silence approves such naked chauvinism.

Mr. Mikhail Mogilyansky himself points out that at the All-Ukraine Student Congress in Lvov some Ukrainian Social-Democrats, Ukrainian émigrés from Russia, also spoke against the slogan of political independence for the Ukraine; they spoke against the Social-Democrat Dontsov, who proposed the resolution on "an independent Ukraine" that was adopted at the congress by a majority of all present against two.

It follows, therefore, that there is no question of all Social-Democrats agreeing with Dontsov. But the Social-Democrats disputed the matter with Dontsov, put forward their own arguments, discussed the matter from the same platform and attempted to convince the same audience.

Mr. Mikhail Mogilyansky lost all sense of elementary political decency when he hurled his coarse invective drawn from the lexicon of the Black Hundreds against Dontsov and against the entire congress of Ukrainian students, knowing full well that it was impossible for his opponents to refute the views of *Rech*, that it was impossible for them to speak to the Russian audience from the same platform and just as resolutely, openly and freely.

They are pitiful democrats, our Cadets! And those who tolerate, without a violent protest, such sallies by the Cadets are pitiful democrats, too. Marxists will never allow their heads to be turned by nationalist slogans whether they are Great-Russian, Polish, Jewish, Ukrainian or any other. Nor do Marxists ever forget the elementary duty of any democrat to struggle against any persecution of any nation for "separatism", the duty to fight for the recognition of the full and unqualified equality of nations, and their right to self-determination.

Views may differ on what this self-determination should be, from the point of view of the proletariat, in each individual case. One can and must dispute with social-nationalists of the Dontsov type, but base persecution for "separatism", the persecution of people who are unable to defend themselves, is the very limit of shamelessness on the part of our Cadets.

Rabochaya Pravda No. 3,
July 16, 1913
Signed: *M*.

Published according to
the *Rabochaya Pravda* text

FRESH DATA ON GERMAN POLITICAL PARTIES

The German statistical office has published some interesting data on the 1912 parliamentary (Reichstag) elections. It is particularly instructive to compare the strength of the various parties in the *towns* and *villages*.

German statistics, like those of most European states, regard all inhabited centres having less than 2,000 inhabitants as villages, unlike Russia which still retains the senseless, arbitrary distinction made by officials and policemen, by which certain inhabited centres are "called" towns irrespective of the number of inhabitants.

German statistics regard inhabited centres with a population of between 2,000 and 10,000 as small towns and those with 10,000 or more inhabitants as big towns.

There proves to be a strikingly regular correlation between the *progressive nature* of a party ("progressive" in the broadest economic and political sense) and the *increase* in the strength of that party in the *towns* and bigger inhabited centres in general.

Four groups of political parties in Germany stand out clearly in this respect:

1) Social-Democrats—the only completely progressive and, in the best sense of the word, "popular" mass party of wage-workers;

2) Progressive People's Party—a petty-bourgeois democratic party, something like our Trudoviks[95] (only under conditions of a fully bourgeois and not a feudal society);

3) National Liberals—the party of the big bourgeoisie, the German Octobrist-Cadet party;

4) all conservative parties, Black-Hundred landowners, clericals, reactionary urban petty bourgeois and peasants

(anti-Semites, "the Centre", i.e., Catholics, conservatives proper, Poles, and so on).

Share of the Votes (%%) Obtained by Parties

	Social-Democrats	Progressists	National Liberals	All conservative parties	Fragmentary and unde-fined	Totals
In villages	19.0	8.8	12.8	58.6	0.8	100.0
In small towns	35.8	12.1	15.0	36.4	0.7	100.0
In big towns	49.3	15.6	13.8	20.0	1.3	100.0
All Germany	34.8	12.3	13.6	38.3	1.0	100.0

Universal franchise exists in Germany. The above table shows clearly that the German village, the German peasantry (like those of *all* European, constitutional, civilised countries) are still, to the present day, *almost completely* enslaved by the landowners and priests, spiritually and politically.

In the German villages almost three-fifths (58.6%) of the votes go to the conservative, i.e., landowner and priest, parties! Everywhere in Europe the peasant *was* revolutionary when he fought against the feudals, the serf-owners and landowners. Once the peasant had obtained his freedom and a little piece of land he, as a general rule, *made his peace* with the landowners and priests and became a reactionary.

The development of capitalism, however, begins in its turn to pull the peasant out of the embraces of reaction and leads him to the Social-Democrats. In 1912, the German Social-Democrats had *already* obtained *almost one-fifth* (19%) of all rural votes.

The political picture in the German countryside today is, therefore, the following. *One-fifth* for the Social-Democrats, *one-fifth* for the more or less "liberal" bourgeoisie and *three-fifths* for the landowners and priests. There is still quite a lot to be done for the political education of the countryside. By ruining the small peasant and putting the screw on him, capitalism, one might say, is knocking reactionary prejudices out of his head by force.

There is already a different picture in the small towns; the Social-Democrats have overtaken the liberal bourgeoisie (35.8% of the votes as compared with 27%) but have not quite caught up with the conservatives, who obtained 36.4% of the votes. The small towns are the stronghold of the urban petty bourgeoisie engaged mainly in commerce and manufacturing. The petty bourgeoisie waver most of all and do not give a stable majority either to the conservatives, or to the socialists or to the liberal bourgeoisie.

In the big towns there has been a Social-Democratic victory. The Social-Democrats have a following of *half* the population (49.3% of the votes), as many as the conservatives and liberals combined (15.6+13.8+20=49.4%). The conservatives here are supported by only *one-fifth* of the population, the liberal bourgeoisie by *three-tenths* and the Social-Democrats by *a half*. If we were to take the biggest towns there would be an incomparably wider predominance of Social-Democracy.

We know that towns in all modern states and even in Russia grow more rapidly than villages, that the towns are centres of the economic, political and spiritual life of the people and are the chief vehicles of progress. The predominance of Social-Democracy in the towns gives a clear demonstration of its significance as the party of the advanced masses.

Of Germany's population of 65,000,000 only 25,900,000 people were living in rural areas in 1912; 12,300,000 were living in small towns and 26,800,000 in the bigger towns. In recent decades, since Germany became a completely capitalist state, relatively free and possessing a stable constitution and universal franchise, the urban population has grown more rapidly than that of the countryside. In 1882, only 18,900,000 of the 45,000,000 population lived in towns, i.e., 41.8%; in 1895 the total population was 52,000,000, the urban population 26,000,000, i.e., 49.8%; in 1907 out of the 62,000,000 population, 36,000,000 lived in towns, i.e., 58.1%. The population of the biggest towns, those with 100,000 or more inhabitants, was in the same years 3,000,000 7,000,000 and 12,000,000 respectively, i.e., 7.4%, 13.6% and 19.1% of the total population. In the course of twenty-five years the entire population has increased by 36.5%, the urban population by 89.6% and the population of the biggest towns by 254.4%.

Finally, it is interesting to note that the purely bourgeois parties in present-day bourgeois Germany are supported by a *minority* of the population. In 1912, the Social-Democrats obtained in the whole of Germany *more than one-third* of the total number of votes cast (34.8%), the conservatives (mainly the landowners and priests) somewhat less than *two-fifths* (38.3%), and all the liberal-bourgeois parties *only one-quarter* of the votes cast (25.9%).

How is this to be explained? Why is it that in bourgeois Germany, in a country in which capitalism is developing with particular rapidity, more than sixty years after the revolution (the bourgeois revolution of 1848), landowners' and clerical parties and not purely bourgeois political parties predominate?

The key to the explanation of this phenomenon was provided by Karl Marx as far back as 1848—the German bourgeoisie, frightened of the independence of the proletariat and seeing that the workers were using democratic institutions *for themselves* and against the capitalists, turned its back on democracy, shamefully betrayed the liberty that it had previously defended and began to fawn upon the landowners and clericals.[96] We know that since 1905 the Russian bourgeoisie has been developing these slavish political inclinations and these slavish political ideas more zealously than the German bourgeoisie.

Rabochaya Pravda No. 3
July 16, 1913
Signed: *V. I.*

Published according to
the *Rabochaya Pravda* text

EXPOSURE OF THE BRITISH OPPORTUNISTS

A Parliamentary by-election recently took place in Leicester, England.

This election is of enormous importance in principle, and every socialist interested in the very important question of the attitude of the proletariat towards the liberal bourgeoisie in general, and the British socialist movement in particular, should ponder deeply over the Leicester election.

Leicester is a *two*-member constituency and each elector has *two* votes. There are only a few constituencies of this kind in Britain, but they particularly favour a tacit *bloc* between the Socialists and the Liberals, as is emphasised by the correspondent in Britain of the *Leipziger Volkszeitung.* It was precisely in such constituencies that the most prominent of the leaders of the so-called Independent (independent of socialism, but dependent on liberalism) Labour Party were elected to Parliament. The I.L.P. leaders, Keir Hardie, Philip Snowden and Ramsay MacDonald, were returned by such constituencies.

And in these constituencies the Liberals, who are in the ascendancy, call on their supporters to cast one vote for the Socialist and one for the Liberal, provided, of course, that the Socialist is a "reasonable", moderate, "independent" one and not an irreconcilable Social-Democrat, whom the British Liberals and liquidators, no less than the Russian, know how to curse as an anarcho-syndicalist, etc.!

What actually takes place, therefore, is the formation of a bloc between the Liberals and the moderate, opportunist Socialists. Actually, the British "independents" (for whom our liquidators express such tender feelings) *depend* on the

Liberals. The conduct of the "independents" in the British Parliament constantly confirms this dependence.

It happened that the I.L.P. member for Leicester, none other than the party leader, MacDonald, resigned for personal reasons.

What was to be done?

The Liberals, of course, put forward their candidate.

Leicester is a factory town with a predominantly proletarian population.

The local I.L.P. organisation called a conference which by 67 votes against 8 decided *to put forward a candidate*. No sooner said than done. Banton, a Town Councillor and prominent member of the I.L.P., was nominated.

Then the Executive Committee of this Party, which assigns the money for the election campaign (and elections in Britain are very costly!), *refused* to endorse Banton's candidature!

The opportunist Executive Committee opposed the local workers.

The Leicester branch of the other British socialist party, which is not opportunist and is *really* independent of the Liberals, then sent its representative to the Leicester I.L.P. and invited them to support *its* candidate, Hartley, a member of the British Socialist Party, a very popular figure in the labour movement, an ex-member of the Independent Labour Party, who left it because of its opportunism.

The members of the Leicester branch of the I.L.P. were in an awkward position: they were heart and soul in favour of Hartley, but ... but what of the discipline in their party, the decision of their Executive Committee? The Leicester people found a way out: they closed the meeting, and *each in his private capacity* declared for Hartley. Next day a huge meeting of workers endorsed Hartley's candidature. Banton himself sent a telegram stating that he would vote for Hartley. The Leicester trade unions declared for Hartley.

The I.L.P. Parliamentary group intervened and published *a protest* in the *Liberal* press (which, like our *Rech* and *Sovremenka*, helps the opportunists) against Hartley's candidature, against "undermining" MacDonald!

The election, of course, resulted in a victory for the Liberals. They obtained 10,863 votes, the Conservatives 9,279, and Hartley 2,580.

Class-conscious workers in various countries quite often adopt a "tolerant" attitude toward the British I.L.P. This is a great mistake. The *betrayal* of the workers' cause in Leicester by the I.L.P. is no accident, but the result of the *entire* opportunist policy of the Independent Labour Party. The sympathies of all *real* Social-Democrats should be with those British Social-Democrats who are determinedly combating the Liberal corruption of the workers by the "Independent" Labour Party in Britain.

Rabochaya Pravda No. 3,
    July 16, 1913
    Signed: *K. T.*

                                    Published according to
                                    the *Rabochaya Pravda* text

THE IDEAS OF AN ADVANCED CAPITALIST

One of the richest and most eminent American merchants, a certain Edward Albert *Filene*, Vice-Chairman of the International Congress of Chambers of Commerce, is now touring Paris, Berlin and other big European centres to make personal contact with the most influential people of the commercial world.

At the banquets arranged, as is fitting, by the richest people of Europe in honour of one of the American rich, the latter is developing his "new" ideas on the *world power* of the merchant. *Frankfurter Zeitung*,[97] the organ of German finance capital, reports in detail the ideas of this "advanced" American millionaire.

"We are experiencing a great historic movement," he proclaims, "that will end in the transfer of all power over the modern world to representatives of commercial capital. We are the people who bear the greatest responsibility in the world and we should, therefore, be politically the most influential.

"Democracy is growing, the power of the masses is growing," argued Mr. Filene (rather inclined, it seems, to regard those "masses" as simpletons). "The cost of living is rising. Parliamentarism and the newspapers, distributed in millions of copies a day, are providing the masses of the people with ever more detailed information.

"The masses are striving to ensure for themselves participation in political life, the extension of franchise, the introduction of an income-tax, etc. Power over the whole world must pass into the hands of the masses, that is, *into the hands of our employees*," is the conclusion drawn by this worthy orator.

"The natural leaders of the masses should be the *industrialists and merchants*, who are learning more and more to understand the community of their interests and those of the masses." (We note in parenthesis that the cunning Mr. Filene is the owner of a gigantic commercial house employing 2,500 people, and that he has "organised" his employees in a "democratic" organisation with profit-sharing, etc. Since he considers his employees hopeless simpletons, Mr. Filene is sure that they are completely satisfied and infinitely grateful to their "father-benefactor" ....)

"Wage increases, the improvement of labour conditions, that is what will bind our employees to us," said Mr. Filene, "that is what will guarantee our power over the whole world. Everybody in the world who is at all talented will come to us to enter our service.

"We need organisation and still more organisation— strong, democratic organisation, both national and international," the American exclaimed. He called upon the commercial world of Paris, Berlin, etc., to reorganise *international chambers of commerce*. They should unite the merchants and industrialists *of all* civilised countries in a single, mighty organisation. All important international problems should be discussed and settled by that organisation.

Such are the ideas of an "advanced" capitalist, Mr. Filene.

The reader will see that these ideas are a paltry, narrow, one-sided, selfishly barren *approximation* to the ideas of Marxism propounded over sixty years ago. "We" are great masters at upsetting and refuting Marx; "we", the civilised merchants and professors of political economy, have refuted him completely!... And at the same time we steal little bits and pieces from him and boast to the whole world of our "progressiveness"....

My worthy Mr. Filene! Do you really believe that the workers of the whole world are actually such simpletons?

Rabochaya Pravda No. 4,   Published according to
July 17, 1913 ·   the *Rabochaya Pravda* text
Signed: *W*.

WHAT CAN BE DONE FOR PUBLIC EDUCATION

There are quite a number of rotten prejudices current in the Western countries of which Holy Mother Russia is free. They assume there, for instance, that huge public libraries containing hundreds of thousands and millions of volumes, should certainly not be reserved only for the handful of scholars or would-be scholars that uses them. Over there they have set themselves the strange, incomprehensible and barbaric aim of making these gigantic, boundless libraries available, not to a guild of scholars, professors and other such specialists, but to the masses, to the crowd, to the mob!

What a desecration of the libraries! What an absence of the "law and order" we are so justly proud of. Instead of *regulations*, discussed and elaborated by a dozen committees of civil servants inventing hundreds of formalities and obstacles to the use of books, they see to it that even *children* can make use of the rich collections; that readers can read publicly-owned books at home; they regard as the pride and glory of a public library, not the number of rarities it contains, the number of sixteenth-century editions or tenth-century manuscripts, but *the extent* to which books are distributed *among the people*, the number of new readers enrolled, the speed with which the demand for any book is met, the number of books issued to be read at home, the number of children attracted to reading and to the use of the library.... These queer prejudices are widespread in the Western states, and we must be glad that those who keep watch and ward over us protect us with care and circumspection from the influence of these prejudices, protect our rich public libraries from the mob, from the *hoi polloi*!

I have before me the report of the New York Public Library for 1911.

That year the Public Library in New York was moved from two old buildings to new premises erected by the city. The total number of books is now about two million. It so happened that the first book asked for when the reading-room opened its doors was in Russian. It was a work by N. Grot, *The Moral Ideals of Our Times*. The request for the book was handed in at eight minutes past nine in the morning. The book was delivered to the reader at nine fifteen.

In the course of the year the library was visited by 1,658,376 people. There were 246,950 readers using the reading-room and they took out 911,891 books.

This, however, is only a small part of the *book circulation* effected by the library. Only a few people can visit the library. The rational organisation of educational work is measured by the number of books issued to be read at home, by the conveniences available to *the majority of the population*.

In three boroughs of New York—Manhatten, Bronx and Richmond—the New York Public Library has *forty-two* branches and will soon have a forty-third (the total population of the three boroughs is almost *three* million). The aim that is constantly pursued is to have a branch of the Public Library within *three-quarters of a verst*, i.e., within ten minutes' walk of the house of every inhabitant, the branch library being *the centre* of all kinds of institutions and establishments for public education.

Almost *eight million* (7,914,882 volumes) were issued to readers at home, 400,000 more than in 1910. To each hundred members of the population of all ages and both sexes, 267 books were issued for reading at home in the course of the year.

Each of the forty-two branch libraries not only provides for the use of reference books in the building and the issue of books to be read at home, it is also a place for evening lectures, for public meetings and for rational entertainment.

The New York Public Library contains about 15,000 books in oriental languages, about 20,000 in Yiddish and about 16,000 in the Slav languages. In the main reading-room there are about 20,000 books standing on *open* shelves for general use.

The New York Public Library has opened a special, central, reading-room for children, and similar institutions are gradually being opened at all branches. The librarians do everything for the children's convenience and answer their questions. The number of books children took out to read at home was 2,859,888, slightly under three million (more than a third of the total). The number of children visiting the reading-room was 1,120,915.

As far as losses are concerned—the New York Public Library assesses the number of books lost at 70-80-90 per 100,000 issued to be read at home.

Such is the way things are done in New York. And in Russia?

Rabochaya Pravda No. 5,
July 18, 1913
Signed: *W.*

Published according to
the *Rabochaya Pravda* text

PETTY PRODUCTION IN AGRICULTURE

The peasant question in modern capitalist states most frequently gives rise to perplexity and vacillation among Marxists and to most of the attacks on Marxism by bourgeois (professorial) political economy.

Petty production in agriculture is doomed to extinction and to an incredibly abased and downtrodden position under capitalism, say the Marxists. Petty production is dependent on big capital, is backward in comparison with large-scale production in agriculture, and can only keep going by means of desperately reduced consumption and laborious, arduous toil. The frittering away and waste of human labour, the worst forms of dependence of the producer, exhaustion of the peasant's family, his cattle and his land—this is what capitalism everywhere brings the peasant.

There is *no* salvation for the peasant except by joining in the activities of the proletariat, primarily those of the wage-workers.

Bourgeois political economy, and the Narodniks and opportunists who champion it (though they may not always be conscious of the fact), on the contrary, try to prove that petty production is viable and is more profitable than large-scale production. The peasant, who has a firm and assured position in capitalist society, must gravitate, not towards the proletariat, but towards the bourgeoisie; he must not gravitate towards the class struggle of the wage-workers but must try to strengthen his position as a proprietor and master—such, in substance, is the theory of the bourgeois economists.

We will try to test the soundness of the proletarian and bourgeois theories by means of precise data. Let us take the data on *female* labour in agriculture in Austria and Germany. Full data for Russia are still lacking because the government is unwilling to take a scientifically based census of all agricultural enterprises.

In Austria, according to the census of 1902, out of 9,070,682 persons employed in agriculture 4,422,981, or 48.7 per cent, were women. In Germany, where capitalism is far more developed, women constitute the *majority* of those employed in agriculture—54.8 per cent. The more capitalism develops in agriculture the more it employs female labour, that is to say, *worsens* the living conditions of the working masses. Women employed in German industry make up 25 per cent of the total labour force, but in agriculture they constitute more than 50 per cent. This shows that industry is absorbing the *best* labour and leaving the weaker to agriculture.

In developed capitalist countries agriculture has already become mainly a women's occupation.

But if we examine statistics on farms of various sizes we shall see that it is in *petty* production that the exploitation of female labour assumes particularly large proportions. On the other hand, even in agriculture, large-scale capitalist production employs mainly male labour, although in this respect it has not caught up with industry.

The following are the comparative figures for Austria and Germany:

Type of farm	Group according to size of farm	Per cent of women employed	
		Austria	Germany
Proletarian	Up to half a hectare*	52.0	74.1
	½ to 2 hectares	50.9	65.7
Peasant	2 to 5 ”	49.6	54.4
	5 to 10 ”	48.5	50.2
	10 to 20 ”	48.6	48.4
Capitalist	20 to 100 ”	46.6	44.8
	100 hectares and over	27.4	41.0
For all farms		48.7	54.8

In both countries we see the operation of the same law of capitalist agriculture. The smaller the scale of production the *poorer* is the composition of the labour force, and the greater the number of women among the total number of persons employed in agriculture.

---

* One hectare = 0.9 of a dessiatine.—*Ed.*

The general situation under capitalism is the following. On proletarian farms, i.e., those whose "proprietors" live mainly by means of wage-labour (agricultural labourers, day-labourers, and wage-workers in general who possess a tiny plot of land), *female labour predominates over male labour*, sometimes to an enormous extent.

It must not be forgotten that the number of these proletarian or labourer farms is enormous: in Austria they amount to 1,300,000 out of a total of 2,800,000 farms, and in Germany there are even 3,400,000 out of a total of 5,700,000.

On peasant farms male and female labour is employed in nearly equal proportions.

Finally, on capitalist farms, male labour *predominates over female labour*.

What does this signify?

It signifies that the composition of the labour force in petty production is inferior to that in large-scale capitalist production.

It signifies that in agriculture the working woman—the proletarian woman and peasant woman—must exert herself ever so much more, must strain herself to the utmost, must toil at her work to the detriment of her health and the health of her children, in order to keep up as far as possible with the male worker in large-scale capitalist production.

It signifies that petty production keeps going under capitalism only by *squeezing out* of the worker a *larger* amount of work than is squeezed out of the worker in large-scale production.

The peasant is more tied up, more entangled in the complicated net of capitalist dependence than the wage-worker. He thinks he is independent, that he can "make good"; but as a matter of fact, in order to keep going, he must work (for capital) harder than the wage-worker.

The figures on *child* labour in agriculture prove this still more clearly.*

Rabochaya Pravda No. 5,
July 18, 1913
Signed: *V. I.*

Published according to the *Rabochaya Pravda* text

---

* See pp. 209-12 of this volume.—*Ed.*

A "FASHIONABLE" BRANCH OF INDUSTRY

Capitalist production develops spasmodically, in fits and starts. At times there is "brilliant" prosperity in industry and then comes collapse, crisis and unemployment. It cannot be otherwise under a system of economy in which individual, isolated proprietors, independent of each other, "work" for an unknown market and have the joint labour of thousands and thousands of workers in big enterprises at their disposal as private property.

An example of a "fashionable" industry that is now developing with particular rapidity and rushing full steam ahead toward a crash is the automobile industry. In Germany, for instance, the number of motor vehicles of all kinds, including motor cycles, was 27,000 in 1907 and 70,000 in 1912.

In France and Britain motor vehicles are still more widespread. Here are the figures for comparison: Germany, 70,000, France, 88,000 and Britain, 175,000.

In proportion to the population, therefore, Germany has *only one-quarter* the number of motor vehicles that Britain has, while Russia is lagging behind to an immeasurably greater extent.

Under the capitalist organisation of economy, motor-cars are available only to an extremely narrow circle of rich people. Industry *could* produce hundreds of thousands of motor vehicles but the poverty of the *masses* hampers development and brings about crashes after a few years of "brilliant" growth.

In passing. Motor vehicles, provided they were in the service of the majority of the population, would be of great significance because an association of united workers could use them instead of a large number of draught animals in farming and in carting. Such a replacement would enable *millions of dessiatines* now used to produce fodder for horses to be used to produce grain, meat and milk and improve the population's food supply.

Bourgeois economists are only trying to frighten people when they say that agriculture cannot produce sufficient grain!

Rabochaya Pravda No. 8,
        July 21, 1913
        Signed: *N.*

Published according to
the *Rabochaya Pravda* text

DEAD LIQUIDATIONISM AND THE LIVING *RECH*

The first issue of the liquidators' newspaper *Zhivaya Zhizn** carried an article by L. M.[98] entitled "On an Old Theme". We will leave until another occasion the little tricks the enthusiastic author got up to in his haste to "grab by the coat-tails" the Kautsky who argued with Rosa Luxemburg. L. M. copies the worn-out method of the liberals —that of exaggerating *this sort of* dispute and depicting it as important in principle by maintaining a *complete silence* on the position of the German opportunists (reformists)!

Mr. L. M. likes holding Kautsky by the coat-tails, but when speaking of "German Social-Democratic literature" he prefers not to mention—out of modesty, no doubt—the extensive and, indeed, fundamentally important literature put out by reformists related in type to L. M. and *Zhivaya Zhizn*.

I repeat, this will be dealt with another time.

L. M. drags the Germans into Russian affairs by the hair, as the saying goes. The first issue of *Zhivaya Zhizn* informs us of these affairs through the lips of L. M.:

... without a struggle for freedom of association "Russian workers cannot get out of the intolerable situation that dooms them to run like squirrels in a cage, to spend tremendous effort in periodical mass actions of one and the same kind that are rewarded neither by organisational growth nor a strengthening of the political positions gained". The efforts of the advanced proletarians (writes L. M., outlining the *ideas* of advanced *liberals*) should be directed toward "making the working class capable of giving battle and winning victories, not only in one-day strikes but also in all other possible fields".

---

* Literally, "Living Life".—*Ed.*

These words contain the essence of the "theory" of the
liquidators of the working-class party. "Running like a
squirrel in a cage"—those words will become famous. They
should be repeated in every issue of *Zhivaya Zhizn*, they
should become the motto of its whole trend. This is the "slogan" of the liquidators!

In his wisdom, L. M. probably regards making petitions
as "other fields" and not "running like a squirrel in a cage"?
Then say so straight out, don't be ashamed, gentlemen!

And here you have the real *live* newspaper *Rech*—live because it advocates not the dead doctrine of the liquidators
but living class interests (the interests of the bourgeoisie,
of course, and not the proletariat). Compare the passages
from *Zhivaya Zhizn* of July 11 quoted above with the leading article in *Rech* of July 6.

The *Rech* leading article declares that the working-class
movement in 1905 was "national, but in 1913 is a class movement" and with ecstatic enthusiasm repeats the attacks
made by the liquidators on the "strike craze", repeats the
statement made by the liquidators that "the workers can and
must struggle for freedom of speech, assembly and association by other more complicated [really?] political means
and not by strikes alone".

It stands to reason that the liberals, like L. M., maintain a modest silence on precisely what "complicated" means
they have in mind. The liberals, on the other hand, say
straight out that with the introduction of freedom of association and so on, it will be possible, they are convinced,
"to conduct *a serious struggle* against the chaotic, casual
strikes that disorganise industry" (the same *Rech* leading
article).

We shall permit ourselves only one remark—everybody
has now recognised the fact of a new wave of strikes, even
purely economic strikes. There is nothing more ridiculous
and pitiful than to speak of them as "casual".

The class position of the liberals is clear. Any worker
will immediately understand their position, will immediately discern the interests of the bourgeoisie in the vague phrases
about "complicated" methods. The living *Rech* expresses
the interests of the bourgeoisie. Dead liquidationism in
Zhivaya Zhizn is helplessly limping along behind the

liberals and is unable to say anything clear and straight-forward about "other fields" and can only get angry and churn out abuse of the "running like squirrels in a cage" variety....

A noteworthy and at the same time shameful slogan that the liquidators have descended to!

Rabochaya Pravda No. 10,
July 24, 1913
Signed: *P. Osipov*

Published according to
the *Rabochaya Pravda* text

MOBILISATION OF ALLOTMENT LANDS

A few days ago the official newspaper *Rossiya* published the results of an investigation carried out by the Ministry of the Interior in the summer of 1912 on the question of the mobilisation of allotment lands, that is, their sale and purchase, their transfer from one owner to another.

The Ministry of the Interior selected four gubernias for its investigation—Vitebsk, Perm, Stavropol and Samara (Nikolayev Uyezd). It is typical that the gubernias of the Great-Russian agricultural "centre" of European Russia, the gubernias where the traces of serfdom are the strongest and where the condition of the peasants is worst and the oppression by the feudal landowners is greatest, *were not included* in the investigation! It is obvious that the Ministry did not wish so much *to investigate* as *to deceive*, did not wish so much *to study* the matter as *to distort it*.

The statistics collected by the Ministry of the Interior and summarised in *Rossiya* are remarkably slipshod, haphazard and primitive; we have before us the usual "official work" produced by Russian civil servants, who can be relied on to bungle the simplest task. For the whole of Russia they examined something like a hundred thousand households but they could not devise a comprehensive programme, or engage competent statisticians, or ensure the uniform application of even a partial consistent programme to all areas!

The general results of the investigation are the following. In the four gubernias mentioned, on January 1, 1912, a total of 108,095 peasant households had left the communes and had acquired titles to their land. This means that of the total number of title-holding households, which now probably amounts to 2,000,000 in the whole of Russia (out of a total of 12,000,000-13,000,000 households), something like one-twentieth have been investigated. Even such an investigation would, of course, be valuable if it were done conscientiously, that is, if it were done not by Russian civil servants and not under Russian political conditions.

Of the *hundred* thousand or so households holding titles, 27,588, i.e., *more than a quarter* (25.5 per cent) sold land. This huge number of sales by peasant owners shows straightaway that in Russia the notorious "private ownership" of land is primarily a means of *liberating* the peasants from the land. In fact, over *ten thousand* (10,380) households out of those that sold land *were not* engaged in farming at all. They had been artificially bound to the soil by the old, semi-medieval commune. The demand made by the Social-Democrats—to grant the right of free exit from the commune—was the only correct one; that alone could have given the peasants without any interference on the part of the police, rural superintendents[99] and similar kindly "authorities" what life in capitalist society insistently demands. You cannot keep anyone on the land who cannot farm it, and to try to do so is absurd.

If the number of title-holding households in the whole of Russia amounts to two million, the above data lead one to suppose that *about 200,000* of them did not engage in farming and immediately sold their land. "Private ownership" immediately threw hundreds of thousands of fictitious farmers out of the countryside! The Ministry of the Interior statistics do not say a word about the price (probably a nominal one) at which these poor people sold their land. Pitiful statistics!

What caused these farmers to sell land to which they had obtained the title? Out of 17,260 such peasants only 1,791, i.e., a tiny minority, sold land in order to improve their farms or to buy new lots. The remaining mass of peasants sold land because they *could not* remain on it—4,117 households sold out to migrate to Siberia; 768 because they were going over to other types of employment; 5,614 from necessity, "drunkenness" (as the official statisticians say!) and bad harvests; 2,498 because of illness, old age and lack of family help; 2,472 for "other" reasons.

These unscrupulous statisticians try to make it seem that only 5,614 households "have actually lost their land"! This, of course, is the despicable kind of trick people who have been ordered to raise a cheer would use. As we have seen, the vast majority of those who sell land are ruined and become landless. It is not for nothing that the peasants who sell out are mostly those owning small plots; even official statistics recognise this fact although, needless to say, they avoid giving any precise and complete figures. Pitiful statistics....

Of the 27,588 title-holders who sold out, more than a half (14,182) sold *all* their land, the remainder selling only part of it. Purchasers of land numbered 19,472. A comparison of the number of purchasers with the number of sellers clearly shows that a concentration of land is taking place, that it is being concentrated in the hands of a *smaller* number of owners. The poor sell land and the rich buy it. Despite their efforts, official scribblers are powerless to minimise the significance of this fact.

In Stavropol Gubernia, 14,282 title-holders sold land to 7,489 purchasers. Of the latter, 3,290 bought *more than 15 dessiatines*—580 bought from 50 to 100 dessiatines, 85 bought from 100 to 500 dessiatines and 7 bought from 500 to 1,000 dessiatines. In Nikolayev Uyezd of Samara Gubernia, 142 purchasers bought from 50 to 100 dessiatines, 102 from 100 to 500 dessiatines and 2 from 500 to 1,000 dessiatines.

In Perm Gubernia, 201 purchasers bought two or more lots of land; in Stavropol Gubernia, 2,957 purchasers bought more than two; of these, 562 bought from 5 to 9 lots, and 168 even *ten or more*!

The concentration of land is taking place on a grand scale. We can see clearly how pitiful, senseless and reactionary are the attempts to *curtail* the mobilisation of the land made by the Third Duma and the government and *defended* by "liberal" *civil servants* through the Cadet Party. There is nothing that reveals the retrograde nature of the Cadets and their civil-service stupidity so much as their defence of "measures" against the mobilisation of peasant lands.

The peasant does not sell his land except from dire need. Attempts to limit this right are despicable hypocrisy and *worsen* the selling conditions for the peasant, because in reality such limitations are evaded in thousands of ways.

The Narodniks, who do not understand the inevitability of land mobilisation under capitalism, hold a much more democratic view when they demand the abolition of private property in land. But only an ignoramus could call such abolition a socialist measure. There is absolutely nothing socialist in it. In England, one of the most developed capitalist countries, the farmers (capitalist tenant farmers) farm land belonging to landlords (big landowners). If this land belonged to the state, capitalism would develop more freely and extensively in agriculture. There would be no hindrances from the landowners. There would be no need to withdraw capital from production to invest in land purchases. The mobilisation of the land, drawing it into circulation, would be *still easier* because the transfer of the land from one person to another would take place more freely, simply and cheaply.

The poorer a country is, and the more it is crushed and stifled under the yoke of feudal landed proprietorship, the more urgent (from the standpoint of the *development* of capitalism and the growth of the productive forces) is the abolition of private property in land, complete freedom for its mobilisation, and the break-down of the old spirit of routine and stagnation in agriculture.

Our Stolypin land legislation, however, far from delivering the peasant from ruin and his land from mobilisation, makes that ruin a hundred times more acute and worsens (to a far greater extent than the "general" capitalist standard) the condition of the peasant, compelling him to accept worse conditions when selling his land.

Rabochaya Pravda No. 12,
July 26, 1913
Signed: *V. I.*

Published according to
the *Rabochaya Pravda* text

HOW CAN PER CAPITA CONSUMPTION
IN RUSSIA BE INCREASED?

A few days ago the organ of our satraps of industrial capital, *Promyshlennost i Torgovlya*, published a leading article under the above heading. The question they raise is basic, that of the causes of Russia's economic (and every other) backwardness. It deserves the most serious attention.

Our industrial and commercial satraps declare that "it is at first glance paradoxical" for Russia to be among the great and advanced powers as far as her output of iron, oil and a number of other items is concerned, while her level of *per capita consumption* (i.e., the total amount of important items produced per head of the population) *"makes her the neighbour of Spain"*, one of the most backward countries.

In 1911, for instance, the amount of iron consumed per head of the population was: 233 kilograms in the United States of America, 136 in Germany, 173 in Belgium and 105 in England, while *in Russia it was a mere 25 kilograms* (one and a half poods). In the half century since the liberation of the peasants the consumption of iron in Russia has increased fivefold, but Russia still remains an unbelievably, unprecedentedly backward country, poverty-stricken and half-savage, four times worse-off than Britain, five times worse-off than Germany and ten times worse-off than America in terms of modern means of production.

What is the reason? The journal is forced to admit that the reason lies wholly in rural living conditions. The rural areas consume a mere quarter of a pood of iron per head of the population and "the peasant, rural population constitutes five-sixths of the population of Russia".

"A certain statistician has calculated that if the Chinese were to lengthen their national costume by the width of one finger it would be sufficient to provide work for all the cotton mills in England for a whole year."

An apt and eloquent remark!

What must be done to make the tens of millions of Russian peasants "lengthen their national costume", or, putting all metaphors aside, increase their consumption, cease being beggars and become, at long last, just a little bit like human beings?

Our industrial satraps answer with empty phrases—"the general cultural development of the country", the growth of industry, of towns, etc., "increased productivity of peasant labour", etc.

Empty phrase-mongering, pitiful excuses! This development, this "increase" *has been going on* in Russia for more than half a century, no one doubts it has been going on. *All* classes are shouting their heads off about "culture". *Even* the Black Hundreds and the Narodniks are taking their stand on the side of capitalism. For a long time the question to raise has been a different one—*why* is the development of capitalism and culture proceeding at a snail's pace? Why are we falling farther and farther behind? Why does this increasing backwardness make exceptional speed and "strikes" necessary?

Our industrial satraps are afraid to answer this question, which is quite clear to any politically conscious worker, because they are satraps. They are not the representatives of capital that is free and strong, like that of America; they are a handful of monopolists protected by state aid and by thousands of intrigues and deals with the very Black-Hundred landowners whose medieval land tenure (about 70 million dessiatines of the best land) and oppression condemn five-sixths of the population to poverty, and the entire country to stagnation and decay.

"We must work," exclaims Mr. I. B—n in the journal of the satraps, "to approximate the rate of per capita consumption to that of the United States of America and not that of Spain." This hired scribbler of the satraps does not want to see that subservience to the Black-Hundred landowners *inevitably* "approximates Russia to Spain" and that approximation to America requires a ruthless, devoted struggle against that class all along the line.

Severnaya Pravda No. 3,   Published according to
       August 3, 1913   the *Severnaya Pravda* text
       Signed: *W. Frey*

AUGUST BEBEL

With the death of Bebel we lost not only the German Social-Democratic leader who had the greatest influence among the working class, and was most popular with the masses; in the course of his development and his political activity, Bebel was the embodiment of a whole historical period in the life of international as well as German Social-Democracy.

Two big periods are to be distinguished in the history of international Social-Democracy. The first period was that of the birth of socialist ideas and the embryonic class struggle of the proletariat; a long and stubborn struggle between extremely numerous socialist theories and sects. Socialism was feeling its way, was seeking its true self. The class struggle of the proletariat, which was only just beginning to emerge as something different from the common mass of the petty-bourgeois "people", took the shape of isolated outbursts, like the uprising of the Lyons weavers. The working class was at that time also only feeling its way.

This was the period of preparation and of the birth of Marxism, the only socialist doctrine that has stood the test of history. The period occupied approximately the first two-thirds of the last century and ended with the complete victory of Marxism, the collapse (especially after the Revolution of 1848) of all pre-Marxian forms of socialism, and the separation of the working class from petty-bourgeois democracy and its entry upon an independent historical path.

The second period is that of the formation, growth and maturing of mass socialist parties with a proletarian class composition. This period is characterised by the tremendous spread of socialism, the unprecedented growth of all kinds of organisations of the proletariat, and the all-round preparation of the proletariat in the most varied fields for the fulfilment of its great historic mission. In recent years a third period has been making its appearance, a period in which the forces that have been prepared will achieve their goal in a series of crises.

Himself a worker, Bebel developed a socialist world outlook at the cost of stubborn struggle; he devoted his wealth of energy entirely, withholding nothing, to the cause of socialism; for several decades he marched shoulder to shoulder with the growing and developing German proletariat and became the most gifted parliamentarian in Europe, the most talented organiser and tactician, the most influential leader of international Social-Democracy, Social-Democracy hostile to reformism and opportunism.

Bebel was born in Cologne on the Rhine on February 22, 1840, in the poor family of a Prussian sergeant. He imbibed many barbarous prejudices with his mother's milk and later slowly but surely rid himself of them. The population of the Rhineland was republican in temper in 1848-49, the period of the bourgeois revolution in Germany. In the elementary school only two boys, one of them Bebel, expressed monarchist sympathies and were beaten up for it by their schoolfellows. "One beaten is worth two unbeaten" is a Russian saying that freely translates the "moral" Bebel himself drew when relating this episode of his childhood years in his memoirs.

The sixties of the last century brought a liberal "springtide" to Germany after long, weary years of counter-revolution, and there was a new awakening of the mass working-class movement. Lassalle began his brilliant but short-lived agitation. Bebel, by now a young turner's apprentice, hungrily devoured the liberal newspapers published by the old people who had been active in the 1848 Revolution, and became an ardent participant in workers' educational associations. Having got rid of the prejudices of the Prussian barracks, he had adopted liberal views and was struggling against socialism.

Life, however, took its course and the young worker, through reading Lassalle's pamphlets, gradually found his way to Marx despite the difficulties involved in getting to know Marx's writings in a Germany that had suffered the oppression of the counter-revolution for more than ten years. The conditions of working-class life, the serious and conscientious study of the social sciences, pushed Bebel towards socialism. He would have arrived at socialism himself, but Liebknecht, who was fourteen years older than Bebel and had just returned from exile in London, helped to accelerate his development.

Evil tongues among Marx's opponents were saying at that time that Marx's party consisted of three people—Marx, the head of the party, his secretary Engels, and his "agent" Liebknecht. The unintelligent shunned Liebknecht as the "agent" of exiles or foreigners, but Bebel found in Liebknecht just what he wanted—living contact with the great work done by Marx in 1848, contact with the party formed at that time, which, though small, was genuinely proletarian, a living representative of Marxist views and Marxist traditions. "There is something to be learnt from that man, damn it!" the young turner Bebel is said to have remarked, speaking of Liebknecht.

In the later sixties Bebel broke with the liberals, separated the socialist section of the workers' unions from the bourgeois-democratic section and, together with Liebknecht, took his place in the front ranks of the Eisenacher party, the party of Marxists that was to struggle for many long years against the Lassalleans, the other working-class party.

To put it briefly, the historical reason for the split in the German socialist movement amounts to this. The question of the day was the unification of Germany. Given the class relationships then obtaining, it could have been effected in either of two ways—through a revolution, led by the proletariat, to establish an all-German republic, or through Prussian dynastic wars to strengthen the hegemony of the Prussian landowners in a united Germany.

Lassale and his followers, in view of the poor chances for the proletarian and democratic way, pursued unstable tactics and adapted themselves to the leadership of the Junker Bismarck. Their mistake lay in diverting the workers' party on to the Bonapartist-state-socialist path. Bebel and Liebknecht, on the other hand, consistently supported the democratic and proletarian path and struggled against any concessions to Prussianism, Bismarckism or nationalism.

History showed that Bebel and Liebknecht were right, *despite* Germany's having been united in the Bismarckian way. It was only the consistently democratic and revolutionary tactics of Bebel and Liebknecht, only their "unyielding" attitude towards nationalism, only their "intractability" in respect of the unification of Germany and her renovation "from above", that helped provide a sound basis for a genuinely Social-Democratic workers' party. And in those days the essential thing was the *basis* of the party.

That the Lassalleans' flirting with Bismarckism, or their "accommodations" to it, did not harm the German working-class movement was due *only* to the very energetic, ruthlessly sharp rebuff dealt to their intrigues by Bebel and Liebknecht.

When the question was settled historically, five years after the foundation of the German Empire, Bebel and Liebknecht were able to unite the two workers' parties and ensure the hegemony of Marxism in the united party.

As soon as the German parliament was set up, Bebel was elected to it, although at the time he was still quite young—only twenty-seven years old. The fundamentals of parliamentary tactics for German (and international) Social-Democracy, tactics that never yield an inch to the enemy, never miss the slightest opportunity to achieve even small improvements for the workers and are at the same time implacable on questions of principle and always directed to the accomplishment of the final aim—the fundamentals of these tactics were elaborated by Bebel himself or under his direct leadership and with his participation.

Germany, united in the Bismarckian way, renovated in the Prussian, Junker way, responded to the successes of the workers' party with the Anti-Socialist Law. The legal conditions for the existence of the working-class party were destroyed and the party was outlawed. Difficult times were at hand. To persecution by the party's enemies was added an inner-party crisis—vacillation on the basic questions of tactics. At first the opportunists came to the fore; they allowed themselves to be frightened by the loss of the party's legality, and the mournful song they sang was that of rejecting full-blooded slogans and accusing themselves of having gone much too far, etc. Incidentally, one of the representatives of this opportunist trend, Höchberg, rendered financial aid to the party, which was still weak and could not immediately find its feet.

Marx and Engels launched a fierce attack from London against disgraceful opportunist shilly-shallying. Bebel showed himself to be a real party leader. He recognised the danger in good time, understood the correctness of the criticism by Marx and Engels and was able to direct the party on to the path of implacable struggle. The illegal newspaper *Der Sozialdemokrat* was established and was published first in Zurich and then in London; it was delivered weekly in Germany and had as many as 10,000 subscribers.[100] Opportunist waverings were firmly stopped.

Another form of wavering was due to infatuation with Dühring at the end of the seventies of the last century. For a short time Bebel also shared that infatuation. Dühring's supporters, the most outstanding of which was Most, toyed with "Leftism" and very soon slid into anarchism. Engels's sharp, annihilating criticism of Dühring's theories met with disapproval in many party circles and at one congress it was even proposed to close the columns of the central newspaper to that criticism.

All the viable socialist elements—headed, of course, by Bebel—soon realised that the "new" theories were rotten to the core and broke away from them and from all anarchist trends. Under the leadership of Bebel and Liebknecht the party learned to combine illegal and legal work. When the majority of the legally-existing Social-Democratic group in parliament adopted an opportunist position on the famous question of voting *for* the shipping subsidy, the illegal *Sozialdemokrat opposed* the group and, after a battle four weeks long, proved victorious.

The Anti-Socialist Law was defeated in 1890 after having been in operation for twelve years. A party crisis, very similar to that of the mid-seventies, again occurred. The

opportunists under Vollmar, on the one hand, were prepared to take advantage of legality to reject full-blooded
slogans and implacable tactics. The so-called "young ones",
on the other hand, were toying with "Leftism", drifting
towards anarchism. Considerable credit is due to Bebel
and Liebknecht for offering the most resolute resistance to
these waverings and making the party crisis a short-lived
and not very serious one.

A period of rapid growth set in for the party, growth
in both breadth and depth, in the development of the trade
union, co-operative, educational and other forms of organisation of the forces of the proletariat, as well as their
political organisation. It is impossible to assess the gigantic practical work carried out in all these spheres by
Bebel as a parliamentarian, agitator and organiser. It
was by this work that Bebel earned his position as the
undisputed and generally accepted leader of the party, the
one who was closest to the working-class masses and most
popular among them.

The last crisis in the German party in which Bebel took
an active part was that of the so-called Bernsteinism. At
the very end of the last century, Bernstein, formerly an
orthodox Marxist, adopted purely reformist, opportunist
views. Attempts were made to turn the working-class party
into a petty-bourgeois party of social reforms. This new
opportunism found many supporters among the function-
aries of the working-class movement and among the intelligentsia.

Bebel expressed the mood of the working-class masses
and their firm conviction that a fight should be put up for
full-blooded slogans, when he revolted with great vigour
against this new opportunism. His speeches against the
opportunists at the congresses in Hanover and Dresden will
long remain as a model of the defence of Marxist views
and of the struggle for the truly socialist character of the
workers' party.[101] The period of preparation and the mustering of working-class forces is in all countries a necessary
stage in the development of the world emancipation struggle
of the proletariat, and nobody can compare with August
Bebel as a brilliant personification of the peculiarities and
tasks of that period. Himself a worker, he proved able to

break his own road to sound socialist convictions and became a model workers' leader, a representative and participant in the mass struggle of the wage-slaves of capital
for a better social system.

Severnaya Pravda No. 6,
        August 8, 1913
        Signed: *V. I.*

Published according to
the *Severnaya Pravda* text

THE SEPARATION OF LIBERALISM
FROM DEMOCRACY

The separation of liberalism from democracy in Russia is one of the basic questions of the entire emancipation movement.

What is the cause of the movement's weakness? Is it because democracy has been *insufficiently* aware and definite in separating from liberalism and has allowed itself to become infected by liberalism's importance and wavering? Or is it because democracy separated from liberalism too soon (or too sharply, etc.) and thus weakened the "force of the common onslaught"?

There can scarcely be anybody interested in the cause of freedom who will argue that this is not a question of fundamental importance. One cannot be a conscious champion of freedom without giving a definite answer to this question. To settle it one must understand which social forces, which classes support liberalism and which support democracy, and what political strivings have their roots in the nature of these classes.

In this article we want to throw some light on this fundamental question from the point of view of current foreign political events. The burning question is naturally that of the Second Balkan War, the defeat of Bulgaria, the Bucharest peace that was so humiliating for her, and Russia's unsuccessful attempt to blame France for not having supported "us", and to obtain a revision of the peace terms.

As we know, *Novoye Vremya* and *Rech* are in agreement about these accusations against France, about this attempt to renew Russia's "active" policy in the Balkans. This means that there is agreement between the feudal landowners and reactionary nationalist ruling circles on the one hand, and the most politically conscious, most organised circles of the liberal bourgeoisie, who have long been gravitating towards an imperialist policy on the other.

Apropos of this, *Kievskaya Mysl*, a provincial newspaper with a large circulation, which expresses the views of certain sections of petty-bourgeois democracy, said the following in a very instructive editorial on August 1:

"It is not that the opposition and nationalism have changed places [as Mr. Milyukov asserted in his well-known foreign policy speech in the Duma] but that liberalism has *separated* [*Kievskaya Mysl*'s italics] from democracy and has entered, at first timidly, with backward glances, and then with head held high, upon the same path, the path of political adventure, along which nationalism leads the way under the same Slavophile banner."

And the newspaper in all justice recalls the generally known facts—how *Rech* displayed "chauvinist enthusiasm", how that newspaper, permeated, in general, with "imperialist tendencies", called for an advance to Armenia, to the Bosphorus.

"Liberalism," said *Kievskaya Mysl*, "by supporting at its own risk Russian foreign policy, which cannot be anything but a reactionary nationalist policy as long as home policy remains such, has also taken upon itself political responsibility for that support."

An incontestable truth. It only has to be fully *analysed*. If it is true that the Russian foreign political line is determined by the line in home policy (and it undoubtedly is), does this refer only to the reactionaries? Obviously not. Obviously it refers to liberalism as well.

Liberalism could not have "separated from democracy" in foreign policy if it was not separated from democracy in home policy. *Kievskaya Mysl* itself has to admit this when it says that "the character of the political mistake of liberalism ... is evidence of profound organic disorders".

That is just it! We should have put it differently—profound class interests of the bourgeoisie—instead of using that somewhat high-sounding and obscure expression. It was these class interests of liberalism that made it fear (especially in 1905) the democratic movement, and that made it turn *to the right* both in home and foreign policy.

It would be ridiculous for anyone to think of denying the connection between Cadet imperialism and chauvinism today and the Cadet-Octobrist slogan to save the Duma in the spring of 1907, between the Cadet vote against local land committees in the spring of 1906 and the Cadet decision to enter the Bulygin Duma[102] in the autumn of 1905. This is the *same* policy of one and the same class, which fears revolution more than it does reaction.

One of the main causes of the weakness of the Russian emancipation movement is the lack of understanding of this truth by the broad sections of the petty bourgeoisie in general, and by petty-bourgeois politicians, writers and ideological leaders in particular.

Contrary to the tales of the liberals who, in order to cover the steps they were taking towards reconciliation with the Rights, pointed to the "implacability" of the Lefts, working-class democrats have never lumped the liberals and Rights together in "one reactionary mass",[103] have never refused *to use* their differences (at the second stage of the Duma elections, for example) in the interests of the emancipation movement. But working-class democrats considered—and must always consider—their task to be one of *neutralising* the wavering liberals, who are capable of becoming "infatuated" with imperialism under Stolypin or Maklakov.

Russian democracy cannot make a serious advance if it does not recognise the deep-going class roots that *separate* liberalism from democracy, if it does not spread the consciousness of this among the *masses*, if it does not learn to neutralise in this way the waverings of the liberals and their betrayals of the cause of "people's freedom". Without this all talk of the successes of the emancipation movement is meaningless.

Severnaya Pravda No. 9,   Published according to
        August 11, 1913   the *Severnaya Pravda* text
        Signed: *V. I.*

A FINE BUSINESS!

There are still many corners of Holy Mother Russia where it is as if serfdom reigned but yesterday. Take the Urals, for example. Landowners there possess tens of thousands of dessiatines of land. The factories (i.e., the same landowners) prevent handicraftsmen from developing small industry. The peasants are still dependent on the landowners and up to now have not been allotted any land.

And the Urals is not a tiny "corner", it is a huge and very rich region.

Litigation between the Stroganov factory workers in the Urals and the management of the factories owned by that very rich landowner over the allotment of land to the peasants according to the law of 1862 (*eighteen sixty-two*!) dragged on for many years.

At last an end was put to the case by a decision of the "supreme institution", the Senate, taken in the spring of 1909. The Senate directed the Perm Gubernia authorities to allot land to the peasants, *to apply* the law of 1862.

Thus, forty-seven years after the promulgation of the law the Senate instructed the landowners to apply it.

And what happened?

What happened was that the landowners lodged a complaint with the landowner Stolypin, who was Minister of the Interior at the time. The Senate is, by law, higher than the Minister of the Interior, but Stolypin "clamped down on the law" and sent the Governor of Perm a telegram—suspend fulfilment of the Senate's instructions!

The Governor suspended it. More correspondence ensued, more red tape.

At last the Council of State agreed with the opinion of the Senate and the decision of the Council of State was "granted supreme sanction", i.e., was confirmed by the highest authority.

And what happened?

What happened was that the landowners applied to the landowner N. A. Maklakov, who had become Minister of the Interior in place of Stolypin. A deputation from the Urals landowners "convinced" the Minister. The Minister declared that the decision of the Senate and the Council of State was "unclear".

More correspondence ensued, more red tape.

In May 1913 the Senate again adopted a decision that was not in the Minister's favour.

The Urals landowners again wrote to the Minister....

That is how the matter still stands. Although more than half a century has elapsed since the promulgation of the law of 1862 allotting land to the Urals workers, the land has not been allotted.

In relating this instructive story the liberal newspapers come to the conclusion that all is not right with the "rule of law" in Russia. That is true, but it is not the whole truth.

It is ridiculous to speak of "law" when the landowners both make the laws and in practice apply or annul them. There is, therefore, a class that itself creates the "law" and itself annuls it. Liberal speeches about "law" and "reforms", therefore, are empty chatter.

The landowners are also in favour of "law", but it is landowners' law, their own law, the law of their class that they favour.

If the liberals still renounce the "theory" of the class struggle, call it a mistake, etc., in face of these instructive facts, it only goes to show that the liberal conscience is not clear. Do not the liberals want to *share* privileges with the landowners? If so, it is understandable that they do not like the "theory" of the class struggle!

But in what way are the workers to blame if their "theory" is proved correct by real events?

Severnaya Pravda No. 14,   Published according to
August 18, 1913   the *Severnaya Pravda* text
Signed: *I*.

THE NATIONALISATION OF JEWISH SCHOOLS

The politics of the government are soaked in the spirit of nationalism. Attempts are made to confer every kind of privilege upon the "ruling", i.e., the Great-Russian nation, even though the Great Russians represent a *minority* of the population of Russia, to be exact, only 43 per cent.

Attempts are made to cut down still further the rights of all the other nations inhabiting Russia, to segregate one from the other and stir up enmity among them.

The extreme expression of present-day nationalism is the scheme for the nationalisation of Jewish schools. The scheme emanated from the educational officer of Odessa district, and has been sympathetically considered by the Ministry of Public "Education". What does this nationalisation mean?

It means segregating the Jews into *special* Jewish schools (secondary schools). The doors of all other educational establishments—both private and state—are to be completely closed to the Jews. This "brilliant" plan is rounded off by the proposal to limit the number of pupils in the Jewish secondary schools to the notorious "quota"!

In all European countries such measures and laws against the Jews existed only in the dark centuries of the Middle Ages, with their Inquisition, the burning of heretics and similar delights. In Europe the Jews have long since been granted complete equality and are fusing more and more with the nations in whose midst they live.

The most harmful feature in our political life generally, and in the above scheme particularly, apart from the oppression and persecution of the Jews, is the striving to fan the flames of nationalism, to segregate the nationalities

20*

in the state one from another, to increase their estrangement, to separate their schools.

The interests of the working class—as well as the interests of political liberty generally—require, on the contrary, the fullest equality of all the nationalities in the state without exception, and the elimination of every kind of barrier between the nations, the bringing together of children of all nations in the same schools, etc. Only by casting off every savage and foolish national prejudice, only by uniting the workers of all nations into one association, can the working class become a force, offer resistance to capitalism, and achieve a serious improvement in its living conditions.

Look at the capitalists! They try to inflame national strife among the "common people", while they themselves manage their business affairs remarkably well—Russians, Ukrainians, Poles, Jews, and Germans together in one and the same corporation. Against the workers the capitalists of all nations and religions are united, but they strive to divide and weaken the workers by national strife!

This most harmful scheme for the nationalisation of the Jewish schools shows, incidentally, how mistaken is the plan for so-called "cultural-national autonomy", i.e., the idea of taking education out of the hands of the state and handing it over to each nation separately. It is not this we should strive for, but for the unity of the workers of all nations in the struggle against *all* nationalism, in the struggle for a truly democratic *common* school and for political liberty generally. The example of the advanced countries of the world—say, Switzerland in Western Europe or Finland in Eastern Europe—shows us that only consistently-democratic state institutions ensure the most peaceable and human (not bestial) coexistence of various nationalities, *without* the artificial and harmful separation of education according to nationalities.

Severnaya Pravda No. 14,
August 18, 1913
Signed: *V. I.*

Published according to
the *Severnaya Pravda* text

IRON ON PEASANT FARMS

Promyshlennost i Torgovlya, the organ of our industrial millionaires, the organ of the Council of Congresses, recently gave vent to a sort of foolishly hypocritical or hypocritically foolish sigh because Russia turns out to be the neighbour of one of the most backward countries, Spain, as far as the per capita consumption of the most important items of production is concerned.

With regard to iron, one of the most important products of modern industry, one of the foundations of civilisation, one might say, Russia's backwardness and barbarism is particularly great.

"A cart with iron tyres is still a rarity in the Russian countryside," the organ of the millionaires admitted.

However, on the question of whether this cultural "rarity" in the Russian village depends on the *incidence* of serf relations and the omnipotence of the feudal landowners (on whom the "aces" of Russian capitalism fawn), the millionaires maintain a modest silence.

We greatly love to chatter about culture, about the development of productive forces, about improving the peasant farm, and so on, and we are past masters at it. Yet whenever it comes to removing the stone that lies in the way of "improving the lot" of millions of impoverished, downtrodden, hungry, ragged, savage peasants, our millionaires become tongue-tied.

Here are some figures from Hungarian agricultural statistics that clearly show the significance the oppression of the peasantry by the landowners has in regard to the extent to which iron is used, *that is*, in regard to the solidity of the iron foundation of culture in the country concerned.

Hungary, of course, is the country closest to Russia, not only geographically, but on account of the omnipotence of the reactionary landowners, who have retained a tremendous quantity of land from medieval times.

In Germany, for instance, there are 23,000 properties out of 5,500,000 that are more than 100 hectares in extent and together they make up less than a quarter of the total land area; in Hungary there are 24,000 such properties out of 2,800,000 and they make up 45 per cent of the country's total land area! Four thousand Hungarian landowners have more than a thousand dessiatines each, and together they own almost *a third* of all the land. As you can see that is not far removed from "Mother Russia".

Hungarian statistics (1895) made a particularly detailed investigation of the question of iron on peasant farms. It was shown that out of 2,800,000 farms, *a million and a half* belonging to labourers (or proletarians, with up to 5 Joch or 2.85 dessiatines) and also *one million* small peasant farms (up to 20 Joch, that is, up to 11 dessiatines) have to make do with *wooden* implements.

These 2,500,000 farms (out of a total of 2,800,000) no doubt use mainly ploughs with a wooden shaft, harrows with wooden frames and on almost half of them the carts in use are without iron tyres.

There are no complete figures for Russia. The figures available for separate localities show that the poverty, primitiveness and neglect on most Russian peasant farms are incomparably greater than on Hungarian farms.

And it cannot be otherwise. If the tyred cart is not to be a rarity there must be a free, educated, bold farmer who is capable of dealing with the feudal landowners, who is capable of getting away from routine methods and has all the land in the state at his disposal. "Culture" is as much to be expected of the peasant who is still oppressed by the Markovs and Purishkeviches with their landed estates, as humanity is to be expected of the Saltykovas.[104]

The millionaires of our industry prefer to share medieval privileges with the Purishkeviches and to sigh about the deliverance of "the fatherland" from medieval lack of culture....

Severnaya Pravda No. 16,
August 21, 1913
Signed: *N. N.*

Published according to
the *Severnaya Pravda* text

METALWORKERS' STRIKES IN 1912

The Association of Factory Owners in the Moscow Industrial Area has this year published (Moscow, 1913, P. P.
Ryabushinsky's Press) something in the nature of a report
on its activities for 1912. Perhaps the most interesting
part of the report is that giving data on the strike movement in various parts of Russia.

I

The total number of strikers in Russia is estimated by
the Association of Moscow Factory Owners as 96,750 in
1911 and 211,595 in 1912. These figures are for economic
strikes *only*. The Association estimates political strikes as
affecting 850,000 workers in 1912, 8,000 in 1911 and 4,000
in 1910.

Note that "for convenient comparison with official information", which does not cover enterprises not under the
Factory Inspectorate, the Association of Moscow magnates
has omitted the 6,000 Lena strikers. It goes without saying
that we still have no guarantee that such a comparison has
been done correctly—the factory owners decided to copy the
bad aspects of our official statistics and not worry about
the completeness of their data or even about the accuracy
of those who compiled them. The summary table of the
number of strikers (page 23 of the report), for instance,
is astonishingly full of crude errors, which we have endeavoured to correct in giving the totals quoted above. That
table assessed the metalworkers participating in strikes
in the Kingdom of Poland *for the whole of* 1912 as 2,390,
and on page 56 we are told that for *seven months* of 1912

a total of 3,790 metalworkers took part in strikes in the Kingdom of Poland!

One cannot help wishing that our Kit Kityches would hire writers able to count or would send their statistics to workers' trade unions to be checked and corrected.

Let us see what role the metalworkers played in the economic strike movement of 1912 according to the factory owners' statistics.

These data distribute the total number of strikers, 211,595, as follows: metalworkers, 78,195; textile workers, 89,540; workers of all other branches of industry, 43,860. Since there are far fewer metalworkers than textile workers in Russia, these figures show immediately that in 1912 the *metalworkers* conducted a most stubborn and persistent strike struggle as compared with workers in other branches of industry. To give this conclusion clearer expression, let us compare the total number of workers in Russia with the number of strikers in 1912.

	Total number of workers in Russia according to statistics		Number of strikers in 1912 (according to the factory owners' data)
	1908 (including miners)	1910 (excluding miners)	
Metalworkers	529,274	280,194	78,195
Textile workers	823,401	840,520	89,540
Others	901,112	831,241	43,860
Totals	2,253,787	1,951,955	211,595

These data show clearly that the metalworkers hold first place for the vigorous nature of their strike struggle; the second place is held by the textile workers, and the workers in other branches of industry take last place.

If the "other" workers had been as energetic in striking as the metalworkers, the number of strikers would have been increased by some 90,000.

There is no doubt that the relatively more favourable market conditions in 1912 facilitated the strike struggle of the metalworkers, but, although the metalworkers outdid everyone else in persistence, the "others", as we shall see later, fared best of all as far as *success* of the economic strikes was concerned.

II

The persistence of the strike struggle is determined, among other things, by the average duration of the strikes. This average is obtained by dividing the total number of days lost through strikes by the number of strikers.

Here are the figures given by the Association of Factory Owners:

	Average duration of strike
1895-1904	4.8 days
1909	6.5　"
1911	8.2　"
1912	13.4　"

"It turns out that the resistance of the workers," says the report, "was almost twice as great in 1912 as that of 1911." To this we must add that if we take the last seven months of 1912 (and, indeed, only for this period are the data in the report under review reasonably well processed), we get an average of *16 days* as the length of a strike.

It therefore follows that the stubbornness of the workers in the strike struggle is undoubtedly increasing and is becoming greater as time goes on.

The duration of the strikes in the different branches of industry was as follows:

	1911	1912	The last seven months of 1912
Metalworkers	10.0 days	14.2 days	18.8 days
Textile workers	9.2　"	11.9　"	14.0　"
Others	5.0　"	15.6　"	16.8　"
All industries	8.2　"	13.4　"	16.0　"

From this we see that as far as concerns the duration of strikes, metalworkers held first place in 1911 and in the second half of 1912; it was only in the first half of 1912 that the "others" took first place and the metalworkers found themselves in the second place. Throughout the whole of the period under review the textile workers have been in the second place as far as the duration of their strikes is concerned.

The factory owners assess the general outcome of the strikes by a computation of "*losses* to industry" from strikes. Our capitalists do not wish to compute what the working class has gained through strikes! Here is a summary of the factory owners' statistics:

Branches of industry	Direct losses to industry from strikes (economic)	Loss of workers' wages	Loss to country in underproduction
	(thousand rubles)		
Metal	558	1,145	4,959
Textiles	479	807	6,010
Others	328	529	3,818
Totals for 1912	1,365	2,481	14,787
" " 1911	402	716	4,563

We see from this table that in 1912 the capitalists' losses were *three times* greater than in 1911.

Representatives of bourgeois political economy will object—but, they will say, did not the "country" lose three times as much and were not the workers' wage losses three times as much, and are not the workers' losses in wages of more significance than the factory owners' losses?

According to factory owners' statistics, and bourgeois logic, too, these foolish workers are only doing themselves harm with their strikes, and the solicitous authorities and capitalist benefactors who persecute them for striking are only acting in the interests of the workers....

The same factory owners tell us that they have succeeded in assessing the results of the 1911 strikes in respect of 96,730 strikers.

In the strike struggle 47,369 workers (49 per cent) were *defeated* and 49,361 (51 per cent) achieved the complete or partial *satisfaction* of their demands, i.e., were successful.

This is the result of strikes that factory owners' statistics and bourgeois economy prefer not to take into account! And, indeed, it cannot be reckoned in rubles, for apart from the workers' direct gain in increased wages when a strike is successful, there is still another "gain". The entire working class, and, therefore, the entire *country* (the country of the working masses and not of the bourgeois minority) gains from the resistance offered by striking workers to the exploiters. Without that resistance the workers would have become downright paupers, crushed by the high cost of living; without that resistance they would be transformed from human beings into the hopeless slaves of capital.

According to the factory owners' statistics, strikes were less successful in the second half of 1912; 52 per cent of the workers on strike suffered *defeat*, only 36 per cent were *successful*, and for 11 per cent the outcome was not determined. At this point we must make a more thorough examination of the role of striking metalworkers in Russia in general and in the various districts in particular.

IV

The Association of Moscow Factory Owners provides fairly well processed information on strikes, as we have said, only for the last seven months of 1912. The information covers five areas of Russia—the Moscow, St. Petersburg, Baltic and Southern areas, and the Kingdom of Poland.

The metalworkers striking during these months are distributed by areas as follows:

Area	Number of strikers in the last seven months of 1912	
	Total	Metalworkers
Moscow	48,140	3,760
St. Petersburg	35,390	15,160
Baltic	13,210	1,160
Southern	22,195	16,605
Kingdom of Poland	12,690	3,790
Totals	131,625	40,475

In the Southern area, therefore, metalworkers predominate among the total number of strikers. In the St. Petersburg area they constitute a very significant section of the strikers (over 40 per cent) and are second only to the textile workers (16,770 strikers in the St. Petersburg area). In the Moscow, Baltic and Polish areas, the metalworkers were but a small minority among the strikers.

By comparing the first five months of 1912 with the last seven months we get:

	Number of strikers:	
	First 5 months	Last 7 months
	1912	
Metalworkers	37,720	40,475
Textile workers . . .	22,950	66,590
Others	19,300	24,560
Totals	79,970	131,625

In the second half of the year the vigour with which the metalworkers engaged in strikes was somewhat less—the strike movement greatly increased among the textile workers while that of workers in other branches of industry remained at approximately the same level.

V

To assess the outcome of strikes the Moscow Association of Factory Owners divides strikers into three groups—those defeated, those successful (whose demands were wholly or partially acceded to) and those whose strikes ended without definite results.

This is one of the most interesting of all questions of strike statistics. The millionaires' association has handled the question badly; for example, there are no data on offensive strikes (when the workers demand an *improvement* in their living and working conditions) and defensive strikes (when workers resist changes introduced by the capitalists *worsening* living and working conditions). Nor is there any detailed information on the causes of strikes (such information is given even in our official statistics), etc.

The way the Association of Moscow Factory Owners have handled what information they do give is, furthermore, extremely unsatisfactory. There are even obvious cases of out-and-out distortion of figures; in the Moscow area, for instance, the number of metalworkers successful in strikes is assessed at 40 (with 3,420 defeated and 300 with undetermined results).

But in the letterpress of the report, page 35, we find that at the beginning of July 1912, there was a strike of workers in a number of art metalware workshops involving *more than 1,200 workers* in 15 enterprises. It was an offensive strike—the workers demanded a nine-hour day with a seven-hour day on the eve of holidays, as well as higher wages and better sanitary conditions. The owners of the workshops tried to organise resistance and decided unanimously not to make concessions and not to accept orders from the shops on strike. The workers had apparently chosen a favourable moment—it was the height of the building season, "it was hard to find unengaged workers. *By the end of July the owners of the majority of workshops made concessions".*

This is what the report says! And in the statistical table the number of metalworkers winning strikes is shown ,as 40 (*forty*!). One begins to wonder whether the factory owners' statisticians were not only too willing "to forget" the *victories* of the workers. Did they not strive—unwittingly, of course—to please the Kit Kityches by understating the number of victorious workers?

In any case, organised, class-conscious workers must approach the factory owners' statistics with caution and scepticism and must persist in their attempts to compile *their own,* workers' strike statistics.

The overall figures on the outcome of strikes given by the factory owners are:

Number of strikers	Metal-workers	Textile workers	Others	Totals
Defeated	19,990	43,085	7,150	70,225
Successful	17,860	20,285	9,520	47,665
Outcome unknown . . .	2,625	3,220	7,890	13,735
Totals	40,475	66,590	24,560	131,625

We see from this that the most successful of all were workers in *other* branches of industry—*more* workers won their strikes than lost them. Second place is held by the metalworkers; the number of successful strikers is nevertheless very considerable—over 40 per cent of the total. The textile workers had the worst results—their losses were more than twice as great as their gains.

VI

Taking them by and large, the results of the strike struggle in 1912 were not bad, although they were not so good as those of 1911. To make it easier to compare the data for different years let us divide the number of strikers, the outcome of whose strikes is unknown, equally between the successful and unsuccessful strikers. In this way we obtain for the last seven months of 1912, a total of 77,000 unsuccessful (i.e., 58.4 per cent) and 55,000 successful (i.e., 41.6 per cent) strikers out of 132,000.

It cannot be guaranteed that these figures are identical in kind with those of official statistics for previous years. We shall, however, quote these figures so that workers will be able to judge the *general* outcome of strikes in Russia in the best and worst years of the working-class movement.

| | Number of strikers (thousands) | | | | |
	Suc-cessful	%	Unsuc-cessful	%	Totals
1895-1904 (total for ten years)	159	37.5	265	62.5	424
1905	705	48.9	734	51.1	1,439
1906	233	50.9	225	49.1	458
1907	59	29.5	141	70.5	200
1908	—	—	—	—	—
1909	—	—	—	—	—
1910	—	—	—	—	—
1911	49	51.0	47	49.0	96
1912 (seven months)	55	41.6	77	58.4	132

Thus, the results of the strikes in the second half of 1912 were *not so good* as those of 1905, 1906, and 1911 but *better* than those of 1895-1904 and *better* than those of 1907. We must repeat that the figures at our disposal for the various years are probably not fully comparable, but they can give some idea of the situation.

Let it be noted that according to British strike statistics for the ten years 1900-09 the average annual percentage of workers winning strikes was 26.8, defeated 31.7, and ending their strikes in a compromise 41.3. If the last figure is divided equally between successful and unsuccessful strikers we get: *successful*, 47.5 per cent, *unsuccessful*, 52.3 per cent. Strikes in Russia in 1905 and 1906, and again in 1911, were more successful than the average British strikes despite the tremendous advantages possessed by the British workers in respect of organisation and political liberty.

VII

It is rather interesting to compare the results of metal-workers' strikes in different parts of Russia.

The Moscow and St. Petersburg areas differ from all others in this respect. The strikes of both metalworkers and all other workers were, in general, relatively unsuccessful in the last seven months of 1912 in the Moscow and St. Petersburg areas. The opposite is true of other areas.

Here are the figures for the Moscow and St. Petersburg areas.

	Number of striking metalworkers in the last seven months of 1912	
	Moscow area	St. Petersburg area
Defeated	3,420	10,840
Successful	40	4,170
Outcome unknown	300	150
Totals	3,760	15,160

The number of defeated is much greater than the number of successful strikers. The same is true of the textile workers in both areas and of "the others" in St. Petersburg. Only in the Moscow area did "the others" show a greater number of successful (4,380) than unsuccessful strikers (1,230).

Apparently there were certain general conditions in the Moscow and St. Petersburg districts that were unfavourable to workers' strikes in nearly all branches of industry.

In the South, on the contrary, and in the Baltic and Polish districts, the strikes of all workers in general, and of metalworkers in particular, were successful.

| | Number of striking metalworkers in the last seven months of 1912 | | |
	South	Baltic area	Kingdom of Poland
Defeated	4,390	440	900
Successful	10,040	720	2,890
Outcome unknown	2,175	—	—
Totals	16,605	1,160	3,790

The metalworkers had their greatest success in Poland; in general, the economic conditions for a strike movement in that district turned out most favourable for the workers. They were successful there in *all* branches of industry (in the South "the others" suffered a defeat and in the Baltic area the textile workers' struggle ended in "a draw"—there were 1,485 each successful and unsuccessful strikers). Even the textile workers, who were, in general, most severely defeated throughout Russia in the second half of 1912 (43,000 defeated and 20,000 successful) scored a brilliant victory in the Kingdom of Poland—only 390 defeated as compared with 8,060 successful.

In the West and South of Russia the workers attacked the capitalists and scored big victories; in Moscow and St. Petersburg they also attacked but in most cases their attacks were warded off. Unfortunately, the data we are analysing are too scanty to permit a comparison with 1911 and it is impossible to draw a definite conclusion as to the causes of the difference.

VIII

As we have seen, the metalworkers come first as far as the persistence of their strikes is concerned and the textile workers are in the last place. It is interesting to compare

the persistence of the successful strikes of metalworkers
with that of the unsuccessful. Here are the figures:

	Number of metalworker strikers	Number of days lost (thousands)	Average number of days lost per striker
Defeated	19,990	230.7	11.5
Successful	17,860	387.3	21.7
Outcome unknown	2,625	145.3	55.4
Totals	40,475	763.3	18.8

We see that the distinguishing feature of successful metalworkers' strikes is that they were almost twice as persistent as the unsuccessful strikes (21.7 days as compared
with 11.5 days). Victory was not easily achieved. Only by
tremendous vigour and persistence was it possible to break
the resistance of the capitalists. The strikes whose outcome
was not clearly defined were apparently those in which
the strength of the "contestants" was more or less equal and
the struggle was extraordinarily stubborn; the average
length of strikes leading to indefinite results was 55.4 days.

Be it noted that among "the other" workers we also observe greater stubbornness in successful strikes and among
textile workers we see the opposite—the unsuccessful strikes
of the latter were the most stubborn.

A comparison of the persistence of metalworkers' strikes
in the different areas of Russia gives the following results:

	Average length of strikes per striking metalworker				
	Moscow area	St. Petersburg area	Baltic area	South	Kingdom of Poland
Defeated	11.5	12.1	5.9	12.0	5.2
Successful	7.5	37.2	23.7	14.9	22.4
Outcome unknown . . .	12.0	261.3	—	47.1	—
Totals	11.5	21.4	17.0	18.4	18.3

First place for duration of strikes among the metalworkers in general is taken by the St. Petersburg area; next
comes the South, then the Polish and Baltic areas and,

lastly, the Moscow area. With the exception of the Moscow area all other successful strikes were more stubborn than the unsuccessful.

Judging by the persistence of their strikes and also by the percentage of workers participating in the strike struggle, the St. Petersburg metalworkers play the role of vanguard to the metalworkers of all Russia. And the metalworkers in general play the same role to the workers of the other branches of industry.

IX

Extreme brevity is the distinguishing feature of the descriptions of individual strikes in the report by the Moscow Association of Factory Owners. We shall quote a few of these descriptions so that metalworkers may see *how* the gentlemen who compile reports for factory owners depict their struggle.

In the Moscow area the strike of 1,200 workers in art metalware workshops is a remarkable case. We have already mentioned this.

The factory owners regard the strike at Siemens and Halske, lasting 14 weeks and ending on August 19, as one of the most stubborn in the St. Petersburg area. The Factory Owners' Association reports that 1,600 workers took part. The factory management did not agree to withdraw the fine imposed for May Day but "in exchange expressed the wish to pay the workers a Christmas bonus of three rubles. Then the factory management agreed to include May Day in the list of holidays if the government did not put any obstacles in the way" (page 38 of the report). "During the strike," we read in the report, "there were several cases of workers attacking the newly employed with the help of whom work was partially resumed."

Most noteworthy of the metalworkers' strikes in the South was that of 3,886 Nikolayev shipyard workers that caused the loss of more than 155,000 working days. The workers demanded the eight-hour day, a fifty per cent increase in wages, the annulment of fines and all overtime, and the institution of elected shop stewards, etc. The strike lasted all the month of June. "At the end of June an agreement was reached between the workers and the shipyard management under which all workers returned to their places; the shipyard recognised the shop stewards, a messroom was opened and wages were increased by 18 per cent." There were clashes between strikers and blacklegs.

The strike that broke out at a locomotive works in Kharkov in November involving 2,000 workers was exceptionally stubborn. The works had urgent government orders to fulfil and "suffered heavy losses on account of the stoppage".

Among the strikes in the Urals area, which were *completely omitted* from the Association of Factory Owners' statistics, we must make special mention of the strike at the Sysert factories. The workers won a wage increase. "At the government munitions factory in Zlatoust the strike was caused by the death of three workers from injuries inflicted by machines. The strikers demanded the installation of safety devices and also an increase in wages."

X

Even a cursory glance at the scanty figures provided by the factory owners' statistics must reveal the following.

Strike statistics that are complete, accurate, intelligently processed and published in good time have tremendous importance, both theoretical and practical, for the workers. They provide valuable information that illuminates every step of the great road the working class is travelling towards its world-wide goals, and also the closer, current tasks of the struggle.

In countries that are to some extent democratic and free, tolerable government statistics are possible. This is out of the question in Russia. Our government statistics are poor, they are absurdly split up among "departments", they are unreliable and their publication is delayed. The factory owners' statistics are little better and still less complete, although sometimes they are published somewhat earlier than those of the sleepy Russian civil servant.

The workers must consider producing *their own*, workers' strike statistics. The difficulties involved in compiling such statistics are, of course, exceedingly great in view of the persecution of workers' associations and the working-class press in Russia. It is impossible to overcome these difficulties at once. Workers, however, are not accustomed to showing fear of persecution or retreating in face of difficulties.

Even partial strike statistics by workers, i.e., those that cover separate areas, separate branches of industries and relatively short periods, will be of great value. Such statistics will teach the workers how to compile something fuller and better and will at times enable them to compare the factory owners' or civil servants' picture with their own.

We therefore permit ourselves to conclude this analysis of factory owners' statistics with the wish that workers should, despite all the obstacles, again and again attempt to compile their own, workers' strike statistics. Two or three class-conscious workers could compile an accurate description of each strike, the time it begins and ends, the number of participants (with distribution according to sex and age wherever possible), the causes and the results of the strike. Such a description should be sent in one copy to the headquarters of the workers' association concerned (trade union or other body, or the office of the trade union newspaper); a second copy should be sent to the central workers' newspaper; lastly, a third copy should be sent to a working-class deputy of the State Duma for his information.

Both factory owners' and government statistics will *always* contain not only gaps but also distortions. Even in the press that sympathises with the workers we often come across monstrously false, absurd appraisals of strikes as manifestations of "a craze", etc., appraisals permeated with the bourgeois spirit.

Only by getting down to business themselves will the workers—in time, after stubborn work and persistent effort—be able to help towards a better understanding of their own movement and thus ensure bigger successes for that movement.

Metallist Nos. 7,8 and 10;
August 24, September 18,
and October 25, 1913
Signed: V. *Ilyin*   Published according to
the *Metallist* text

THE RUSSIAN BOURGEOISIE AND RUSSIAN REFORMISM

The working-class press has already reported and given its appraisal of the appeal to the Prime Minister made by Mr. Salazkin in Nizhni-Novgorod on behalf of the merchants of Russia in respect of the "urgent necessity" for radical political reforms. It is, however, worth while returning to the subject on account of two important circumstances.

How rapidly the United Nobility and the merchants of Russia have exchanged roles! For forty years or more, prior to 1905, the nobility played at liberalism and made respectful references to a constitution, while the merchants seemed more satisfied, less oppositional.

After 1905 the situation was reversed. The nobility turned arch-reactionary. The June Third constitution left them quite satisfied and they desired changes only insofar as they were farther to the right. The merchants, on the contrary, became a definitely liberal opposition.

All at once Russia became, as it were, "Europeanised", i.e., fitted into the usual European relations between feudals and bourgeoisie. It stands to reason that this happened only because purely capitalist relations had long been the basis of political grouping in Russia. They had been maturing since 1861 and rapidly reached full maturity in the fires of 1905. All the Narodnik phraseology about Russia's fundamental exceptionalism and all attempts to argue about Russian politics and Russian economics from a supra-class or extra-class position immediately lost all their interest and became boring, inept, ridiculously old-fashioned rubbish.

A step forward has been made; the harmful self-deception has been got rid of; the childish hope of achieving anything worth while and serious without class battles has been got rid of. Take the side of one class or another, help the consciousness and development of one class policy or another—such is the stern but useful lesson taught in an affirmative form by the year 1905 and confirmed in a negative form by the experience of the June Third system.

The extra-class nonsense of the liberal intellectuals and petty-bourgeois Narodniks has been swept aside from the path of history. And a good thing too. It should have been done long ago!

On the other hand, take a look at the reformism of the liberal merchants of Russia. They announce the "urgent necessity for the reforms" recorded in the Manifesto of October Seventeenth. Everybody knows that the Manifesto speaks of "the unshakable foundations of civil liberty", "real inviolability of person", "freedom of conscience, speech, assembly and association", and also "the further development of the principle of universal franchise".

Obviously, this is really a list of radical political reforms. Obviously, the implementation of even one of those reforms alone would constitute a great change for the better.

And now *all* the merchants of Russia, economically the most powerful class in capitalist Russia, demand *all* these reforms. Why is it that these demands have been treated by everyone with complete indifference, why does everyone think they lack seriousness—everyone, from the Prime Minister who listened to them, ate and drank, replied, expressed his thanks and went away, down to that Moscow merchant who said that Salazkin's words were excellent but would not amount to anything?

Why is this?

It is because Russia is in that peculiar historical situation, which for a long time the big European states have not experienced (but which, at some time or other, occurred in each one of them), when reformism is particularly dull, ridiculous, impotent and, therefore, repellent. There is no doubt that the implementation of any of the reforms demanded by the merchants—either freedom of conscience or freedom of association or any other freedom—would mean a great change for the better. Every advanced class—first and foremost the working class—would grasp with both hands the slightest reformist possibility of effecting any change for the better.

That is a simple truth that the opportunists just cannot understand when they make such a fuss about their sapient "partial demands", although the example of the excellent way the workers seized upon the "partial" (though real) insurance reform should have been a lesson to everybody.

But the point is that there is nothing *"real"* in the reformism of the liberals as far as political reforms are concerned. In other words—everybody knows full well, both the merchants and the Octobrist-Cadet majority in the Duma, that there is not and cannot be the tiniest reformist path to any one of the reforms demanded by Salazkin. Everybody knows, understands and feels it.

For this reason there is more historical realism, historical reality and efficacy in a simple indication of the absence of a reformist path than there is in widely-broadcast, inflated, high-sounding nonsense about any reforms you like. He who knows that there is no reformist path and passes that knowledge on to others is doing a thousand times more *in deed* to utilise insurance and any other "possibility" for purposes of democratic progress than those who chatter about reforms and do not believe what they themselves say.

The truth that reforms are possible only as a by-product of a movement that is completely free of all the narrowness of reformism has been confirmed a hundred times in world history and is *particularly* true for Russia today. That is why liberal reformism is so dead. That is why the contempt for reformism on the part of democrats and of the working class is so much alive.

Severnaya Pravda No. 21,
August 27, 1913;
Nash Put No. 3,
August 28, 1913
Signed: *V. Ilyin*

Published according to
the *Severnaya Pravda* text

THE ROLE OF SOCIAL ESTATES AND CLASSES
IN THE LIBERATION MOVEMENT

Statistical data on crimes against the state in Russia have been published in a legal journal. The statistics are very instructive, they provide precise figures on the question of the role of the social estates and classes in the liberation movement at different historical epochs.

Unfortunately, the data are incomplete. The epochs dealt with are: 1827-46 (the epoch of serfdom); 1884-90 (the epoch of the *raznochintsi** movement, the merging of the bourgeois-liberal and liberal-Narodnik movements). Lastly there is the epoch immediately preceding the revolution (1901-03) and the revolutionary epoch (1905-08), that is, the epochs of the bourgeois-democratic and proletarian movements.

The figures on the role played by the social estates are the following; out of one hundred persons charged with crimes against the state there were:

Epoch	Nobility	Urban petty bourgeoisie and peasants	Clergy	Merchants
1827-46	76	23	?	?
1884-90	30.6	46.6	6.4	12.1
1901-03	10.7	80.9	1.6	4.1
1905-08	9.1	87.7	?	?

From these figures it can be seen how rapidly the nineteenth-century liberation movement became democratised

---

* *Raznochintsi* (sing. *raznochinets*)—professional class not drawn from the nobility many of whom took part in the revolutionary democratic movement.—*Ed.*

and how sharply its class composition changed. The epoch of serfdom (1827-46) saw the absolute predominance of the nobility. That is the epoch from the Decembrists to Herzen. Feudal Russia is downtrodden and motionless. An insignificant minority of the nobility, helpless without the support of the people, protested. But these, the best of the nobility, helped *to awaken* the people.

In the epoch of the *raznochintsi* or the bourgeois-liberal epoch (1884-90), the nobility were already a smaller group in the liberation movement. If, however, we add to them the clergy and merchants we get 49 per cent, i.e., *almost a half.* The movement still remains half a movement of the privileged classes—of the nobility and the top-level bourgeoisie. Hence the impotence of the movement, despite the heroism of individuals.

The third (1901-03) and fourth (1905-08) epochs are those of the peasant and proletarian democrats. The role of the nobility is a very small one. The urban petty bourgeoisie and the peasantry make up eight-tenths of the whole before the revolution and nine-tenths during the revolution. The masses have awakened. Hence the two results: (1) the possibility of obtaining something of a serious nature and (2) the liberals' hatred of the movement (the appearance of counter-revolutionary liberalism).

Still more interesting are the data on occupations, available only for the last three epochs. Out of each hundred participants in the liberation movement (charged with state crimes) there are people engaged in:

Epoch	Agriculture	Industry and commerce	Liberal professions and students	No definite occupation or no occupation
1884-90	7.1	15.1	53.3	19.9
1901-03	9.0	46.1	28.7	8.0
1905-08	24.2	47.4	22.9	5.5

These are extraordinarily instructive figures. The role of the *raznochintsi* in the epoch of the Narodniks and the Narodnaya Volya Party (1884-90) is immediately revealed; the *majority* of the participants (53.3 per cent) were students or people following liberal professions. A mixed bourgeois-liberal and liberal-Narodnik movement with students and intellectuals playing an outstanding role—such is the class essence of the parties and the movement of that time. The peasants ("agriculture") and industrial workers ("industry and commerce") provided a small minority (7 and 15 per cent). The so-called declassed people, that is, those who have been squeezed out of their own class and have lost contact with any definite class—this group of people constitutes *one-fifth* (19.9 per cent), they are more numerous than the peasants and more numerous than the workers!

This accounts for the peculiar forms taken by the movement, the magnificence of its heroism, and its impotence.

Then we come to the pre-revolutionary epoch (1901-03). The leading role is played by the urban workers ("industry and commerce"). Although they were a minority of the population they provided *almost a half* (46.1 per cent) of the participants. The intelligentsia and the students were *already* in the second place (despite the fables of the liberals and liquidators about the workers' party). The role of the peasants was insignificant ("agriculture" 9 per cent) but was growing.

The last epoch, 1905-08. The proportion of the urban workers increased from 46.1 to 47.4 per cent. They had already aroused the peasant masses, whose share in the movement increased more than that of all other classes—from 9 to 24.2 per cent, that is, by *almost three times*. The peasantry had now outstripped the liberal intellectuals and the students (22.9 per cent). The role of the declassed elements, those who had been ejected from their own class, was very insignificant (5.5 per cent). The deliberately libellous character of the liberal theory on the "intellectual" nature of our revolution here stands out in bold relief.

The proletariat and bourgeois democrats (the peasantry)—these were the social forces of the movement. But the peasantry, who constitute an overwhelming majority of the population as compared with the workers and town dwellers, lagged a long way behind and provided only *a quarter* (24.2 per cent) of the participants because so far they had been only slightly aroused.

All that remains is to end on a note of praise for the June Third (Stolypin) agrarian policy that is very successfully, rapidly and energetically arousing the others....

Severnaya Pravda No. 22,
  August 28, 1913;
  Nash Put No. 4,
  August 29, 1913
  Signed: *V. Ilyin*

Published according to
the *Severnaya Pravda* text

CLASS WAR IN DUBLIN

In Dublin, the capital of Ireland—a city of a not highly industrial type, with a population of half a million—the class struggle, which permeates the whole life of capitalist society everywhere, has become accentuated to the point of class war. The police have positively gone wild; drunken policemen assault peaceful workers, break into houses, torment the aged, women and children. Hundreds of workers (over 400) have been injured and *two killed*—such are the casualties of this war. All prominent workers' leaders have been arrested. People are thrown into prison for making the most peaceful speeches. The city is like an armed camp.

What has happened? How could such a war have flared up in a peaceable, cultured, civilised free state?

Ireland is something of a British Poland, only rather more like Galicia than the Poland represented by Warsaw, Lodz and Dombrowski. National oppression and Catholic reaction have turned the proletarians of this unhappy country into paupers, the peasants into toilworn, ignorant and dull slaves of the priesthood, and the bourgeoisie into a phalanx, masked by nationalist phrases, of capitalists, of despots over the workers; finally, the administration has been turned into a gang accustomed to every kind of violence.

At the present moment the Irish nationalists (i.e., the Irish bourgeoisie) are the victors. They are buying up the lands of the English landlords; they are getting national *self-government* (the famous Home Rule for which such a long and stubborn struggle has been going on between Ireland and England); they will freely govern "their own" country jointly with "their own" Irish priests.

Well, this Irish nationalist bourgeoisie is celebrating its "national" victory, its maturity in "affairs of state" by declaring a war to the death on the Irish labour movement.

An English Lord-Lieutenant lives in Dublin, but in fact he has less power than the Dublin capitalist leader, a certain Murphy, publisher of the *Independent* ("Independent"—my eye!), principal shareholder and director of the Dublin tramways, and a shareholder in many capitalist enterprises in Dublin. Murphy has declared, on behalf of all the Irish capitalists, of course, that he is ready to spend three-quarters of a million pounds (nearly seven million rubles) to destroy the Irish trade unions.

And these unions have begun to develop magnificently. The Irish proletariat, awakening to class-consciousness, is pressing the Irish bourgeois scoundrels engaged in celebrating their "national" victory. It has found a talented leader in the person of Comrade *Larkin*, Secretary of the Irish Transport Workers' Union. Larkin is a remarkable speaker, a man of seething Irish energy, who has performed miracles among the unskilled workers—that mass of the British proletariat which in Britain is so often cut off from the advanced workers by the cursed petty-bourgeois, liberal, aristocratic spirit of the British skilled worker.

A new spirit has been aroused in the Irish workers' unions. The unskilled workers have brought unparralleled animation into the trade unions. Even the women have begun to organise—a thing hitherto unknown in Catholic Ireland. So far as organisation of the workers is concerned Dublin looks like becoming one of the foremost towns in the whole of Great Britain. The country that used to be typified by the fat, well-fed Catholic priest and the poor, starving, ragged worker who wore his rags even on Sunday because he could not afford Sunday clothes, that country, though it bears a double and triple national yoke, has begun to turn into a country with an organised army of the proletariat.

Well, Murphy proclaimed a crusade of the bourgeoisie against Larkin and "Larkinism". To begin with, 200 tramwaymen were dismissed in order to provoke a strike during the exhibition and *embitter* the whole struggle. The Transport Workers' Union declared a strike and demanded the reinstatement of the discharged men. Murphy engineered lock-outs. The workers retaliated by downing tools. War raged all along the line. Passions flared up.

Larkin—incidentally, he is the grandson of the famous Larkin executed in 1867 for participating in the Irish liberation movement—delivered fiery speeches at meetings. In these speeches he pointed out that the party of the English bourgeois enemies of Irish Home Rule was openly calling for resistance to the government, was threatening revolution, was organising armed resistance to Home Rule and with absolute impunity was flooding the country with revolutionary appeals.

But what the reactionaries, the *English* chauvinists Carson, Londonderry and Bonar Law (the English Purishkeviches, the nationalists who are persecuting Ireland), may do the proletarian socialist may not. Larkin was arrested. A meeting called by the workers was banned.

Ireland, however, is not Russia. The attempt to suppress the right of assembly evoked a storm of indignation. Larkin *had to be* tried. At the trial Larkin became the accuser and, in effect, put Murphy in the dock. By cross-questioning witnesses Larkin proved that Murphy had had long conversations with the Lord-Lieutenant on the eve of his, Larkin's, arrest. Larkin declared the police to be in Murphy's pay, and no one dared gainsay him.

Larkin was released on bail (political liberty cannot be abolished at one stroke). Larkin declared that he would appear at a meeting no matter what happened. And indeed, he came to one disguised, and began to speak to the crowd. The police recognised him, seized him and beat him up. For two days the dictatorship of the police truncheon raged, crowds were clubbed, women and children were brutally treated. The police broke into workers' homes. A worker named *Nolan*, a member of the Transport Workers' Union, was beaten to death. Another died of injuries.

On Thursday, September 4 (August 22, O. S.), Nolan's funeral took place. The proletariat of Dublin followed in a procession 50,000 strong behind the body of their comrade. The police brutes lay low, not daring to annoy the crowd, and exemplary order prevailed. "This is a more magnificent demonstration than when they buried Parnell" (the celebrated Irish nationalist leader), said an old Irishman to a German correspondent.

The Dublin events mark a turning-point in the history of the labour movement and of socialism in Ireland. Murphy has threatened to destroy the Irish trade unions. He has succeeded only in destroying the last remnants of the influence of the Irish nationalist bourgeoisie over the Irish proletariat. He has helped to steel the independent revolutionary working-class movement in Ireland, which is free of nationalist prejudices.

This was seen immediately at the Trades Union Congress which opened on September 1 (August 19, O. S.), in Manchester. The Dublin events inflamed the delegates—despite the resistance of the opportunist trade union leaders with their petty-bourgeois spirit and their admiration for the bosses. The Dublin workers' delegation was given an ovation. Delegate Partridge, Chairman of the Dublin branch of the Engineers' Union, spoke about the abominable outrages committed by the police in Dublin. A young working girl had just gone to bed when the police raided her house. The girl hid in the closet, but was dragged out by the hair. The police were drunk. These "men" (if one may call them such) beat up ten-year-old lads and even five-year-old children!

Partridge was twice arrested for making speeches which the judge himself admitted were peaceful. "I am sure," said Partridge, "that I would now be arrested if I were to recite the Lord's Prayer in public."

The Manchester Congress sent a delegation to Dublin. The bourgeoisie there again took up the weapon of nationalism (just like the bourgeois nationalists in Poland, or in the Ukraine, or among the Jews!) declaring that "Englishmen have no business on Irish soil!" But, *fortunately*, the nationalists have already lost their influence over the workers.*

Speeches delivered at the Manchester Congress were of a kind that had not been heard for a long time.

---

* The Irish nationalists are already expressing the fear that Larkin will organise an independent Irish workers' party, which will have to be reckoned with in the first Irish national parliament.

A resolution was moved to transfer the whole Congress to Dublin, and to organise a general strike throughout Britain. Smillie, the Chairman of the Miners' Union, stated that the Dublin methods would compel all British workers to resort to revolution and that they would be able to learn the use of arms.

The masses of the British workers are slowly but surely taking a new path—they are abandoning the defence of the petty privileges of the labour aristocracy for their own great heroic struggle for a new system of society. And once on this path the British proletariat, with their energy and organisation, will bring socialism about more quickly and securely than anywhere else.

Severnaya Pravda No. 23,
August 29, 1913;
Nash Put No. 5,
August 30, 1913
Signed: *V.*

Published according to
the *Severnaya Pravda* text

NEW LAND "REFORM" MEASURES

The government has drafted a new bill on peasant land tenure. It is proposed to speedily "limit the fragmentation" of individual farmsteads and non-commune holdings. The landowners want to "protect small landed properties" from scattering, disintegration and fragmentation.

In essence the law prohibits the break-up of *medium-sized* peasant holdings—farmsteads and non-commune properties. When such lands are sold or inherited they must pass into the hands of a single owner. Co-heirs are to receive a cash "indemnity", to be assessed by landowners' survey commissions.

Cash for the indemnity payments is to be advanced on especially favourable terms by the Peasant Bank with the land as security. The size of the average (undivided) holdings is to be determined on the basis of the 1861 feudal laws on the size of the decree allotment.[105]

The significance of this bill is obvious. The landowners want to create privileged landed properties protected against capitalism for the peasant bourgeoisie. Realising that their privileges and their feudal system of land tenure are shaky, the landowners are trying to win over to their side the richest section of the peasant bourgeoisie, insignificant in numbers as it is. I will share a small part of my privileges with you, says the landowner to the kulaks and rich peasants, I will help you grow richer at the expense of the masses of peasants, who are being ruined, and you will protect me from those masses, you will be the bulwark of law and order. Such is the class meaning of the new bill.

Here we have absolutely perfect conformity with the general tendency of the June Third agrarian policy, otherwise known as the Stolypin agrarian policy. It is one and the same landowners' policy, and the landowners as a class have not been able to pursue any other policy in Russia since 1905. There is no other way in which they can uphold their privileges or even their existence.

Democrats, both working-class and bourgeois (i.e., the peasantry as a mass), must recognise this indisputable truth of class relationships and draw from it the inevitable conclusion. There is nothing more foolish and reactionary than the bureaucratic point of view held by the liberals and the Narodniks, who fear the *mobilisation* of peasant lands, i.e., their free sale and purchase. *Rech*, for instance, in two editorials, states in reference to the new bill that "the protection of small landed properties is a necessity". The trouble, you see, was that the June Third agrarian policy was adopted "suddenly, as a sharp political weapon".

This is the sapient liberal, in the role of a "supra-class" civil servant, reproaching Stolypin, the leader of the landowners, for having used a political weapon for the benefit of the landowners! The cowardly desire to escape the inevitable class struggle is hidden by whimpering about the connection between the interests of a class and the politics of a class. No wonder Stolypin only laughed at *such* opponents.

"The protection of small landed properties", that favourite formula of the liberals (Russian) and the Narodniks, is a reactionary phrase. The working class supports the peasantry (and guides it) only when, and only to the extent that, its actions are democratic, that is, when they are in the interests of social development and of capitalist development, when they are in the interests of the country's deliverance from the yoke of the feudals and from their privileges. Every curtailment of the mobilisation of peasant lands is, first, a foolish measure, incapable of halting capitalism, a measure that can only worsen the condition of the masses, make their life more difficult and compel them to evade the law. Secondly, it is a measure that actually creates a small section of *privileged* petty bourgeois, the most hidebound and backward enemies of progress.

The working class does not counterpose to the class politics of the feudal landowners phrases in the "supra-class" spirit, it counterposes the interests of the other classes that constitute nine-tenths of the population. The peasantry, as a petty-bourgeois mass, will for a long time waver between the consistent democracy of the proletariat and hopes of obtaining concessions from the landowners, hopes of sharing their privileges.

However, the conditions provided by the Russian landowners are so burdensome for the peasants, starvation for millions is so common under these conditions, that there can be no doubt whatsoever which side everything that is alive, viable and politically conscious will follow.

Nash Put No. 4, August 29, 1913; *Severnaya Pravda* No. 24, August 30, 1913 Signed: V. *Ilyin*

Published according to the *Severnaya Pravda* text

THE MERCHANT SALAZKIN AND THE WRITER F. D.

The speech delivered by the merchant Salazkin is undoubtedly of great social significance. Gone for ever is that historical epoch, the epoch of "primitive accumulation", in which the landed nobility grumbled and appealed for "faith", and the merchant bowed and expressed his gratitude.

Gone, too, is the first period of the June Third, counterrevolutionary epoch, when the merchant, terrified to death by the movement of the masses, gazed upon Stolypin with admiration and tender emotion. The second period has begun, the period of working-class upswing, "social" revival and merchant liberalism.

A correct appraisal of this liberalism, something between Octobrism and the Cadet Party, is to an increasing extent being *forced* (by the course of events) even *upon* petty-bourgeois democrats. *Severnaya Pravda* recently quoted the just arguments of *Kievskaya Mysl* (see *Severnaya Pravda* No. 9,* August 11) on the *separation* of liberalism from democracy, on the *rapprochement* between the liberalism of the Cadets—to say nothing of the "Progressists"—and reactionary nationalism.

There are, however, some writers who lag behind even petty-bourgeois democracy because they are held in bondage by their own opportunist doctrine. At the head of these writers, of course, stands the liquidator F. D.

In his appraisal of Salazkin's speech, F. D. wrote (*Novaya Rabochaya Gazeta*, August 23) that the Black Hundreds were right to raise an outcry against Salazkin, "but the

* See pp. 302-04 of this volume.—*Ed.*

Left-wing [meaning liberal] press was also right in pointing out the organic inability of the bureaucracy to meet the pressing requirements of the country. *Rossiya* alone was not right."

"Salazkin's speech is not to be explained by love for radical programmes," says F. D., "but by the absence of law and order. The merchant has revolted.... And if such is the case, no matter how hostile the merchant may be towards radical programmes he will be compelled, if not today then tomorrow, to combine his efforts with those of the more radical sections of the country."

Such is F. D.'s appraisal. He goes no further than combining liberalism with the workers.

Very original! F. D. does not notice the combination of the efforts of the merchant with those of the Black-Hundred landowner. He does not notice that Salazkin is upholding the "fundamentals" of the June Third regime and within the framework of those fundamentals wants to push Purishkevich into the background.

Nor does he notice the difference between the *reformist* position of the liberals and Salazkin, and the position of the working class, which is alien to the wretched narrowness of reformism. The writer F. D. has overlooked the substance of the present difference between democracy and liberalism.

F. D. is interested in *one thing alone*—"combining" the liberals and the workers. An interesting ... speciality!

Regard F. D.'s article as a political document, regard it from the "all-Europe" point of view (for, indeed, F. D. and his friends are fond of talking about their Europeanism...). You will see that F. D. shares in full the position of Lloyd George and the extreme opportunists of the "workers' party" (on a British scale); or the position of Combes and Jaurès (on a French scale); or the position of the *Berliner Tageblatt*, the organ of the Left liberals in Berlin, and of Bernstein, Kolb and Vollmar.

There is nothing in F. D.'s article that is unacceptable to a Left Cadet who is doing his best "to combine" "the efforts of the Salazkins with those of the more radical sections of the country".

The Marxist tells the workers—take advantage of the disagreement between the Salazkins and the Purishkeviches by neutralising the vacillation of the Salazkins, who are much more closely "combined" with the Purishkeviches than with the opposition. The liberal tells the workers— the Salazkins will be compelled to combine their efforts with yours.

How comes it that the writer F. D. forgot to explain the class roots of the reformism of the liberals in general and of Salazkin in particular? How did F. D. even forget to point out the whole absurd, ridiculous, ugly narrowness of the reformism of Salazkin-type merchants under Russian conditions?

Was it not because the writer, *despite* his Marxist "signboard", upholds the very same reformist point of view that the merchant Salazkin holds *in conformity* with the interests of his class and his progressist, i.e., semi-Octobrist, signboard?

Severnaya Pravda No. 26,   Published according to
   September 1, 1913   the *Severnaya Pravda* text
Signed: *Para-conciliator*

THE STRUGGLE FOR MARXISM

Recently there has been a lively discussion in the newspapers about collections made by St. Petersburg workers for the working-class press. It must be admitted that a most detailed and serious discussion of this question is essential since it is one of tremendous importance from the point of view of political principles.

How does the matter stand? The liquidators (*Novaya Rabochaya Gazeta*) insist on the equal division of funds collected. The Marxists (*Severnaya Pravda*) demand division according to the wishes of the workers who contribute their pence. The workers must themselves decide, by a discussion on the trend represented by each newspaper, *for whom* they have made their contributions.

The resolution of twenty-two Vyborg supporters of the liquidators, the first *document* on the question, said simply (see *Novaya Rabochaya Gazeta* No. 2, August 9): "Take collections for the benefit of working-class newspapers on a parity basis." Then the resolutions of some of the workers of the Nobel Works and the Putilov Works (ibid., Nos. 6, 8, 9, 10) upheld and actually put into practice the division of collections into *three equal* parts—one part each for the Marxists, liquidators and Narodniks. The *Novaya Rabochaya Gazeta* editors tacitly approved and defended it in an article by G. R.[106] (No. 9).

Severnaya Pravda, on the contrary, showed that equal division is an incorrect method and one that does not correspond to the aims and purposes of Marxism.

Every class-conscious worker, we repeat, must study this question with care and quite independently.

What are the arguments in favour of equal division? Reference is made to the "sacred slogan of Marxist workers—Workers of all countries, unite!"

The question arises—does this slogan demand the alliance of Marxist workers, who are members, say, of a Marxist party, with those who support *bourgeois* parties? Any worker who gives this a little thought will agree that it does not.

In all countries, even in the most advanced, there are workers who support bourgeois parties—they are for the Liberals in Britain, for the Radical-Socialists in France, for the Catholics, and the liberal "people's" party in Germany, for the Reform (petty-bourgeois) Party in Italy, etc., including the petty-bourgeois P. S. P. (Polish Socialist Party) in neighbouring Poland.

The great slogan calls upon workers to unite in a proletarian, independent, class party, and *not one* of the parties mentioned above is proletarian.

Take the basic principle of our Narodniks. From the Narodnik point of view, the abolition of the private ownership of land and its equalitarian division is socialism or "socialisation", but it is an erroneous and *bourgeois* point of view. Marx long ago showed that the more daring *bourgeois* economists can and do demand the abolition of private property in land.[107] It is a *bourgeois* reform that *extends* capitalism's field of action. We support the peasants as *bourgeois* democrats in their struggle for land and freedom against the feudal-minded landowners.

However, unity between a proletarian organisation of wage-workers and petty-bourgeois peasant democrats is a flagrant violation of the great Marxist slogan. Attempts at such unity would do great damage to the working-class movement and always end in an early collapse.

The history of Russia (in the years 1905, 1906 and 1907) has demonstrated that there is not and cannot be any mass, class support for the Narodniks, except that of the Left-wing peasantry.

The liquidators and the workers who follow them, therefore, have retreated from Marxism, have left the *class* path and entered on the path of non-party unity between wage-workers and a petty-bourgeois party. For it is, indeed, a *non-party* alliance when the worker is told: don't try to find out which is the proletarian and which is the petty-bourgeois party, fork out equally for both!* The masses "cannot get at the root of things", wrote G. R. in *Novaya Rabochaya Gazeta* No. 9. That is precisely why we need an old, tried and tested Marxist newspaper *to develop the political consciousness* of the masses who "cannot get at the root of things", *to help* them get at that root and *understand* it.

The reference made by G. R. and similar writers who *oppose* organised, Marxist unity (but never raise the question of uniting the two parties!)—their reference to "masses who cannot get at the root of things" is nothing but the *preaching* of non-party tendencies, is a *retreat* from Marxism, is the underhanded pursuit of petty-bourgeois views and policies.

By such a policy the liquidators justify their name, i.e., they are deserters from the Marxist organisation, its destroyers.

Another argument (see G. R.'s article and the discussion by the editors of *Novaya Rabochaya Gazeta* in No. 6) is that collections taken in accordance with political trends would disrupt "unanimous opposition to the reactionaries", who persecute workers' newspapers.

---

* The way in which some workers respond to the liquidators' unprincipled preaching may also be judged from the following resolution published in *Novaya Rabochaya Gazeta* No. 21.

"We find this decision [to divide collections equally between the three newspapers] to be necessary and the only just one; first, because all three newspapers are, as workers' newspapers, equally subjected to penalties and persecution and, secondly, the overwhelming majority of workers, both here and in other parts of the country, have not yet gained a full understanding of the specifics of the various party trends and cannot with full knowledge attach themselves to any one of them, but are equally in sympathy with all of them."

The liquidators' newspaper has never made an attempt to explain to its readers, has never given them an opportunity of finding out, whether a Narodnik newspaper may be considered a working-class newspaper, and whether it should be confused with a Marxist or even with a liquidators' newspaper. *Novaya Rabochaya Gazeta* prefers to stick to the "elemental", to plod along behind those who do not understand, as long as it can be "a nuisance" to the Marxists.

When a politically conscious worker has thought this over he will see that it is the old liberal argument about disrupting "unanimity against reaction" by the separation of the democrats from the liberals. It is a bourgeois argument and is profoundly erroneous.

The non-party masses "who cannot", as G. R. asserts, "get at the root of things", learn splendidly from examples. One who is still ignorant and not politically conscious, who cannot think or is too lazy to think and "get at the root of things" will wave his hand and say "I also protest, give them all an equal share". But one who *begins* to think and "get at the root of things", will *also* go to listen to *a discussion on platforms*, to the defence of the views of each trend, and, by listening to those who are *more* politically conscious, will himself gradually learn, and his indifference and his broad sympathy for all will change to a definite, thoughtful attitude to the newspapers.

The liquidators have forgotten all these elementary truths that "every worker should know and remember". They have proved by their *plan* to "divide equally" that they are *correctly* regarded as the vehicle of the non-party spirit, as renegades from Marxism and advocates of the "bourgeois influence over the proletariat" (see the unanimous decision of the Marxists, January 1910).

The Marxist organisation unites *politically conscious* workers by its common programme, common tactics, common decisions on the attitude to reaction, capitalists, bourgeois democrats (Narodniks), etc. All these *common* decisions—among others, the decisions of 1908, 1912 and 1913 on the absurdity and harmfulness of *reformism*—are upheld and are persistently implemented by the Marxists.

Discussions (talks, debates, disputes) about parties and about common tactics are essential; without them the masses are disunited; without them common decisions are *impossible* and, therefore, unity of action is also impossible. Without them the Marxist organisation of those *workers* "who can get at the root of things" *would disintegrate* and the influence of the bourgeoisie on the unenlightened would thereby be facilitated.

In advocating collections in accordance with political trends, collections accompanied by a discussion on platforms, the best St. Petersburg workers are struggling for Marxism against the champions of a non-party spirit.

We are confident that the workers will always and everywhere bend all their efforts to uphold *only* the Marxist system of collections and discussions, which *educate* the masses.

Severnaya Pravda No. 27,
   September 3, 1913
   Signed: *V. Ilyin*

                              Published according to
                           the *Severnaya Pravda* text

A WEEK AFTER THE DUBLIN MASSACRE

On Sunday, September 7 (August 25, O. S.), exactly a week after the police massacre, the Dublin workers organised a huge meeting to protest against the conduct of the Irish capitalists and the Irish police.

The meeting took place in the same street (O'Connell Street) and at the same spot where the meeting banned by the police was to have taken place the previous Sunday. It is a historic spot, a spot where it is most convenient to organise meetings and where they are most frequently held in Dublin.

The police kept out of sight. The streets were filled with workers. There were crowds of people, but complete order prevailed. "Last Sunday," exclaimed an Irish speaker, "the police truncheon reigned here without reason; today reason reigns without the police truncheon."

Britain *has* a constitution—and the authorities did not dare to bring their drunken policemen into action for the second time. Three platforms were put up and six speakers, including representatives of the English proletariat, condemned the crime perpetrated against the people, called upon the workers to display international solidarity, to wage a common struggle.

A resolution was unanimously adopted demanding freedom of assembly and association, and calling for an immediate investigation—under the direction of independent persons and with a guarantee of publicity for all the proceedings—of the conduct of the police the previous Sunday.

In London a magnificent meeting was held in Trafalgar Square. Groups of socialists and workers came with their banners. There were many posters with cartoons and slogans on topical events. The crowd particularly applauded a poster depicting a policeman waving a red flag with the inscription, "Silence!"

Outstanding speeches were made by Ben Tillett, who showed that the "Liberal" government of Britain is no better than a reactionary one, and Partridge, Dublin Secretary of the Engineers' Union, who described in detail the shameless acts of police violence in Dublin.

It is instructive to note that the principal slogan at the London and Dublin meetings was the demand for freedom of association. This is quite understandable. Britain *has* the foundations of political liberty, *has* a constitutional regime, generally speaking. The freedom of association demanded by the workers is one of the reforms absolutely necessary and quite achievable under the present constitutional regime (just as achievable as, say, the partial reform of workers' insurance in Russia).

Freedom of association is equally indispensable to the workers of Britain and of Russia. And the British workers quite rightly advance this slogan of a political reform essential to them, perfectly well aware of the path to be followed for its achievement and of its complete feasibility under the British Constitution (just as the Russian workers would be right in advancing the partial demand for amendments to the Insurance Act).

In Russia, however, precisely those general foundations of political liberty are absent *without which* the demand for freedom of association is simply ridiculous and is merely a current liberal phrase designed to deceive the people by suggesting that the path of reform is possible in our country. In Russia the fight for freedom of association— freedom most urgently needed by both the workers and the entire people—cannot be conducted *without* contrasting the impotent and false reformism of the liberals with the consistent democracy of the workers, who have no reformist illusions.

Severnaya Pravda No. 27,   Published according to
    September 3, 1913;   the *Severnaya Pravda* text
    Nash Put No. 8,
    September 3, 1913
        Signed: V.

QUESTIONS OF PRINCIPLE IN POLITICS

THE LIBERAL BOURGEOISIE AND REFORMISM

In the name of the merchants of all Russia, the millionaire Salazkin made an appeal for extensive political reforms in a speech at Nizhni-Novgorod Fair. At a meeting of three thousand metalworkers in St. Petersburg, the reformists suffered a decisive defeat, receiving only 150 votes for their candidates for membership of the executive body.[108]

These two facts, which simply cry out for comparison, make even quite unprincipled people ask questions of principle concerning present-day Russian politics. There are masses of people in all classes in Russia that are interested in politics, but few of them realise the significance of the theoretical principles involved in the presentation of questions of politics. Few people realise the significance of political parties that always give well-considered, precise and properly formulated answers to these questions. When the parties are connected with definite classes, such answers are given on the basis of work among the masses and are verified by years of such work.

The answers given by the Marxists were precisely of this type when four and a half years ago they appraised the June Third system and their tasks in relation to it.* Workers who for years and years have been acting conscientiously in the spirit of those answers in every possible sphere are divided by a deep gulf from those confused intellectuals who fear any sort of definite answer and who, at every step, slide into reformism and liquidationism.

---

* See present edition, Vol. 15, pp. 321-24.—*Ed.*

One can only pity those people who, watching the struggle of the Marxists against the liquidators, avoid the issue with miserable words about the harmfulness of disputes, squabbles, internecine struggles, factionalism.... Many self-styled Marxists and all "Left" Narodniks belong to this category!

Those who, in principle, are champions of the bourgeoisie and enemies of Marxism, the liberals from the newspaper *Rech*, have been unable to ignore the above facts. They repeat all their tired, pitiful phrases in an editorial article (in issue No. 234), but now they go further.

The liberals are forced to admit that "the struggle between the Bolsheviks and the liquidators is going on everywhere", and that "it has percolated all the pores of the working-class organism".

So what of it? Could it be accidental?

No....

"Important disagreements on matters of principle have long been apparent; in the final analysis they may be reduced to the question of the course to be taken in the further development of the country."

At last they have thought it out! The Marxists explained this in December 1908, the liberals have begun to realise it in August 1913. Better late than never.

"Is the path of reforms conceivable," continues the liberal newspaper, "or are 'reforms possible only as a by-product of a movement that is completely free of all the narrowness of reformism' [quoted from *Severnaya Pravda*]. That is how the question is presented."

Precisely! The question of liquidationism is merely part of the question of the non-party reformists who have broken away from Marxism.

It will be interesting to see how the liberals, the champions of reformism in principle, defend it.

"There is, of course, a great deal of metaphysics and fatalism in the opinion that reforms are possible only as a 'by-product'. There can be no reforms without reformers and reformism, even if only as a 'by-product'"....

There again you have a sample of angry words and an attempt to evade an answer! What have metaphysics got to do with it, when historical experience, the experience of England, France, Germany and Russia, the experience of all modern history in Europe and Asia, shows that serious reforms have always been merely the by-product of a movement completely free of the narrowness of reformism?

And what has fatalism to do with it, when that same experience says clearly that it is the very classes hostile to reformism that have produced the greatest effect?

Or perhaps there is more "fatalism" to be observed in the conduct of the Russian working class in the early years of the twentieth century than there was in the conduct of the liberal Zemstvo people and bourgeoisie in the last thirty years of the nineteenth century? You liberal gentlemen make yourselves ridiculous!

Can you possibly be such ignoramuses that you do not see the connection between the interests of the bourgeoisie as a class and their desire to confine themselves to reformism, between the condition of the working class and its contrary desire?

Indeed, gentlemen, you are poor advocates of reformism in general! But perhaps your defence of reformism in present-day Russia is better?

"It must be admitted," continues *Rech*, "that the situation now obtaining, one that has time and again demonstrated to the most modest reformers the futility of their efforts, turns people's thoughts, and especially their feelings, towards the negation of reformism."

So there you have it! It seems that even you, who make a principle of advocating reformism, cannot find support either in historical experience or in "the situation now obtaining" in Russia. Even you have to admit that the situation is against you!

What metaphysicians and fatalists you are, gentlemen— or what blind slaves to the narrow, selfish, cowardly moneybag—if you continue to uphold the unprincipled position of reformism in contradiction to the experience of history, in contradiction to the experience of "the situation now obtaining"! Are not you, who do not believe in reforms yourselves, actually defending that bourgeoisie that strives to gain profit at other people's expense?

It is understandable that an advanced contingent of the working class of Russia, the metalworkers of St. Petersburg, have dealt a crushing defeat to the reformists and liquidators among their number. According to the figures of the liberal and reformist *Rech*, the reformist liquidators obtained 150 out of 2,000 votes, that is, seven and a half per cent of the total. Does this not show again and again—after the elections of workers to the Fourth Duma, after the history of the emergence of the working-class press in St. Petersburg and Moscow—that the liquidators represent only confused and half-liberal intellectuals, and that the mass of the politically conscious workers have firmly and resolutely condemned and rejected them?

Severnaya Pravda No. 28,
September 4, 1913;
Nash Put No. 9,
September 4, 1913
Signed: *V. I.* ·

Published according to
the *Severnaya Pravda* text

LIBERALS AND DEMOCRATS
ON THE LANGUAGE QUESTION

On several occasions the newspapers have mentioned the report of the Governor of the Caucasus, a report that is noteworthy, not for its Black-Hundred spirit but for its timid "liberalism". Among other things, the Governor objects to artificial Russification of non-Russian nationalities. Representatives of non-Russian nationalities in the Caucasus are *themselves* striving to teach their children Russian, as, for example, in the Armenian church schools, in which the teaching of Russian is not obligatory.

Russkoye Slovo (No. 198), one of the most widely circulating liberal newspapers in Russia, points to this fact and draws the correct conclusion that the hostility towards the Russian language in Russia "stems exclusively" from the "artificial" (the right word would have been "forced") implanting of that language.

"There is no reason to worry about the fate of the Russian language. It will itself win recognition throughout Russia," says the newspaper. This is perfectly true, because the requirements of economic exchange will always compel the nationalities living in one state (as long as they wish to live together) to study the language of the majority. The more democratic the political system in Russia becomes, the more powerfully, rapidly and extensively capitalism will develop, the more urgently will the requirements of economic exchange impel various nationalities to study the language most convenient for general commercial relations.

The liberal newspaper, however, hastens to slap itself in the face and demonstrate its liberal inconsistency..

"Even those who oppose Russification," it says, "would hardly be likely to deny that in a country as huge as Russia there must be one single official language, and that this language can be only Russian."

Logic turned inside out! Tiny Switzerland has not lost anything, but has gained from having not *one single* official language, but three—German, French and Italian. In Switzerland 70 per cent of the population are Germans (in Russia 43 per cent are Great Russians), 22 per cent French (in Russia 17 per cent are Ukrainians) and 7 per cent Italians (in Russia 6 per cent are Poles and 4.5 per cent Byelorussians). If Italians in Switzerland often speak French in the common parliament they do not do so because they are compelled by some savage police law (there are none such in Switzerland), but because the civilised citizens of a democratic state themselves prefer a language that is understood by a majority. The French language does not excite hatred in Italians because it is the language of a free civilised nation, a language that is not imposed by disgusting police measures.

Why should "huge" Russia, a much more varied and terribly backward country, *inhibit* her development by the retention of any kind of privilege for any one language? Should not the contrary be true, liberal gentlemen? Should not Russia, if she wants to overtake Europe, put an end to every kind of privilege as quickly as possible, as completely as possible and as vigorously as possible?

If all privileges disappear, if the imposition of any one language ceases, all Slavs will easily and rapidly learn to understand each other and will not be frightened by the "horrible" thought that speeches in different languages will be heard in the common parliament. The requirements of economic exchange will themselves *decide* which language of the given country it is to the *advantage* of the majority to know in the interests of commercial relations. This decision will be all the firmer because it will be adopted voluntarily by a population of various nationalities, and its adoption will be the more rapid and extensive the more consistent the democracy and, as a consequence of this, the more rapid will be the development of capitalism.

The liberals approach the language question in the same way as they approach all political questions—like hypocritical hucksters, holding out one hand (openly) to democracy and the other (behind their backs) to the serf-owners and police. We are against privileges, shout the liberals, and under cover they haggle with the serf-owners for first one, then another, privilege.

Such is the nature of *all* liberal-bourgeois nationalism—not only Great-Russian (it is the worst of them all because of its violent character and its kinship with the Purish-keviches) but Polish, Jewish, Ukrainian, Georgian and every other nationalism. Under the slogan of "national culture" the bourgeoisie of *all* nations, both in Austria and in Russia, are *in fact* pursuing the policy of splitting the workers, emasculating democracy and haggling with the serf-owners over the sale of the people's rights and the people's liberty.

The slogan of working-class democracy is not "national culture" but the international culture of democracy and the world-wide working-class movement. Let the bourgeoisie deceive the people with various "positive" national programmes. The class-conscious worker will answer the bourgeoisie—there is only one solution to the national problem (insofar as it can, in general, be solved in the capitalist world, the world of profit, squabbling and exploitation), and that solution is consistent democracy.

The proof—Switzerland in Western Europe, a country with an old culture, and Finland in Eastern Europe, a country with a young culture.

The national programme of working-class democracy is: absolutely no privilege for any one nation or any one language; the solution of the problem of the political self-determination of nations, that is, their separation as states by completely free, democratic methods; the promulgation of a law for the whole state by virtue of which any measure (Zemstvo, urban or communal, etc., etc.) introducing any privilege of any kind for one of the nations and militating against the equality of nations or the rights of a national minority, shall be declared illegal and ineffective, and any citizen of the state shall have the right to demand that such a measure be annulled as unconstitutional, and that those who attempt to put it into effect be punished.

Working-class democracy counterposes to the nationalist wrangling of the various bourgeois parties over questions of language, etc., the demand for the unconditional unity and complete solidarity of workers of *all* nationalities in *all* working-class organisations—trade union, co-operative, consumers', educational and all others—in contradistinction to any kind of bourgeois nationalism. Only this type of unity and solidarity can uphold democracy and defend the interests of the workers against capital—which is already international and is becoming more so—and promote the development of mankind towards a new way of life that is alien to all privileges and all exploitation.

Severnaya Pravda No. 29,
September 5, 1913;
Nash Put No. 12,
September 7, 1913
Signed: *V. I.*

Published according to
the *Severnaya Pravda* text

THE LANGUAGE OF FIGURES[109]

I

It is well known that particularly in 1905 and after factory workers' wages throughout Russia soared. The factory inspectors' reports say that the average wages of factory workers in Russia for the five years 1901-05 were 206 rubles and for the following five years, 1906-10, were 238 rubles.

The wages of workers in Moscow Gubernia are somewhat below the average for Russia. According to Factory Inspector Kozminykh-Lanin, they averaged 201 rubles in the 1901-05 period and 235 rubles for the succeeding four years, 1906-09.

As a result of 1905, therefore, the wages per worker in Moscow Gubernia increased by an average of *34 rubles*, i.e., by almost 17 per cent. Estimating the number of factory workers in Moscow Gubernia at between 300,000 and 350,000, this constitutes a total *annual* gain for all workers of something like *11,000,000 rubles*.

We see that the sacrifices made by the workers during the strikes of 1905 have been repaid by a considerable improvement in their economic position.

Although the victory of the June Third system, i.e., the counter-revolutionary system, led to the withdrawal of a number of the workers' gains, capital did not succeed in reducing workers' wages to the former low level. Workers' wages in Moscow Gubernia averaged about 200 rubles from 1901 to 1905, fluctuating between 197 rubles (1902) and 203 rubles (1905). In 1906, when the results of 1905 first made themselves felt, wages rose to 228 rubles, and in 1907, to 237 rubles; in 1908 there was a slight drop (236.5 rubles) and in 1909 they again rose to 237 rubles.

The figures show that without the gains of 1905-06 the workers would have been subjected to intolerable poverty since the cost of living has been rising throughout the past decade.

II

Wages at the bigger factories in Moscow Gubernia are, as a rule, higher than those paid at the smaller establishments. The textile workers, who constitute 68 per cent, i.e., more than two-thirds, of the total number of factory workers in our gubernia, received the following average annual wages for the year 1909.

					Rubles	Per cent
Factories employing more than 1,000 workers				. .	219	100
"	"	from 501 to 1,000	"	. .	204	93
"	"	" 101 " 500	"	. .	197	90
"	"	" 51 " 100	"	. .	188	86
"	"	" 21 " 50	"	. .	192	88
"	"	" 20 or less	"	. .	164	75
Totals					211	96

The bigger the factory, the higher the wages. The same is to be found among the metalworkers. It is easier for the workers at a big factory to unite, repulse the capitalist and uphold their own demands collectively. To catch up with their more advanced comrades the workers in small factories and workshops must unite more strongly in associations (trade union, educational, co-operative and others) and rally more closely around their working-class newspaper.

Strikes are more easily organised and are conducted more successfully at big factories because of the greater solidarity of the workers. The big factories took part in the strike movement of 1905 and 1906 to a greater extent than the small factories.

We see that on account of this the workers in the biggest factories *gained more* from the strikes of those years than the workers at small establishments. Here are the figures for workers in all industries in Moscow Gubernia:

Average annual wages per worker

Category of factory	Five years 1901-05	Four years 1906-09	Ruble increase
Employing more than 1,000 workers	196	234	+38
" from 501 to 1,000 "	186	231	+45
" " 101 " 500 "	211	238	+27
" " 51 " 100 "	215	240	+25
" " 21 " 50 "	216	241	+25
" " 20 or less "	193	207	+14
Totals	201	235	+34

First of all we must explain, in respect of these figures, the (apparent) exception ᵥto the rule formulated above, according to which wages at the bigger factories are higher than at smaller establishments. The point is that metalworkers, printers and some others earn much more than textile workers (360 rubles, 310 rubles as compared with 211 rubles, etc.). The *share* of the textile workers in the total number of workers at big factories is much greater than their share at the medium and small establishments. This accounts for the apparent exception to the rule, which makes it appear that wages are higher at medium and small than at big factories.

What conclusion are we to draw concerning increased wages at big and small factories since 1905?

At the big factories (those employing 500 or more workers) the increase amounts to about 40 rubles a year, that is, about 20 kopeks to a ruble.

At medium and small factories, employing from 21 to 500 workers, the increase amounts to about 25 rubles, that is, about 12 kopeks to a ruble.

At the very smallest factories (20 workers and less) the increase is a mere 14 rubles, that is, 7-8 kopeks to a ruble.

Thus the more vigorous and united strike struggle by workers at the big factories resulted in a greater increase in wages. We have already said that workers in small factories can catch up with the workers in big factories in this respect by uniting in associations.

III

Increased wages were not the only gains made by workers in the strike movement of 1905. The position of the workers has, in general, changed for the better.

It is impossible to express the exact extent of this improvement in figures, but in 1905-06 every worker realised the improvement and felt it strongly.

The data given by Factory Inspector Kozminykh-Lanin enable us to determine the influence of 1905 only on the *fining* of workers. By fining workers the capitalist is taking upon himself the role of judge. For this reason fines are always accompanied by particularly extensive arbitrary action in respect of the workers and at times even by direct humiliation of the workers. It is natural that the workers always demand the *annulment* of fines, the abolition of the capitalists' right to be judges in the workers' affairs.

The following are the figures for fines levied on all workers in Moscow Gubernia year by year.

Year	Average fine per worker (kopeks)
1901	30
1902	27
1903	27
1904	29
1905	17
1906	12
1907	15
1908	18
1909	21

We see how successfully the workers "reduced" the amount of the fines. Before 1905 the fines amounted to 27-30 kopeks a worker.

But then comes the year 1905. Fines immediately drop to almost a half—to 17 kopeks. In 1906 the results of 1905 are more clearly demonstrated—fines drop to 12 kopeks.

The revolution passes. The capitalists grow bolder. The fines again rise to 15-18-21 kopeks.

But even in 1909—the year of the longest and deepest lull—the capitalists did not succeed in raising fines to the former disgraceful level. No matter how the capitalist may fawn upon Purishkevich, these two "dear friends" have not succeeded in going back to the good old days—the *worker in Russia has changed.* The worker in Russia has learned a thing or two!

If we compare the total fines with the total wages of the workers—and such a comparison is essential for it is not the same thing to pay twenty kopeks out of wages of one ruble as paying twenty kopeks out of wages of a ruble and a half—the victory of the workers in 1905 becomes still more obvious.

Out of every 100 rubles of the workers' wages, the fines per annum averaged in kopeks:

1901	15	1906	5
1902	14	1907	6
1903	13	1908	8
1904	14	1909	9
1905	9		

It follows, therefore, that the workers of Moscow Gubernia achieved a reduction of atrocious fines to *one-third* as a result of 1905. They will succeed in obtaining the complete abolition of fines.

IV

In conclusion let us take a brief glance at the question of what share of his wages the Moscow worker obtains in cash.

The Moscow workers are in a difficult position in this respect. In 1909 their total wages amounted to 73,000,000 rubles; of this sum they received 61,500,000 rubles, that is, 84.2 per cent, in cash. Almost a tenth of their wages, 7,200,000 rubles, was paid in the shape of groceries and other commodities from the factory shops. This type of wages places the workers in serf-like dependence on the owners and gives those owners "superprofits".

The position of workers in the cotton industry is particularly bad—over one-fifth of their wages (5,900,000 rubles out of 28,800,000) is paid in foodstuffs. If the workers were to win for themselves free workers' co-operatives there would not only be a saving of hundreds of thousands of rubles for the slaves of capital, but the semi-serf dependence of the workers on the *factory owners'* shops would be removed.

To continue: 3,750,000 rubles (5 per cent) of the workers' wages went to pay for products they took from the shops of consumers' associations, etc. Lastly, 680,000 rubles (0.9 per cent) of the wages went for the maintenance of workers boarded by factory owners.

This form of payment, which dooms the workers to a thousand forms of dependence of a serf character, has been preserved most noticeably in industries processing silk and flax, and after them in those processing food and livestock products.

As for the influence of 1905 on the forms in which wages are paid, we may say that there have been practically no gains. Here are the figures, as from 1901:

Percentages of wages paid in:

Year	Workers' total wages (million rubles)	Cash	Goods from factory shops	Goods from consumers' associations	Boarding of workers by factory owners
1901	53	81.4	8.9	7.3	2.4
1902	54	81.5	9.1	7.0	2.4
1903	57	83.0	8.3	6.6	2.1
1904	55	82.7	9.0	6.5	1.8
1905	57	82.8	9.2	6.5	1.5
1906	64	85.1	7.6	5.8	1.5
1907	71	83.8	9.4	5.3	1.5
1908	73	82.9	10.4	5.2	1.5
1909	73	84.2	9.8	5.1	0.9

Since 1905 payment in cash has increased to an extremely insignificant extent. The system of boarding workers by factory owners has been reduced to an equally small extent. And payment of wages through factory shops, on the contrary, has somewhat increased.

Taking it by and large, the situation has remained as bad as it was before. Moscow workers must struggle for the payment of wages in cash and for the replacement of factory shops by free workers' consumers' associations.

Nash Put Nos. 13 and 14,
September 8 and 10, 1913
Signed: *V. Ilyin*

Published according to
the *Nash Put* text

BOURGEOIS GENTLEMEN ON "FAMILY" FARMING

At the Kiev Agricultural Congress, before an audience of 1,000 landowners from all parts of Russia, Professor Kosinsky read the first paper, in which he tried to prove that "family farming" had become paramount in agriculture.

The question of "family" farming is one of the most important when one is seeking an explanation of capitalist relations in agriculture. In Russia, moreover, there is the Narodnik bourgeois party (this includes the Left Narodniks), which tries to make the workers believe it is a socialist party and most zealously advocates "family" farming. It is, therefore, necessary for every class-conscious worker to understand what this "family" farming is.

Mr. Bourgeois Professor Kosinsky, producing no data of any kind, asserted that peasant farming is growing and large-scale farming, which exploits wage-labour, is collapsing and dying out. The professor

"distinguished three forms of peasant farms: (1) parcellised (dwarf) farms, when the peasant works at a factory, and at home, in his own village, has only a vegetable garden or an allotment attached to his house, the cultivation of which provides a small addition to his income; (2) subsistence farms, with a somewhat larger allotment, the cultivation of which does not meet all the requirements of the family, some members of which work elsewhere; (3) family farms, peasant farms proper, on which the entire family works.

"Agrarian evolution is leading to the break-up of the second category and its replacement by family and parcellised farms. The future is assured mainly for the family farms. The average size of these farms, expressed in Russian measure, is about 50 dessiatines. The triumph of family farming is in no way accompanied by the proletarianisation of the rural districts" (*Kievskaya Mysl* No. 242).

These, then, are the principles of the bourgeois theory of "family" farming borrowed by the Narodniks. Every worker who is in any way familiar with political economy will immediately see that what Mr. Bourgeois calls parcellised or dwarf farms are the *proletarian*, labourer farms, the "farms" of *wage*-workers.

Evidently by "subsistence" farms he means small peasant farms which do not produce mainly for exchange; not commercial farms, but natural economy farms (on which the peasant produces his own food). In admitting that these farms are being ousted our uninformed bourgeois professor admits the victory of capitalism, the growth of exchange, and the squeezing out of small farming. By *what kind* of farming is it being ousted? Firstly by proletarian farming. This is precisely what is called proletarianisation, Mr. Uninformed Professor! Secondly by "family" farming, in which the average size of farms is about 50 dessiatines.

It remains for me to prove to the uninformed professor and to his Socialist-Revolutionary (Narodnik) pupils that "family" farming is precisely *petty-bourgeois, capitalist* farming.

What is the principal feature of capitalism? The employment of wage-labour. It is time our professors and Socialist-Revolutionaries learnt this truth.

What do European, scientific statistics tell us about wage-labour in peasant farming? They tell us that not only 50-dessiatine farms, but even farms of *over 10 hectares* (a hectare is about the same as a dessiatine), *in the majority of cases*, cannot dispense with wage-labour!

Germany. The last census (1907). Number of farms from 10 to 20 hectares—412,741. These employ 711,867 wage-workers. Even the farms from 5 to 10 hectares employ a total of 487,704 wage-workers on 652,798 farms. In other words: even here the number of wage-workers equals more than half the total number of farms. And everybody knows that in the overwhelming majority of cases the small farmer does not employ more than one hired worker.

Austria. The last census (1902). Number of farms from 10 to 20 hectares—242,293. Of these the *majority*, 142,272, i.e., nearly three-fifths, employ wage-workers. We will add that the development of capitalism in Austria is far behind that of Germany. Taking Austrian agriculture as a whole, the percentage of wage-workers employed is *half* the German percentage (14 per cent as against 30 per cent).

Switzerland. The last census (1905). Number of farms from 10 to 15 hectares—19,641. Of these, 11,148, i.e., the *majority*, employ wage-workers. Of the farms of 5 to 10 hectares about 36 per cent in Switzerland and 33 per cent in Austria employ wage-workers.

One can judge from this how profoundly ignorant, or extremely unconscientious, is the bourgeois professor in whose train the Narodniks follow, a professor who *denies* the proletarianisation of the rural districts and *admits* that "subsistence" farms are being ousted, firstly, by proletarian farms, and secondly, by "family" farms, applying this sentimental catchword to farms employing wage-workers!

All those who praise the successes of "family" farming under capitalism (including our Left Narodniks) are bourgeois, who deceive the workers. The deception lies, firstly, in painting the bourgeoisie in bright colours. The exploiter of wage-labour is called a "working" farmer! Secondly, the deception lies in concealing the gulf that divides the overwhelming majority of the proletarian farms from the insignificant minority of capitalist farms.

The interests of the bourgeoisie demand the embellishment of capitalism and the concealment of the gulf that divides the classes. The interests of the proletariat demand the exposure of capitalism and of the exploitation of wage-labour; they demand that the eyes of the masses be opened to the immensity of the gulf that divides the classes.

Here are brief figures taken from the census of 1907, showing the gulf that divides the classes in German agriculture. Total number of farms—5,700,000. Of these, proletarian farms (up to two hectares) number 3,400,000. The overwhelming majority of these "farmers" are *wage-workers* who possess small plots of land.

Then follow the petty farmers (2 to 5 hectares per farm; total number of farms, 1,000,000). These are the poorest peasants. Less than half of them (495,000) are independent tillers *without* any other occupation. The majority are in need of outside employment, i.e., they have to sell their labour-power. These peasants join the proletariat most easily.

We will combine these to make up *Group I*: proletarian and small peasant farms.

Group II: middle peasant farms (5 to 10 hectares). As we have seen, a fairly large number of these exploit wage-workers. The middle peasant is a petty bourgeois who wavers between the proletariat and the bourgeoisie.

Group III: the rest, i.e., the capitalists (20 hectares and over) and big peasants (10 to 20 hectares). As we have seen, the *majority* of the big peasants exploit wage-workers.

Thus, Group I consists of proletarian and small peasant farms; Group II consists of middle peasant farms; Group III consists of big peasant and pure capitalist farms. Let us see how much land and livestock these groups own.

Group	Number of farms (000,000)	Number of workers (000,000)	Area of land (000,000 hectares)	Number of livestock (in terms of cattle) (000,000)	Number of machines (000,000)
I	4.4	7.3	5.0	7.0	0.2
II	0.6	2.5	4.6	5.1	0.4
III	0.7	5.4	22.2	17.3	1.2
Total	5.7	15.2	31.8	29.4	1.8

Such is the picture of modern agriculture; not the picture drawn by the professor, or by the Narodniks, but the real picture. *Most* of the land, livestock and machines belong to an insignificant minority (less than one-eighth—0.7 out of 5.7) of capitalists and peasant bourgeois. The *overwhelming majority* of the "farmers" (4.4 million out of 5.7 million) have less than two workers, less than two dessiatines and less than two head of livestock per farm. These are paupers. Their share in the total agricultural production is insignificant. They are led by the nose with promises of salvation under capitalism.

Compare the productivity of labour in the various groups (i.e., the number of workers per dessiatine of land and per head of livestock), and you will see a barbarous dissipation and waste of labour on the small farms. The capitalist farms own nearly all the machines and labour productivity is high.

Compare the number of livestock with the amount of land (including meadow land, land under fodder crops, etc.)

in the various groups. You will see starving cattle in the small farms and capitalist "prosperity" among the small group at the top.

The Marxists champion the interests of the masses and say to the peasants: there is no salvation for you except by joining in the proletarian struggle. The bourgeois professors and the Narodniks are deceiving the masses with fables about small "family" farming under capitalism.

Nash Put No. 15,
September 11, 1913;
Pravda Truda No. 4,
September 14, 1913
Signed: *V. Ilyin*

Published according to
the *Pravda Truda* text

HARRY QUELCH

On Wednesday, September 17 (September 4, O. S.), Comrade Harry Quelch, leader of the British Social-Democrats, died in London. The British Social-Democratic organisation was formed in 1884 and was called the Social Democratic Federation. In 1909 the name was changed to Social-Democratic Party, and in 1911, after a number of independently existing socialist groups amalgamated with it, it assumed the name of the British Socialist Party.

Harry Quelch was one of the most energetic and devoted workers in the British Social-Democratic movement. He was active not only as a Social-Democratic Party worker, but also as a trade-unionist. The London Society of Compositors repeatedly elected him its Chairman, and he was several times Chairman of the London Trades Council.

Quelch was the editor of *Justice*,[110] the weekly organ of the British Social-Democrats, as well as editor of the party monthly journal, the *Social-Democrat*.

He took a very active part in all the work of the British Social-Democratic movement and regularly addressed party and public meetings. On many occasions he represented British Social-Democracy at international congresses and on the International Socialist Bureau. Incidentally, when he attended the Stuttgart International Socialist Congress he was persecuted by the Wurtemburg Government, which *expelled* him from Stuttgart (without trial, by police order, as an alien) for referring at a public meeting to the Hague Conference as a "thieves' supper". When, the day following Quelch's expulsion, the Congress resumed its session, the British delegates left empty the chair on which Quelch had sat, and hung a notice on it bearing the inscription:

"Here sat Harry Quelch, now expelled by the Wurtemburg Government."

The South Germans often boast of their hatred for the Prussians because of the Prussian red tape, bureaucracy and police rule, but they themselves behave like the worst Prussians where a proletarian socialist is concerned.

The historical conditions for the activities of the British Social-Democrats, whose leader Quelch was, are of a very particular kind. In the most advanced land of capitalism and political liberty, the British bourgeoisie (who as far back as the seventeenth century settled accounts with the absolute monarchy in a rather democratic way) managed in the nineteenth century to *split* the British working-class movement. In the middle of the nineteenth century Britain enjoyed an almost complete monopoly in the world market. Thanks to this monopoly the profits acquired by British capital were extraordinarily high, so that it was possible for some crumbs of these profits to be thrown to the aristocracy of labour, the skilled factory workers.

This aristocracy of labour, which at that time earned tolerably good wages, boxed itself up in narrow, self-interested craft unions, and isolated itself from the mass of the proletariat, while in politics it supported the liberal bourgeoisie. And to this very day perhaps nowhere in the world are there so many liberals among the advanced workers as in Britain.

In the last quarter of the nineteenth century, however, things began to change. Britain's monopoly was challenged by America, Germany, etc. The economic basis for the narrow, petty-bourgeois trade-unionism and liberalism among British workers has been destroyed. Socialism is again raising its head in Britain, getting through to the masses and growing irresistibly *despite* the rank opportunism of the British near-socialist intelligentsia.

Quelch was in the front ranks of those who fought steadfastly and with conviction against opportunism and a liberal-labour policy in the British working-class movement. True, isolation from the masses sometimes infected the British Social-Democrats with a certain sectarianism. Hyndman, the leader and founder of Social-Democracy in Britain, has even slipped into jingoism. But the party of the Social-

Democrats* has fought him on this, and over the whole of Britain the Social-Democrats, and they *alone*, have for decades been carrying on systematic propaganda and agitation in the Marxist spirit. This is the great historical service rendered by Quelch and his comrades. The fruits of the activities of the Marxist Quelch will be reaped in full measure by the British working-class movement in the next few years.

In conclusion we cannot refrain from mentioning Quelch's sympathy for the Russian Social-Democrats and the assistance he rendered them. Eleven years ago the Russian Social-Democratic newspaper had to be printed in London. The British Social-Democrats, headed by Quelch, readily made their printing-plant available. As a consequence, Quelch himself had to "squeeze up". A corner was boarded off at the printing-works by a thin partition to serve him as editorial room. This corner contained a very small writing-table, a bookshelf above it, and a chair. When the present writer visited Quelch in this "editorial office" there was no room for another chair....

Pravda Truda No. 1,
September 11, 1913;
Nash Put No. 16,
September 12, 1913
Signed: *V. I.*

Published according to
the *Pravda Truda* text

---

* The party here referred to is the British Socialist Party, founded in 1911.—*Ed.*

MARXISM AND REFORMISM

Unlike the anarchists, the Marxists recognise struggle for reforms, i.e., for measures that improve the conditions of the working people without destroying the power of the ruling class. At the same time, however, the Marxists wage a most resolute struggle against the reformists, who, directly or indirectly, restrict the aims and activities of the working class to the winning of reforms. Reformism is bourgeois deception of the workers, who, despite individual improvements, will always remain wage-slaves, as long as there is the domination of capital.

The liberal bourgeoisie grant reforms with one hand, and with the other always take them back, reduce them to nought, use them to enslave the workers, to divide them into separate groups and perpetuate wage-slavery. For that reason reformism, even when quite sincere, in practice becomes a weapon by means of which the bourgeoisie corrupt and weaken the workers. The experience of all countries shows that the workers who put their trust in the reformists are always fooled.

And conversely, workers who have assimilated Marx's theory, i.e., realised the inevitability of wage-slavery so long as capitalist rule remains, will not be fooled by any bourgeois reforms. Understanding that where capitalism continues to exist reforms cannot be either enduring or far-reaching, the workers fight for better conditions and use them to intensify the fight against wage-slavery. The reformists try to divide and deceive the workers, to divert them from the class struggle by petty concessions. But the workers, having seen through the falsity of reformism, utilise reforms to develop and broaden their class struggle.

The stronger reformist influence is among the workers the weaker they are, the greater their dependence on the bourgeoisie, and the easier it is for the bourgeoisie to nullify reforms by various subterfuges. The more independent the working-class movement, the deeper and broader its aims, and the freer it is from reformist narrowness the easier it is for the workers to retain and utilise improvements.

There are reformists in all countries, for everywhere the bourgeoisie seek, in one way or another, to corrupt the workers and turn them into contented slaves who have given up all thought of doing away with slavery. In Russia, the reformists are liquidators, who renounce our past and try to lull the workers with dreams of a new, open, legal party. Recently the St. Petersburg liquidators were forced by *Severnaya Pravda** to defend themselves against the charge of reformism. Their arguments should be carefully analysed in order to clarify an extremely important question.

We are not reformists, the St. Petersburg liquidators wrote, because we have not said that reforms are everything and the ultimate goal nothing; we have spoken of movement to the ultimate goal; we have spoken of advancing through the struggle for reforms to the fulness of the aims set.

Let us now see how this defence squares with the facts.

First fact. The liquidator Sedov, summarising the statements of all the liquidators, wrote that of the Marxists' "three pillars" two are no longer suitable for our agitation. Sedov retained the demand for an eight-hour day, which, theoretically, can be realised as a reform. He deleted, or relegated to the background the very things that go beyond reforms. Consequently, Sedov relapsed into downright opportunism, following the very policy expressed in the formula: the ultimate goal is nothing. When the "ultimate goal" (even in relation to democracy) is pushed further and further away from our agitation, that is reformism.

Second fact. The celebrated August Conference (last year's) of the liquidators likewise pushed non-reformist demands further and further away—until some special occasion—instead of bringing them closer, into the heart of our agitation.

---

* See pp. 325-27 of this volume.—*Ed.*

Third fact. By denying and disparaging the "old" and dissociating themselves from it, the liquidators thereby confine themselves to reformism. In the present situation, the connection between reformism and the renunciation of the "old" is obvious.

Fourth fact. The workers' economic movement evokes the wrath and attacks of the liquidators (who speak of "crazes", "milling the air", etc., etc.) as soon as it adopts slogans that go beyond reformism.

What is the result? In words, the liquidators reject reformism as a principle, but in practice they adhere to it all along the line. They assure us, on the one hand, that for them reforms are not the be-all and end-all, but on the other hand, every time the Marxists go beyond reformism, the liquidators attack them or voice their contempt.

However, developments in every sector of the working-class movement show that the Marxists, far from lagging behind, are definitely in the lead in making practical use of reforms, and in fighting for them. Take the Duma elections at the worker curia level—the speeches of our deputies inside and outside the Duma, the organisation of the workers' press, the utilisation of the insurance reform; take the biggest union, the Metalworkers' Union, etc.,— everywhere the Marxist workers are ahead of the liquidators, in the direct, immediate, "day-to-day" activity of agitation, organisation, fighting for reforms and using them.

The Marxists are working tirelessly, not missing a single "possibility" of winning and using reforms, and not condemning, but supporting, painstakingly developing every step beyond reformism in propaganda, agitation, mass economic struggle, etc. The liquidators, on the other hand, who have abandoned Marxism, by their attacks on the very existence of the Marxist body, by their destruction of Marxist discipline and advocacy of reformism and a liberal-labour policy, are only disorganising the working-class movement.

Nor, moreover, should the fact be overlooked that in Russia reformism is manifested also in a peculiar form, in identifying the fundamental political situation in present-day Russia with that of present-day Europe. From the liberal's point of view this identification is legitimate, for the liberal believes and professes the view that "thank

God, we have a Constitution". The liberal expresses the interests of the bourgeoisie when he insists that, after October 17, every step by democracy beyond reformism is madness, a crime, a sin, etc.

But it is these bourgeois views that are applied in practice by our liquidators, who constantly and systematically "transplant" to Russia (on paper) the "open party" and the "struggle for a legal party", etc. In other words, like the liberals, they preach the transplanting of the European constitution to Russia, *without* the specific path that in the West led to the adoption of constitutions and their consolidation over generations, in some cases even over centuries. What the liquidators and liberals want is to wash the hide without dipping it in water, as the saying goes.

In Europe, reformism actually means abandoning Marxism and replacing it by bourgeois "social policy". In Russia, the reformism of the liquidators means not only that, it means destroying the Marxist organisation and abandoning the democratic tasks of the working class, it means replacing them by a liberal-labour policy.

Pravda Truda No. 2,
September 12, 1913
Signed: *V. I.*

Published according to
the *Pravda Truda* text

THE LAND QUESTION AND THE RURAL POOR

A paper on this important subject was read by Minin, a Chernigov agronomist, at the All-Russian Agricultural Congress on September 3 in Kiev.

Mr. Minin, apparently a Narodnik (who agreed, incidentally, with the bourgeois professor Kosinsky on the viability of "family" farming), demonstrated in all justice that agronomy helps the affluent peasant. The agrarian regulations help the strong and ruin the poor. They are a chariot in which the strong sit and crush the defeated.

There can be no doubt that this is an absolute truth. Only people without a conscience could deny it. But in what does Mr. Minin see "salvation"?

He said (according to the report in *Kievskaya Mysl* No. 244):

"The only thing that will save the smallest farms after the reallocation is for them to form themselves into voluntary co-operatives for the joint exploitation (collective tilling) of their own land."

Obviously, this Narodnik remedy is simply childish. The landowners and kulaks are driving millions of peasants from the land and ruining millions more. World capitalism as a whole, the entire power of international commerce, the might of capital to the tune of thousands of millions in the hands of the bourgeoisie of all countries are pulling Russia along with them, sustaining and supporting her bourgeoisie in the towns and in the *countryside*, including those within the village communes. And now we are told that the collective tilling of "their own scraps of land" by ruined peasants is "salvation"! This is like trying to beat a railway train with a wheelbarrow—in speed and carrying capacity.

It won't work, my Narodnik gentlemen! You are right, of course, when you say that the railway train is crushing the poor, but wheelbarrows are not what you should be thinking about.

Not backward from the train to the wheelbarrow, but onward from the capitalist train to that of the united proletarians.

The innocent dreams of the Narodniks are not only childishly naïve, they are actually harmful because they divert the minds of the poor from the class struggle. There is no salvation for the rural poor *outside* the class struggle of the proletariat against the bourgeoisie for the reconstruction of the entire capitalist system. All these unions, co-operatives, associations, etc., can only be of use if they participate consciously in that class struggle.

Although it is beyond all shadow of doubt that the development of capitalism and the proletarianisation of the countryside must inevitably continue in Russia, as in the rest of the world, it would be the greatest mistake to confine oneself to this truth.

There are various kinds of capitalism—the semi-feudal capitalism of the landowners with its host of residual privileges, which is the most reactionary and causes the masses the greatest suffering; there is also the capitalism of free farmers, which is the most democratic, causes the masses less suffering and has fewer residual privileges.

What influence, for example, would the transfer of all the land to the peasants without compensation have on the development of capitalism in Russia? That would not be socialism. That would *also* be capitalism, yet it would not be Purishkevich-Guchkov but democratic, Narodnik-peasant capitalism. The development of capitalism would proceed more rapidly, more extensively, more freely and with less suffering for the masses.

That is the *real substance* of the present, existing agrarian problem in Russia. That is what the advocates of landowners' solution of the land question and bourgeois agronomy on the one hand, and the Narodniks and Left Cadets (such as Shakhovskoi) on the other, were arguing about in Kiev (without understanding the substance of the issue). They were arguing about whether bourgeois democrats

should leave the Purishkeviches to complete the organisation of the new Russia on feudal-capitalist lines, or whether
they should take that organisation into their own hands,
into the hands of the masses, into the hands of the peasants,
and continue it without the Purishkeviches on free, democratic, capitalist lines.

It is not difficult to understand the position of the politically conscious worker on this issue. We know perfectly
well that both the Stolypin path of development and that of
the Narodniks mean the development of capitalism, which
will in any case lead to the triumph of the proletariat. We
shall not lose heart, no matter which turn history takes. But
we shall not allow history to take any turn without our participation, without the active intervention of the advanced
class. The working class is not indifferent to the clashes between the Purishkeviches and the peasant democrats; its
attitude is one of heartiest, most devoted defence of the interests of peasant democracy and democracy for the entire
people in their most consistent form.

Not the least concession to the alleged socialism (but
actually petty-bourgeois dreaming) of the Narodniks, which
is rotten through and through, but the greatest attention
to the peasant democrats, to their education, to awakening
and rallying them, to liberating them from every kind of
stifling prejudice—such is the line taken by the politically
conscious worker.

Do you want to dream of the victory of the wheelbarrow
over the train? Then your way is not ours, we are the enemies of banal Manilovism.[111] Do you want to fight against
the Purishkeviches? Then your way is ours, but remember
that the workers will not forgive the slightest vacillation.

But the working class treats those who, in obsequious
haste, declare the "complete" success of Stolypin's solution
of the land question with the contempt that advanced,
strong classes hostile to reformism always display towards
opportunists and towards the knights of transient success.

Pravda Truda No. 3,
September 13, 1913
Signed: *V. Ilyin*

Published according to
the *Pravda Truda* text

HOW DOES BISHOP NIKON DEFEND
THE UKRAINIANS?

It is reported in *Kievskaya Mysl* that Bishop Nikon, deputy to the State Duma, Right, was the first to put his signature to the bill on the Ukrainian school and Ukrainian associations submitted to the Duma.

The bill says: teaching in elementary schools in the Ukrainian language shall be permitted; Ukrainian teachers shall be appointed; the teaching of the Ukrainian language and the history of the Ukraine shall be introduced; Ukrainian associations shall not be persecuted and they shall not be closed "at the discretion of the authorities, which is frequently undisguised lawlessness".

Thus Purishkevich's party comrade, Bishop Nikon, does not like *lawlessness* in *certain* cases.

Bishop Nikon is quite right in assuming that the question he raises "is one of outstanding importance, one that concerns the perversion of the thirty-seven million Ukrainians"; in saying that "the rich, beautiful, talented, flourishing and poetic Ukraine is being condemned to degeneration, gradual stultification and slow extinction".

The protest against the oppression of the Ukrainians by the Great Russians is a perfectly just one. But let us look at the arguments Bishop Nikon puts forward in defence of the Ukrainian demands.

"The Ukrainian people do not seek any of this notorious autonomy, re-establishment of the Zaporozhye Sech or something of that kind; the Ukrainians are not separatists.... The Ukrainians are not people of foreign extraction, they are our own people, our blood brothers, and as such should not suffer any limitations in respect of their language and the development of their national culture; otherwise we equate them, our brothers, with the Jews, Poles, Georgians and others, who actually are people of foreign extraction."

And so it boils down to this—the Ukrainian Bishop Nikon and others of his school of thought are begging the Great-Russian landowners to grant *privileges* to the Ukrainians on the grounds that they are their brothers, while the Jews are people of foreign extraction! To put it simply and forthrightly—because the Jews and others are of foreign extraction we agree to oppress them, if you make concessions to us.

The picture is the familiar one of the defence of "national culture" *by all* bourgeois nationalists, from the Black Hundreds to the liberals, and even to the bourgeois-democratic nationalists!

What Bishop Nikon refuses to understand is that the Ukrainians cannot be protected from oppression unless all peoples, without exception, are protected from all oppression, unless the concept "people of foreign extraction" is completely expunged from the life of the state, unless the complete equality of rights of all nationalities is upheld. No one can be protected from national oppression unless the most extensive local and regional autonomy and the principle of settling *all* state questions in accordance with the will of the majority of the population (that is, the principle of consistent democracy) are consistently put into practice.

Bishop Nikon's slogan of "national culture" for the Ukrainians means nothing more than the propagation of Black-Hundred ideas in the Ukrainian language; it is the slogan of Ukrainian-clerical culture.

Politically conscious workers have understood that the slogan of "national culture" is clerical or bourgeois deception—no matter whether it concerns Great-Russian, Ukrainian, Jewish, Polish, Georgian or any other culture. A hundred and twenty-five years ago, when the nation had not been split into bourgeoisie and proletariat, the slogan of national culture could have been a single and integral call to struggle against feudalism and clericalism. Since that time, however, the class struggle between the bourgeoisie and the proletariat has gained momentum everywhere. The division of the "single" nation into exploiters and exploited has become an accomplished fact.

Only the clericals and the bourgeoisie can speak of national culture in general. The working people can speak only of the international culture of the world working-class movement. That is the only culture that means full, real, sincere equality of nations, the absence of national oppression and the implementation of democracy. Only the unity and solidarity of workers of all nations in *all* working-class organisations in the struggle against capital will lead to "the solution of the national problem".

Pravda Truda No. 3,
September 13, 1913

Published according to
the *Pravda Truda* text

NOTES OF A PUBLICIST

I. NON-PARTY INTELLECTUALS AGAINST MARXISM

The editors of *Novaya Rabochaya Gazeta* have come out in defence of the non-Party agitation to divide collections equally between the liquidators, the Narodniks and the Marxists.

When it was pointed out to them that such a division is an absolutely unprincipled method that undermines the foundations of the Marxist attitude to petty-bourgeois trends,* the editors did not know what to say in reply and tried to pass it off with a joke. We, they said, don't know anything about a "Marxist system of collections".

The renegades want to "make amiable jokes" about our old decisions.

The workers, however, will allow no joking on such a question.

That same twenty-third issue of *Novaya Rabochaya Gazeta* informs us that the liquidators' agitation has attracted two working-class groups in Russia—a group of printing workers in the town of Dvinsk and a group at the Nemirov-Kolodkin factory in Moscow. These groups contributed their collections *equally* to the liquidators', Narodniks' and Marxist newspapers.

Let the renegade intellectuals laugh off the question; the workers, however, must and will decide it.

To preach the equal division of collections means preaching non-partisanship and confusing (or equating) newspapers that hold the proletarian class point of view with

---

* See pp. 343-47 of this volume.—*Ed.*

those of the petty bourgeoisie, the Narodnik newspapers. The "amiable jokers", those who write for the liquidators' newspaper, cannot raise any objection to this elementary truth, although their jokes and sniggers probably arouse the admiration of the bourgeois public. A person who has suffered a complete fiasco among the workers often recompenses himself with the admiration expressed by the bourgeoisie when he ridicules the very idea of a consistently Marxist solution to questions of current practice.

The liquidators have taken comfort—at a meeting of metalworkers they suffered a complete defeat. At any meeting of the bourgeois gentry the liquidators are awarded an amiable smile for amiable jokes directed against the position held by a workers' newspaper.

Let everyone have what he wants. Let the liquidators console themselves with their successes among the bourgeoisie. The workers, however, will explain to the masses the indubitable truth that to preach the equal division of workers' collections is preaching non-partisanship, is preaching the confusion or the equation of the proletariat's Marxist newspaper with an intellectual and petty-bourgeois newspaper, like that of the Narodniks.

II. LIBERAL BLINDNESS

The usual method adopted by West-European opportunists, from the time of Eduard Bernstein, whose views were vigorously rejected by German Social-Democracy, is the following:

"Take a look at things as they are," said Bernstein and the other opportunists, "have the courage to say outright what is—in Germany we are all engaged in a struggle for reforms, we are all reformists in essence, we are a party of reforms. And the abolition of wage-slavery in a series of crises is all words, an empty utopia."

Since then the opportunists have repeated this trick of theirs a hundred times and the entire bourgeois press (our Cadet *Rech* above all) is constantly making use of this argument of the opportunists *against* Marxism. Anyone seriously interested in the fate of the working-class move-

ment should have a proper knowledge of this worn-out manoeuvre of the downright enemies and false friends of the
proletariat.

In St. Petersburg quite recently (September 4) the not
unknown liquidator D. repeated in the liquidators' newspaper the all-Europe bourgeois manoeuvre with a crude-
ness or arrogance that is worthy·of attention.

Let the reader judge for himself.

"We open any workers' newspaper, say even *Severnaya Pravda,*"
wrote D., "and what do we see? We read of the activities of workers'
organisations, trade unions, clubs and co-operatives; of the meetings
of the members of those organisations and of their leading committees,
of insurance agents, etc.; of lectures and reports organised by workers; of strikes and strike committees; of the organisation of various
collections; of attempts at political action on the part of groups of
workers in defence of the workers' press, to honour the memory of
Bebel or for some other immediate purpose."

That is what D. and others like him have "seen" and
still "see" in *Severnaya Pravda.* And just like Bernstein,
of course, he exclaims: "It will do no harm to look first
at what is" (D.'s italics). Whereupon he comes to the conclusion that all this is the struggle for freedom of association. "The slogan of struggle for freedom of association as
the most important current demand", "epitomises *what is*"
(D.'s italics).

Bernstein maintained that he was "generalising what
is" when he asserted that the working-class struggle was
a struggle for reforms.

D. maintains that he is "generalising what is" when he
asserts that the working-class movement in Russia is reformist.

Bernstein tried to give a *liberal* content to the workers'
struggle for reforms, a struggle filled with a far from reformist content. D. is acting in literally the same fashion.
He sees *nothing* but liberal reformism and tries to pass off
his blindness as reality.

Severnaya Pravda, of course, did fight for even the slightest improvement in the workers' life and in the conditions of
the workers' struggle, but did not do it in the liberal way,
as gentlemen like D. do! There *was* a lot in *Severnaya Pravda*
that they missed—there was the struggle against reformism,
there was defence of the "old", defence of full-blooded slo-

gans, etc. Gentlemen like D. are of the opinion that such things are not important. They *"fail to see"* them, they do not want to see them, just because they are liberals. Like all liberals, they cannot understand the *connection*, the close, inseverable connection the Marxists make between defence of the slightest improvement and defence of the slogans of their organisation, etc. It is not clear to them that this connection determines the radical difference between the world outlook of the liberal (he is also in favour of freedom of association) and that of the working-class democrat.

Divorce the struggle for reforms from the struggle for the final goal—that is what Bernstein's preaching actually amounts to. Divorce the struggle for improvements, for freedom of association, etc., from the struggle against reformism, from the defence of Marxism, from its spirit and its political trend—that is what the preaching of D. and the other liquidators actually amounts to.

They want to impose their liberal blindness (not seeing the connection with the past, not seeing its trend, not seeing the struggle against reformism) on the working class. As the meeting of metalworkers on August 25 showed again and again, advanced workers have already seen through the liberal nature of D. and his petty group.

III. A NECESSARY EXPLANATION

In issue No. 24 of *Novaya Rabochaya Gazeta* we came across an amusing sally against our description of the Dublin events.* It would probably not have been worth while responding to an amusing item had the liquidators' newspaper not gone so far as to offer an explanation that is extremely important and instructive for the workers. Judge for yourselves. We made a distinction between Britain, where the workers' demand for the *reform* of trade union legislation (laws on freedom of association) is of very serious and real importance because the general basis of political liberty exists in that country, and Russia, where such a demand

---

* See pp. 348-49 of this volume.—*Ed.*

is not serious, is an empty liberal phrase, but where such
reforms as insurance are seriously practicable under the
existing political system.

The liquidators do not understand the difference. Let
us try to explain it by asking two questions: 1. Why is
a bourgeois-democratic revolution, a revolution for political liberties, impossible in England? 2. Why was it that
in Russia, towards the end of the last century, in 1897, for
example, partial *reforms* of the factory laws were quite
possible, and nobody disputed the partial demands of the
workers in this sphere, whereas all Marxists in those days
considered that the demand for partial political reforms was
a liberal deception?

When the liquidators have given these questions some
thought they may be able to guess the reasons for taking a
different attitude to various reforms in Russia and in Britain.

And now for the important explanation given in the
liquidators' newspaper.

"But," it says (*No. 24, page 2, column 1*) *"if this basis* [*i.e., the
general basis of political liberties*] *is not necessary for partial changes
in insurance legislation, why is it necessary for a partial change
in the law of March 4, 1906 and certain articles of the decree on
strikes of December 2, 1905?"*

We congratulate you on your frankness and thank you
for it! You have hit the mark—"a partial change in the
laws of March 4, 1906 and December 2, 1905"[112] is quite
possible *without* anything general! Superb.

Only—do you know what?—that "partial change in the
laws of March 4, 1906 and December 2, 1905" is not called
"freedom of association" but Octobrist deception of the
people.

The *Novaya Rabochaya Gazeta* writers have admitted
exactly what was to be proved.

By the "freedom of association" that the liberals and
liquidators treat you to, must be understood:

*"A partial change in the laws of March 4, 1906 and December 2,
1905."*

Once again we thank you for your frankness. And so we
shall put it on record that the main, central, chief, primary,
etc., etc., slogan of the liquidators is, by their own admis-

sion, the demand for *a partial change in the laws of March 4, 1906 and December 2, 1905.*

Novaya Rabochaya Gazeta has brilliantly refuted its association with the liberals, has it not?

It is not for nothing that the liquidators have been called Social-Democratic Octobrists!

Pravda Truda No. 3,
September 13, 1913
Signed: *N—k*

Published according to
the *Pravda Truda* text

CIVILISED BARBARISM

Britain and France are the most civilised countries in the world. London and Paris are the world's capitals, with populations of six and three million, respectively. The distance between them is an eight- to nine-hour journey.

One can imagine how great is the commercial intercourse between these two capitals, what masses of goods and of people are constantly moving from the one to the other.

And yet the richest, the most civilised and the freest countries in the world are now discussing, in fear and trepidation—by no means for the first time!—the "difficult" question of whether a tunnel can be built under the English Channel (which separates Britain from the European Continent).

Engineers have long been of the opinion that it can. The capitalists of Britain and France have mountains of money. Profit from capital invested in such an enterprise would be absolutely certain.

What, then, is holding the matter up?

Britain is afraid of—invasion! A tunnel, you see, would, "if anything should happen", facilitate the invasion of Britain by enemy troops. That is why the British military authorities have, not for the first time, wrecked the plan to build the tunnel.

The madness and blindness of the civilised nations makes astonishing reading. Needless to say, it would take only a few seconds with modern technical devices to bring traffic in the tunnel to a halt, and to wreck the tunnel completely.

But the civilised nations have driven themselves into the position of barbarians. Capitalism has brought about a situation in which the bourgeoisie, in order to hoodwink the workers, is *compelled* to frighten the British people with idiotic tales about "invasion". Capitalism has brought about a situation in which a whole group of capitalists who stand to lose "good business" through the digging of the tunnel are doing their utmost to wreck this plan and hold up technical progress.

The Britishers' fear of the tunnel is fear of themselves. Capitalist barbarism is stronger than civilisation.

On all sides, at every step one comes across problems which man is quite capable of solving *immediately*, but capitalism is in the way. It has amassed enormous wealth—and has made men the *slaves* of this wealth. It has solved the most complicated technical problems—and has blocked the application of technical improvements because of the poverty and ignorance of millions of the population, because of the stupid avarice of a handful of millionaires.

Civilisation, freedom and wealth under capitalism call to mind the rich glutton who is rotting alive but will not let what is young live on.

But the young is growing and will emerge supreme in spite of all.

Pravda Truda No. 6,
September 10. 1913
Signed: *W.*

Published according to
the *Pravda Truda* text

THE BLACK HUNDREDS

There is in our Black-Hundred movement one exceedingly original and exceedingly important feature that has not been the subject of sufficient attention. That feature is ignorant peasant democracy, democracy of the crudest type but also extremely deep-seated.

No matter how much the commanding classes try to fence our political parties off from the people both by means of the June Third election law and by thousands of "peculiar features" of our political system, reality has its way. Every political party, even of the extreme Right, has to seek some sort of link with the people.

The extreme Rights constitute the party of the landowners. They cannot, however, confine themselves to links with the landowners alone. They have to conceal those links and pretend that they are defending the interests of the entire people, that they stand for the "good old", "stable" way of rural life. They have to appeal to the most deep-rooted prejudices of the most backward peasant, they have to play on his ignorance.

Such a game cannot be played without risk. Now and again the voice of the real peasant life, peasant democracy, breaks through all the Black-Hundred mustiness and cliché. Then the Rights are compelled to get rid of the "inconvenient" peasant democrat. Naturally this banishment of the most faithful Black Hundreds, their expulsion from their own camp by the extreme Rights because of their democracy, is not without its educational effect on the masses.

Bishop Nikon, an extreme Right-winger has, for instance, been forced to abandon his Duma work. Why?

A letter from Bishop Nikon himself, published in *Yeniseiskaya Mysl*,[113] gives a clear answer to this. It stands to reason that Bishop Nikon dare not speak openly about the reasons for his withdrawal. But Bishop Nikon, quoting a letter from a peasant, does write: "The land, bread and other important questions of our Russian life and of the region do not appear to reach either the hands or the hearts of the authorities or the Duma. These questions and such solution of them as is possible are regarded as 'utopian', 'hazardous', untimely. Why do you keep silent, what are you waiting for? For moods and revolts for which those same 'undernourished', hungry, unfortunate peasants will be shot down? We are afraid of 'big' issues and reforms, we limit ourselves to trivialities and trifles, good though they may be."

That is what Bishop Nikon writes. And that is what very many Black-Hundred peasants think. It is quite understandable why Bishop Nikon *had* to be removed from Duma affairs and Duma speeches for such statements.

Bishop Nikon expresses his Black-Hundred democracy in arguments that are, in essence, very far from correct. The land, bread and all other important questions *do* reach the hands and hearts (and pockets) of the "authorities" and the Duma.

The "authorities" and the Duma *provide* "such solution" to these questions "as is possible"—and it is indeed the *possible* solution, the one that accords with the interests and power of the landowners who are dominant among the authorities and in the Duma.

Bishop Nikon realises that his Black-Hundred views are being undermined by the real state of affairs; they are being destroyed by what he observes in the Duma and in the attitude of the "authorities", etc. Bishop Nikon, however, cannot *understand* the reason for all this, or is afraid to understand it.

But reality will win through, and out of ten in any village who think as Bishop Nikon does, nine will, in the long run, most likely prove less obtuse in mastering the lessons of life than the bishop.

Pravda Truda No. 14,
September 26, 1913

Published according to
the *Pravda Truda* text

RUSSIAN GOVERNMENT
AND RUSSIAN REFORMS

There is a little magazine called *Grazhdanin*[114] compiled by Prince Meshchersky. The Prince, who has been through fire and water in the various higher civil service "spheres" of St. Petersburg, usually preaches in this magazine the most reactionary things.

The magazine is interesting primarily because in it the talkative Prince is continually divulging the secrets of the higher administration of Russia. For Russia is actually administered by those landowner dignitaries in whose society Prince Meshchersky moved and is still moving. And they actually do administer Russia in exactly the way, in exactly the spirit, by exactly the means advised, assumed and suggested by Prince Meshchersky.

In the second place, the magazine is interesting because its courtly editor, confident that it will never *reach the people*, often exposes the Russian administration in the most ruthless manner.

Here are two interesting admissions made by this princely dignitary:

"A very typical phenomenon," he writes. "From time to time people come to us from France, or Belgium, or England, nice people who show a sympathy for Russia and the Russians, they stay in luxurious circumstances in a hotel, submit their letters of introduction to some official or another ... and quite soon, in perhaps ten days or so, these newly arrived foreigners are received by some minister and are given hopes of receiving some concession, which they take off home with them.... Then back they come again and a week later they have already acquired a concession somewhere in Russia and are counting up the foreseeable profits with such energy that they have dreams of millions."

That is what Prince Meshchersky writes. By way of exception he writes the truth. Features of Asiatic primitiveness, governmental graft, the schemes of financiers who share their monopoly incomes with highly-placed officials, are still boundlessly strong in Russian capitalism. When our Narodniks fight, and fight with good reason, against such disgusting and shameless swindles, they often regard it as a war against capitalism. Their mistake is obvious. They are actually fighting *for the democratisation* of capitalism.

"When I was abroad," the arch-reactionary Prince writes in another place, "I was in contact with people in different walks of life.... I do not remember that any sort of social or state reforms ever constituted the subject of the conversation.... I read the newspapers ... but found no articles about reforms.... As soon as I crossed the frontier and reached home, I found the reverse; I took up the first Russian newspaper I came across and on the first, the second and even the third page there were articles about some sort of reforms."

Correctly observed. The bourgeoisie does not need reforms in Europe. In Russia they are necessary. The princely dignitary cannot understand the reason for this difference—just as some wise people cannot understand that the strongly anti-reformist tactics of the workers are justified because of the bourgeoisie's need for reforms.

Pravda Truda No. 14,   Published according to
September 26. 1913   the *Pravda Truda* text
Signed: *Observer*

HOW VERA ZASULICH DEMOLISHES LIQUIDATIONISM

Zhivaya Zhizn No. 8 (July 19, 1913), carried an excellent article by Vera Zasulich in defence of liquidationism ("Apropos of a Certain Question"). We ask all those interested in questions affecting the working-class movement and democracy to pay careful attention to this article, which is valuable both because of its contents and because of the forthrightness of its authoritative author.

I

In the first place, Vera Zasulich, like all liquidators, does her best to calumniate the Party, but her frankness as a writer exposes her so clearly that it is amazing. "The Russian Social-Democratic Labour Party," we read in the article, "is an underground organisation of intellectuals for propaganda and agitation among the workers, which was founded at the Second Congress, and which split immediately." Actually, the Party was founded in 1898 and based itself on the awakening of a mass working-class movement in the 1895-96 period. Dozens and hundreds of workers (like the late Babushkin in St. Petersburg) not only attended lectures at study circles but as early as 1894-95 *themselves carried on agitation* and then founded workers' organisations in other cities (the Ekaterinoslav organisations founded by Babushkin when he was exiled from St. Petersburg, etc.).

The relative dominance of intellectuals in the early days of the movement was to be observed everywhere and not only in Russia. By using this fact to slander the workers' party, Vera Zasulich crushes liquidationism among all thinking workers who experienced the agitation and strikes of 1894-96.

"In 1903," writes Vera Zasulich, "the underground study circles engaged in this work were united to form a secret society with hierarchical rules. It is difficult to say whether the new organisation as such helped or hindered current work...."

Anyone who does not wish to be accused of having a short memory, must know that groups of intellectuals and workers, not only in 1903, but beginning from 1894 (and in some cases even earlier) *helped* both in economic and political agitation, in strikes and in propaganda. To assert publicly that "it is difficult to say whether the new organisation helped or hindered the work" is not merely stating a tremendous and obvious historical untruth—it means *renouncing the Party*.

What value, indeed, can one place on the Party if it is difficult to say whether it helped or hindered the work? Is it not clear that the sabbath was made for man and not man for the sabbath?

The liquidators have to renounce the Party in retrospect in order to justify their renunciation of it at the present time.

Vera Zasulich, speaking of this present time, the June Third epoch, says: "I have heard reports of the district branches of the organisation losing members...."

There is no disputing that fact. The district and all other branches of the organisation have lost members. The question is one of how this phenomenon of flight from the organisation is to be explained, what attitude is to be adopted towards that phenomenon.

Vera Zasulich answers: "they lost their members because at that time there was nothing to do in them."

The answer is definite and may be equated with a definite condemnation of the underground and justification of flight from it. How does Vera Zasulich prove her statement? 1) There was nothing for propagandists to do because "many workers had collected whole libraries" of books published in the days of freedom, "which the police had not yet succeeded in confiscating".

Vera Zasulich has an interesting knack of not noticing how she refutes her own words. If the police were "confiscating" the libraries, *it means* that discussions on what had been read, the assimilation of it and further study *was giving rise* precisely to underground work! Vera Zasulich wants to prove that there "was nothing to do", while her own admission shows that there *was* something to do.

2) "Underground political agitation was out of the question at that time. Furthermore, it was neither the right, nor the duty of the districts to take the initiative in such 'actions'."

Vera Zasulich repeats the liquidators' words without knowing the state of affairs. That the period under discussion was a difficult one, more difficult than before, there is no denying. The work of the Marxists, however, is *always* "difficult" but the thing that makes them different from the liberals is that they do not declare what is difficult to be impossible. The liberal calls difficult work impossible so as to conceal his renunciation of it. The difficulty of the work compels the Marxist to strive for greater solidarity among the best elements in order to overcome the difficulties.

The objective fact that the work in the period under discussion was *possible* and was conducted is proved, for example, by the elections to the Third and Fourth Dumas, if by nothing else. Surely Vera Zasulich does not believe that supporters of the underground movement could have been elected to the State Duma *without* the participation of the underground.

3) "There was nothing to do in the underground groups, but outside them there was a mass of essential social work to be done." Clubs, various associations, congresses, lectures, etc.

Such is the argument put forward by all liquidators and repeated by Vera Zasulich. Her article could simply be recommended for use in workers' circles as an object-lesson on the misadventures of the liquidators!

The underground was necessary because, among other things, Marxist work in clubs, associations, at congresses, etc., was connected with it.

Compare this argument of mine with that of Vera Zasulich. Ask yourself, *what grounds* has Vera Zasulich for depicting work in legal associations as something carried on *"outside"* the work of the underground groups? Why "outside" and not "in close contact with", why not "in the same direction"?

Vera Zasulich has no factual grounds whatsoever, because everybody knows that there was probably not a single legal association, etc., in which members of the underground groups did not take part. The only grounds Vera Zasulich has for her assertions is the subjective mood of the liquidators. The liquidators did get the feeling that there was nothing *for them* to do in the underground, that *they* sympathised only with work that was *outside* the underground, only if it was *outside* the ideological line of the underground. In other words, Vera Zasulich's "grounds." amount to *justification* of the liquidators' flight from the underground!

Pitiful grounds indeed.

We cannot, however, confine ourselves to pointing out the subjective grounds for Vera Zasulich's writings, the errors of fact and logic with which literally every phrase of her article teems. We must seek the objective grounds for the undoubted fact that the "districts lost their members", that there was a flight from the underground.

We have not far to look. It is well enough known that the bourgeois and petty-bourgeois society of Russia at the time under discussion was carried away to a very great extent by counter-revolutionary temper. It is well enough known what profound antagonism between the bourgeoisie and the proletariat came to the surface in the days of freedom and engendered that counter-revolutionary temper and also confusion, despondency and loss of spirit among many vacillating friends of the proletariat.

This objective relationship between classes in the period under discussion explains fully enough why the bourgeoisie in general and the liberal bourgeoisie in particular (for domination over the masses of the people had been snatched out of their hands) *were bound* to hate the underground, declare it worthless and "ineffective" (Vera Zasulich's expression), condemn and reject underground political agitation and also the conduct of legal work in the spirit of the underground, in accordance with the slogans of the *underground* and in direct ideological and organisational contact with it.

The first to flee from the underground were the bourgeois intellectuals who succumbed to the counter-revolutionary mood, those "fellow-travellers" of the Social-Democratic working-class movement who, like those in Europe, had been attracted by the liberating role played by the proletariat (in Europe—by the plebs in general) in the bourgeois revolution. It is a well-known fact what a mass of Marxists left the underground after 1905 and found places for themselves in all sorts of legal cosy corners for intellectuals.

No matter what subjective "good" intentions Vera Zasulich may have had, her repetition of the arguments of the liquidators amounts objectively to a rehash of the petty ideas of the counter-revolutionary liberals. The liquidators, who are so loud in their talk of "independent action by the workers", etc., actually represent and defend the intellectuals who have defected from the working-class movement and gone over to the side of the bourgeoisie.

The flight of some people from the underground could have been the result of their fatigue and dispiritedness. Such individuals may only be pitied; they should be helped because their dispiritedness will pass and there will again appear an urge to get away from philistinism, away from the liberals and the liberal-labour policy, to the working-class underground. But when the fatigued and dispirited use journalism as their platform and announce that their flight is not a manifestation of fatigue, or weakness, or intellectual woolliness, but that it is to their credit, and then put the blame on the "ineffective", "worthless", "moribund", etc., underground, these runaways then become disgusting renegades, apostates. These runaways then become the worst of advisers for the working-class movement and therefore its dangerous enemies.

When one finds the liquidators defending and lauding such elements and at the same time coming out with vows and assurances that they, the liquidators, stand for unity, one can only shrug one's shoulders and ask oneself whom they hope to deceive with this blissful idiocy and hypocrisy. Is it not obvious that a working-class party cannot possibly exist without a determined struggle against the lauding of defection from the Party?

The liquidators (with Vera Zasulich following them) enjoy calling these apostates and runaways "the living forces of the working class". But these evasions of the liberal intellectuals have long been refuted by indisputable facts on a country-wide scale. Of the deputies from the worker curias 47 per cent were Bolsheviks in the Second Duma, 50 per cent in the Third Duma and 67 per cent in the Fourth Duma. This is an irrefutable proof that the workers left the liquidators in the period between 1907 and 1913. The emergence of the first working-class daily newspaper and the events now to be observed in the trade unions add still further proofs to this. If we glance at the objective facts and not at the empty, boasting declarations of the liberal intellectuals, we shall see that the living forces of the working class are those of the supporters of the underground, the opponents of the liquidators.

All Vera Zasulich's discourse on the past is, however, only the beginning. There is something better to come. Her defence of renegation and defection from the Party is only the introduction to her defence of the destruction of the Party. It is these important sections of her article that we shall now examine.

II

"The underground organisation," we read in the article, "has always been the weakest feature of Social-Democracy in Russia ..." ("always"—neither more nor less). Bold historians, our liquidators. "Always" means in 1882-93, before the mass working-class movement under the organised leadership of the Party; it means in 1894-1904. And in the 1905-07 period?

"But even if it had been ten times better, it would not have survived the revolution and counter-revolution. In the history of Europe I cannot remember a single revolutionary organisation that, after living through a revolution, proved effective in the moment of reaction."

This argument provides such a rich collection of "gems" that one does not know where to begin sorting them out!

Zasulich "cannot remember" in European history the case she is discussing. But can she remember "in the history of Europe" a bourgeois revolution that took place when there were independent working-class parties with hundreds of thousands, a million members in neighbouring countries, and with capitalism highly developed and having created in the country in question a united industrial proletariat and a working-class movement on a national scale?

Vera Zasulich cannot "remember" a case of this kind because there has not been one "in the history of Europe". Mass political strikes did not and could not play a decisive role in any bourgeois revolution in European history before the twentieth century.

And so what do we get? We get this. The liquidators refer to "the history of Europe" as an example, where at the time of the bourgeois revolutions, *there were no* independent proletarian parties with mass strikes; they cite that example *for the purpose of renouncing* the tasks, or of *belittling*, clipping, curtailing, docking the tasks to be done in a country in which the two above-mentioned basic conditions (an independent proletarian party and mass strikes of a political nature) *were present* and still are present!

Vera Zasulich fails to understand—and this failure to understand is extremely typical of the liquidators— that she has *repeated the idea of the liberal* Prokopovich, using different words, for a different reason and approaching the subject from a different angle. That liberal, at the time when he, as an extreme Economist (1899), was breaking away from the Social-Democrats, expressed the idea that "the political struggle is for the liberals, the economic struggle for the workers".

All opportunists in the working-class movement of Russia from 1895 to 1913 have been drawn towards this idea and have lapsed into it. It is in struggle against this idea that the Social-Democratic Party in Russia has grown; only in struggle against this idea *could* it have grown. The struggle against this idea, the liberation of the masses from the influence of this idea is, in fact, the struggle for an independent working-class movement in Russia.

Prokopovich expressed the idea in its application to present tasks, using the imperative or the desiderative mood.

Vera Zasulich repeats the idea in the form of an allegedly-historical, retrospective discourse, or a review of events.

Prokopovich spoke forthrightly, frankly, clearly and sharply—abandon your idea of political independence, brother workers! Vera Zasulich, not realising whither liquidationism was leading her, has reached the same abyss by a zigzag route; the example of Europe also shows you, brother workers, that you cannot expect to have an "effective" organisation of your old tested *type*, of the same type as your organisation in 1905. Since 1905 the liberals have abandoned empty dreams of an "underground" and have created an "effective" organisation, an open one, which, although not legalised by the June Third system, is tolerated by it, retains its parliamentary group, its legal press and its local committees, which are actually known to everybody. Your old organisation, brother workers, is ineffective, and according to the lessons taught by "the history of Europe" *was bound to be*, but we liquidators promise you and offer you a new "open party" every day. What more do you want? Be content with our, the liquidators', promises, curse your old organisation in stronger terms, spit upon it, deny it and remain for the time being (until you get the "open party" we have promised) *without any organisation*!

This is exactly the real meaning of Vera Zasulich's liquidationist arguments, the meaning determined *not* by her will and mind, but by the relation of the classes in Russia, the objective conditions of the working-class movement. That is exactly what the liberals want. Vera Zasulich is only *echoing* Prokopovich!

Unlike late eighteenth-century Europe and Europe in the first half of the nineteenth century Russia provides an example of a country in which the old organisation has demonstrated its viability and efficiency. This organisation has been preserved even in times of reaction despite the defection of the liquidators and a host of the philistines. This organisation, while preserving its basic type, has been able to adapt *its form* to the changing conditions, has been able to vary that *form* to meet the requirements of the moment that marks "another step in the transformation into a bourgeois monarchy".[115]

An objective proof of this adaptation of the old organisation is to be seen—if we take one of the simplest, most obvious proofs, a proof that is most easily understood by the liberals—in the results of the elections to the Fourth Duma. Two-thirds of the deputies elected by the worker curias proved to be members of the old organisation, among them the six from the main industrial gubernias. In those gubernias there are about a million factory workers. Everything vital, all those politically conscious and influential among the genuine *masses*, the proletarian masses, participated in the elections, and in so doing changed the *form* of their old organisation, modifying the *conditions* of its activity but preserving its general line, the ideological and political basis and *content* of its activity.

Our position is clear. It was delineated irrevocably in 1908. The liquidators, however—and this is their misfortune—have no position as long as they have no *new* organisation. They can do nothing but sigh over the bad past and dream of a better future.

III

"Organisation is essential to the Party," writes Vera Zasulich. She is not content even with the Stockholm (1906) decision, adopted at a time when the Mensheviks *predominated and were forced* to accept the famous Clause One of the Rules.

If that is true (and it most certainly is), Vera Zasulich is wrong and she will have to renounce the *Mensheviks'* Stockholm decision. Organisation is not only "essential to the Party"—that is recognised by every liberal and every bourgeois who wishes to "use" the working-class party for politics directed against the working class. The Party *is* the sum-total of its organisations linked together in a single whole. The Party *is* the organisation of the working class divided into a long chain of all kinds of local and special, central and general organisations.

Here, again, the liquidators find themselves without any position. In 1903, they put forward their idea of Party membership, according to which not only those belonging to its organisations but those who were working (outside the organisations) under their control were regarded as Party members. Vera Zasulich recalls this episode, apparently deeming it important.

"... as far back as the Second Congress ten years ago," she writes, "the Mensheviks felt that it was impossible to tack away the whole Party in the underground...."

If the Mensheviks felt a revulsion against the underground in 1903, why was it that *in 1906*, in the period of an immeasurably more "open" Party, they *themselves*, having a majority at the Congress, reversed the Menshevik formulation they had adopted in 1903 and *accepted* the Bolshevik formulation? Vera Zasulich writes Party history in such a way that one comes across an amazing, unbelievable distortion of the facts at every step!

It is an indisputable fact that at Stockholm in 1906 the Mensheviks accepted the Bolshevik definition of the Party as the sum of its organisations; if Vera Zasulich and her friends have *again* changed their views, if they now consider that *their* 1906 decision was a mistake, why do they not say so straight out? In general, Vera Zasulich seems to regard this question as one of importance since she has raised it herself and herself has recalled the year 1903!

The reader can see that there is nothing more feeble and confused than the liquidators' views on the question of organisation. It is a complete absence of views. It is a model of characterlessness and confusion. Vera Zasulich exclaims crossly: "Organisational opportunism is a foolish expression." But "being cross" won't help. Did not Cherevanin *himself* say in a published statement that "organisational anarchy" had been noted among the future liquidators at the meetings of the *Menshevik* group in London in 1907. At that time, the most prominent liquidators found themselves (and find themselves again today) in the highly original situation of slaying liquidators.

"Organisation is essential to the Party," writes Vera Zasulich. "But it will only be possible for the organisation to embrace the whole Party for any lengthy period and exist peacefully [!] in one and the same form and with one and the same set of rules [listen to this!] when Russian social life has achieved and consolidated [if it is ever consolidated in Russia] a system of legality and at last travels a smooth road, leaving behind the mountainous path that it has been following at an accelerating pace for a whole century, at times ascending, at times crashing into the abyss of reaction, whence, having recovered from injuries received, it starts scrambling uphill again...."

26*

Here is an argument put forward by the liquidators that deserves a prize as a model of confusion. Try and understand what the author is getting at.

A change in the "Rules"? Then for God's sake, gentlemen, say what changes in the Rules you are talking about! And don't make fools of yourselves, don't try to prove "philosophically" that the Rules are not something unchangeable.

But although she speaks of "one and the same set of Rules" (incidentally they were changed in 1912*) Vera Zasulich proposes *no* changes at all.

What does she mean? She means that the Party will become an organisation when the mountainous path comes to an end and Russia travels a smooth road. That is an exceedingly respectable idea and it belongs to the liberals and *Vekhi*; until the *smooth road* is reached everything is nasty and evil, the Party is not a party and politics are not politics. On the "smooth road" everything will be "in order" and on the "mountainous path" there is nothing but chaos.

We read this argument long ago, put forward by the liberals. This argument is understandable, natural and legitimate from the point of view of the liberals' hatred of the underground and the "mountainous path". The facts are distorted (for there have been a number of *organised parties* in the underground in Russia), but we realise that the liberals' hatred of the underground blinds them to the facts.

But again, what does Vera Zasulich mean? Apparently, according to her, the organised party is impossible in Russia. Therefore? Indistinct ideas and things left unsaid, the confusion of the issue by long, heavy, tortuous periods, endless beating about the bush. The only thing one senses is that the author is worming her way towards renunciation of all organisation. And as she worms her way closer to this, Vera Zasulich speaks out—here is her crowning idea:

"We have a broad section of workers who would have every right to join any socialist party in the West. All our forces are in this rapidly growing section of the workers, who lack only the opportunity of formally joining a party to found one, and no matter what we call this section we shall both think of it and speak of it as the party."

---

* See present edition, Vol. 17, p. 482.—*Ed.*

When arguments concern the liquidation of the Party, therefore, we must realise that by the word *party* the liquidators mean *something quite different*. What do they mean by party?

Here it is—"a broad section of workers ... who lack only [!] the opportunity of formally joining a party to found one [!!]".

Incomparable! The party consists of those "who lack the opportunity of formally joining it". The party is those who remain outside the party.

Truly, Vera Zasulich has gathered some wonderful gems for us by saying frankly what all the liquidators are wandering about *on the verge of*.

IV

There are about a million Party members in Germany today. The Social-Democrats there receive about 4,250,000 votes and there are about 15,000,000 proletarians. Here is a simple and vivid example that will untangle what the liquidators have tangled. One million—that is the *party*, one million in the party organisations; 4,250,000 is the "broad section". It is actually much broader because women are disfranchised, as are many workers who do not possess the residential qualification, age qualification, etc., etc.

The "broad section" consists almost entirely of Social-Democrats and without it the party would be powerless. When any action is taken, this broad section expands to two or three times that size because on such occasions a mass of those who are not Social-Democrats follow the party.

Surely this is clear? It really is a little awkward to have to point out something so elementary!

In what way does Germany differ from Russia? Certainly not because in Russia there is *no* difference between the "party" and the "broad section"! To understand this let us first look at France. There we see (approximately—more accurate figures would only *strengthen* my argument):

Party . . . .   about 70,000*
"Broad section" (voting for the
  Social-Democrats) . . . . .   about 1,000,000
Proletarians . . ..   about 10,000,000

And in Russia? Party—150,000 in 1907 (calculated and
verified at the London Congress). Today the number is not
known, probably much less, 30,000 or 50,000, we cannot
say definitely.

Our "broad section" is 300,000-500,000 if we add up
the number of those voting for the Social-Democrats. Lastly,
proletarians—probably about 20,000,000. I repeat that these
are approximate figures, but *any other* figures that anybody
might arrive at through closer calculation would only add
strength to my argument.

My argument is that in all countries, everywhere and
always, there exists, *in addition* to the party, a "broad section" of people *close to the party* and the huge mass of the
class that founds the party, causes it to emerge and nur-
tures it. By not understanding this simple and obvious
point, the liquidators are repeating the error of the Economists of 1895-1901; the Economists simply could not
understand the difference between the "party" and the
"class".

The party is the politically conscious, advanced section
of the class, it is its vanguard. The strength of that vanguard is ten times, a hundred times, more than a hundred
times, greater than its numbers.

Is that possible? Can the strength of hundreds be greater
than the strength of thousands?

It can be, and is, *when the hundreds are organised.*

Organisation increases strength tenfold. God knows this
is no new verity. But it is not our fault if for the benefit
of Vera Zasulich and the liquidators we have to begin at
the beginning.

The political consciousness of the advanced contingent
is, incidentally, manifested in its ability to organise. By
organising it achieves *unity of will* and this united will
of an advanced thousand, hundred thousand, million *becomes* the will of the class. The intermediary between the

---

* The exact figure given at the last Congress in Brest (1913) was
68,903.[116]

party and the class is the "broad section" (broader than the party but narrower than the class), the section that votes Social-Democrat, the section that helps, sympathises, etc.

The *relationship* of the party to the class differs in different countries, depending on historical and other conditions. In Germany, for example, about one-fifteenth of the class is organised in the party; in France about a hundred-and-fortieth part. In Germany there are four or five Social-Democrats of the "broad section" to every Party member; in France there are fourteen. In France there has never actually been a party 100,000 strong—and this in conditions of "open" organisation and political liberty.

Any reasonable person will understand that there are historical conditions, objective causes, which made it possible to organise one-fifteenth of the class in the party in Germany, but which make it more difficult in France, and *still more difficult* in Russia.

What would one think of the Frenchman who declared that "our party is a narrow circle and not a party; you cannot tuck the party away in an organisation; the party is the broad section, *all forces* are in it, etc."? You would probably express surprise at the fact that this Frenchman was not in a mental hospital.

And here in Russia we are expected to take people seriously who feel, see and know that our path is *still mountainous*, that is, the conditions for organisation are *more difficult*, and nevertheless declare that they "will think and speak of the broad section [the unorganised!] as the party". These people are confused runaways from the Party, confused Social-Democrats *outside the Party* or *close to the Party* who have not withstood the pressure of the liberal ideas of decline, despondency and renunciation.

V

"For the underground to be a useful force," writes Vera Zasulich in the conclusion to her excellent article, "the underground, even if it alone is called the party, must display an attitude towards the worker Social-Democrats [i.e., towards the broad section in which Zasulich sees "all forces", and of which she declared: "we shall think of it and speak of it as the party"] similar to that of party officials to the party."

Think carefully over this statement, the gem of gems in an article so rich in gems. First Zasulich knows very well what is meant by a *party* in present-day Russia. But dozens of liquidator writers are continually assuring the public that they do not know it, with the result that disputes on the liquidation of the *Party* are so unbelievably confused by these gentry. Let readers who are interested in the fate of the working-class movement and oppose vulgar, commonplace liquidators turn to Vera Zasulich's article and gain from it the answer to the question that has been and is still being obscured—what is a party?

Secondly, examine Vera Zasulich's conclusion. The underground's attitude to the broad section should be that of party officials to the party, she tells us. May we ask what is the essence of the attitude of the officials of any association to that association? Obviously it is that the official does not carry out his own will (or that of a group or circle), but the will of the association.

How is the will of a broad section of several hundred thousands, or several million, to be determined? *It is absolutely impossible to determine the will of a broad section that is not organised in an association*—even a child would understand that. It is Vera Zasulich's misfortune, and that of the other liquidators, that they have taken a position on the inclined plane of organisational opportunism and are constantly sliding down into the swamp of the worst anarchism.

For anarchism is precisely what it is, in the fullest and most accurate meaning of the word, when Vera Zasulich declares that the liquidators *will think and speak* of the broad section as the party, and that the underground should display the attitude towards it that it would to a higher organisation, to a supreme arbiter on the question of "officials", etc., although she herself admits that the "broad section lacks only the opportunity of formally joining a party" and therefore "lacks the opportunity of *forming a party*".

When an appeal is made to broad sections or to the masses *against* the organisation and at the same time the impossibility of organising those sections or masses *is admitted*, that is pure anarchism. The anarchists constitute one of the most harmful elements of the working-class movement be-

cause they are always shouting about the mass of the oppressed classes (or even about the oppressed masses in general), always ruining the good name of any socialist organisation but are themselves unable to create *any* other
organisation as an alternative.

The Marxists have a fundamentally different view of the
relation of the unorganised (and unorganisable for a lengthy
period, sometimes decades) masses to the party, to organisation. It is to enable the mass of a *definite class* to learn
to understand its own interests and its position, to learn to
conduct its own policy, that there must be an organisation
of the advanced elements of the class, immediately and at
all costs, even though at first these elements constitute only
a tiny fraction of the class. To do service to the masses and
express *their* interests, having correctly conceived those
interests, the advanced contingent, the organisation, must
carry on all its activity among the masses, drawing from the
masses all the best forces without any exception, at every
step verifying carefully and objectively whether contact
with the masses is being maintained and whether it is a live
contact. In this way, and *only* in this way, does the advanced
contingent train and enlighten the masses, expressing
their interests, teaching them organisation and directing
all the activities of the masses along the path of conscious
class politics.

If the political activity of the masses as a whole, when
directly or indirectly drawn into elections, or participating
in them, should result in *all* the elected· representatives of
the workers being supporters of the underground and its
political line, supporters of the Party, we have an objective
fact *proving* the viability of our contact with the masses,
proving the right of that organisation to be and to call itself the *sole* representative of the masses, and *sole* vehicle
for the expression of the class interests of the masses. *Every*
politically conscious worker, or rather, every group of workers, *was able* to participate in the elections and direct them
one way or the other; and if the result is that the organisation that is ridiculed, cursed and treated with disdain by
the liquidators has been *able to lead the masses*, that means
that the attitude of our Party to the masses is correct in
principle, it is the Marxist attitude.

The theory of the *"broad section . . .* who lack *only* the opportunity of formally joining a party to found one" is an anarchist theory. The working class in Russia cannot consolidate and develop its movement if it does not struggle with the greatest determination against this theory, which corrupts the masses and destroys the very concept of organisation, the very principle of organisation.

The theory of the "broad section" *to replace* the party is an attempt to justify an extremely high-handed attitude towards and *mockery* of the mass working-class movement (furthermore, the mockers never fail to speak of the "masses" in their every phrase and to use "mass" freely as an adjective in all its cases). Everyone realises that the liquidators are using this theory to make it appear that *they*, their circle of intellectuals, represent and express the will of the "broad section". What, they would say, does the "narrow" party mean to us when we represent the "broad section"! What does an underground mean to us, an underground that carries with it a million workers to the polls, when we represent the broad section numbering, perhaps, millions and tens of millions!

The objective facts—the elections to the Fourth Duma, the appearance of workers' newspapers and the collections made on their behalf, the Metalworkers' Union in St. Petersburg, the shop assistants' congress[117]—serve to show clearly that the liquidators are a group of intellectuals that have fallen away from the working class. But the "theory of the broad section" enables the liquidators to get round all objective facts and fills their hearts with pride in their unacknowledged greatness....

VI

Vera Zasulich's article is such a collection of oddities from the point of view of logic and of the ABC of Marxism that the reader naturally asks himself—is it possible that there is no *other* meaning to all these meaningless phrases? Our review would be incomplete if we did not point out that *there is a point of view* from which the article is quite comprehensible, logical and correct. That is the point of view of the split.

The history of the working-class movement is full of examples of unsuccessful, useless and even harmful parties. Let us suppose for a moment that our Party is one of them. In that case it is harmful and criminal to tolerate its existence, and still more so to tolerate its representatives. It is then obligatory to struggle *for the destruction* of that party and its replacement by a new party.

From the point of view of a profound conviction of the harmfulness of the underground, such statements as "it is not known whether it (the Party) helped or hindered", whether it now helps or hinders, are natural and understandable. We shall justify and praise* those who leave it and put it down to the "ineffectiveness" of the old party. We shall appeal to *non-party people against* that old party so that they will join the new party.

Vera Zasulich did not express this point of view of the split in full. Perhaps this fact is subjectively important and noteworthy to the author. Objectively, however, it is of little importance. If a writer says A, B, C, and then *all* the letters of the alphabet except the last, it is a safe bet that 999 readers out of 1,000 will add (aloud or to themselves) the last letter. The liquidators are all in this ridiculous position; they produce a whole collection of arguments for a split and then either say nothing at all or say that they "favour unity".

Apropos of Vera Zasulich's article and of a dozen similar articles by L. S., Dan, Levitsky, Yezhov, Potresov and Martov we have only one answer—the first condition for unity is the absolute condemnation of the "theory of the broad section in place of the party", the condemnation of all acts against the underground, the condemnation of Vera Zasulich's article and the definite discontinuance of all such sallies. The party cannot be "united" without struggling against those who question the necessity for its existence.

From the point of view of a split Vera Zasulich's article is logical and correct. If the liquidators succeed in founding

---

* In passing. This *defence* of the renegades is implicit in Vera Zasulich's phrase "the broad section only lack the opportunity of formally joining a party to found one". There are thousands of facts that prove the opposite. By speaking of "lack of *opportunity*", Vera Zasulich is actually defending philistinism, or worse.

a new party and if that new party turns out better than the old, Vera Zasulich's article (and all the liquidators' literature) will be justified historically. It would be foolish sentimentality to deny the founders of a better, genuine, truly working-class party the right *to destroy* the old, ineffective, useless party. If the liquidators do not establish any new party at all, if they do not create any new working-class organisation, then all their literature and Vera Zasulich's article will remain as a monument to the confusion of those who dropped out of the Party, of those characterless intellectuals who were carried away by the counter-revolutionary stream of despondency, disbelief, and philistinism and went plodding along behind the liberals.

One thing or the other. There is no middle way. There is nothing here to "reconcile"; you cannot "slightly bury" the old party and "slightly create" a new one.

The specific nature of the time through which Russia is now living is demonstrated, among other things, by the fact that a relatively small Party nucleus which was able to hold out during the storm and to remain in existence despite the breaking of individual organisational ties here and there, a nucleus that has ensured for itself an uncommonly strong influence among the overwhelming mass of the workers (not as compared with present-day Europe, of course, but with the Europe of 1849-59), that this nucleus is surrounded by a multitude of anti-Party, non-Party, extra-Party and near-Party Social-Democrats and near-Social-Democrats.

And that is precisely how matters should stand in a country with the Mont Blanc of the German Social-Democratic Party next to it, while inside that country ... inside even the liberals do not see any other road except the "mountainous path", Messrs. Struve & Co. having for more than ten years trained hundreds and thousands of petty-bourgeois intellectuals, wrapping up their petty liberal ideas in almost Marxist words.

Take Mr. Prokopovich. A notable figure in journalism and in public activities in Russia. In essence, undoubtedly, a liberal. There is, however, reason to fear that he regards himself as a Social-Democrat—an anti-Party Social-Democrat. Take Mr. Makhnovets (Akimov). A liberal of a more melancholy temperament and with a more strongly expressed love for the workers. He no doubt considers himself a Social-Democrat—a non-Party Social-Democrat. Take the writers in *Kievskaya Mysl*, *Nasha Zarya*, *Luch*, etc. They form a whole collection of extra-Party and near-Party Social-Democrats. Some of them are engaged mainly in dreaming about the foundation of a new, open party, but have not yet made a final decision on the question of whether they will disgrace themselves too much if they set about fulfilling this plan of genius *"prematurely"*. Others specialise in solemnly declaring that they do not want to liquidate anything, that they are for unity and in complete agreement with ... the German Social-Democrats.

Take the Social-Democratic Duma group. One of its most prominent figures, Chkheidze, whom Nekrasov seems to have had prophetically in mind when he wrote:

> *But at times avoids an issue,*
> *That is painful, hard to solve.*[118]

The years 1911 and 1912 were the most difficult and painful period for the Social-Democrats in the epoch of the Third and the beginning of the Fourth Duma. The working-class press—liquidators' and anti-liquidators'—took shape. Chkheidze "avoided the issue". He did not go with either one or the other. He was a near-Party Social-Democrat. He seemed to be waiting and watching; on the one hand, there was no party but the old one, and on the other hand, it might happen that "they" would bury the party a little bit.... You read his speeches and quite often applaud a sally against the Rights that is often witty and stinging, his heated and astringent words, his defence of the old traditions, and at the same time you have to hold your nose when you open a liquidators' newspaper that thunders against "crazes", waves tradition carelessly aside and teaches the workers disdain for organisation—all apparently with the approval of Chkheidze, whose name is an ornament to the list of contributors. You come across an article by An accompanied by a sharp criticism of him from the *Luch* editors and cannot help but wonder—have not our poor Chkheidze and our kindly An suffered a tragi-comic defeat in their attempt to cast off the yoke of Dan....

There are people who, in the name of the great principle of proletarian unity, advise the Party to come to an
agreement with one of the groups of near-Party, almost-
Social-Democrats, that wants to "avoid", or is wavering on,
the question of whether to bury or to strengthen the old
organisation. It can well be understood that these people
are themselves wavering or have a very poor acquaintance
with the real state of affairs. A party that wants to exist
cannot allow the slightest wavering on the question of
its existence or any agreement with those who may bury
it. There is no end to those who want to act as intermediaries in such an agreement, but they are all people, who,
to use an old expression, are burning their oil in vain and
wasting their time.

P.S.
P. B. Axelrod's concluding article in No. 13 of *Zhivaya
Zhizn* (July 25, 1913) headed "Then and Now" provided
an amazingly vivid confirmation of our words. The real
essence of this well-padded article is not, of course, in its
amusing boosting of the liquidators' August Conference,
but in the resurrection of the labour congress question.
It goes without saying that Axelrod prefers to say nothing about his bitter and painful experience with the idea
of a labour congress in 1906 and 1907—why rake up the
past? Nor does Axelrod mention the specific conditions
of the *present day*, when it appears possible to hold labour congresses of a special character, as it were, and for
special reasons (a shop-assistants' congress today, perhaps an
insurance or trade union congress tomorrow, etc.). Axelrod is probably not pleased with the experience of the shop-
assistants' congress, at which the majority (as the liquidators have been forced to admit in *Zhivaya Zhizn*) was *against*
the liquidators.
Axelrod does not say anything about what has been and
what is. He prefers to let his imagination run wild on the
future "thaw"—luckily we cannot know anything about
its concrete conditions! He toys with the idea of convening
"a Social-Democratic labour congress if not of all Russia,
then one of all Russians"—which is then called exactly
that, a congress of all Russians.

Thus there are two changes to the former brilliant plan; first, it is not merely a labour congress, but a Social-Democratic labour congress. That is progress. Let us congratulate Axelrod on having taken a step forward in six years. Let us congratulate him if he has become convinced of the harm caused by fantastic plans to "unite" with the Left Narodniks. Secondly, he replaces "all-Russia congress" by "congress of all Russians". That signifies rejection of complete unity with workers of *non-Russian* nationality in Russia (Axelrod regards the collapse among them of the idea of a labour congress as being final!). That is two steps backward. That is the hallowing of separatism in the working-class movement.

But this is still not the best part. Why was Axelrod dreaming of a labour congress? This is why:

> "The labour congress will complete the liquidatory process that has been going on during the past few years, the liquidation of the old party regime that grew up on the outdated historical basis of the feudal state and the hierarchical socio-political regime and at the same time will mark the beginning of a completely new epoch in the historical life of Russian Social-Democrats, the epoch of development on exactly the same lines as the Social-Democratic parties in the West."

Everybody knows that "exactly the same lines" are the lines of a *legal* party. Speaking without equivocation, this means that the liquidators need the labour congress to *"complete the liquidation"* of the old party and to found a *new, legal* party.

Such, in brief, is the idea behind Axelrod's long disquisitions.

Here you have the last word in near-Party Social-Democracy! For the members of the party to work in the party and strengthen it is an old, outdated idea that Axelrod has banished to the archives. We are not liquidating anything, that is libel, we only "stand aside" and shout for all to hear about the "completion of the liquidation of the Party". We vow and swear that tomorrow we shall be excellent members of the future legal party.

These sweet near-Party Social-Democrats of 1913 are very much like those liberals of 1903 who assured us that they were proper Social-Democrats and would certainly become members of the Social-Democratic Party—when it became legal, of course.

We do not for a moment doubt that there will be a period of political liberty in Russia and that we shall have a legal Social-Democratic Party. Probably some of those near-Party Social-Democrats of today will become members of it.

And so—until we meet again in the ranks of the future, legal party, our future comrades! In the meantime, excuse us, we are not going the same way, because as yet you, near-Party Social-Democrats, are carrying on liberal and not Marxist work.

Prosveshcheniye No. 9,
September 1913
Signed: *V. Ilyin*

Published according to
the *Prosceshcheniye* text

RESOLUTIONS OF THE SUMMER, 1913, JOINT CONFERENCE OF THE CENTRAL COMMITTEE OF THE R.S.D.L.P. AND PARTY OFFICIALS [119]

Written September 1913

Published in 1913 in the pamphlet
*Notification and Resolutions
of the Summer, 1913,
Joint Conference of the Central
Committee of the R.S.D.L.P.
and Party Officials.*
Issued by the Central Committee

Published according to
the text of the illegal
mimeographed edition
of the resolutions collated
with the text of the pamphlet

THE TASKS OF AGITATION IN THE PRESENT SITUATION

1. The situation in the country is becoming increasingly acute. The rule of the reactionary landowners is causing increasing discontent even among the most moderate sections of the population. The obstacle to anything like real political liberty in Russia is still the tsarist monarchy, which is hostile to all real reform, protects only the power and revenues of the feudal landowners, and suppresses with exceptional cruelty every manifestation of the working-class movement.

2. The working class continues to act as the leader of the revolutionary struggle for nation-wide liberation. The mass revolutionary strike movement continues to grow. The genuine struggle waged by the advanced contingents of the working class is proceeding under revolutionary slogans.

Owing to the very circumstances of the struggle the mass economic movement, which in many cases starts with the most elementary demands, is to an increasing degree merging with the revolutionary working-class movement.

It is the task of the advanced workers to accelerate by their agitational and educational activities the process of uniting the proletariat under the revolutionary slogans of the present epoch. Only in this way will the advanced workers succeed in fulfilling their other task of rousing the peasant and urban democrats.

3. The working-class struggle, which is proceeding under revolutionary slogans, has compelled the liberal-Octobrist bourgeoisie and a section of the manufacturers to talk volubly about the need for reforms in general, and for limited freedom of association in particular. While feverishly organising in employers' associations, introducing insurance

against strikes and calling upon the government to harass the working-class movement systematically, the bourgeoisie is at the same time urging the workers to abandon their revolutionary demands and to confine themselves *instead* to individual constitutional reforms and a semblance of freedom of association. The working class should take advantage of every sign of vacillation on the part of the government as well as of disagreements between the bourgeoisie and the reactionary camp, to intensify its attack in both the economic and political fields of struggle. But to be able to make good use of the situation the working class must continue to adhere to the platform of full-blooded revolutionary slogans.

4. This being the general state of affairs, the task of the Social-Democrats is to continue to conduct extensive revolutionary agitation among the masses for the overthrow of the monarchy and the establishment of a democratic republic. Vivid examples from real life must be used continuously to demonstrate all the harmfulness of reformism, i.e., the tactics of putting demands for partial improvement to the fore *instead* of revolutionary slogans.

5. In their agitation in favour of freedom of association and for partial reforms in general, the liquidators descend to liberalism. Actually, they deny that it is necessary to conduct revolutionary agitation among the masses, and in their press they frankly declare that the slogans "democratic republic" and "confiscation of the land" cannot serve as subjects for agitation among the masses. They advocate freedom of association as the all-inclusive slogan of the day, and, in fact, urge it as a substitute for the revolutionary demands of 1905.

6. This Conference, giving warning of the pernicious, reformist agitation of the liquidators, points out again that the R.S.D.L.P. long ago advanced in its minimum programme the demands for freedom of association, freedom of speech, freedom of the press, etc., closely linking these demands with the revolutionary struggle for the overthrow of the tsarist monarchy. This Conference confirms the resolution of the January 1912 Conference, which states: "The Conference calls upon all Social-Democrats to explain to the workers the paramount importance to the proletariat of

freedom of association; this demand must always be closely linked up with our general political demands and our revolutionary agitation among the masses."*

The main slogans of the epoch still are: (1) a democratic republic; (2) confiscation of the landed estates; (3) an 8-hour day. Freedom of association is included here as part of the whole.

RESOLUTION ON THE ORGANISATIONAL QUESTION AND ON THE PARTY CONGRESS

1. The reports from the localities have shown that the most urgent organisational task is not only to consolidate the leading Party organisations in every town, but also to link up the towns with each other.

2. As a first step towards regional amalgamation this Conference recommends the organisation of meetings (and where possible conferences) of comrades from different centres of the working-class movement. Every effort must be made to have all branches of Party activity represented at these meetings: political, trade union, insurance, co-operative, etc.

3. This Conference affirms that for the purpose of co-ordinating activities throughout Russia, the system of having representatives of the Central Committee is absolutely essential. A beginning has only just been made in applying the decision on representatives adopted by the February Conference. Advanced workers in the districts should see to it that such representatives are appointed at least in every large centre of the working-class movement, and as many of them as possible.

4. This Conference places on the order of the day the question of convening a Party congress.[120] The growth of the working-class movement, the maturing of a political crisis in the country and the need for united working-class actions on a nation-wide scale, make it necessary and possible to convene such a congress—after adequate preparations for it have been made.

5. This Conference invites the comrades in the districts, when discussing this subject, to make suggestions for the

---

* See present edition, Vol. 17, p. 480.—*Ed.*

congress agenda, for the desirable date of convocation, for draft resolutions, etc.

6. This Conference points out that apart from other difficulties, the problem of meeting the expenses of the congress can also be solved only by the workers themselves.

This Conference calls upon the comrades to start a fund for the convocation of the Party congress.

THE STRIKE MOVEMENT

1. This Conference confirms the resolutions of the January 1912 Conference, and of the February 1913 Conference,* which contains an appraisal of the strike movement fully borne out by the experience of the past few months.

2. Characteristic of the new stage of revival of the revolutionary strike is the movement in Moscow and the rising temper in several districts hitherto unaffected by the movement.

3. This Conference welcomes the initiative taken by the St. Petersburg Committee and by a number of Party groups in Moscow in raising the question of a general political strike, and in taking steps in this direction in July and September this year.**

4. This Conference affirms that the movement is approaching the moment when it will be opportune to bring up the question of a general political strike. Systematic agitation in preparation for this strike must be started everywhere immediately.

5. The slogans for these political strikes, which must be vigorously disseminated, should be the fundamental revolutionary demands of the day: a democratic republic; an 8-hour day; confiscation of the landed estates.

6. This Conference calls upon all local Party officials to develop an extensive leaflet propaganda and to establish the most regular and closest communication possible

---

* See present edition, Vol. 17, pp. 465-68 and Vol. 18, pp. 456-58. —*Ed.*

** The Editorial Board of the Central Organ, which was instructed to publish the resolutions of the Conference, added a reference to the September events that fully confirmed the correctness of these resolutions.

between the political and other working-class organisations of the various cities. It is particularly necessary to secure co-ordination of activities primarily between the St. Petersburg and Moscow workers, so that the political strikes that are likely to arise from various causes (persecution of the press, strikes to enforce insurance, etc.) may as far as possible take place simultaneously in both cities.

THE PARTY PRESS

1. This Conference points to the vast importance of the legal press for Social-Democratic agitation and organisation, and therefore calls upon Party bodies and upon all class-conscious workers to increase their assistance to the legal press by securing for it the widest possible circulation, and by organising mass collective subscriptions and regular collections of contributions. The Conference reaffirms that such contributions are counted as Party membership dues.

2. Special efforts must be made to consolidate the legal workers' newspaper in Moscow[121] and to issue a workers' newspaper in the South at the earliest possible date.

3. This Conference expresses the desire that the closest possible contact be established between the existing legal working-class periodicals by means of an exchange of information, arrangement of conferences, etc.

4. Recognising the importance of a theoretical organ of Marxism and the need for one, this Conference expresses the desire that all the organs of the Party and trade union press should make the workers familiar with the magazine *Prosveshcheniye*, and urge them to subscribe to it regularly and to render it their systematic support.

5. This Conference draws the attention of Party publishing houses to the great need to publish an extensive series of popular, Social-Democratic agitation and propaganda pamphlets.

6. In view of the recent intensification of the revolutionary mass struggle, and of the need to report on it in the fullest detail (which the legal press cannot do), this Conference calls special attention to the need to stimulate in every way the development of underground Party publishing activities; in addition to publishing illegal leaflets,

pamphlets, etc., it is absolutely essential to secure the more
frequent and regular issue of the illegal Party organ (the
Central Organ).[122]

SOCIAL-DEMOCRATIC ACTIVITIES IN THE DUMA

Having examined in detail the resolution of the
R.S.D.L.P. on the Social-Democratic group in the Duma,
adopted at the December 1908, Conference, and having
discussed all the facts concerning the activities of the
Social-Democrats in the Fourth Duma, this Conference
affirms:

1. that the aforesaid resolution quite correctly defined
the aims and objects of Social-Democratic activities in the
Duma, and that this resolution must therefore continue to
serve as a guide to these activities in the future;

2. that the last subsection of Point 3 (3 h) of the December
resolution (on voting or abstaining from voting on questions
concerning the improvement of the conditions of the workers)[123] should be interpreted as follows. If bills, motions,
etc., concern immediate and direct improvements in conditions for workers, minor salaried employees and working
people generally (for example, reduction of hours, increase
of wages, the removal of even minor evils in the lives of the
workers and of broad sections of the population in general,
etc.), the clauses that provide for such improvements
should be voted for.

In cases when the conditions the Fourth Duma attaches
to these improvements make them dubious, the group
should abstain from voting, but must *unfailingly* formulate
its motives for so doing, after having first discussed the
question with representatives of workers' organisations.

This Conference affirms that:

on all questions, important bills, etc., the Socialist-Demo-
cratic group in the Duma must independently formulate
its own motion to pass on to next business.

In cases of the group's vote against the government, after
the Social-Democratic motion has been rejected, coinciding
with the vote of other parties, the group must endeavour
to formulate its own motives for voting for another party's
motion, or part of a motion.

THE SOCIAL-DEMOCRATIC GROUP IN THE DUMA

This Conference is of the opinion that united action on the part of the Social-Democratic group in the Duma is possible and essential.

This Conference affirms, however, that the conduct of the seven deputies gravely jeopardises the unity of the group.

Taking advantage of their accidental majority of one, the seven deputies encroach on the elementary rights of the six workers' deputies, who represent the overwhelming majority of the workers of Russia.

The seven deputies, guided by narrow factional interests, deprive the six deputies of the opportunity to speak in the Duma on very important questions affecting the lives of the workers. In several cases, when the Social-Democratic group put up two or more speakers, the six deputies were not given an opportunity in spite of repeated demands to put up their own speaker.

Similarly, in appointing representatives to various Duma committees (for example, the Budget Committee) the seven deputies refuse to allow the six to have one of the two places.

When the group elects representatives to bodies that are of importance to the working-class movement, the seven deputies, by a majority of one, deprive the six of all representation. The staff that serves the group is always elected in a biased manner (for example, the demand for a second secretary was rejected).

This Conference is of the opinion that such conduct on the part of the seven deputies inevitably gives rise to friction in the group, which hinders united action and threatens to split the group.

This Conference protests most emphatically against this conduct on the part of the seven deputies.

The six deputies represent the overwhelming majority of the workers of Russia and act in complete harmony with the political line of its organised vanguard.

This Conference is therefore of the opinion that united action on the part of the Social-Democratic group in the Duma is possible only if the two sections of the group enjoy equal rights, and if the seven deputies abandon their steam-roller tactics.

Notwithstanding irreconcilable disagreements in spheres of activity outside as well as inside the Duma, this Conference demands that the group should maintain unity on the basis of the aforesaid equality of rights of its two sections.

This Conference invites class-conscious workers to express their opinion on this important question and to exert all efforts to help preserve the unity of the group on the only possible basis, that of equal rights for the six workers' deputies.

WORK IN LEGAL ASSOCIATIONS

1. In the present period of revival of the economic and political struggle of the working class it is particularly necessary to intensify activities in all the legal working-class associations (trade unions, clubs, sick benefit societies, co-operative societies, and so forth).

2. All activities in legal working-class associations must be conducted not in a neutral spirit, but in keeping with the spirit of the decisions of the London Congress of the R.S.D.L.P. and of the International Congress in Stuttgart.[124] Social-Democrats should recruit members for all working-class associations from the widest possible working-class circles, and urge all workers to join them irrespective of their party opinions. But the Social-Democrats in these associations should form themselves into Party groups and by prolonged and systematic activities secure the establishment of the closest relations between the associations and the Social-Democratic Party.

3. The experience of the international and of our Russian working-class movement teaches that it is necessary from the very inception of such working-class organisations (trade unions, co-operative societies, clubs, etc.) to strive to convert every one of them into a stronghold of the Social-Democratic Party. This Conference urges all Party members to bear this important task in mind, for it is a particularly urgent one in Russia, where the liquidators are making systematic efforts to utilise the legal societies *against* the Party.

4. This Conference is of the opinion that in electing delegates to the sick benefit societies, in all trade union activities, etc., it is necessary, while upholding the complete

unity of the movement and the submission of the minority to the majority, to pursue the Party line, secure the election of supporters of the Party for all responsible posts, etc.

5. For the purpose of summing up the experience of practical activities in legal working-class societies it is desirable to arrange more frequent conferences with active participants in the work of local legal working-class organisations and to invite to general Party conferences as large a number as possible of representatives of Party groups operating in these legal societies.

RESOLUTION ON THE NATIONAL QUESTION

The orgy of Black-Hundred nationalism, the growth of nationalist tendencies among the liberal bourgeoisie and the growth of nationalist tendencies among the upper classes of the oppressed nationalities, give prominence at the present time to the national question.

The state of affairs in the Social-Democratic movement (the attempts of the Caucasian Social-Democrats, the Bund and the liquidators to annul the Party Programme,[125] etc.) compels the Party to devote more attention than ever to this question.

This Conference, taking its stand on the Programme of the R.S.D.L.P., and in order to organise correctly Social-Democratic agitation on the national question, advances the following propositions:

1. Insofar as national peace is in any way possible in a capitalist society based on exploitation, profit-making and strife, it is attainable only under a consistently and thoroughly democratic republican system of government which guarantees full equality of all nations and languages, which recognises no compulsory official language, which provides the people with schools where instruction is given in all the native languages, and the constitution of which contains a fundamental law that prohibits any privileges whatsoever to any one nation and any encroachment whatsoever upon the rights of a national minority. This particularly calls for wide regional autonomy and fully democratic local self-government, with the boundaries of the self-governing and autonomous regions determined by the local

inhabitants themselves on the basis of their economic and social conditions, national make-up of the population, etc.

2. The division of the educational affairs of a single state according to nationalities is undoubtedly harmful from the standpoint of democracy in general, and of the interests of the proletarian class struggle in particular. It is precisely this division that is implied in the plan for "cultural-national" autonomy, or for "the creation of institutions that will guarantee freedom for national development" adopted in Russia by all the Jewish bourgeois parties and by the petty-bourgeois, opportunist elements among the different nations.

3. The interests of the working class demand the amalgamation of the workers of all the nationalities in a given state in united proletarian organisations—political, trade union, co-operative, educational, etc. This amalgamation of the workers of different nationalities in single organisations will alone enable the proletariat to wage a victorious struggle against international capital and reaction, and combat the propaganda and aspirations of the landowners, clergy and bourgeois nationalists of all nations, who usually cover up their anti-proletarian aspirations with the slogan of "national culture". The world working-class movement is creating and daily developing more and more an international proletarian culture.

4. As regards the right of the nations oppressed by the tsarist monarchy to self-determination, i.e., the right to secede and form independent states, the Social-Democratic Party must unquestionably champion this right. This is dictated by the fundamental principles of international democracy in general, and specifically by the unprecedented national oppression of the majority of the inhabitants of Russia by the tsarist monarchy, which is a most reactionary and barbarous state compared with its neighbouring states in Europe and Asia. Furthermore, this is dictated by the struggle of the Great-Russian inhabitants themselves for freedom, for it will be impossible for them to create a democratic state if they do not eradicate Black-Hundred, Great-Russian nationalism, which is backed by the traditions of a number of bloody suppressions of national move-

ments and systematically fostered not only by the tsarist monarchy and all the reactionary parties, but also by the Great-Russian bourgeois liberals, who toady to the monarchy, particularly in the period of counter-revolution.

5. The right of nations to self-determination (i.e., the constitutional guarantee of an absolutely free and democratic method of deciding the question of secession) must under no circumstances be confused with the expediency of a given nation's secession. The Social-Democratic Party must decide the latter question exclusively on its merits in each particular case in conformity with the interests of social development as a whole and with the interests of the proletarian class struggle for socialism.

Social-Democrats must moreover bear in mind that the landowners, the clergy and the bourgeoisie of the oppressed nations often cover up with nationalist slogans their efforts to divide the workers and dupe them by doing deals behind their backs with the landowners and bourgeoisie of the ruling nation to the detriment of the masses of the working people of all nations.

*   *
*

This Conference places on the agenda of the Party congress the question of the national programme. It invites the Central Committee, the Party press and the local organisations to discuss (in pamphlets, debates, etc.) the national question in fullest detail.

THE NARODNIKS

1. The London Congress, in summing up the activities of the Narodnik parties—including, among others, the Socialist-Revolutionary Party—in the period of revolution, definitely stated that these parties constantly vacillated between submission to the hegemony of the liberals and determined struggle against landed proprietorship and the feudal state; and it also pointed to the pseudo-socialist character of their propaganda, which tones down the antagonism between the proletarian and the small proprietor.

2. The period of reaction has brought out these features still more strongly, for, on the one hand, the Socialist-Revolutionary Party has abandoned a consistently democratic policy, and certain elements in it are even criticising the revolution, thereby following in the footsteps of the liberals; on the other hand, this party has been reduced to a mere group of intellectuals divorced from the life of the masses.

3. The Socialist-Revolutionary Party officially continues to advocate terrorism, the history of which in Russia has fully confirmed the correctness of Social-Democratic criticism of this form of struggle, and which ended in complete defeat. Furthermore, its boycott of the elections and the complete inability of this organisation of intellectuals to exercise systematic influence on the course of the social development of the country have brought it about that nowhere has this party been in the slightest degree a factor in the new revival of the revolutionary movement.

4. The petty-bourgeois socialism of the Narodniks reduces itself to the pernicious preaching to the working class of ideas that obscure the ever-widening gulf between the interests of labour and capital and tone down the acuteness of the class struggle; it fosters petty-bourgeois utopias in the sphere of co-operation.

5. The Narodniks are greatly hindered in conducting republican-democratic propaganda among large masses of the peasantry by their vacillation in the struggle for democratic slogans, their narrow group character and their petty-bourgeois prejudices. The interests of this propaganda itself therefore demand, in the first place, strong criticism of the Narodniks by the Social-Democrats.

This Conference does not by any means reject the joint action with the Narodnik parties especially provided for by the London Congress, but suggests that the tasks of the Social-Democrats are:

a) to expose the vacillations and tendency to abandon consistent democracy that are manifesting themselves in the Narodnik parties;

b) to combat the petty-bourgeois socialism of the Narodniks, which tends to obscure the gulf between capital and labour;

c) to support the republican-democratic trends among the peasant masses and constantly point out to them that only the consistently democratic socialist proletariat can serve as a reliable leader of the masses of the poorer peasants in their struggle against monarchy and landed proprietorship;

d) to devote greater attention to the propagation of Social-Democratic ideas among the groups of workers—although these are not numerous—who have not yet rid themselves of the obsolete theories of Narodism.

THERE'S A TRUDOVIK FOR YOU!

Zavety[126] is an out-and-out Narodnik, *Left*-Narodnik, publication with Mr. Chernov himself on the staff. It is a bulky and serious magazine. And if the celebrated *"family labour* principle" that all Trudoviks,* all Narodniks, including all the Socialist-Revolutionaries, have constantly on their lips is to be found anywhere it is in this magazine.

Some people even assert that the "family labour principle" is a socialist principle, and that its theoreticians are socialists.

Let us see how Mr. S. Zak, a Left Narodnik who has made a special study of the question of industrial capitalism, discusses the *"family labour* principle" in industry.

Mr. S. Zak distinguishes three types of industry: (1) "family labour" industry; (2) "transitional" industry which stands midway between "family labour" and capitalist industry, and (3) capitalist industry. Enterprises employing over 50 workers he classifies as capitalist; those employing from 11 to 50 workers come under the heading "transitional industry" and *those employing no more than 10* he classifies as *"family labour"* industry.

Why does he classify the last-named enterprises as "family labour"? The reason, if you please, is that "since these undertakings do not employ on the average even one clerk and one technician per undertaking, it is absurd to say that they are capitalist undertakings".

This theory is worthy of a semi-literate clerk, but not of an author who wants to be regarded as a socialist! Until Mr. Zak and the other Narodniks have invented *"their own"*,

---

* See Note 95.—*Ed.*

new, truly Russian political economy, we shall stick to the old view that capitalism means production of *commodities*, in which *labour-power* is also transformed into a commodity.

This is elementary, and to be ignorant of it is disgraceful. The Narodniks say that they subscribe to Marx's theories, and that they are opposed to bourgeois political economy, but what they offer the public is nothing more than the views of the most banal philistine, who has learnt nothing and who repeats scraps of bourgeois phrases, such as: if the owner has an "office", he is a capitalist. But if my plant is a small one, how can I be a capitalist? I am a working man!

The defence of such views in the press is a rejection of the science of political economy, it is the defence of ignorance.

Capitalists may be small or big, foolish or clever, but this is not a criterion of capitalism. Capitalism means producing *commodities* and hiring wage-labour.

In the opinion of our Narodnik another criterion of "family labour" industry is—do the members of the owner's family take part in the work? Anybody who is familiar with the rudiments of political economy knows that family labour is typical of *petty-bourgeois* industry. Exalting the petty bourgeoisie with the title of "family labour" industry shows a complete failure to understand what socialism is.

Here are Mr. Zak's own figures. For every group of 100 factories, we find on the average the following numbers of members of owners' families employed: (1) 28 in the factories employing up to 3 workers; (2) 34 in the factories employing 4 to 5 workers; (3) 22 in the factories employing 6 to 10 workers.

Our "neo-Narodnik" is splendid, is he not? He himself quotes figures which show that wage-labour *predominates*, and yet he calls it "family labour" industry!

Mr. Zak skips over the returns of various industrial censuses, waxes enthusiastic over the "numerous" "working" masters he finds, and asserts that this proves the "unsoundness of the orthodox theory"—as the Narodniks ironically call Marx's doctrine. We shall quote the complete figures of the German census returns, to which Mr. Zak primarily refers. We shall take industry in the broad sense of the term, including commerce and transport.

Enterprises	Number	%	Number or quantity (millions)					
			Workers	%	H. P.	%	Kilowatts	%
One-man workshops	1,452,000	44.4	1.4	10.1	—	—	—	—
Small (2 to 5 workers)	1,524,000	46.7	3.8	26.2	0.7	7.4	0.1	7.1
Medium (6 to 50 workers)	259,000	8.0	3.5	24.3	1.5	17.3	0.2	15.7
Large (51 workers and over)	31,000	0.9	5.7	39.4	6.6	75.3	1.2	77.2
Total	3,266,000	100	14.4	100.	8.8	100	1.5	100

Look closely at this picture of capitalism in industry. One-man, petty-bourgeois workshops are very "numerous": *one and a half million*. Their *share* of industry? *One-tenth* of the workers and *none* of the machinery, either steam or electrically driven!

What about the big capitalists? They account for *one-hundredth* of the factories, but they employ nearly two-fifths (39 per cent) of the total number of workers and have *over* *three-fourths* (75-77 per cent) of the total machinery.

Every intelligent worker will see at once that these figures fully confirm his everyday experience: the existence of a vast number of miserable petty bourgeois crushed by capital, and the *most complete predominance* of a handful of large capitalist enterprises.

To proceed. The statistics, so hopelessly garbled by this "Left" Narodnik, reveal a very rapid growth of capitalism and the elimination of small production. We shall compare the returns of three German censuses, that of 1882, 1895 and 1907 (the last). So as not to weary the reader with figures, we shall take only the most important of them; we shall compare the one-man workshops with the capitalist plants, taking medium and large together.

Year	One-man workshops		Medium and large capitalist plants	
	% of total number of plants	% of total number of workers	% of total number of plants	% of total number of workers
1882	62	26	4	41
1895	54	17	7	53
1907	42	10	9	63

Twenty-five years ago the one-man workshop owners constituted the majority of the masters (three-fifths). Now they constitute the minority (two-fifths). Formerly, they employed one-fourth of the total number of workers; they now employ only one-tenth.

On the other hand, the share of the capitalist plants shows a rapid increase. Twenty-five years ago they employed only a minority of the workers (two-fifths), but they now employ the *majority*, nearly two-thirds of the total number of workers (63 per cent). And we have already seen that the concentration of steam, to say nothing of electrically driven *machinery*, in the hands of a small number of capitalists is *far greater* than the concentration of workers.

Thus, the industrial censuses of the free and rapidly developing countries are the best proof of the correctness of Marx's theory. Capitalism rules everywhere. Everywhere it is squeezing out small production. Everywhere the masses of peasants and small artisans and handicraftsmen are being ruined. Big capital forces down and crushes the small master in a thousand ways that are still poorly reflected in statistics. There is no salvation for the small master. His only way of escape is to join the struggle of the proletariat.

From first to last the theory of the "family labour principle" and "family labour industry" is a repetition of the old bourgeois prejudices, prejudices that are being shattered all the time by the experience of every country.

In trying to prove to the workers that the capitalist or small master who employs from five to ten wage-workers is a "working master", the Left Narodniks only reveal their own bourgeois nature.

Pravda Truda No. 18,
October 1, 1913
Signed: *V. Ilyin*

Published according to
the *Pravda Truda* text

28*

BEWILDERED NON-PARTY PEOPLE

One of the most widespread and unhealthy symptoms of our public life is the contempt (if not open hostility) that is displayed towards adherence to a party.

It is characteristic of political free lances, political adventurers and political Manilovs to repudiate party affiliations and to talk pompously about party "bigotry", "dogmatism", intolerance, and so on, and so forth. As a matter of fact, the use of such expressions merely reflects the ridiculous and paltry conceit or self-justification of intellectuals who are shut off from the masses and feel compelled to cover up their feebleness. Serious politics can only be promoted by the *masses*; non-party masses that do not follow the lead of a strong party are, however, disunited, ignorant masses, without staying power, prone to become a plaything in the hands of adroit politicians, who always emerge "opportunely" from the ranks of the ruling classes to take advantage of "favourable" circumstances.

Russia is one of the most petty-bourgeois countries in the world and is least accustomed to free political activities. This, and this alone, explains the contempt that is so widespread in this country for adherence to a party. One of the tasks of class-conscious workers in Russia (and one of the great historical services they must render) is to wage a systematic and persevering struggle against this attitude.

The following is one of the latest examples of the smug non-partisanship that reigns among the *near-Party* intellectuals.

The workers have organised the collection of funds for working-class newspapers on an extensive scale. It is not difficult to understand that when the masses have consciously decided for themselves *which* newspaper to assist and which *trend* to support, such collections *teach* them ideologically sound and principled politics.

The liquidators, who so often descend to non-party politics, have launched their notorious campaign for the *collections to be shared equally*. In this they were prompted solely by the desire to cover up their own weakness, and in their haste they did not have time to think and realise that the principle underlying such a campaign is precisely the principle of *non-partisanship*.

They were immediately exposed by the real state of affairs. Russian petty-bourgeois society *made the liquidators'* slogan its own: share and share alike with everybody, with the liquidators and with the Narodniks!

When their political gamble is exposed, these non-party people who have renounced the Marxist past for the sake of visions of something as "broad" as it is unprincipled, begin to twist and turn. G. R., in No. 24 of the liquidators' newspaper, assures us that the liquidators are not at all in favour of uniting with the Narodniks, and alleges that such union has been "systematically advocated" by the Marxists.

A cruder distortion of the truth could scarcely be imagined. If G. R. and Co. were not non-party, if they did not treat the *history* of Marxism like philistines, they would know that it was *only* due to the Marxists (supporters of *Pravda*) that the question of the attitude the workers should adopt to the various parties was *settled* quite officially more than six years ago.* The Marxists alone gave a precise definition of the *class* basis of *all* the important parties in Russia; the liquidators have never been able to do this. The Marxists alone of all the parties in Russia, *six years* ago, defined the exact nature of the various "trends" and the attitude that should be adopted towards them in place of a chaotic, unprincipled attitude ("as circumstances demand") towards individual parties.

Since then, events have brilliantly confirmed the correctness of this definition in the most unquestionable manner.

The definition states clearly and precisely that the Narodniks are petty-bourgeois democrats with whom "joint

---

* See present edition, Vol. 12, pp. 136-38.—*Ed.*

action" is possible only against reaction and against liberalism.

Now, G. R. and Co., in asserting that they are opposed to uniting with the Narodniks, want to wriggle out of it by saying: "We are in favour of the collections being shared equally between the *two* newspapers when 'mass collections' are made, but we are opposed to this when collections are made 'among groups of politically conscious supporters'!" (See *Novaya Rabochaya Gazeta* No. 24.)

In the first place, it has already been proved by actual experience that a non-party plan emerges from your advocacy of share and share alike. This is a fact. This very issue, No. 24, contains a resolution adopted by one workers' group which says: *equally with the Narodniks, too*. As is always the case with them, our non-partisans or independents, find themselves in the wrong box!

In the second place, can a group of politically conscious supporters be called such if it is unable to enlighten the masses? No, gentlemen, non-partisans, it cannot! Politically conscious supporters will say to the masses—let everybody contribute, let everybody unite, but *try*, in doing so, *to distinguish* the trends of the different newspapers!

To contribute and say "share and share alike" means being non-party, indifferent and not politically conscious. To contribute and say, "*for such and such a trend*", means being politically conscious, and taking part consciously in a *common* action.

G. R. distorts this political ABC. The result is that G. R. and Co., the liquidators, while asserting that they are opposed to uniting with the Narodniks, are *actually* continuing their policy of uniting with them on a *non-party* basis; they are continuing a *non-party* policy extremely harmful to the workers, one which cannot be tolerated.

Worker democrats have more than once offered determined resistance to the advocacy of non-partisanship and must do so again in the future, for it dulls the political consciousness of the workers and makes it easier for all sorts of frauds to be perpetrated upon them.

Za Pravdu No. 3,   Published according to
October 4, 1913   the *Za Pravdu* text
Signed: *Kar—ov*

THE LIBERALS
AND THE LAND PROBLEM IN BRITAIN

On Saturday, October 11 (September 28, O.S.), the British Liberal Minister, Lloyd George, opened his "Land Campaign"in two "brilliant" speeches delivered in the town of Bedford. Just as our Kit Kitych Guchkov promised "to settle accounts" with the Russian privileged and all-powerful landowners, so the British Liberal Minister promised to start a campaign on the land question, to expose the landlords and appeal to the people on the issue of a "radical" (Lloyd George is extremely radical!) land reform.

The Liberal press in Britain tried to give their leader's campaign as impressive an appearance as possible. Publicity, publicity at all costs! If the speech is too long, let us publish a brief "summary" of it, let us call it a land "charter", let us embellish it in such a way as to conceal the diplomatic subterfuges of the parliamentary huckster behind a long list of reforms—a minimum wage, 100,000 cottages for the workers, and the "compulsory alienation of the land at its *net* [!!] value to the landlords".

In order to show the reader *how* the Minister of the British Liberal bourgeoisie carries on agitation among the people, we shall quote several passages from Lloyd George's Bedford speeches.

"There is no question more vital, ... than the question ... of the land!" exclaimed the speaker. "It enters into everything—the food the people eat, the water they drink, the houses they dwell in, the industries upon which their livelihood depends." And to whom does the land belong in Britain? To a handful of rich people! One-third of all the land belongs to members of the House of Lords. "Landlordism is

the greatest of all monopolies in this land." The power of
the landlords is boundless. They may evict their tenants,
and devastate the land worse than an enemy would. "Now,
I am not attacking the landlords either individually or as
a class," the Minister took pains to declare, "but can such a
state of affairs be allowed to continue?"

During the last few decades the agricultural population
has declined from over two million to one and a half million, while the number of gamekeepers has increased from
9,000 to 23,000. There is no other country in the world
where there is so much uncultivated land and where the
farmers suffer so much from game bred by the rich for their
amusement.

The wealth of Britain is increasing at an astonishing rate.
But what about the farm labourers? Nine-tenths of them earn
less than twenty shillings and sixpence (about 10 rubles)
per week, a sum which in workhouses is considered to be
barely sufficient to prevent an inmate from starving. Sixty
per cent of the farm labourers earn less than eighteen shillings (about 9 rubles) per week.

The Conservatives propose that the land be purchased
in small holdings. "But him who talks about purchase,"
thundered the British Rodichev,[127] "I shall ask: *at what
price?*" (*Laughter.*)

Will not the high price crush the small buyer? Will he
not be crushed by high rates? There is a Small Holdings
Act which is supposed to provide land for workers. Here
is an example. The total rates and taxes on a plot of land
are assessed at £30 (nearly 270 rubles). This land is bought
and resold to poor people in small holdings. The price they
pay turns out to be £60!

The depopulation of rural England threatens to make our
country defenceless—without a strong peasantry there can
be no strong army. Now, can either a Russian or a British
Liberal get along without playing on crude nationalist and
chauvinist sentiments?

"The landlords did not create the land," exclaimed Lloyd
George, "the country must choose between the power of
the landlords and the welfare of the workers. We must act
firmly and determinedly against monopoly—and property
in land is the greatest monopoly. The tenant farmer must

obtain guarantees that he will not be evicted, or deprived of the fruits of his energy and skill." (A voice: "What is the remedy?") "We must act, enough of timid attempts at half-measures. We must deal with it thoroughly, we must do as businessmen do. It is no use tinkering and mending, we must put the land monopoly under better control.

"We must secure a minimum wage for the labourer, shorten the working day, give him a decent, comfortable cottage and a plot of land so that he can grow a certain amount of produce for his family. We must secure for him a *ladder of progress* in order that the 'enterprising' labourer may rise from the small allotment, the kitchen garden, to the small holding. And the most enterprising might look forward to taking their position as one of the substantial farmers in the community. You are tempted with the charms of emigration to America and Australia. But we want the British worker to find sustenance for himself, a free life and comfort for himself and for his children right here, in England, in our own country."

Thunderous applause.... And one can almost hear the isolated voices of those in the audience who were not fooled (like the one who shouted: "What is the remedy?") saying: "He sings well; but will he do anything?"

He sings well, this British Liberal Minister, this favourite of the petty-bourgeois crowd, a past master in the art of breaking strikes by brazen deception of the workers, the best servant of British capital, which enslaves both the British workers and the 300 million population of India. What power, however, induced this hardened politician, this lackey of the money-bags, to make such "radical" speeches?

The power of the labour movement.

In Britain there is no conscripted army. The people cannot be restrained by violence—they can be restrained only by deception. The labour movement is growing irresistibly. The people's attention must be diverted, the masses must be "engaged" with high-sounding schemes for reform, a pretence must be made of waging war on the Conservatives, sops must be promised to prevent the masses from losing faith in the Liberals, to ensure that they follow the industrial and financial capitalists like sheep following shepherds.

And the promises of reform ... does not the English proverb say that promises are like pie-crusts, made to be broken? Lloyd George makes promises and the Liberal Cabinet as a whole will cut them to a fifth before setting about their realisation. The Conservatives, in their turn, will make a *further* cut, the result being a tenth.

The reformism of the British bourgeoisie is the clearest indication of the growth of a deep-going revolutionary movement among the British working class. No eloquent orator, no Liberal charlatan can stop this movement.

Za Pravdu No. **8,**
October 12, 1913
Signed: *V. I.*

Published according to
the *Za Pravdu* text

A WEAK DEFENCE OF A WEAK CASE

A certain G. Golosov is mortally offended over the fact that I, in *Prosveshcheniye*, referred to Chkheidze as a "near-Party Social-Democrat".*

G. Golosov is in a towering rage; he hurls invectives right and left and burdens his lines with exclamation marks and marks of interrogation. But the greater the anger he displays the more evident it becomes that his angry outcries are merely a screen to cover up his lack of proof.

I did refer to Chkheidze as a near-Party Social-Democrat. It should not be difficult for Golosov to realise that he could refute me if he proved that Chkheidze is a *Party* Social-Democrat.

I mentioned the fact that at the most critical moment in the history of the Social-Democratic group (and in the history of the regeneration of the Party) Chkheidze "avoided the issue". When the liquidator and anti-liquidator press came into being (1911 and beginning of 1912) Chkheidze was *neither on one side nor on the other*.

Does my angry opponent disprove this precisely indicated fact?

He does not. Angry G. Golosov does not disprove this fact, nor can he do so. Poor Golosov; he is wrathful, but he is weak! He timidly evades the fact that proves that Chkheidze's behaviour (notwithstanding his oratorical talent and parliamentary experience) was the behaviour of a *near-Party* man.

If irate G. Golosov were able to think, he would realise that a man proves his party allegiance by taking a most

* See p. 413 of this volume.—*Ed.*

energetic, direct, and open part in the affairs of his party
(and not only of its group in the Duma). The rise of a liquidator and anti-liquidator press marked an extremely important moment in the modern history of the Marxist organisation. Hence, I proved up to the hilt that Chkheidze is a near-
Party man.

In a fit of hysterical rage G. Golosov exclaims: "The Party
is supposed to be where V. Ilyin and G. Zinoviev are."

Thus, good Golosov adds to his troubles by raising the
extremely interesting and important question as to *where*
the Party is. If G. Golosov cannot think, the workers can,
and they have all thought and are thinking about this question.

The Party is *where* the majority of the class-conscious
worker Marxists who take an active part in political life
are to be found.

G. Golosov's anger rises to the pitch of hysteria simply
because he realises he is unable to disprove this plain truth.

The elections to the Fourth Duma, the history of the inception and growth of *Pravda*, the election to the Executive
Committee of the Metalworkers' Union, the insurance campaign and the resolutions passed by the workers in support of the six worker deputies—all *proved* that the Party
is on the side of the six, that it supports their line. *Their*
slogans have been adopted and tested by the *mass* actions
of workers in all branches of the working-class movement.

Irate Golosov is angry simply because he is unable to
disprove the precise, obvious and indisputable fact that the
Marxists beat the liquidators in the elections, in the trade
unions, in the effort to establish daily newspapers and in the
insurance campaign.

Those against whom *all* the facts speak have no alternative but to "get angry" and go into hysterics.

The Party is where the majority of the workers have
rallied around the Party's decisions which provide complete,
systematic and accurate answers to the most important
problems. The Party is where the majority of class-conscious workers are united by the singleness of these decisions
and by a single will to implement them conscientiously.

In defending the "right" of Chkheidze (and of the seven)
to flout these decisions and the will of the working class,

G. Golosov, like all the liquidators, is trying to break up the Marxist organisation in the interests of non-partisanship.

There can be no doubt that the workers will continue to back the position of *their* six deputies as against the *near-Party* position of the seven.

Za Pravdu No. 12,
   October 17, 1913
Signed: V. *Ilyin*

Published according to
the *Za Pravdu* text

DECLARATION[128]

Dear Comrades,

Our joint activities in the State Duma during the past year revealed a number of disagreements and points of friction between our group and yours—the other seven Social-Democratic deputies. Matters have reached the stage of open polemics in the press; and the last decisions you adopted just before the adjournment of the State Duma in June 1913, when some of the deputies had already left, revealed to the full that the situation had become intolerable and had reached an impasse. These decisions which you adopted by a vote of seven against six, are: refusal to allow the Bolsheviks (i.e., the six deputies) to have one of the two seats on the Budget Committee, and the election of one delegate (instead of two) to a certain important body.

After repeatedly, by seven votes against six, depriving the six workers' deputies of the right to nominate one of the two speakers put up in the Duma, the aforesaid decisions were the last drop that filled the cup to overflowing.

You are aware that we have been, and still are, acting entirely in keeping with the spirit of consistent Marxism, and ideologically adhere to all its general decisions.

You are aware, comrades, that absolutely objective facts prove that it is no exaggeration to say that our activities have been in complete harmony with the political consciousness and will of the overwhelming majority of the Marxist advanced workers in Russia. This was proved by the case of *Pravda*, the first workers' newspaper which was brought into being by the revival of the working-class movement in April and May 1912, and which rallied to its side the majority of the workers. It was proved by the circulation of *Pravda*, which reached 40,000. It was proved by the collection of funds for *Pravda* by workers' groups, the progress of which that newspaper always openly reported. It was proved by the Fourth Duma elections in the worker curia, which resulted in the Bolsheviks winning all the seats in the curia, and which revealed an indisputable and undisputed enormous growth of Marxist and anti-liquidator convictions among the class-conscious workers of Russia as compared with the elections in the worker curia to the Second and Third Dumas. Lastly, it was proved by the election of the Executive Committee of the Metalworkers' Union in St. Petersburg and by the case of the first workers' newspaper in Moscow this year. It goes without saying that we regard it as our absolute duty to act in strictest harmony with the will of the majority of the workers of Russia who are united by Marxism.

You seven deputies, however, act independently of this will and contrary to it. You boldly adopt decisions that run counter to the will of the majority of the class-conscious workers. We shall mention, for example, your acceptance on vague terms, of Jagiello, who is not a Social-Democrat, and to this day has not been recognised by a single Social-Democrat in Poland; and your adoption—contrary to the will of the majority of the workers—of nationalist slogans, such as so-called cultural-national autonomy, and so forth. We do not know exactly your attitude towards the liquidator trend, but we think that you incline towards liquidationism rather than fully support it. Be that as it may, it nevertheless remains an indisputable fact that you do not feel bound by the opinions and demands of the majority of the class-conscious workers of Russia, with whom we go hand in hand.

Needless to say, under these circumstances, every socialist in every country in the world, every class-conscious worker, will regard as monstrous your efforts to suppress us by means of one vote, to deprive us of one of the two seats on Duma committees, or other bodies, to deprive us of spokesmen in the Duma, etc., and to foist upon us tactics and a policy that have been condemned by the majority of the class-conscious workers of Russia.

We affirm, and cannot but affirm at the present time, that our disagreements are irreconcilable in other spheres of activity besides that of the Duma. We are compelled to regard your efforts to suppress us and to deprive us of one of the two seats as being undoubtedly aimed at a split and, as such, precluding all possibility of co-operation between us. Nevertheless, respecting as we do the strong desire of the workers that the unity of the Social-Democratic deputies be preserved at least in the Duma and in face of the outside world, and bearing in mind our year's experience, which has proved that it *is possible* to achieve such unity in *Duma* activities by means of an *agreement*, we call upon you to declare precisely and unambiguously, once and for all, that the suppression, in any form, of the six deputies from the worker curia by seven votes is impermissible. The unity of the Social-Democratic group in the Fourth Duma can be really maintained only on the condition that the equality of the seven and six is fully and definitely recognised, and that the principle of agreement between them on all questions concerning Duma activities is adhered to.

Za Pravda No. 13,
October 18, 1913

Published according to
the *Za Pravda* text

THE DUMA "SEVEN"

The long-winded statements and arguments of the seven deputies to the State Duma in defence of liquidationism create a very strange impression.

All the time the seven discuss *solely* Duma activities, Social-Democratic activities in the *Duma*!

Outside of the Taurida Palace *nothing* of an organised character exists for the seven! "We, the seven of us, decided; we and Jagiello voted; we appointed speakers; we adopted a declaration"—this is all one hears from the seven. "We members of the Duma", "we in the Duma"—except for this, the seven know and understand nothing.

The seven have already become so thoroughly infected with liquidationist views that they have ceased to understand the ABC of Marxism.

According to Marxist standards, deputies to the Duma should *not* carry out *their own* will, but the will of the Marxist organisation, *not their own* decisions, but those of the Marxist body as a whole, *not their own*, but its tactics. It is a shame and a disgrace that this ABC of Marxism should have to be explained to Duma deputies! What a pass their inclinations towards the liquidators must have brought them to if they dare to act as non-Party people, as subverters of the proletarian political organisation!

The seven pro-liquidators *dare not even ask* "where is the Marxist organisation?"

And yet, this is the crux of the whole question.

All appeals for unity are sheer hypocrisy if those who make them evade the question of the *single* will, the *single* decisions and *single* tactics of the *majority* of the advanced and class-conscious workers of Russia organised on a Marxist basis.

Za Pravdu long ago indicated the criteria by which the Marxist will of the majority of the workers, opposition to which means splits, disorganisation and disruption can (and must) be judged.

These criteria are: (1) the elections to the Fourth Duma in the worker curia; (2) the case of the workers' newspapers; (3) the trade unions. In Europe they add to these what is the most important—the number of openly registered members of political parties. Everybody will understand that data of the latter kind cannot be obtained in Russia; they are partly compensated for by *common decisions*, which every honest worker regards as binding.

The liquidators and the seven *do not say* a word about this, not a word about the characteristics of the Marxist organisation, about its decisions and its tactics! The liquidators and the seven want "unity", that is, they want the six workers' deputies *to submit to the seven non-Party* deputies; that is, *they want to flout the will of the Marxist body as a whole.*

The liquidators and the seven want the Social-Democratic Duma group to act on its own according to its own sweet will, *in isolation from and opposed* to this body as a whole. And this disgraceful, disruptive demand they call a demand for unity.

The appeals for unity made by the seven remind one of a well-known quip: the seven want to "unite" with the six in the same way as a man "unites" with a piece of bread. He *swallows* it.

The seven non-Party men want to swallow the six Marxists; and they demand that this should be called "unity".

The destruction of the Marxist organisation by the seven deputies who have *alienated themselves* from the majority of the workers, by the seven *pro-liquidator* deputies, by the seven who have forgotten that in the Duma they are only the *vehicles* of the will of the majority of the workers—this is what the liquidators and the seven deputies are aiming at!

The working class protests against this astounding, disruptive behaviour of the arrogant enemies of working-class organisation, and emphatically demands subordination in Duma activities *as in all else*.

Za Pravdu No. 19,
October 25, 1913
Signed: *V. F.*

Published according to
the *Za Pravdu* text

THE LIBERAL BOURGEOISIE
AND THE LIQUIDATORS

The Cadet Party, the leading party of the liberal bourgeoisie in Russia, has a number of men at its headquarters who have received a European education. In our day a man cannot be regarded as educated if he is not generally familiar with Marxism and the West-European working-class movement.

Since they have a large number of bourgeois intellectuals in their ranks, the Russian Cadets are, of course, familiar with Marxism; among them there are even some who were Marxists, or near-Marxists in their youth, but who grew "wiser" as they grew older and became liberal philistines.

All this explains the difference between the attitude of the old, European liberals, and that of the new, Russian liberals towards Social-Democracy. The former tried to prevent the emergence of Social-Democracy and denied its right to existence; the latter have been obliged to resign themselves to the *fact*: "We have no doubt," says the leading article in *Rech* (No. 287), "that Social-Democracy is destined to become the open political party of the proletariat in Russia." That is why the fight our liberals are waging *against* Social-Democracy has assumed the form of a struggle *in favour of opportunism in the ranks* of Social-Democracy.

Impotent to prevent the rise and growth of Social-Democracy, our liberal bourgeois are doing their best *to make it grow in the liberal way*. Hence, the prolonged and systematic efforts of our Cadets to foster opportunism (and liquidationism in particular) in the ranks of the Social-Democrats; the liberals *rightly* regard this as the *only* way of retaining their influence over the proletariat and of making the working class dependent upon the liberal bourgeoisie.

The liberals' appraisal of the fight waged by the six workers' deputies against the seven pro-liquidator deputies is therefore very instructive. As onlookers, the liberals are compelled candidly to admit the main fact: the seven are the "parliamentary elements of Social-Democracy", they are a "party of parliamentary activity", they have in their ranks "the entire intelligentsia of the Duma Social-Democrats". Their line is that of the "evolution of Social-Democracy into an open parliamentary party", a line connected with a special "trend in tactics". "*Novaya Rabochaya Gazeta* is the organ of the Social-Democrat parliamentarians."

Za Pravdu, on the contrary, is the "organ of the irreconcilables", says *Rech*, who are not a party of parliamentary activity but are the "antithesis of such a party".

The party of "*intellectual deputies*" versus "*workers' deputies*", such is *Rech*'s verdict. *Rech* says superciliously that it is impossible to tell whom the majority of the workers support, but it refutes itself in the very next breath by the following illuminating passage:

"The longer the transition to this normal existence" (i.e., open, legal existence) "is delayed," it says, "the more reason will there be to anticipate that the *parliamentary majority of the Social-Democratic intellectuals will be compelled to yield to the non-parliamentary workers' majority* and to its present mood. We saw the deplorable consequences of such a divergence of trends at the end of 1905. And whatever one's opinion may be of the future upshot of the present impasse, it is hardly likely that anyone will be found to justify the blunders committed by the inexperienced leaders of the spontaneous mass temper in those winter months." This is what *Rech* writes.

We have stressed what interests us now particularly in this admission.

The non-parliamentary workers' **majority** versus the "parliamentary majority of the Social-Democratic intellectuals",—even the liberals perceive this as the issue in the controversy between the six and the seven.

The seven and *Novaya Rabochaya Gazeta* represent the majority of the self-styled Social-Democratic intelligentsia *as opposed* to the "non-parliamentary workers' majority", *as opposed to the Party.*

The old party has disappeared; we don't need the old party; we will do without the party, we will make shift with one newspaper and activities in the Duma, and advocate the formation of an open party in the future—such, virtually, is the position of the seven and the position of all liquidators.

One can understand, therefore, why the liberals speak so kindly of the seven and of the liquidators, why they praise them for understanding parliamentary conditions, and refer to their tactics as "intricate, thoughtful and not oversimplified". The seven and the liquidators carry *liberal slogans* into the ranks of the working class—why should not the liberals praise them? The liberals could not wish for anything better than the erection of a bulwark of intellectuals, parliamentarians and legalists *against* the old party, *against* the "non-parliamentary workers' majority".

Let this bulwark call itself Social-Democratic; its name is not important, what is important is its liberal-labour policy—that is the way the enlightened bourgeoisie argues, and from its point of view it argues quite correctly.

The liberals have realised (and have blurted out) what all class-conscious, advanced workers realised long ago— that the *Novaya Rabochaya Gazeta* group and the seven that follow its lead, are this bulwark of liberal intellectuals who have split off from the Social-Democratic Party, repudiate the Party, denounce its "underground" activities and pursue a systematic policy of concessions to bourgeois reformism, bourgeois nationalism, etc.

The unity of the "non-parliamentary workers' majority", which is the genuine Party majority and is really independent of the liberal bourgeoisie, is *inconceivable* unless this bulwark of intellectual liquidators of the workers' party is vigorously combated.

Za Pravdu No. 20,
October 26, 1913

Published according to
the *Za Pravdu* text

CAPITALISM AND WORKERS' IMMIGRATION

Capitalism has given rise to a special form of migration of nations. The rapidly developing industrial countries, introducing machinery on a large scale and ousting the backward countries from the world market, raise wages at home above the average rate and thus attract workers from the backward countries.

Hundreds of thousands of workers thus wander hundreds and thousands of versts. Advanced capitalism drags them forcibly into its orbit, tears them out of the backwoods in which they live, makes them participants in the world-historical movement and brings them face to face with the powerful, united, international class of factory owners.

There can be no doubt that dire poverty alone compels people to abandon their native land, and that the capitalists exploit the immigrant workers in the most shameless manner. But only reactionaries can shut their eyes to the *progressive* significance of this modern migration of nations. Emancipation from the yoke of capital is impossible without the further development of capitalism, and without the class struggle that is based on it. And it is into this struggle that capitalism is drawing the masses of the working people of the *whole* world, breaking down the musty, fusty habits of local life, breaking down national barriers and prejudices, uniting workers from all countries in huge factories and mines in America, Germany, and so forth.

America heads the list of countries which import workers. The following are the immigration figures for America:

Ten years 1821-30 99,000
  " " 1831-40 496,000
  " " 1841-50 1,597,000
  " " 1851-60 2,453,000
  " " 1861-70 2,064,000
  " " 1871-80 2,262,000
  " " 1881-90 4,722,000
  " " 1891-1900 3,703,000
Nine " 1901-09 7,210,000

The growth of immigration is enormous and continues to increase. During the five years 1905-09 the average number of immigrants entering America (the United States alone is referred to) was *over a million* a year.

It is interesting to note the change in the place of origin of those emigrating to America. Up to 1880 the so-called *old* immigration prevailed, that is, immigration from the old civilised countries, such as Great Britain, Germany and partly from Sweden. Even up to 1890, Great Britain and Germany provided more than half the total immigrants.

From 1880 onwards, there was an incredibly rapid increase in what is called the *new* immigration from Eastern and Southern Europe, from Austria, Italy and Russia. The number of people emigrating from these three countries to the United States was as follows:

Ten years 1871-80 201,000
  " " 1881-90 927,000
  " " 1891-1900 1,847,000
Nine " 1901-09 5,127,000

Thus, the most backward countries in the old world, those that more than any other retain survivals of feudalism in every branch of social life, are, as it were, undergoing compulsory training in civilisation. American capitalism is tearing millions of workers of backward Eastern Europe (including Russia, which in 1891-1900 provided 594,000 immigrants and in 1900-09, 1,410,000) out of their semi-feudal conditions and is putting them in the ranks of the advanced, international army of the proletariat.

Hourwich, the author of an extremely illuminating book, *Immigration and Labour*, which appeared in English last year, makes some interesting observations. The number of people emigrating to America grew particularly after the 1905 Revolution (1905—1,000,000; 1906—1,200,000; 1907—1,400,000; 1908 and 1909—1,900,000 respectively). Workers who had participated in various strikes in Russia introduced into America the bolder and more aggressive spirit of the mass strike.

Russia is lagging farther and farther behind, losing some of her best workers to foreign countries; America is advancing more and more rapidly, taking the most vigorous and able-bodied sections of the working population of the whole world.*

Germany, which is more or less keeping pace with the United States, is changing from a country which released workers into one that attracts them from foreign countries. The number of immigrants from Germany to America in the ten years 1881-90 was 1,453,000; but in the nine years 1901-09 it dropped to 310,000. The number of foreign workers in Germany, however, was 695,000 in 1910-11 and 729,000 in 1911-12. Dividing these immigrants according to occupation and country of origin we get the following:

	Foreign workers employed in Germany in 1911-12 (thousands)		
	Agriculture	Industry	Total
From Russia	274	34	308
" Austria	101	162	263
" other countries	22	135	157
Total	397	331	728

The more backward the country the larger is the number of "unskilled" agricultural labourers it supplies. The advanced nations seize, as it were, the best paid occupations for themselves and leave the semi-barbarian countries the worst paid occupations. Europe in general ("other countries") provided Germany with 157,000 workers, of whom *more than eight-tenths* (135,000 out of 157,000) were industrial workers. Backward Austria provided only *six-tenths*

---

* Other countries on the American Continent besides the United States are also rapidly advancing. The number of immigrants entering the United States last year was about 250,000, Brazil about 170,000 and Canada over 200,000; total 620,000 for the year.

(162,000 out of 263,000) of the industrial workers. The most backward country of all, Russia, provided only *one-tenth* of the industrial workers (34,000 out of 308,000).

Thus, Russia is punished everywhere and in everything for her backwardness. But compared with the rest of the population, it is the workers of Russia who are more than any others bursting out of this state of backwardness and barbarism, more than any others combating these "delightful" features of their native land, and more closely than any others uniting with the workers of all countries into a single international force for emancipation.

The bourgeoisie incites the workers of one nation against those of another in the endeavour to keep them disunited. Class-conscious workers, realising that the break-down of all the national barriers by capitalism is inevitable and progressive, are trying to help to enlighten and organise their fellow-workers from the backward countries.

Za Pravdu No. 22,
October 2 9, 1913
Signed: *V. I.*

Published according to
the *Za Pravdu* text

MATERIAL ON THE CONFLICT WITHIN
THE SOCIAL-DEMOCRATIC DUMA GROUP[129]

A conflict has broken out between the six Social-Democratic deputies from the worker curia in the State Duma—Badayev, Malinovsky, Muranov, Petrovsky, Samoilov and Shagov, on the one side, and the other seven members of the Social-Democratic group in the State Duma, on the other. Both the six and the seven have appealed to the workers to discuss the question and to express their opinions.

The discussion is already under way among the St. Petersburg workers, and to enable it to proceed successfully, we publish the following summary of material and considerations, which will interest all workers who have the fate of their Marxist organisation at heart.

WHOSE WILL?

The main question that confronts the workers in connection with the split in the Social-Democratic group in the Duma is the relation between the Duma group and the Marxist body as a whole. Whose will should determine the decisions, tactics and conduct of the Social-Democratic group in the Duma?

The experience of all Social-Democratic parliamentary groups throughout the world provides a clear and absolutely indisputable answer to this question. Social-Democrat parliamentary deputies are the vehicles of the will of the class-conscious and organised proletariat of the country in question. The decisions adopted by the advanced proletariat, and which it carries out in all its economic and political struggle, are *binding* for Social-Democrat representatives in parliament. Parliamentary deputies who disagree with the will of the class-conscious, organised and advanced proletariat, resign, i.e., surrender their title of deputy.

These general and fundamental principles, to which all Marxists all over the globe subscribe, must first of all be clearly understood and thoroughly assimilated so that no unscrupulous persons may confuse and obscure the point at issue.

Anyone who attempts to defend the conception that Social-Democrat parliamentary deputies should be independent of the will of the majority of the organised and class-conscious workers at once exposes himself as an enemy of the Marxist organisation and a disruptor of all unity, of all united action on the part of worker Social-Democrats.

The question now is, how can we Russian workers determine what are the will and decisions of the majority of the class-conscious and united worker Social-Democrats of Russia?

WHAT IS THE WILL OF THE MAJORITY OF THE CLASS CONSCIOUS WORKERS OF RUSSIA?

In all countries in the world the following criteria determine the will of the politically organised proletariat.

First, the workers' newspapers. The support which the proletariat renders the different workers' newspapers reveals its political will and indicates the trend it stands for.

Second, parliamentary elections. Election laws in different countries vary, but it is often possible to determine without error *which deputies* the working class elects. The *trend* to which the deputies elected by the workers belong *indicates the will* of the proletariat.

Third, various workers' associations and societies, especially the trade unions, which wage a struggle against capital, give an indication of the will of the proletariat.

Fourth, in Western Europe, the most precise index of the will of the proletariat is the decisions of the socialist parties, which conduct their activities openly, and whose membership is known.

It is common knowledge that there is no open Social-Democratic Party in Russia. In this country even the Constitutional-Democratic Party is presumed to be banned. In Russia, those who attack or renounce the "underground", or justify renouncing it, are therefore called liquidators, i.e., renegades, disruptors of the workers' organisation.

Let us now examine *facts* concerning the will of the advanced workers of Russia.

WHAT DID THE ELECTIONS TO THE SECOND,
THIRD AND FOURTH DUMAS REVEAL CONCERNING
THE WILL OF THE PROLETARIAT?

For the reactionary purpose of separating the workers from the peasants, the Russian election law provides for the establishment of worker curias, i.e., the separate election of workers' deputies. But this enables us all the more easily to ascertain the will of the workers, who return to the Duma men who agree with their views and trend.

That is why *all* the candidates elected by the *worker curias* at the elections to the Second, Third and Fourth Dumas were *Social-Democrats*. All informed people (except the politically unscrupulous) were therefore compelled to draw the conclusion that it was the will of the workers of Russia to march solidly in step with the Social-Democrats.

But *which* trend *inside* the Social-Democratic movement did the workers support?

A clear-cut reply to this question is provided by the returns which show to which *trends* the candidates elected by the worker curias belonged. In the Second Duma there were 23 deputies elected by the worker curia; of these 11(i.e., 47 per cent) were Bolsheviks. It is common knowledge that at that very time, the spring of 1907, a certified majority in the workers' party supported the Bolsheviks.

To the Third Duma, after the election reform, the worker curia elected only eight deputies. Of these, four (i.e., 50 per cent) were Bolsheviks. To the Fourth Duma the worker curia elected nine deputies, of whom six (i.e., 67 per cent) were Bolsheviks.

Thus, over a period of six years, from 1907 to 1912, when the intelligentsia *deserted* Social-Democracy, the workers *in increasing numbers* came over to the side of the Bolsheviks.

Over two-thirds of the workers of Russia support the views and line of the *six* deputies from the worker curia in the Fourth Duma—Badayev, Malinovsky, Muranov, Petrovsky, Samoilov and Shagov. These deputies are backed by the *overwhelming majority* of the class-conscious workers who take an active part in politics.

The intellectuals deserted the Marxist organisation; they tried to liquidate it. The workers deserted the liquidators. Only unscrupulous people can deny the truth of this.

WHO ARE THE DEPUTIES?

On the very day that the declaration of the six deputies* appeared in the newspapers, the liquidators' newspaper (issue No. 60) hastened to the defence of the seven deputies and argued that the latter had received *no fewer* workers' votes than the six.

At that time our paper (issue No. 13) published figures which completely shattered the liquidators' position and knocked the bottom out of the "argument" they advanced.

These figures showed the number of workers in the gubernias which returned Social-Democratic deputies to the Duma; they also gave a perfectly clear idea of which section of the Social-Democratic group in the Duma received the highest number of workers' votes, and even how much higher.

Here are the figures:

---

* See pp. 446-48 of this volume.—*Ed.*

Gubernia	Name of deputy	Thousands		
		Number of workers according to factory inspectors' reports	Mining industry	Totals
Moscow	Malinovsky . . .	348	3	351
Vladimir	Samoilov	202	3	205
St. Petersburg	Badayev	170	27	197
Ekaterinoslav . .	Petrovsky . . .	33	85	118
Kostroma . . .	Shagov	91	—	91
Kharkov	Muranov	45	1	46
	Totals . . .	889	119	1,008
Warsaw	Jagiello	78	—	78
Don Region . . .	Tulyakov . . .	18	41	59
Ufa	Khaustov . . .	6	31	37
Taurida	Buryanov . . .	10	10	20
Irkutsk	Mankov	2	11	13
Tiflis	Chkheidze . . .	5	—	5
Kars and Batum Region	Chkhenkeli . . .	1	1	2
	Totals . . .	120	94	214

Since deputy Jagiello is not really a member of the group of seven deputies, for he does not belong to the Social-Democratic Party and has no voice in the relations between the six and the seven deputies, and furthermore, since he was elected to the Duma contrary to the wishes of the majority of the worker electors of the city of Warsaw, the number of workers in the Warsaw Gubernia cannot be counted as having voted in favour of the seven deputies.

The upshot is that out of 1,144,000, the seven deputies can claim only 136,000, or 11.8 per cent, or about *one-tenth*, whereas the six deputies can claim 1,008,000, or 88.2 per cent, or about *nine-tenths*.

The liquidators' emphatic statement that the workers' vote was equal is utterly refuted.

What do they say in answer to that?

Their answer is worth repeating in full, and it can be explained only by the hopelessness of their case.

"Leaving aside the question as to whether these figures are correct or significant, we assert..." says Mr. F., in No. 61 of *Novaya Rabochaya Gazeta.*

Gentlemen, you raised the question of the number of workers' votes. The figures are presented to you, but you leave them aside.

Barely had he finished saying this, when another statement appeared in the next issue (No. 62), at which one can only wonder.

"Our newspaper yesterday expressed its opinion on the arithmetical side of this assertion."

Leaving aside means "expressing an opinion". Who are the simpletons that the liquidators count on fooling?

In quoting these figures, which the liquidators have not been able to refute, we have not said a word about the particularly important place in our electoral system occupied by the gubernias which elected the six workers' deputies. Discouraged by the *facts,* the liquidators are now talking about the special privileges provided for the six deputies by the law of June 3, about our being supposed to stand in awe of Stolypin's curias, about our regarding only the six deputies as Social-Democrats, etc.

Assertions of this kind have a very definite "if unflattering" name.... We will not soil our lips!...

The numbers of workers in the various gubernias remain unchanged. They can and must be compared.

The German Social-Democrats count their election gains in spite of the fact that women there are deprived of the franchise.

All this is so clear and simple that one can only wonder whom the liquidators expect to mislead with their "arguments".

WHAT IS THE WILL OF THE WORKERS
AS SHOWN BY WORKERS' NEWSPAPERS IN RUSSIA?

It is common knowledge that workers' newspapers began to appear in Russia after the 1908-10 period of despondency and collapse, i.e., in 1911; and they became firmly established in 1912.

Take the year 1912. The first to appear and become firmly established was the weekly *Zvezda,*[130] which later began to appear twice a week and paved the way for the daily

Pravda. Pravda appeared thanks to the *extraordinarily strong* support of the workers in April 1912. This newspaper rallied around itself the majority of the class-conscious workers. Its line was the line of the *majority* of the united and class-conscious proletarians.

By 1913 there were *two* all-Russian newspapers of the same trend. A tremendous wave of working-class support brought into being *Nash Put*, a Moscow newspaper of *the same* trend.

The other trend, the liquidators, started a daily newspaper, *Luch*, only in the *autumn* of 1912, after publishing very feeble weeklies.

Thus, the facts prove beyond doubt that the *majority* of the workers rallied around *Pravda* very much earlier. The liquidator newspaper was launched later, and it *opposed the will* of the majority, *tried to effect a split*, i.e., it demonstrated the refusal of the minority to submit to the majority.

Every worker will understand that workers' *unity* of action is *thwarted* if a *second* newspaper is published in the same city with the object of undermining the first. *Not a single* Social-Democratic Party anywhere in Europe would tolerate anything of the sort.

WHAT IS THE WILL OF THE WORKERS
AS SHOWN BY COLLECTIONS FOR WORKERS' NEWSPAPERS?

Bourgeois newspapers are maintained by large sums of capital. Workers' newspapers are maintained by funds collected by the workers themselves.

In making contribution to a publication or a newspaper of any particular trend the workers very clearly express their will.

The funds that the workers have contributed to the workers' press in Russia are therefore a most important index of the workers' will. Only absolute ignoramuses or unscrupulous people (like the Cadets and the liquidators) can attempt to brush this aside.

The following figures show how many *collections* were made by *workers' groups*; they have been published more than once, and are open to verification by anyone who can read.

| | Number of collections made by workers' groups | | | |
	For Pravda	For the Moscow newspaper	For both	For Luch
1912	620	5	625	89
1913 to April 1	309	129	438	139
1913, from April 1 to October	1,252	261	1,513	328
Totals for the two years . .	2,181	395	2,576	556

These figures cover a *long* period of time. They cover the *whole* of 1912 and nine months of 1913. They cover the *whole of Russia.**

What do they show? They undoubtedly show that *supporters* of *Za Pravdu*, supporters of the *six workers' deputies*, opponents of liquidationism *clearly predominate* among the class-conscious workers.

All those who refuse to recognise the decisions of this overwhelming majority are schismatics, disruptors, violators of the will of the workers.

WHAT IS THE WILL OF THE WORKERS
AS SHOWN BY THE ST. PETERSBURG TRADE UNIONS?

It is common knowledge that the metalworkers are the most developed and most advanced section of the working class not only in St. Petersburg, but throughout Russia, and not only Russia, but throughout the world.

Nobody can deny—and on the day the metalworkers assembled the liquidators *themselves* admitted it—that the metalworkers are the *vanguard* of the entire Russian proletariat.

What did the metalworkers' meeting in St. Petersburg prove?

The occasion was the election of the Executive Committee. There were two lists of candidates.

One list, published in the liquidators' newspaper and backed by the latter, contained the *names of a number* of well-known liquidators.

---

* In the symposium *Marxism and Liquidationism* there is a footnote to this passage: "By May 1914 *Pravda* had in round figures 6,000 workers' groups. The liquidators had about 1,500."—*Ed.*

The other list, published in *Pravda*, was *anti-liquidationist*.

The liquidators fraudulently gave out their list as the decision of the union, but their fraud did not help them.

The metalworkers' meeting was attended by about *3,000 people*. 'Of these, only some *150* cast their votes for the liquidators' list of candidates.

Obviously, this quite clearly revealed the will of the class-conscious and advanced workers. The workers will not allow any mention of liquidationism.

Of all the trade unions in St. Petersburg, the Printers' Union alone still supports the liquidators,* thereby isolating itself from the rest of the St. Petersburg proletariat. But even there, it must be observed, not everything is "favourable" for the liquidators. Are there many admirers of the liquidators to be found among the shop assistants, woodworkers, gold- and silversmiths, tailors, bakers, builders, tavern employees, and so forth? How many are there, and where are they? Are many of these admirers to be found in the cultural and educational institutions? There is little evidence of them! And yet the liquidators, in denouncing the "underground" and the "strike craze", in pleading for legality in the shelter of Stolypin reforms, assert that everything legal supports them! Whom are the working-class intelligentsia supporting? In our last issue *106 working-class students* expressed their greetings to the six and denounced the liquidators!

In following the lead of the liquidators the seven deputies are *flouting the will* of the majority of the workers. This has been proved by the Duma elections, by the collections for the newspapers, by the meeting of the metalworkers, by all the activities in the legal movement, and by the present insurance campaign (the support rendered the insurance weekly in response to the appeal of the six workers' deputies).

The seven deputies who are *flouting* the will of the majority of the workers must bear in mind the inevitable consequences if they insist on pursuing *their own* will in *opposition to* the majority of the workers.

---

* In the symposium *Marxism and Liquidationism* there is a footnote to this passage: "Evidently even this union is now beginning to shift away from the liquidators."—*Ed.*

IDEOLOGICAL UNITY

The liquidator newspaper writes:

"Social-Democracy constitutes a definite ideologically united body and those who do not subscribe to its ideas do not belong to it."

That is the truth, but not the whole truth, for Social-Democracy is not only an *ideologically but also an organisationally* united body. This can be forgotten only by liquidators, i.e., by those who refuse to recognise precisely the organised body, who ignore its will, flout its decisions, etc.

Our liquidators, those who wrote for *Luch* and are now writing for *Novaya Rabochaya Gazeta*, exposed themselves most vividly to the masses of the workers by opposing and strongly combating the Russian Marxist organisation.

The liquidators have been strongly condemned in a number of decisions adopted by this, the only existing political organisation of the workers of Russia. They have been condemned for their intolerable, disruptive and schismatic attitude towards this organisation. These decisions were passed in 1908, in 1910 and in 1912. Russian workers who take an interest in the affairs of their class are familiar with them. But the liquidators not only did not consider it necessary to abide by these decisions, they have unceremoniously flouted them by all their actions and their propaganda.

That explains why the liquidationist newspaper, in discussing the question of *organisation*, concealed from its readers the fact that Social-Democracy represents not only an ideologically but also an organisationally united body. Operating in complete isolation from the organisation, flouting its decisions, making its very existence the subject of derision, the liquidators, naturally, prefer not to remind the workers of this.

But although the liquidator writer conceals this circumstance from his readers, he has nevertheless had to admit that those who do not subscribe to the ideas of the Social-Democratic organisation cannot possibly be regarded as belonging to it. But the liquidators are the very people who come under this category. Their ideas are not Social-Democratic but liberal-labour ideas. The ideas of opportunists and legalists, the ideas of those who trim down consistent Marxist slogans and advocate the destruction of the old organisation and the formation of an open party under the June Third regime, can nowhere ever be regarded as Social-Democratic by anybody.

Both in their organisational activities and in their propaganda of non-Marxist ideas, the liquidators have *gone beyond the bounds* of Social-Democracy.

Social-Democracy is a definite organisationally united body and those who refuse to submit to the discipline of this organisation, who ignore it and flout its decisions, do not belong to it. Such is the basic rule.

But the liquidator who let the cat out of the bag is also right. He is right when he says that *those who do not subscribe to Social-Democratic ideas do not belong to Social-Democracy.* Precisely, Mr. Liquidator. Only you fail to see that these words apply primarily and most aptly to yourself and your liquidator ideas.

THE LIQUIDATORS AND THE BOURGEOISIE

If anybody has any doubts about this let him watch the attitude of the bourgeois politicians and the bourgeois press towards liquidationism, its ideas and the struggle it is waging against the Marxist working-class organisation. Anybody who does this will very soon become convinced that *the bourgeoisie greets every pronouncement by the liquidators against the Marxists with paeans of praise and admiration.* It welcomed the liquidators' pronouncements against the old organisation; gleefully it took up their campaign against the workers on strike and their denunciation of the "strike craze".

But while admiring and praising the liquidators, the bourgeois press could not close its eyes to a very sad circumstance. It was obliged to admit that liquidationism, which is so pleasing to the bourgeois liberals (birds of a feather flock together!), is only an intellectualist trend and meets with no success among the masses of the workers. The liberals deplore this very much, but every class-conscious worker should rejoice at it!

See how *Rech*, the leading organ of the bourgeois liberals, appraised what happened in the Social-Democratic group in the Duma.

It stated plainly that the seven are the "parliamentary elements of Social-Democracy", that they belong to the "party of parliamentary activity", that "the position of the intellectualist deputies is more thoughtful". To put it briefly, the position of the liquidators and of *Novaya Rabochaya Gazeta* suits the liberal gentlemen more than that of the six workers' deputies.

"All of them were elected directly by the workers", say the liberals in respect of the workers' deputies; they constitute a group of "irreconcilables", and their slogans are much more "intelligible" to the masses of the workers.

Now it is precisely this "irreconcilability" of the workers' deputies and their direct contact with the masses that the liberal gentlemen do not like. And they tearfully declare that "there is reason to anticipate that the parliamentary majority of the Social-Democratic intellectuals will be compelled to yield to the non-parliamentary workers' majority".

In this controversy the liberal gentlemen desire from the bottom of their hearts to see the victory of the "moderates", the liquidators, the advocates of "parliamentary" tactics; and they would like to see the irreconcilable workers' deputies with their "straightforward" slogans tied hand and foot!

But even the liberals have an inkling that the working class and its devotion to the uncurtailed slogans will prevent the realisation of the liquidator and liberal dream of a victory of the opportunists in the ranks of Social-Democracy.

DECISION OF THE UNITED MARXISTS

The seven deputies, who oppose the will of the majority of the proletariat, furtively evade the fact that the six are acting in harmony with that will.

The following is an already published decision of the Marxists:

"This Conference is of the opinion that *united action* on the part of the Social-Democratic group in the Duma is *possible and essential.*

"This Conference affirms, however, that the *conduct of the seven deputies* gravely *jeopardises the unity* of the group.

"Taking advantage of their accidental majority of one,

the seven deputies encroach on the elementary rights of the six workers' deputies who represent the overwhelming majority of the workers of Russia.

"The seven deputies, guided by narrow factional interests, deprive the six deputies of the opportunity to speak in the Duma on very important questions affecting the lives of the workers. In several cases, when the Social-Democratic group put up two or more speakers, the six deputies were not given an opportunity in spite of repeated demands to put up even one of theirs.

"Similarly, in appointing representatives to various Duma committees (for example, the Budget Committee) the seven deputies refuse to allow the six to have one of the two places.

"When the group elects representatives to bodies that are of importance to the working-class movement, the seven deputies, by a majority of one, deprive the six of all representation. The staff that serves the group is always elected in a biased manner (for example, the demand for a second secretary was rejected).

"This Conference is of the opinion that such conduct on the part of the seven deputies inevitably gives rise to friction in the group, which hinders united action and threatens to split the group.

"This Conference protests most emphatically against this conduct on the part of the seven deputies.

"The six deputies represent the overwhelming majority of the workers of Russia and act in complete harmony with the political line of the organised vanguard of the working class. This Conference is therefore of the opinion that united action on the part of the Social-Democratic group in the Duma is possible *only* if the two sections of the group *enjoy equal rights*, and if the seven deputies abandon their steam-roller tactics.

"Notwithstanding irreconcilable disagreements in spheres of activity outside as well as inside the Duma, *this Conference demands that the group should maintain unity* on the basis of the aforesaid equality of rights of its two sections.

"This Conference invites class-conscious workers *to express their opinion* on this important question *and to exert all efforts to help preserve the unity* of the group on the only possible basis, that of equal rights for the six workers' deputies."*

This decision clearly and precisely expressed through the medium of workers' representatives the will of the majority that we discussed in detail above.

Only *non-Party* Social-Democrats can act contrary to this will. *Only liquidators* can advise the seven to act as *they think fit*, as schismatics and disruptors of the workers' organisation.

OUR WORK WITHIN THE DUMA GROUP

The six deputies submitted to the judgement of the workers the question of their being suppressed in the Duma group by the accidental majority within the group.

They quoted astonishing facts about the group. What have the seven deputies said in reply?

Instead of making a clear and straightforward statement refuting the cases of their being restricted in the Duma activities, enumerated by the six, the seven deputies quoted a number of cases when there was no restriction or suppression.

No doubt there were cases in the activities of the group when the rights of the six deputies were respected; if this were not so it would have been nothing short of an insult to the proletariat, and such a situation in the Duma group would be intolerable even for a single day.

That the unity of the group is possible and that agreement is essential is proved by the experience of the year the group has been in existence.

But this experience also shows that within the group the six deputies were tied hand and foot by the seven who inclined towards liquidationism and ignored the majority of the workers.

The facts which are quoted by the six deputies, and which clearly depict the state of affairs in the group, have not been refuted.

The seven deputies: 1) attempted to change the Programme of the Social-Democratic Party. In the Duma, for example,

---

* See pp. 425-26 of this volume.—*Ed.*

they advocated the cultural-national autonomy rejected by all Marxists in 1903.

2) Accepted deputy Jagiello into the group with the right to vote on Duma affairs and wanted to grant him a vote on Party affairs although he belongs to another organisation and does not belong to the Social-Democrats.

3) Refused to allow the six deputies to have their own secretary in spite of their repeated demands for one.

4) Restricted the six deputies in every way as regards speaking in the Duma.

5) Refused to allow the six deputies representation on a certain important body.

6) Restricted the right of the six deputies to be represented on Duma committees, including the Budget Committee.

To all these charges the seven deputies have but one reply—for *the benefit of the cause.*

Obviously, the suppression and restriction of the activities of the six deputies, who represent the overwhelming majority of the workers of Russia, cannot be shown to benefit the *workers' cause and the cause of Social-Democracy.*

The following facts and figures on Social-Democrat representation on Duma committees, show convincingly how the six deputies were suppressed in the Duma group.

Of the 26 committees on which the Social-Democrats are represented:

the six deputies are represented on *seven*; the other seven deputies are represented on *thirteen*—nearly *twice as many.*

Of the 20 committees on which there is one Social-Democratic representative:

the six deputies are represented on *seven*; the other seven are represented on *thirteen*—nearly *twice as many.*

Of the committees on which there are two Social-Democratic representatives:

the six deputies are represented on *three*; the other seven are represented on *six*—*twice as many.*

On each of three of these committees the seven had two representatives.

Not one of the six deputies sits on more than two committees. Of the seven, *Chkhenkeli sits on six committees; Skobelev sits on six, and Mankov sits on four.*

WHAT DO THE SIX DEMAND?

The six demanded the right to have their own secretary, one *of the two* seats on the Budget Committee, and the election of two representatives instead of one to a certain important body.

The seven *have admitted* that they *have not conceded these demands to this day, and have even rejected them.*

Every worker will agree that these demands are quite fair.

The seven will forfeit all confidence if they refuse to yield to these fair demands.

The seven are in duty bound to grant *equal rights, complete equality* to the six workers' deputies who act in conformity *with the will of the majority.*

Only in this way can the seven—who act *contrary to the will* of the majority—take a step towards unity, at least in Duma activities.

The workers must compel the seven to respect the will of the majority!

UNITY INSIDE AND OUTSIDE THE DUMA

There is only one way of ensuring unity outside the Duma, and that is, by maintaining the unity of the workers' cells, by bringing into these cells all those who sincerely and honestly desire to work for the benefit of the working class under the leadership of its political organisation. Entry is open to all. All those who desire to work in harmony with the organisation can and should join. Only in this way can we ensure unity in the working-class movement; *unity from below, unity in practical activities, in the struggle, under mutual control.*

Our newspaper issued this slogan long ago, and has always championed it. There is no evidence, however, that the liquidators are following the same road, which is always open to them if they really want Social-Democratic activity and unity.

But what about unity in Duma activities?

Everywhere unity in parliamentary activities is always achieved in one way only: by the parliamentary representatives submitting to the majority of the organised workers. But the seven deputies who are inclining towards liquidationism refuse to respect the will of this majority. They refuse to respect the clear-cut decisions of the organised workers. They prefer to use their accidental majority of one vote to suppress the six deputies who express the will of the overwhelming majority of the workers and are operating in complete ideological harmony with the Marxist organisation.

The only proper thing for those who refuse to respect the Marxist body as a whole to do is to say so openly.

But they prefer to stick tight to their position of alleged non-responsibility. Not only do they refuse to respect the decisions of the organised workers, but they want to use their *majority in the Duma* to violate the decisions that express the will of the proletariat outside the Duma.

Unity in the Duma will be possible only if the seven deputies abandon this line of conduct.

The six deputies demand no more than that.

Our comrades say: unity of action will be possible in the Duma if the seven deputies, who do not feel bound by the decisions of the Marxists, abandon their tactics of suppressing us, who desire to keep in step with these ideological decisions.

On this basis unity is possible.

But only on this basis. The seven deputies' refusal to accede to these demands indicates that they are deliberately and openly heading for a split. The overwhelming majority of the organised workers, who, as the above-quoted figures show, support the six, *offer* to work with the seven deputies on the basis of agreement. That the latter reject this offer, shows that they have completely and definitely *broken away* from the Marxist workers' organisation. It shows that the seven vacillating deputies have entirely gone over to schismatic liquidationism.

Za Pravdu No. 22,
October 29, 1913

Published according to
the *Za Pravdu* text
collated with the symposium
Marxism and Liquidationism,
Part II, St. Petersburg, 1914

A CADET PROPERTY-OWNER ARGUES "ACCORDING TO MARX"

Mr. Velikhov, property-owner, member of the State Duma and the Cadet Party, editor and publisher of *Gorodskoye Dyelo*,[131] published in his magazine an article in defence of the Kiev congress of urban representatives of "the intellectualist bureaucracy".

This malicious phrase, borrowed from the reactionary press, denotes the democratic intelligentsia, who, be it known, have given offence to the poor property-owners by analysing the "property-owners' institutions" and demanding political clarity. "The intellectualist bureaucracy," complains Mr. Velikhov, tried "primarily to impose a general-political role on the congress."

Mr. Velikhov calls this trend at the congress "political" and contrasts it to another trend, *"municipal"*.

The views of the latter he outlines as follows:

"The revolution, said the urban representatives, has passed and is not likely to be repeated in the near future. It is probable that it was not completely successful because the revolutionary-minded classes [which classes? Say what you mean, Mr. Velikhov!] acted at that time without having acquired sufficient knowledge and experience and were not trained to take over state power. The broad road of meetings, slogans, tub-thumping speeches and resolutions of protest no longer satisfies anyone, and has apparently outlived itself. Ahead of us there is tremendous cultural work of a practical nature."

That is how a property-owner speaks. He shows the point of view of the serf-owner both in his morals and in his urge to forget that at the decisive moment the bourgeoisie went over to the side of the feudalists. He repeats in a peculiar way some "would-be Marxist" phrases that he has heard somewhere, probably among the liquidators:

"In Russia," he writes, "where the working-class proletariat is still small in numbers and weak, where, even according to Marx's *Capital*, government should pass from the landed aristocracy to the urban bourgeoisie at the next stage of historical development, to attack the bourgeoisie, to disdain them, to hinder their attempts to struggle against the present political system and regime means putting the brake on natural progress." (*Gorodskoye Dyelo*, 1913, No. 20, pp. 1341-1342.)

Quite, quite "according to Marx"!

My dear progressive and even Constitutional-Democratic property-owner! "The attempts of the bourgeoisie to struggle against the present political system" have *never* been hindered by the Marxists. You will never be able to show a single case of "struggle" in which the "weak proletariat" did not participate *more* energetically. The Marxists and the workers *have not disdained a single case* of bourgeois "struggle" against the feudal landowners.

But do you not recall, you who quote Marx, those historical examples that have been increasingly frequent since 1848, of the bourgeoisie *betraying* the struggle against the feudal landowners and going over *to their side?*

Russian history, too, teems with such examples, especially in 1904 and still more so in the autumn of 1905, still more so in the winter of that year and then in the spring of 1906, and so on and so forth.

Can you not understand, Mr. Property-Owner who quotes Marx, that the interests of *the struggle* against the feudal landowners demand that *those* bourgeois who talk about struggle and, by their actions, betray it should be exposed, attacked and discredited?

Za Pravdu No. 23,
October 30, 1913
Signed: *V. Ilyin*

Published according to
the *Za Pravdu* text

THE WORKING-CLASS MASSES
AND THE WORKING-CLASS INTELLIGENTSIA

The liquidators' journal *Nasha Zarya* No. 9 carried an article under this heading by G. Rakitin in which the author is forced to admit that which the liquidators' newspaper brushes aside in impotent wrath. Rakitin is superior to the various F. D.'s because he at least tries *to think some things over and get an understanding of the issue* instead of treating the reader to boring invective.

"The victory"—that is how Rakitin begins his article—"the victory won by the supporters of *Pravda* at the general meeting of the St. Petersburg Metalworkers' Union, and several other facts that bear witness to the growing influence of Bolshevism in the working-class milieu (especially in St. Petersburg) provide food for thought; how has it come about that strongholds of the Menshevik trend, and specifically of the so-called 'liquidationism', have begun to escape from the influence of the trend that laid the foundation of open working-class organisations in Russia, and that has alone worked actively in them during the past few years?"

Notice has to be taken of this passage to show the reader a rare case of "a bright interval" where the liquidators are compelled to admit the truth. In the articles by F.D.& Co., *Novaya Rabochaya Gazeta* merely frets and fumes when shown the exact figures on the elections to the Second, Third and Fourth Dumas, or on the collections made by workers' groups, etc., figures which *prove* the dominance of the *Pravda* trend among politically conscious (those participating in political life) workers.

G. Rakitin admits the fact. He also admits the victory at the metalworkers' meeting and "*other facts*" (although he modestly refrains from saying what those facts are—a method that is purely literary-intellectual and is calculated *to hide* from the workers *exact* figures that would make *independent* verification possible). Rakitin, in general, admits "the growing influence of Bolshevism in the working-class milieu, especially in St. Petersburg"; he admits that "strongholds" of liquidationism "have begun to escape from the influence" of that "trend".

Rakitin strives *to explain* this fact, a sad one for the liquidators, in a way most *comforting* to them.

What is his explanation?

"The working-class masses" are going through a "Bolshevik stage of the movement" admits G. Rakitin (p. 59). But "the working-class intelligentsia", he declares (p. 57) "are in the majority of cases supporters of the so-called 'liquidator' trend". Hence, of course, the conclusion that "comforts" the liquidators—"the Bolshevik stage of the movement" is a "temporary infatuation of the masses and the rising generation of workers with Bolshevik slogans", an influence "rather of instinct and intuition than consciousness and calculation"; the addiction of the working masses to "the primitive peasant world outlook", the "overestimation of the significance of spontaneous outbursts"; the failure to understand the "flexible class tactics" (of the liquidators) and its replacement by "the simplified tactics of Bolshevism", etc., etc.

In short, the *Nasha Zarya* contributor provides a magnificent explanation—*Pravda*'s majority is immature, undeveloped, spontaneous, feeble and the liquidator minority is intellectualist, flexible, politically conscious, etc. In exactly the same way all reactionary writers always explain that the masses have democratic convictions because they are foolish, undeveloped and so on, while the nobility and the bourgeoisie are developed and intelligent!

But please show us, my dear Rakitin, where your proofs are. You admitted yourself that *facts* bear witness to the victory of the *Pravda* supporters, to the masses "going through a Bolshevik stage of the movement"! Where are the *facts* proving that the overwhelming majority of the working-class intelligentsia support the liquidators? Where are facts such as the elections to the State Duma, or the number of collections by workers' groups, or the victory of some list of candidates in the trade unions?

Rakitin does not adduce *a single* fact, not even a single argument!

We therefore permit ourselves to disagree with Rakitin. It is *gratifying* to him, of course, to regard the Bolshevik *working-class masses* as undeveloped and stupid ("instinct and not consciousness") and the liquidator minority as developed and intelligent. But to write history, to provide *an explanation of the stages of the working-class movement* basing oneself on what is gratifying to the person of the historian and not on facts—that, if Rakitin will excuse me, is simply amusing puerility. I cannot say, of course, whether it is "instinct and intuition" that compel the liquidator Rakitin to consider the liquidator minority particularly intelligent, clever and advanced, but is it proper for *a writer* to be guided by "instinct and intuition" and not by *"consciousness and calculation"*?

Written at the beginning
of November 1913

First published in 1938
in the journal *Proletarskaya
Revolutsia* No. 9

Published according to
the manuscript

THE SPLIT IN THE RUSSIAN SOCIAL-DEMOCRATIC DUMA GROUP[132]

Dear Comrades,

In issue No. 266 of your newspaper, you published an article by your "Russian correspondent" on the split in the Russian Social-Democratic Duma group. Unfortunately, that article is far from objective and in a certain respect may mislead the German reader. We hope, Comrades, that you will respond to our request to publish this brief denial so that German workers and the fraternal German party will be correctly informed on these elementary facts.

1) Your Russian correspondent begins by saying that Social-Democracy in Russia "suffers from fragmentation into *many* organisations, groups and trends". This in itself is absolutely untrue. Every Russian Social-Democrat and, in general, everyone interested in the historical struggle in Russia, knows that at present in the Russian working-class movement there are only *two* trends, *two* leading newspapers in St. Petersburg and two political lines—the Marxists and the liquidators. The former, i.e., the Marxists, publish in St. Petersburg the daily newspaper *Za Pravdu* (very recently the government destroyed their second newspaper in Moscow *Nash Put*). The latter publish *Novaya Rabochaya Gazeta* in St. Petersburg. There are *no other* "trends" of any kind in the Russian working-class movement; even among Russian students abroad and among émigrés all other intermediate, so-called "trends" are disappearing. Every Russian Social-Democrat today has to choose between the Marxists and the liquidators.

2) Your "Russian correspondent" defines the difference between the Russian Marxists and the liquidators as being

the same as that between radicals and revisionists in Germany, as being the same as the difference "between a Bebel or a Ledebour on the one hand and a Frank or a David on the other". But that is not quite true. The Russian liquidator, it goes without saying, supports the revisionist platform. He has adopted the worst features of West-European opportunism. Nevertheless, there is a substantial difference between the liquidators and the revisionists. A Frank or a David would never assert that the existence of the present German Social-Democratic Party and its organisation is "harmful". Our liquidators, however, are struggling against the very existence of the Party, they are actually destroying ("liquidating") its underground organisation, they struggle even against its decisions during (political) strikes, and as a reward for this activity enjoy the applause and whole-hearted support of the entire Russian bourgeoisie.

3) Your correspondent writes that "a political disagreement in the Duma group" between the six Marxists and the seven deputies with liquidator tendencies emerged only on one occasion. But that is not so. Disagreements occurred at every step, as has been incontrovertibly proved by the St. Petersburg working-class press. Things went so far that the seven, by a majority of one, voted to renounce the Programme of our Party. In the very first political declaration proclaimed from the Duma rostrum, the seven deputies renounced before the whole of Russia the Programme adopted at the Second Party Congress in 1903. To the joy of those nationalist elements (the Bund) that adhere to the liquidators, they declared that Russian Social-Democrats defend what is known as "cultural-national autonomy". The Party, however, rejects this demand, which in Russia is supported by almost all bourgeois nationalists. When the Programme of the Party was being elaborated this demand was rejected by *all* Russian Social-Democrats. Quite recently Plekhanov described this demand as the "adaptation of socialism to *nationalism*". The six Marxist deputies made a sharp protest against this betrayal of the Programme. The seven deputies, however, stuck to their decision, which was directed against the Party.

4) Your correspondent says it can only be proved "indirectly" that the six Marxist deputies represent the major-

ity of the working class. This is absolutely untrue. We
shall quote a few exact figures to show how many workers are represented by the six and how many by the seven.

Gubernia	Name of Marxist deputy	Number of workers according to factory inspectorate
St. Petersburg	Badayev	197,000
Moscow	Malinovsky	351,000
Vladimir	Samoilov	205,000
Ekaterinoslav	Petrovsky	118,000
Kostroma	Shagov	91,000
Kharkov	Muranov	46,000
	Total	1,008,000

Gubernia	Other deputies	Number of workers according to factory inspectorate
Warsaw	Jagiello	78,000
Don Region	Tulyakov	59,000
Ufa	Khaustov	37,000
Taurida	Buryanov	20,000
Irkutsk	Mankov	13,000
Tiflis	Chkheidze	5,000
Kars Region	Chkhenkeli	2,000
	Total	214,000

The entire worker curia is represented by Marxist deputies.
The six Marxist deputies represent a number of workers
that is *five times* greater, by a conservative estimate, than
that represented by the seven who favour liquidationism.

Is this an "indirect" proof?

Here are some more figures on the number of *workers'
groups* supporting the legal press of the Marxists and of the
liquidators by the collection of funds.

	Pravda	Moscow newspaper	Total for Marxist press	Liquidators' newspaper
1912	620	5	625	89
1913 to April 1	309	129	438	139
1913, from April to October	1,252	261	1,513	328
Totals for the two years	2,181	395	2,576	556

These figures were published in the St. Petersburg newspaper *Za Pravdu* No. 22,* and no one has *disputed them.* Your correspondent should have known them. Contributions from groups are always acknowledged in both newspapers, and the figures are regarded by our enemies in the bourgeois camp as evidence of the alignment of forces of the two trends.

Here, too, the figures show that the Marxists are supported by five times as many workers' groups as the liquidators.

Can this be called "indirect" proof?

Unlike the legal Social-Democratic parties in Western Europe, we cannot at the present time publish the exact strength of our membership. Nevertheless, we also have direct proof of whom the workers support.

In the Second Duma, among the twenty-three deputies from the worker curia (all Social-Democrats) eleven (i.e., 47 per cent) were Bolsheviks. In the Third Duma, four out of eight, i.e., 50 per cent were Bolsheviks. In the Fourth Duma, six out of nine, i.e., 67 per cent. Perhaps these data on the elections to *three Dumas* in *five* years (1907-12) are also "indirect proofs"?

Now that a statement of the six against the seven has been published in the press, all trade unions that have expressed an opinion are on the side of the six deputies against the seven. Every day the Marxist newspaper in St. Petersburg publishes numerous resolutions of many workers, elected representatives, trade unions, and workers' cultural and educational organisations that support the six deputies.

---

* See pp. 461 and 465 of this volume.—*Ed.*

The six workers' deputies, who represent the whole working class of Russia, have formed their own Social-Democratic workers' group in the Duma, which in all respects submits to the will of worker Social-Democrats. The seven deputies act as an "independent" group. The six workers' deputies have proposed to the seven an agreement for work in the Duma. Up to now the seven have bluntly rejected the proposal. An agreement, however, is inevitable.

Such is the true state of affairs.

Editorial Board of the Central Organ of the Russian Social-Democratic Labour Party —"Sotsial-Demokrat"

Written at the beginning
of November 1913

Published on December 24, 1913
in the newspaper *Leipziger
Volkszeitung* No. 298

First published in Russian
on January 21, 1934
in the newspaper *Pravda* No. 21

Published according to
the *Pravda* text.
collated with the
Leipziger Volkszeitung
Translated from the German

THE LEFT NARODNIKS ON THE CONTROVERSIES AMONG THE MARXISTS

Issue No. 3 of *Volnaya Mysl*[133] contains an article bearing the pretentious title: "Unity, Duality or Trinity."

"We openly declare," says this article, "that the claim of the Bolshevik faction that it alone embraces the entire working-class movement is as unreasonable and absurd as the efforts of the two Social-Democratic factions to embody the entire socialist movement in Russia. The future belongs only to the unification of all the socialist trends in a single party.

"And we, who issued this slogan in the beginning of 1900, shall remain true to it to the end."

This is a perfect example of the amusingly irate statements that are made about "unity"! *Not a word* about the principles which underlie the historical struggle that has raged between Marxists and Narodniks for several decades. Nor do we hear a word about the history of the movement of 1905-07, when the open activities of the *masses* of the population of all classes revealed in practice the *fundamental* difference between the Social-Democratic proletariat and the *"working"* (i.e., petty-bourgeois) peasantry.

The existence in Russia of a radical and serious newspaper that formulates the question in *this* way, shows vividly how necessary it still is to wage a long and persistent struggle for the *most elementary* definition of principles.

That the Bolsheviks enjoy the backing of the majority of the class-conscious workers is a fact which their enemies, the liquidators, are compelled to admit, albeit angrily and through their clenched teeth.

This cannot be refuted by sentiment. The workers will not be intimidated if the words: "unreasonable and absurd" are bawled at them—they will only smile.

From the standpoint of ideas, the entire history of Marxism in Russia is the history of the struggle against petty-bourgeois theories, beginning with "legal Marxism" and Economism. This was no chance struggle, nor is its direct continuation at the present time accidental. It is in the struggle against petty-bourgeois liquidationism and Left Narodism that the workers' party in Russia is taking shape and maturing as a genuine proletarian class party in this difficult period of the June Third regime.

"We Left Narodniks have never tried to profit by other people's misfortunes," writes *Volnaya Mysl*, but in the same breath asserts that the split is the cause of "the complete inner weakness of our Social-Democratic movement"!

To write a thing like that, gentlemen, means nothing if not "profiting"—not, however, say we, by other people's "misfortunes", but by "other people's *ideological struggle*"; for it is the ideological conflict between liberal and proletarian policy that lies at the root of the controversies among the Marxists. The workers, unperturbed by angry words or by sentiment, have already learned to detect the basic principles of the struggle.

"There is *less* disagreement in the united parties in the European working-class movement than among us," writes *Volnaya Mysl*. This is a very common, but very fallacious argument. Nowhere in Europe is there any sign of an attempt to replace the proletarian, Marxist organisation by ... talk about a "broad" party formed with Purishkevich's blessing ... etc.

From controversies of *this sort* the workers will learn to *build* a workers' party *in deeds* and not merely in words.

Za Pravdu No. 34,   Published according to
November 13, 1913   the *Za Pravdu* text

THE AGRARIAN QUESTION
AND THE PRESENT SITUATION IN RUSSIA
(NOTES OF A PUBLICIST)

Two interesting articles on this subject appeared in recent magazines. One was in the liquidators' *Nasha Zarya* (No. 6, 1913, N. Rozhkov) and the other in *Russkaya Mysl*, the organ of the Right Cadets (No. 8, 1913, Y. Y. Polferov). There can be no doubt that the two authors wrote their articles knowing nothing about each other, and that they proceeded from entirely different premises.

Nevertheless, the resemblance between the two articles is astonishing. They both clearly demonstrate—and this gives them a special value—the kinship of the principles underlying the ideas of the liberal-labour politicians and those of the counter-revolutionary liberal bourgeoisie.

N. Rozhkov uses exactly the same material as Mr. Polferov, except that the latter's is more copious. Capitalism has been developing in Russian agriculture since the 1905 Revolution. The prices of grain and land are rising; imports of agricultural machinery and of fertilisers, as well as the home manufacture of both, are increasing. Small credit institutions are growing, and so is the number of peasants who are setting up their independent farmsteads. Wages are rising (44.2 per cent from 1890 to 1910, says N. Rozhkov who forgets the rise in the cost of living in the same period!). Commercial stock-breeding, vegetable oil production and grass cultivation are on the increase, and progress is being made in agricultural education.

Needless to say, all this is very interesting. From the point of view of Marxism there has never been the slightest doubt that the development of capitalism cannot be halted.

Had the authors merely adduced new data to explain this they would certainly have deserved our thanks.

But how should these data be appraised; and what conclusions should be drawn from them?—that is the crux of the matter. Here, N. Rozhkov jumps to conclusions with an eagerness that is positively touching. "Feudal serf economy has been transformed into bourgeois capitalist economy ... the transition to bourgeois conditions in agriculture is an accomplished fact, about which there cannot be the slightest doubt.... The agrarian problem in its previous form is now a thing of the past in Russia.... No attempt must be made to galvanise the corpse—the agrarian problem in its old form."

As the reader sees, the conclusions are perfectly clear and just as perfectly—liquidationist. The editors of the liquidator magazine (as has long been the custom in commercialised journals with no principles) appended a small *reservation* to the article, stating: "There is much in this that we do not agree with ... we do not think it is possible to assert *so emphatically*, as N. Rozhkov does, that Russia will proceed precisely along the path mapped out by the law of November 9-June 14...."

The liquidators are "not so emphatic" as N. Rozhkov! What a profound, principled attitude to the question!

In this article N. Rozhkov has proved once again that he *has learned by heart* a number of Marxist propositions, but *has not understood* them. That is why they "popped out" so easily.

The development of capitalism in Russian agriculture was also under way in 1861-1904. All the symptoms of this development that Rozhkov and Polferov now point out were in existence at that time. The development of capitalism did not avert the *bourgeois-democratic* crisis in 1905, but paved the way for it and intensified it. Why? Because the old, semi-feudal, natural, economy had been eroded, while the *conditions for the new*, bourgeois economy had not yet been created. Hence, the unusual intensity of the 1905 crisis.

The ground for *such* crises has disappeared, says Rozhkov. This, of course, could possibly be true if we were to speak abstractly, of capitalism in general, and *not* of Russia, *not* of 1913. Marxists, it goes without saying, recognise the existence of a bourgeois-democratic agrarian problem only under special conditions (*not* always, and *not* everywhere).

But Rozhkov has not the slightest inkling of what propositions he has to prove in order to confirm the *concrete* conclusion he draws.

The peasants are discontented with their conditions? "But the peasants are discontented everywhere," writes Rozhkov.

To compare and identify the discontent of the West-European peasants whose village life and legal status are based on a fully developed bourgeois system, and who have their "parties of law and order", with the *famines* in Russia, with the *complete* degradation of village life caused by the social-estate system with the *complete* domination of feudalism in the sphere of the law, etc., is puerile and absurd. Rozhkov cannot see the wood for the trees.

Capitalism is growing, *corvée* (labour service) is declining, he writes. "The vast majority of landowners," writes the liberal Polferov "... are developing more and more the contract and métayage system, which has arisen exclusively out of the peasants' need of money and land.."

The liberal writing in *Russkaya Mysl* is less of a naïve optimist than the ex-Marxist writing in the liquidator *Nasha Zarya*!

N. Rozhkov did not even attempt to deal with the data showing the *degree* to which métayage, labour service, *corvée*, bondage are prevalent in the rural districts *today*. With amazing unconcern, he ignored the fact that these forms are *still* widespread. But this fact leads to the conclusion that the *bourgeois-democratic* crisis has become still more acute.

Don't galvanise the corpse, writes the liquidator, echoing the liberal, who uses *other* words to indicate that the demands of 1905 are a "corpse".

To this we have replied: Markov and Purishkevich are not corpses. The economic system which engendered them, and is engendering their class to this day, is not a corpse. To fight that class is the living task of living workers who have a live understanding of their class aims.

The renunciation of this task proves that the liquidators are a decomposing *corpse*, for although they do not all speak "so emphatically" as Rozhkov, they *all* forget, or obscure, the struggle against agrarian (and particularly landowner) Purishkevichism and against political Purishkevichism.

The domination of the Purichkeviches in our life is the reverse side of the same medal that in our rural districts is called labour service, bondage, *corvée*, serfdom, the absence of the most elementary general conditions for the bourgeois system of economy. If the millionaire-proprietors at the top (Guchkov and Co.) are grumbling, then the conditions of the millions of small proprietors (the peasants) at the bottom must be absolutely intolerable.

When they set out to deal with the roots of Purishkevichism the workers are by no means neglecting their "own" tasks in order to "galvanise" something that is alien to them. No. In *this way* the democratic aims of *their* struggle, of their class, become clearer to *them* and they teach democracy and the elements of socialism to the broad masses. For only "royal-Prussian socialism" (as Marx called it in his statement against Schweitzer)[134] can leave in the shade the feudal domination of Purishkevichism in general, and of landowner Purishkevichism in particular.

Without noticing it, Rozhkov has descended to the position of Polferov, who says: "The simple allotment of additional land" would not "save" the situation without intensification! As if intensification would not proceed a hundred times faster if Purishkevichism *were abolished!* As if the question were merely one of the peasants, whether they should or should not be "allotted additional land", and not a question of the *entire* nation, of the *entire* development of capitalism, a development which is being distorted and retarded by Purishkevichism!

Rozhkov has blurted out the *real nature* of liquidationism, and revealed the *connection* that exists between the all-embracing slogan "freedom of association" (see how this slogan is dealt with in the *liberal* speech delivered by Tulyakov and in the *Marxist* speech delivered by Badayev in the State Duma on October 23, 1913)—revealed the connection between this slogan and *satisfaction* with the present state of the agrarian problem.

This connection is an objective fact and *Nasha Zarya*'s "small reservations" will not obliterate it.

Stop thinking about the entire nation, about Purishkevichism in every sphere of life, about the famines that afflict the peasantry, about *corvée*, labour service and serfdom; fight "for legality", for "freedom of association" as one of a series of reforms—such are the *ideas* that the *bourgeoisie* fosters in the minds of the workers. Rozhkov and the liquidators are merely trailing unwittingly in the wake of the bourgeoisie.

We, however, think that the proletarians, the foremost representatives of the entire mass of the working people, cannot achieve even their own emancipation except by waging an all-round struggle against Purishkevichism for the sake and in the interests of the struggle against the bourgeoisie; and these are the ideas that distinguish the Marxist from the liberal-labour politician.

Za Pravdu No. 36,
November 15, 1913
Signed: V. *Ilyin*

Published according to
the *Za Pravdu* text

TWO METHODS OF CONTROVERSY AND STRUGGLE

Some controversies and conflicts of opinion in the press help the reader to obtain a better understanding of political problems, to appreciate their importance more profoundly, and to solve them more confidently.

Other controversies, however, degenerate into recrimination, intrigues and squabbling.

The advanced workers, who are aware of the responsibility *they* bear for the progress of the work of educating and organising the proletariat, must keep careful watch to prevent the *inevitable* controversies, the *inevitable* conflict of opinions, from *degenerating* into recrimination, intrigues, squabbling and slander.

This is a question of the workers' cause, the workers' organisation, it is the most serious and important question of combating the slightest attempts at disruption. It cannot be treated lightly. Those who have not learned to cut at the very roots of disruption are useless as organisers; and without an organisation the working class is *nothing*. No movement, including the working-class movement, is possible without debates, controversy and conflict of opinions; and *no* organisation *is possible* if resolute measures are not taken to prevent controversies from degenerating into recrimination and squabbling.

We invite class-conscious workers to examine from this angle the conflict between the six and the seven Social-Democrat Duma deputies.

The six considered it their duty to respect the will and decisions of the Marxist conference. The Duma representatives of the proletariat are duty bound to obey the will of the majority of the class-conscious, organised, Marxist workers outside the Duma.

This is a general principle, the general basis of all our views on the tasks of the working-class movement.

If this view is wrong it must be refuted and rejected. If it is correct, if it is the ABC without which no policy can be pursued, without which *no* organisation is possible, then this view must be accepted and firmly adhered to in spite of all the howling, outcries, attacks and slander.

Worker comrades! Debate this question. Arrange debates, talks and discussions to. obtain absolute clarity on this question, but have no dealings with those who resort to recrimination instead of argument.

What did the liquidators say in reply to the first and fundamental argument of the six deputies?

Their only reply was abuse! They abused the conference; they abused the "underground" a hundred times over, and that is all.

Is that a reply? Is it not simply an attempt to disrupt, to wreck the organisation?

Things have gone so far that F. D. in No. 70, writes literally the following: "Where are the responsible bodies that promoted their candidatures and gave them their instructions?"

Worker comrades, think over what this question means! You will find that it is one worthy of ... those who carry out interrogations!... Will you not realise, F. D. and other liquidators, that we *cannot* argue with you when you put questions of *that sort*.

Examine the substance of the matter. Is the decision of the conference correct; does it correctly express the interests and views of the majority of the workers? *Pravda* answers this question by quoting a series of exact figures (see *Za Pravdu*, Tuesday, October 29, 1913).* These figures show that the *Pravda* trend enjoys the support of the absolute and indisputable *majority* of class-conscious workers, i.e., of those who take an active part in politics.

These figures compared the elections to the Second, Third and Fourth Dumas in the worker curia—and they

---

* See pp. 458 74 of this volume.—*Ed.*

referred to the number of workers represented by the six and the seven, and to the number of workers' groups which openly assisted in collecting funds for the respective newspapers, etc.

What did the liquidators say in reply to this argument on the substance of the question of the majority?

Abuse was their only reply. The liquidators do not refute a single figure, not a single one. They do not even make an attempt to correct them, or quote others in place of them!

The thing is as clear as daylight. Those who evade precise data on the question of the majority *run counter* to the will of the majority; they are disruptors.

The seven Duma deputies are inclining towards liquidationism, for they sanction abuse of the "underground" and take a hand in flouting the will of the majority. This shows that the seven are *non-Party*. And no man in his senses will allow seven non-Party men to suppress Party decisions and the supporters of Party decisions by one vote.

No amount of liquidator abuse will refute this plain and simple fact.

The six deputies performed their duty, and the more the liquidators shout and rave the sooner will all workers and Marxists understand that the six are right, and that the establishment of equality and concord with the non-Party Social-Democratic deputies in the State Duma is inevitable.

Za Pravdu No. 36,
November 15, 1913

Published according to
the *Za Pravdu* text

WOULD-BE "UNITERS"

The Berlin group of Polish Social-Democrats (Rosa Luxemburg, Tyszka and Co.), which the Polish worker Social-Democrats emphatically repudiate, is irrepressible. It persists in calling itself the "Executive Committee" of the Polish Social-Democratic Party, although there is not a person in the world who can say what this miserable Executive *without* a party "administers".[135]

The worker Social-Democrats of Warsaw and Lodz declared long ago that they had dissociated themselves from the aforesaid Berlin group. The State Duma elections in Warsaw and the insurance campaign in that city revealed to all that there is only one Social-Democratic organisation in Poland, namely, the one that has categorically declared it does not recognise the disruptors and slanderers on the Executive Committee. Of the feats performed by this Executive it is sufficient to mention one: these people came out with the *unsupported* statement that the main bulwark of the Polish worker Social-Democrats, the Warsaw organisation, was "in the clutches of the secret police." A year elapsed, but this Executive produced no evidence whatever in support of their atrocious charge. This, of course, was enough in itself to discourage any honest person, active in the working-class movement, from having any dealings whatever with the people in the Tyszka group. As the reader sees, the fighting methods of these people differ very little from those employed by our Martov, Dan and Co....

And it is this group of persons, condemned by *all* the parties working in Poland, that has now decided to act as the saviour of the Russian working-class movement.

Rosa Luxemburg has sent to the International Socialist Bureau[136] a proposal that it should discuss the question of restoring unity in Russia. One of the motives that she advances for this is that the "Lenin group", if you please, is causing disruption in the *Polish* Social-Democratic Party.

This statement gives the Berlin group away at once. It is common knowledge that the Bolsheviks are shoulder to shoulder with the Polish worker Social-Democrats who have repudiated this group of intriguers. That fact keeps our notorious Executive awake at nights, and explains its "unity" campaign, which was opened with attacks on the Russian Marxists and has the object of supporting the Russian liquidators.

Rosa Luxemburg would never have done this if things were "going well". Even her group refused to meet the liquidators at the "August" reconciliation.

But having lost all significance in the Polish and in the Russian working-class movement owing to its lack of principles and to its intrigues, this tiny group of political bankrupts is now clutching at the liquidators' coat-tails. It turns out, of course, that the "Lenin group" is guilty of all mortal sins, and therefore—therefore it is necessary, at all costs, to amalgamate with it. The old, old story!...

What is essentially the Russian Marxists' attitude towards the proposal that the International Socialist Bureau should investigate the disagreements among the Russians?

As far as we know, they will be very pleased if the West-European comrades can be persuaded to investigate the substance of our controversies. We have heard that the Russian Marxists have, for their part, sent to the International Socialist Bureau a proposal that it should also investigate the split in the Polish Social-Democratic Party and the disgraceful conduct of the Tyszka group towards the genuine workers' organisations in Poland. The Marxists will be very pleased if the International Bureau also examines the disagreements between the six and the seven Duma deputies. This will bring before our foreign comrades the question of whether the parliamentary group should be subordinate to the workers' party, or, on the contrary, whether the workers' party should be subordinate to the parliamentary group.

The Marxists will be still more pleased if Rosa Luxemburg's proposal that the question of Russian unity be placed on the agenda of the International Congress to be held in Vienna in 1914 is accepted.

The new International has twice discussed such questions at its congresses. The first occasion was in Amsterdam, in 1904, when the question of unity in France was discussed. The Congress examined the *substance* of the controversy between the Guesdists (Marxists) and Jaurèsists (revisionists) and *condemned* the line of the Jaurèsists, condemned their tactics of joining bourgeois Cabinets, of compromising with the bourgeoisie, etc. And on the basis of this decision on the *substance* of the issue it proposed that the conflicting groups should unite.

The other occasion was in Copenhagen in 1910, when the Czech-Austrian split was discussed. The Congress again discussed the *substance* of the controversy, expressed its opposition to the "Bundist-nationalist" principles of the Czech separatists, and declared that the trade unions in a given country should *not* be organised on a national basis; and it was on the basis of this settlement of the *substance* of the controversy that the Congress recommended the two sides to unite. (Incidentally, the Czech Bundists refused to obey the decision of the International.)

If the Russian question is brought up at the Vienna Congress there can be no doubt that the Congress will express an opinion on the importance of the "underground" in a country like present-day Russia, on the question as to whether, under present conditions, Marxists should be guided by the prospects of "evolution" *or* by the prospects of "uncurtailed" slogans, etc. At all events, it will not be without interest to hear the opinion of the International on all these questions....

Unfortunately, however, this is still a long way off. Meanwhile, we merely have the irate but impotent pronouncement of the Rosa Luxemburg and Tyszka group in Berlin. We advise Mr. F. D. to make good use of this pronouncement against the Marxists and in defence of the liquidators. Although the liquidators' newspapers reported the disgraceful exploits of this Berlin group in its struggle against the Polish workers, Mr. F. D. will not, of course, be able to resist the temptation to drink also from this ... fresh spring.

But the Russian workers will say: *We* ourselves will establish unity in our Russian workers' organisations. As for feeble intrigues, we shall simply laugh at them.

Za Pravdu No. 36,   Published according to
November 15, 1913   the *Za Pravdu* text

A LETTER TO S. G. SHAHUMYAN

December 6, 1913

Dear Friend,

Your letter of November 15 gave me great pleasure. You must realise how highly one in my position appreciates the opinions of comrades in Russia, especially thoughtful people, who are thinking hard studying the subject. I was therefore particularly pleased to get your early reply. One feels less isolated when one receives letters like this. But poetry enough—let's get down to business.

1. You are *in favour* of an official language in Russia. It is "necessary; it has been and will be of great progressive importance". I disagree emphatically. I wrote about this long ago in *Pravda*,* and so far have not been refuted. Your argument does not convince me in the least. Quite the reverse. The *Russian* language has undoubtedly been of progressive importance for the numerous small and backward nations. But surely you must realise that it *would have been* of much greater progressive importance had there been no compulsion. Is not an "official language" a stick that *drives people away* from the Russian language? Why will you not understand the *psychology* that is so important in the national question and which, if the slightest coercion is applied, besmirches, soils, nullifies the undoubtedly progressive importance of centralisation, large states and a uniform language? But the economy is still more important *than* psychology: in Russia we *already* have a *capitalist* economy, which makes the *Russian* language essential. But you have no faith in the power of the economy and want to prop it up with the crutches of the rotten police regime.

---

* See pp. 354-57 of this volume.—*Ed.*

Don't you see that in this way you are *crippling* the economy and hindering its development? Will not the collapse of the wretched police regime multiply tenfold (even a thousand-fold) the number of voluntary associations for protecting and spreading the Russian language? No, I absolutely disagree with you, and accuse you of *königlich-preussischer Sozialismus*!*

2. You are *opposed* to autonomy. You are in favour *only* of regional self-government. I disagree entirely. Recall Engels's explanation that centralisation does not in the least preclude local "liberties".[137] Why should Poland have autonomy and not the Caucasus, the South, or the Urals? Does not the central parliament determine the *limits* of autonomy? We are certainly in favour of democratic centralism. We are opposed to *federation*. We support the Jacobins as against the Girondists. But to be afraid of autonomy in Russia of all places—that is simply ridiculous! It is reactionary. Give me an example, imagine a case in which autonomy *can* be harmful. You cannot. But in Russia (and in Prussia), this narrow interpretation—only local self-government—plays into the hands of the rotten police regime.

3. "The right to self-determination does not imply only the right to secede. It also implies the right to federal association, the right to autonomy," you write. I disagree entirely. It does *not* imply the right to *federation*. Federation means the association of equals, an association that demands *common* agreement. How can *one* side have a *right* to demand that the other side should *agree* with it? That is absurd. We are opposed to federation in principle, it loosens economic ties, and is unsuitable for a single state. You want to secede? All right, go to the devil, if you can break economic bonds, or rather, if the oppression and friction of "coexistence" *disrupt* and ruin economic bonds. You don't want to secede? In that case, excuse me, but don't decide *for* me; don't think that you have a "*right*" to federation.

"Right to autonomy?" Wrong again. We are *in favour of autonomy for all* parts; we are in favour of the *right* to

---

* Royal Prussian socialism.—*Ed.*

secession (and not *in favour* of everyone's *seceding!*). Autonomy is *our* plan for organising a democratic state. Secession is not what we plan at all. We do not advocate secession. In general, we are opposed to secession. But we stand for the *right* to secede owing to reactionary, Great-Russian nationalism, which has so besmirched the idea of national coexistence that sometimes *closer* ties will be established *after* free secession!

The right to self-determination is an *exception* to our general premise of centralisation. This exception is absolutely essential in view of reactionary Great-Russian nationalism; and any rejection of this exception is opportunism (as in the case of Rosa Luxemburg); it means foolishly playing into the hands of reactionary Great-Russian nationalism. But exceptions *must not be* too broadly interpreted. In this case there is *not*, and *must not* be anything more than the *right to secede*.

I am writing about this in *Prosveshcheniye*.* Please do not fail to write to me in greater detail when I have finished these articles (they will appear in three issues). I will send something more. I was mainly responsible for getting the resolution passed. I delivered a series of lectures on the national question in the summer,[138] and have made some little study of it. That is why I intend to "stick tight", although, of course, *ich lasse mich belehren*** from comrades who have studied the question more deeply and for a longer period.

4. So you are opposed to "altering" the Programme; opposed to a "national programme", are you? Here, too, I disagree. You are afraid of *words*. You must not let words frighten you. *Everybody* changes it (the Programme) any way, *surreptitiously*, in an underhand manner, and for the worse. We, however, define, make more precise, develop and consolidate our position in keeping with the spirit of the Programme, with the *consistently* democratic spirit, with the Marxist (anti-Austrian) spirit. This *had to be done*. Let the opportunist (Bundist, liquidator, Narodnik) scum

---

* See present edition, Vol. 20, "Critical Remarks on the National Question".—*Ed.*

** I am willing to take advice.—*Ed.*

have their say, let them give *their* equally *precise* and *complete* answers to *all* the problems raised, and solved, in our resolution. Let them try. No, we have not "given way" to the opportunists, we have *beaten* them on *all* points.

A popular pamphlet on the national question is very much needed. Write. Looking forward to reply, I send you my very heartiest greetings. Regards to all friends.

Yours, *V. I.*

Written November 23
(December 6), 1913

First published March 2 (15),
1918, in the newspaper
Bakinsky Rabochy (*Bahu Worker*) No. 48

Published according to
the manuscript

"CULTURAL-NATIONAL" AUTONOMY

The essence of the plan, or programme, of what is called "cultural-national" autonomy (or: "the establishment of institutions that will guarantee freedom of national development") is *separate schools for each nationality.*

The more often all avowed and tacit nationalists (including the Bundists) attempt to obscure this fact the more we must insist on it.

Every nation, irrespective of place of domicile of its individual members (irrespective of territory, hence the term "extra-territorial" autonomy) is a united officially recognised association conducting national-cultural affairs. The most important of these affairs is education. The determination of the composition of the nations by allowing every citizen to register freely, irrespective of place of domicile, as belonging to any national association, ensures absolute precision and absolute consistency in segregating the schools according to nationality.

Is such a division, be it asked, permissible from the point of view of democracy in general, and from the point of view of the interests of the proletarian class struggle in particular?

A clear grasp of the essence of the "cultural-national autonomy" programme is sufficient to enable one to reply without hesitation—it is absolutely impermissible.

As long as different nations live in a single state they are bound to one another by millions and thousands of millions of economic, legal and social bonds. How can education be extricated from these bonds? Can it be "taken out of the jurisdiction" of the state, to quote the Bund formula, classical in its striking absurdity? If the various nations living in a single state are bound by economic ties, then any attempt to divide them permanently in "cultural" and particularly educational matters would be absurd and reactionary. On the contrary, efforts should be made to *unite* the nations in educational matters, so that the schools should be a preparation for what is actually done in real life. At the present time we see that the different nations are unequal in the rights they possess and in their level of development. Under these circumstances, segregating the schools according to nationality would *actually* and inevitably *worsen* the conditions of the more backward nations. In the Southern, former slave States of America, Negro children are still segregated in separate schools, whereas in the North, white and Negro children attend the same schools. In Russia a plan was recently proposed for the "nationalisation of Jewish schools", i.e., the segregation of Jewish children from the children of other nationalities in separate schools. It is needless to add that this plan originated in the most reactionary, Purishkevich circles.

One cannot be a democrat and at the same time advocate the principle of segregating the schools according to nationality. Note: we are arguing at present from the general democratic (i.e., bourgeois-democratic) point of view.

From the point of view of the proletarian class struggle we must oppose segregating the schools according to nationality far more emphatically. Who does not know that the capitalists of all the nations in a given state are most closely and intimately united in joint-stock companies, cartels and trusts, in manufacturers' associations, etc., which are directed *against* the workers irrespective of their nationality? Who does not know that in *any* capitalist undertaking—from huge works, mines and factories and commercial enterprises down to capitalist farms—we *always*, without exception, see a larger variety of nationalities among the workers than in remote, peaceful and sleepy villages?

The urban workers, who are best acquainted with developed capitalism and perceive more profoundly the psychology of the class struggle—their whole life teaches them or they perhaps imbibe it with their mothers' milk—such workers instinctively and inevitably realise that segregating the schools according to nationality is not only a *harm-ful* scheme, but a downright fraudulent swindle on the part *of the capitalists.* The workers *can* be split up, divided and weakened by the advocacy of such an idea, and still more by the segregation, of the ordinary peoples' schools according to nationality; while the capitalists, whose children are well provided with rich private schools and specially engaged tutors, *cannot in any way* be threatened by any division or weakening through "cultural-national autonomy".

As a matter of fact, "cultural-national autonomy", i.e., the absolutely pure and consistent segregating of education according to nationality, was invented not by the capitalists (*for the time being* they resort to cruder methods to divide the workers) but by the opportunist, philistine intelligentsia of Austria. There is *not a trace* of this brilliantly philistine and brilliantly nationalist idea in any of the democratic West-European countries with mixed populations. This idea of the despairing petty bourgeois could arise only in Eastern Europe, in backward, feudal, clerical, bureaucratic Austria, where *all* public and political life is hampered by wretched, petty squabbling (worse still: cursing and brawling) over the question of languages. Since cat and dog can't agree, let us at least segregate all the nations once and for all absolutely clearly and consistently in "national curias" for educational purposes!—such is the psychology that engendered this foolish idea of "cultural-national autonomy". The proletariat, which is conscious of and cherishes its internationalism, will never accept this nonsense of refined nationalism.

It is no accident that in Russia this idea of "cultural-national autonomy" was accepted *only by all* the Jewish bourgeois parties, then (in 1907) by the conference of the *petty-bourgeois* Left-Narodnik parties of different nationalities, and lastly by the petty-bourgeois, opportunist elements of the *near-Marxist* groups, i.e., the Bundists and the liquidators (the latter were even too timid to do so straightforwardly and definitely). It is no accident that in the State Duma *only* the semi-liquidator Chkhenkeli, who is infected with nationalism, and the petty-bourgeois Kerensky, spoke in favour of "cultural-national autonomy".

In general, it is quite funny to read the liquidator and Bundist references to Austria on this question. First of all, why should the most backward of the multinational countries be taken as the *model*? Why not take the most advanced? This is very much in the style of the bad Russian liberals, the Cadets, who for models of a constitution turn mainly to such backward countries as Prussia and Austria, and not to advanced countries like France, Switzerland and America!

Secondly, after taking the Austrian model, the Russian nationalist philistines, i.e., the Bundists, liquidators, Left Narodniks, and so forth, have themselves changed it *for the worse*. In this country it is the Bundists (plus *all* the Jewish bourgeois parties, in whose wake the Bundists follow without always realising it) that mainly and primarily use this plan for "cultural-national autonomy" in their propaganda and agitation; and yet in Austria, the country where this idea of "cultural-national autonomy" originated, Otto Bauer, the father of the idea, devoted a special chapter of his book top roving that "cultural-national autonomy" *cannot* be applied to the Jews!

This proves more conclusively than lengthy speeches how inconsistent Otto Bauer is and how little he believes in his own idea, for he excludes the *only* extra-territorial (not having its own territory) nation from his plan for extra-territorial national autonomy.

This shows how Bundists borrow *old-fashioned* plans from Europe, multiply the mistakes of Europe tenfold and "develop" them to the point of absurdity.

The fact is—and this is the third point—that at their congress in Brünn (in 1899) the Austrian Social-Democrats *rejected* the programme of "cultural-national autonomy" that was proposed to them. They merely adopted a compromise in the form of a proposal for a union of the nationally delimited *regions* of the country. This compromise did *not* provide either for extra-territoriality or for segregating education according to nationality. In accordance with this compromise, in the most advanced (capitalistically) populated centres, towns, factory and mining districts, large country estates, etc., there are *no* separate schools for each nationality!

The Russian working class has been combating this reactionary, pernicious, petty-bourgeois nationalist idea of "cultural-national autonomy", and will continue to do so.

Za Pravdu No. 46,
November 28, 1913

Published according to
the *Za Pravdu* text

COTERIES ABROAD AND RUSSIAN LIQUIDATORS

Issue No. 86 of *Novaya Rabochaya Gazeta* contains a scurrilous article against Social-Democrats that deserves attention *in spite of* its abusive character and *in spite of* the insinuations of which everybody is sick and tired.

This article is entitled "The German Social-Democratic Press on the Split". It deserves attention because it very clearly explains to Russian workers something they have not known up to now, and which they *ought to know*.

They *ought to know* what intrigues the coteries of Russian Social-Democrats abroad are hatching *against* the Social-Democratic organisation in Russia, for ignorance of these intrigues constantly and inevitably condemns many Russian Social-Democrats to making comic and tragi-comic mistakes.

The liquidators' article commences with italics: "*Not a single* voice has so far been heard in the ranks of the German Social-Democrats" in favour of a split (by "split", the liquidators mean the *building* of a Marxist organisation *in opposition to* the liquidators).

Note the italics in the first sentence of the article: "*Not a single* voice"!

The worn-out trick of the bourgeois hack-writer—not everybody reads a newspaper through to the end, but everybody sees the *first* striking words of an article....

Read the liquidators' article further. It quotes the opinion of a Frankfurt newspaper, which is, of course, *in favour of* the liquidators, but it says nothing about the fact that this newspaper is an opportunist one!

My dear liquidators! Do you think the Russian workers are fools who do not know that there are opportunists among the German Social-Democrats, and that the *Socialist* (*alleged*) *Monthly*, the chief organ of the German opportunists, *constantly* supports *Nasha Zarya*?

We read further. The opinion of a Dresden newspaper. It condemns the split in general. Neither the newspaper's sympathies in Russian affairs, nor its position on German affairs is indicated. The liquidators do not want to enlighten the Russian workers, but to fool them by leaving a number of things unsaid.

We read further. The Leipzig organ of the Social-Democrats

"a fortnight ago published a report from Russia describing the situation in tones rather favourable to the schismatics".

This is literally what is published in the liquidator newspaper; and, of course, not a word in italics.

And, of course, not a word, not a syllable, not a sound on *the substance* of that "unpleasant" report! Oh, we are past masters in the art of petty trickery and miserable intrigue!

On the one hand, we have italics: "*Not a single* voice"; and on the other hand, the *only* report from Russia turns out to be written "in tones rather favourable" to the opponents of the liquidators.

We read further:

"The issue [of the Leipzig Social-Democratic newspaper] of November 15 contains a long *editorial* [liquidators' italics!] article"....

from which *only* the passages that favour the liquidators are quoted.

Russian workers! It is high time you learned to expose the liquidators' lies.

The liquidators print the word "editorial" in italics. This is a *lie*. The article is signed with the initials *J. K.*,[139] i.e., it is *not* an editorial article, but an article by an individual contributor!

The liquidators are deceiving the Russian workers in the most brazen and insolent manner.

This is not all. The liquidators *concealed* the fact that in this very same report the *seven* are called "*shameless splitters*" for admitting Jagiello to the Duma group, in opposition to the will of the Polish Social-Democrats!

And this is still not all. The liquidators *concealed* a fact which is obvious to every politically-informed person. The article signed J. K. was written by one of *Tyszka*'s supporters. All the evidence goes to prove this. Tyszka's supporters are the group of Rosa Luxemburg, Tyszka & Co. in Berlin, those who circulated a most abominable rumour about the presence of provocateurs in the Warsaw Social-Democratic organisation. Even *Luch* (true, this was *after* Jagiello had been smuggled into the Duma group!) admitted that this was abominable. Even *Novaya Rabochaya Gazeta* has admitted more than once that "Tyszka & Co." do not represent the Polish Social-Democratic workers of Warsaw in fighting against the *workers' insurance centre*, to which the Bund, the Lefts and the Polish Social-Democrats (of Warsaw, and not Tyszka & Co., of course) are affiliated.

And now, in order to fool the Russian workers, the liquidators clutch at the coat-tails of the Tyszka crowd. A drowning man clutches at a straw (even at a filthy and rotten one).

The article of the Tyszka supporter, J. K., like all the pronouncements of that group, throbs with but one desire: to hatch an intrigue around the split, to make "a little political capital" out of it. Pretending that coteries "divorced" from the working-class movement in Russia are viable political organisations, hatching intrigues around this, uttering sentimental phrases *instead of* studying events in Russia—such is the nature of "Tyszka-ism", and it is what nine-tenths of the separate and "independent" coteries abroad are engaged in.

They seem now to be reviving in the hope of being able to "play on" the split between the six and the seven....

Vain hope! Russian worker Social-Democrats have matured sufficiently to be able *themselves* to decide the fate of their organisation by a majority vote, and contemptuously to brush aside the intrigues of the coteries abroad. Members of these coteries very often write in the German Social-Democratic press expressing the point of view of these coteries; but it is not at all difficult to recognise this crowd "by their ears".

Za Pravdu No. 46,
November 28, 1913

Published according to
the *Za Pravdu* text

THE CADET MAKLAKOV
AND THE SOCIAL-DEMOCRAT PETROVSKY

It is some considerable time now since the Social-Democrat Petrovsky spoke in the State Duma on the question of the rules and was deprived of the right to speak by the Chairman for "unparliamentary language" addressed to the Minister, and so forth. As a "topic of the day" in the narrow sense of the term this matter is perhaps out of date. But the fact of the matter is that the speeches delivered by Petrovsky and the Cadet Maklakov deserve more attention than ordinary "news of the day".

The Cadet Maklakov spoke in the State Duma on the question of the new rules. This gentleman was the author of the rules and the spokesman for the Rules Committee. On a number of questions the Cadet Maklakov spoke *against* the Cadet group in the Duma, and with the aid of the Octobrists and the Rights secured the adoption of *most reactionary* rules directed *against* the opposition.

This is not new. It has long been common knowledge that V. Maklakov is a favourite of the Octobrists and that he is an Octobrist at heart. But the *extremely important* fact of our public life that is revealed by this long-known circumstance deserves the closest attention.

Here we have one of the most prominent Cadets himself *suppressing the freedom of the Duma* with the aid of the Rights and Octobrists on a question on which the Duma is relatively *less impotent* than on other questions. The Social-Democrat Petrovsky was a thousand times right in speaking sharply against such an old hand at shady politics.

But what is the main point here? Was V. Maklakov's conduct crooked because Mr. V. A. Maklakov is *himself crooked*? Of course, not, and that is not the point, anyway.

Just as the Beilis case[140] was interesting and important because it very vividly revealed what is behind our home politics, its behind-the-scenes "machinery", etc., so this minor (relatively) case of V. Maklakov's speech *against* the Cadets and against the freedom of the Duma reveals for the hundredth and hundred-and-first time what is really behind the policy of the party of our Russian liberal bourgeoisie.

The struggle between the Cadets and the Octobrists is a struggle between *competitors*—that is why it is so sharp and unscrupulous. It was *possible* for V. Maklakov, favourite of the Octobrists and suppressor of the freedom of the Duma, to become a "leading light" among the Cadets *because*, and *only* because, the Cadets have the *same class basis* as the Octobrists. They are two different wings, or representatives of different trends, of the liberal bourgeoisie, who are more afraid of democracy than they are of the Purishkeviches.

This is material. This is important. This is the quintessence of politics. This is the reason our bourgeoisie is astoundingly impotent politically, its economic power notwithstanding.

The Social-Democrat Petrovsky performed his duty as a democrat in opposing V. Maklakov, the suppressor of the freedom of the Duma. There will be no freedom in Russia until the democratic masses learn to despise the Maklakovs as well as the parties that produce gentlemen of this type.

Za Pravdu No. 47,
November 29, 1913
Signed: *M.*

                                        Published according to
                                        the *Za Pravdu* text

ZABERN

Sometimes "incidents" occur in politics when the nature of a certain order of things is revealed, as it were, suddenly, and with extraordinary power and clarity in connection with some relatively minor happening.

Zabern is a small town in Alsace. Over forty years ago Alsace was severed from France by the victorious Prussians (with only one party in Germany, the Social-Democratic Party, emphatically protesting). For over forty years the French population of Alsace has been forcibly "Germanised" and "driven" by every possible form of pressure into the royal Prussian, drill-sergeant, bureaucratic discipline that is called "German culture". But the Alsatians have been retorting to all this with their hymn of protest: "You have taken our Alsace and our Lorraine, you may Germanise our field, but never, never, never will you capture our hearts."

One day a Prussian aristocrat, a young officer named Forstner brought things to a climax. He grossly insulted the Alsatian people (he used the word *Wackes*, a coarse term of abuse). The German Purishkeviches had used this sort of language in barracks a million times without causing any trouble, but the million and first time—the fat was in the fire!

The pent-up anger of decades against tyranny, nagging and insult, against decades of forced Prussianisation, burst out on the surface. It was not a revolt of French culture against German culture. The Dreyfus case[141] showed that there is as much crude militarism capable of every kind of savagery, barbarism, violence and crime in France as in any other country. No, this was not a revolt of French

culture against German culture, but the revolt of the democracy fostered by a number of French revolutions against
absolutism.

The unrest of the population, their resentment against
the Prussian officers, the jeers hurled at these officers by
the proud, freedom-loving French crowd, the rage of the
Prussian militarists, the arbitrary arrests and assaults on
people in the street—all this gave rise in Zabern (and later
throughout Alsace) to "anarchy", as the bourgeois newspapers call it. The landowning, "Octobrist", clerical, German Reichstag, by an overwhelming majority, passed a
resolution *against* the Imperial German Government.

"Anarchy" is a silly catchword. It presupposes that there
has been and still is in Germany an "established" civil,
legal system which, on the instigation of the devil, has been
violated. The catchword "anarchy" is impregnated through
and through with the spirit of official, university German
"scholarship" (with apologies to real scholarship), the
scholarship that cringes before the landowners and the
militarists, and sings the praises of the exceptional *"rule
of law"* in Germany.

The Zabern incident showed that Marx was right when,
nearly forty years ago, he described the German political
system as a "military despotism, embellished with parliamentary forms".[142] Marx's appraisal of the real nature of
the German "constitution" was a hundred thousand times
more profound than those of hundreds of bourgeois professors, priests and publicists who sang the praises of the
"legal state". They all bowed and scraped in face of the successes and triumphs of the German rulers of the day. In
appraising the class nature of politics, Marx was not guided
by the "zigzag" of events, but by the *entire* experience of
international democracy and of the international working-
class movement.

It was not "anarchy" that "burst out" in Zabern; it was
the *true* nature of the German regime, the sabre rule of the
Prussian semi-feudal landowners that was aggravated and
came to the surface. If the German bourgeoisie had possessed
a sense of honour, if it had possessed brains and a conscience,
if it had believed what it said, if its deeds were not in contradiction to its words, in short, if it were *not* a bourgeoisie

confronting millions of socialist proletarians, the Zabern "incident" would have been "incidental" to the bourgeoisie's becoming republican. As it is, the whole affair will be confined to platonic protests by bourgeois politicians—in parliament.

But things will not stop there outside parliament. The mood of the petty-bourgeois masses in Germany has been and is undergoing a change. Conditions have changed, the economic situation has changed, *all the props* of the "peaceful" rule of the aristocratic Prussian sabre have been *undermined*. Whether the bourgeoisie likes it or not, *events* are sweeping it towards a profound political crisis.

The time when the "German Michael" slumbered peacefully under the guardianship of the Prussian Purishkeviches, while the course of Germany's capitalist development was exceptionally favourable, has gone. The general, fundamental collapse is irresistibly maturing and approaching....

Za Pravdu No. 47,
November 29, 1913
Signed: *V. I.*

Published according to
the *Za Pravdu* text

THE QUESTION OF BUREAU DECISIONS[143]

Today, Monday, December 2 (15), yesterday's decision of the Bureau on Russian affairs became known—so far from a brief telegram. Plekhanov has announced his resignation in writing, i.e., resigned *of his own accord.*

The Organising Committee (OC), the liquidators' leading institution, has been affiliated, i.e., has obtained the right to representation in the Bureau.

(Apropos of this it must be mentioned that according to the Rules, not only the most opportunist parties, but even semi-party workers' organisations may affiliate. The most opportunist groups of the British are affiliated; therefore, the affiliation of the OC could not be prevented.)

What is the result? Plekhanov has been squeezed out by the liquidators! If the liquidators try to rejoice over this, they must be answered—*hypocritical supporters of unity.* The liquidators have managed to *replace* Plekhanov. That is the actual result. Let all workers in general, and worker Mensheviks in particular, judge whether the liquidators are sincerely striving for unity, whether sincere supporters of unity would have substituted themselves for Plekhanov. Surely there cannot be anybody so naïve as to believe that the replacement of Plekhanov by a liquidator is a step *towards* unity and not *away* from it.

At all events I can offer the editors an article on the subject if the liquidators have started any foolish jubilation. It can also be added (later) that having become affiliated, the OC members (the liquidators) have committed themselves to becoming an *entity*, i.e., a party. Probably an *open party*, eh gentlemen? Time will show.

At last "unification has been entrusted to the executive"—says the telegram. That means that the Executive Committee of the Bureau (Vandervelde+Bertrand+Anseele+the Secretary Huysmans) has been instructed to take measures or to take steps towards re-establishing unity.

Apparently (or probably) that has been done without any reproach to us. In that case it is quite acceptable to us. It must be said that the Executive Committee of the Bureau *always* and unconditionally must work for unity, and that two years ago, Huysmans, the Secretary of the Bureau, asked Lenin in writing what measures should be adopted as a step towards unity. Entrusting this to the Executive, therefore, is, I repeat, quite acceptable to us, and any possible misinterpretations by the liquidators will be simply untrue.

Nothing is said in the telegram about the seven and the six. It is known from a letter, however, that at the beginning of the Bureau session a liquidator was named during the roll-call. Our representative then said that the six had not elected him, to which Huysmans replied with an explanation of the rules, according to which representation (from socialist parliamentary groups) is granted only to the majority *irrespective* of party membership. It is probable that they left it at that—one liquidator from the seven or the eight. If such are the rules (which we shall verify—*so far* we have had to accept the official explanation of the rules of the Bureau by the Secretary of the Bureau at an official session), then it was a good thing we did not waste our efforts and did not "put in an appearance", did not go there and make demands. It has no practical significance. It is not convenient to speak about it in the press. If the liquidators start rejoicing—we shall again answer them: hypocritical supporters of unity, who contravene the will of the majority of politically conscious workers.

And so the result is as mentioned elsewhere.

We also see from the letter of our representative that the liquidators have been agitating Kautsky (who represented the Germans) to have a *commission* appointed on the question of unity. Kautsky censured Rosa Luxemburg for her attack on Lenin and was of the opinion that nothing could be done from abroad; it was necessary for the Russian workers to demand unity.

We shall await a confirmation of these statements. We are certainly in favour of *unity* in accordance with the will of the *majority* of politically conscious workers in Russia.

Such is the state of affairs according to information at present available.

Written December 2 (15), 1913

First published in the
fourth Russian edition
of the *Collected Works*

Published according to
the manuscript

WORKING-CLASS UNITY

Lately, the polemics that *Novaya Rabochaya Gazeta* has been conducting against the six worker deputies in the Duma have been steadily losing any business-like and ideological character and assuming more and more the character of a "squabble". It is *all the more* necessary, therefore, to *turn* these polemics *back* into the channels of a serious examination of controversial questions. Every class-conscious worker will probably agree with us about this.

We have before us the "big names" that the liquidators always juggle with. Tsereteli and Gegechkori condemn the six; the "leading body" of the August Conference (1912) does the same. For the thousand and first time they call the six splitters, and proclaim "unity".

We, for our part, undeterred by raving and shouting, will, for the thousand and first time, calmly call upon the workers to reflect upon the question and study it.

The working class needs unity. But unity can be effected only by a united organisation whose decisions are conscientiously carried out by all class-conscious workers. Discussing the problem, expressing and hearing different opinions, ascertaining the views of the *majority* of the organised Marxists, expressing these views in the form of decisions adopted by delegates and carrying them out conscientiously—this is what reasonable people all over the world call *unity*. Such a unity is infinitely precious, and infinitely important to the working class. Disunited, the workers are nothing. United, they are everything.

Are there, we ask, data available that will enable every class-conscious worker who desires to study the controversy for himself to judge whether unity *has been maintained*

among worker Social-Democrats during the past few
years?

Efforts must be made to collect such data, to verify them
and to publish them as material for the purpose of enlightening, uniting and organising the workers.

The newspaper *Pravda* has been in existence since April
1912, and its trend has always (and not one of its opponents
has ever denied this) strictly conformed to the decisions
which on *three occasions* in this period (once in 1912 and
twice in 1913) were passed by the leading Marxist body.
How many workers have accepted these decisions (on all
questions of working-class life; altogether there were about
forty decisions) and have carried them out?

The reply to this question—obviously a very important
and interesting one—can be only approximate, but it is
based on absolutely precise and objective and *not* biased data.
In 1912 and 1913 there were basically *two* workers' newspapers, which advocated *different* views to the masses of the
workers. Both of them published reports of the workers'
groups which collected funds for the respective newspapers.
Needless to say, the workers' groups which collected funds
for a *given* newspaper thereby expressed by deeds (and not
merely by words) their sympathies for the policy pursued by
that paper, and their determination to back the decisions
that it supports.

The publication of these data in the two rival newspapers
is the best guarantee against mistakes, which interested
workers can themselves correct. Here are the data, which
have been published *many times* before, have *never* been refuted by anyone, and have never been superseded by other
data. In the course of nearly two years, from January 1912
to October 1913, 556 workers' group collections were made
for *Luch*, 2,181 for *Pravda*, and 395 for the Moscow workers'
newspaper.

One may boldly assert that nobody but a person blinded
by prejudice would hesitate to admit that the majority (and
the overwhelming majority at that) supported *Pravda*.
Slowly but surely the *Pravda* people are building up *real
unity* among the workers, uniting them by uniform decisions, which they conscientiously carry out. *This is the first
time* in Russia that a Marxist daily newspaper, which scru-

pulously defends uniform and precise decisions, has been able for so long to *unite* more and more systematically and closely *workers' groups* scattered all over the country.

This is unity in deeds and not merely in words! Of course, this is not everything but it is actual deeds and not merely words, not a mere advertising.

But Tsereteli, Gegechkori and the "August leading body", like all the other liquidators, *stubbornly* ignore the facts!

They shout about "unity", but say nothing about the fact that it is the liquidators—obviously in the minority among the class-conscious workers—who *are violating unity*, are flouting the will of the majority!

No outcries, no clamour and no abuse can refute this plain and simple fact; and all references made by the "August leading, and so forth", to all sorts of "bodies" and groups, only raise a smile. Just think, gentlemen! What are your "bodies and groups" worth if *no* workers, or only an *obvious* minority, support them? Such "bodies and groups" are *breakaway* bodies if they fail to call upon all the workers to obey the will of the majority.

The experience of the revival of the working-class movement during the past two years increasingly confirms the correctness of the *views* of *Pravda*. The experience of uniting the *workers* of Russia on definite decisions formulated by the Marxists is more and more clearly revealing the successes, growth and strength of our organisation. It goes without saying that we shall proceed along this path more boldly and quickly, undaunted by abuse, by outcries, or by anything else.

Za Pravdu No. 50,
December 3, 1913

Published according to
the *Za Pravdu* text

A STUBBORN DEFENCE OF A BAD CASE

Those gentlemen, the liquidators, are stubbornly defending the Octobrist clause that "slipped" into their Bill on liberties. This is Clause 5, which by a legal twist limits freedom of association by stating that the workers shall not be liable to criminal prosecution for their actions "*if, in general, they are not actions of a nature that renders them criminally-liable*".

The reactionary nature of this clause is obvious. It is obvious that *genuine* Social-Democrats would say the very opposite of this pettifoggery, i.e., they would say that acts committed in the course of a strike, for the purpose of assisting oppressed fellow workers, should not be liable to punishment, or at least, that the penalty should be reduced.

It is obvious that the liquidators will have to delete this reactionary clause from their Bill; the workers will compel them to do so.

But instead of straightforwardly admitting their mistake the liquidators (guided by Burenin-Gamma[144]) twist and turn and resort to petty lying. Mr. Gorsky assures us in *Novaya Likvidatorskaya Gazeta*[145] that the conferences held abroad (three or four years ago)[146] "with the closest cooperation of N. Lenin" adopted similar clauses in a Bill on strikes.

All this is a downright falsehood.

At these conferences abroad the work was divided as follows. Subcommittees drafted the bills, while the general committee discussed certain fundamental questions. Lenin was not even a member of the Strike Subcommittee (he was a member of the Eight-Hour-Day Subcommittee); and on the general committee, Lenin *opposed* every point that conceded or recognised criminal liability!

Mr. Gorsky wants to throw the blame for a Bill drafted by a certain Mr. F. D. (an ex-member of the Strike Subcommittee!) on Lenin. That trick won't work, gentlemen.

In defending this bad case Mr. Burenin-Gamma advanced another bad argument. He wrote:

"They [the Social-Democrats] should keep their class struggle within certain limits, not out of respect for 'bourgeois law', but out of respect for the legal and moral consciousness of the broad masses of the people."

Now this is an argument that is indeed worthy of a philistine!

Out of considerations of *expediency* we wage our class struggle within certain limits, Mr. Liquidator, and avoid everything which may (under certain circumstances) disrupt our ranks or facilitate the enemy's onslaught upon us at a time when this is to his advantage, etc. Failing to understand these real reasons, the liquidator falls into the opportunist morass. What are the broad masses of the people? Those masses are the undeveloped proletarians and petty-bourgeois who are full of prejudices—philistine, nationalist, reactionary, clerical and so on, and so forth.

How can we, for example, *"respect"* the "legal and moral consciousness" of anti-Semitism, which, as everybody knows, has very often proved to be a dominant feature of the consciousness of the "broad masses of the people" even of Vienna (a city that is more cultured than many Russian cities).

The "legal and moral consciousness" of the broad masses of *philistines* will condemn, let us say, a blow struck at a blackleg, when it was struck in the heat of defending a strike called for an increase of a starvation wage. We shall not *advocate* violence in such cases because it is *inexpedient* from the point of view of *our* struggle. But we shall not "respect" this philistine "consciousness"; on the contrary, we shall steadily combat it by all the means of persuasion, propaganda and agitation at our command.

Mr. Burenin-Gamma's appeal for "respect" for the legal and moral consciousness of the broad masses of the people is the appeal of a philistine for respect for philistine prejudices.

It is further proof (in addition to a thousand others) of the philistinism of the liquidators.

Proletarskaya Pravda No. 1,
December 7, 1913

Published according to
the *Proletarskaya Pravda* text

THE CADETS AND "THE RIGHT OF NATIONS TO SELF-DETERMINATION"

Last summer, *Rech*, the chief liberal newspaper in Russia, published an article by Mr. Mikhail Mogilyansky on the All-Ukraine Student Congress in Lvov. *Rabochaya Pravda* at the time pointed out that Mr. Mogilyansky in a manner most reprehensible (for a democrat, or for a man who poses as a democrat) showered *abuse* on the Ukrainian separatism advocated by Mr. Dontsov,* and others. We stated at once that the issue was not whether one agreed or disagreed with Mr. Dontsov, whom many Ukrainian Marxists opposed, we said it was *impermissible* to hurl such epithets at "separatism" as "delirium" and adventurism. We said that this was a chauvinist approach, and that in criticising any particular plan for secession, a Great-Russian democrat must agitate for *freedom* to secede, for the *right* to secede.

As the reader will see, this is a question of principle, of programme, and concerns the duties of democrats in general.

But now, six months later, Mr. Mikhail Mogilyansky again brings this point up in *Rech* (No. 331) but does not reply to us; he replies to Mr. Dontsov, who sharply attacked *Rech* in the Lvov newspaper *Shlyakhi*[147] and incidentally pointed out that "*Rech*'s chauvinistic thrust was properly branded only in the Russian Social-Democratic press".

In replying to Mr. Dontsov, Mr. Mogilyansky states *three times* that "criticism of Mr. Dontsov's recipes *does not imply repudiation of the right of nations to self-determination*".

This statement by a contributor to the liberal *Rech* is extremely important and we invite our readers to pay partic-

---

* See pp. 266-67 of this volume.—*Ed.*

ular attention to it. The more rarely the liberal gentlemen establish and analyse the fundamental and material truths of democracy instead of indulging in common political-oppositional scandal-mongering, the more persistently must we call for a serious appraisal of every case in which they do so.

Does our Constitutional-"Democratic" Party recognise the right of nations to self-determination or not? This is the interesting question that Mr. Mogilyansky inadvertently raises.

He thrice repeats his reservation, but he does not give a straightforward answer to this question! He knows perfectly well that neither the programme of the Constitutional-Democratic Party, nor its daily political sermons (propaganda and agitation) provide a straightforward, precise and clear answer to this question.

"It must be said," writes Mr. Mogilyansky, "that even the 'right of nations to self-determination' is not a fetish that must never be criticised: the unhealthy conditions of life of a nation may engender unhealthy tendencies in national self-determination; and to expose the latter does not mean repudiating the right of nations to self-determination."

This is a beautiful example of a liberal evasion which the Semkovskys repeat in different strains in the columns of the liquidators' newspaper! Oh, no, Mr. Mogilyansky, *no* democratic right is a "fetish", and never must the *class* content, for example, of any of them be forgotten. All general democratic demands are *bourgeois*-democratic demands; but only anarchists and opportunists can deduce from this that it is not the business of the proletariat to back these demands in the most consistent manner possible.

The *right* to self-determination is one thing, of course, and the *expediency* of self-determination, the secession of a given nation under given circumstances, is another. This is elementary. But does Mr. Mogilyansky, do Russian liberals, does the Constitutional-Democratic Party admit that it is the *duty* of a democrat to preach to the masses—particularly the Great-Russian masses—the great significance and urgency of this right?

No, no, and no again. That is what Mr. Mogilyansky evades and conceals. That is one of the roots of the *nationalism and chauvinism* of the Cadets—not only of Struve, Izgoyev and the other outspoken Cadets, but also of the diplomats of the Cadet Party like Milyukov, and the philistines of that party like.... But their names are not important!

The class-conscious workers of Russia will not forget that in addition to national reactionaries we have in this country national liberals, and that the rudiments of national democracy are springing up (recall Mr. Peshekhonov's appeal in *Russkoye Bogatstvo* No. 8, 1906, for "caution" concerning the nationalist prejudices of the Great-Russian muzhik).

Advocacy of the right to self-determination is very important in the fight against the abscess of nationalism in all its forms.

Proletarskaya Pravda No. 4,
December 11, 1913
Signed: *I.*

Published according to
the *Proletarskaya Pravda*
text

A GOOD RESOLUTION AND A BAD SPEECH

All class-conscious workers in Russia undoubtedly showed interest in the resolution on Russian affairs passed by the International Bureau and paid attention to it. It is known that the pivot of this resolution was the decision to organise or arrange a *"general exchange of opinion"* among "all sections of the working-class movement" of Russia, including those which accept the Social-Democratic programme, as well as those whose programmes "are in agreement" (or "in harmony"—*im Einklange*) with it.

The latter definition is extremely broad, for it embraces not only the supporters of Jagiello, but also every group that wishes to declare that its programme "harmonises" or "is in agreement with" the Social-Democratic programme. This broad definition, however, will not do any harm for, of course, it is desirable that the widest possible circle should participate in this *"exchange of opinion"* so as not to exclude any of those with whom even individual groups of Social-Democrats *might desire* to unite. We must not forget that two plans were proposed at the meeting of the International Socialist Bureau: (1) Kautsky's plan to "arrange a general exchange of opinion" and *no more*. An exchange of opinion before impartial colleagues, the Executive Committee of the International Socialist Bureau, will *ascertain* the state of affairs and the depth of the disagreements; (2) The plan proposed by Rosa Luxemburg, but withdrawn after Kautsky's objections. This plan proposed a "unification conference" (*Einigungskonferenz*) "to restore the united party".

This second plan was not so good, of course, for, the first essential is to gather precise data, apart from the fact that Rosa Luxemburg was merely trying to smuggle in "restoration" of the notorious "Tyszka group".

The plan accepted was Kautsky's; it was more cautious and approached the question of unity more systematically, *through* a preliminary "exchange of opinion" and the study of precise data. It is quite natural therefore that Kautsky's resolution should have been adopted unanimously.

But a distinction must be drawn between Kautsky's resolution, which was adopted by the Bureau, and the *speech* he made, in the course of which he said some *monstrous things* on one point. We have already commented briefly on this matter, but the appearance of the report of Kautsky's speech in *Vorwärts* (the chief organ of the German party)[148] compels us to deal with this important question in greater detail.

Objecting to Rosa Luxemburg, Kautsky said that "the old party had disappeared although old names had been retained which, however, in the course of time (*im Laufe der Jahre*—during the past few years) had acquired a new content. Old comrades could not simply be excluded merely because their party (*ihre Partei*) did not bear the old name".

When Rosa Luxemburg objected to this and said that "Kautsky's statement that the Russian party was dead [*sei tot*] was a thoughtless expression", Kautsky limited himself to "protesting that he did not say that Russian Social-Democracy was dead. He merely said that the old forms were broken, and that a new form would have to be created".

This is the translation of the official record of the passages relevant to our question.

It is obvious that Kautsky did not say and could not have said that *Social-Democracy* was dead. But he did say that the *party* had disappeared, and this *he did not withdraw*, in spite of the protest that was made!

This is incredible, but it is a fact.

The confusion Kautsky betrayed here is stupendous. To the exclusion of *which* "old comrades" did he refer? Potresov and Co.? By "*their* party" did he mean liquidator amorphousness?

Or did Kautsky have in mind the "P.S.P. Left wing" which was excluded by Rosa Luxemburg's formula? If so, then his expression "old comrades" is unintelligible, for *never* since the Social-Democratic Party has been in existence,

i.e., since 1898, have the members of the P.S.P. and Social-Democrats been fellow party members.

As far as we are concerned the two interpretations are
the same, for it would be ridiculous indeed to exclude the
liquidators from an "exchange of opinion" on the question
of unity (for the whole question centres round them), just
as it would be ridiculous to exclude the P.S.P. Left wing
(speaking abstractly, the liquidators—anything can be expected of them—are quite capable of making an ultimatum
of their defence of their break-away alliance with the *non*-
Social-Democratic P.S.P.). At all events it must be ascertained exactly not only what the liquidators want of the
party, but also what their allies want.

The undoubted fact remains that at the Bureau, Kautsky
went to the length of saying that the Russian party had disappeared.

How could he have descended to such a monstrous statement? To understand this the Russian workers must know
who informs the German Social-Democratic press about Russian affairs? When the Germans write they usually avoid the
question of our disagreements. When Russians write for
German Social-Democratic publications we either see all the
émigré coteries allied with the liquidators in a campaign
of scurrilous abuse against the "Leninists" (as was the case
in *Vorwärts* in the spring of 1912), or the writings of the
Tyszkas and Trotskys, or a member of some other émigré
coterie, deliberately obscuring the issue. *For years* there has
not been a single document, collection of resolutions, analysis of ideas, or a single attempt to collect the facts!

We regret that the German leaders (who show ability in
collecting and analysing facts when they study theory)
are not ashamed to listen to and repeat the fairy-tales of
their liquidator informants.

The Bureau's *resolution* will be carried out, but Kautsky's
speech will remain a sad curiosity.

Proletarskaya Pravda No. 6,   Published according to
December 13, 1913   the *Proletarskaya Pravda* text

THE NATIONALITY OF PUPILS IN RUSSIAN SCHOOLS

To obtain a more precise idea of the plan for "cultural-national autonomy", which boils down to segregating the schools according to nationality, it is useful to take the concrete data which show the nationality of the pupils attending Russian schools. For the St. Petersburg educational area such data are provided by the returns of the school census taken on January 18, 1911.

The following are the data on the distribution of pupils attending elementary schools under the Ministry of Public Education according to the *native languages* of the pupils. The data cover the whole of the St. Petersburg educational area, but *in brackets* we give the *figures for* the city of St. Petersburg. Under the term "Russian language" the officials constantly lump together Great-Russian, Byelorussian and Ukrainian ("Little Russian", according to official terminology). Total pupils—265,660 (48,076).

Russian—232,618 (44,223); Polish—1,737 (780); Czech—3 (2); Lithuanian—84 (35); Lettish—1,371 (113); Zhmud—1 (0); French—14 (13); Italian—4 (4); Rumanian—2 (2); German—2,408 (845); Swedish—228 (217); Norwegian—31 (0); Danish—1 (1); Dutch—1 (0); English—8 (7); Armenian—3 (3); Gipsy—4 (0); Jewish—1,196 (396); Georgian—2 (1); Ossetian—1 (0); Finnish—10,750 (874); Karelian—3,998 (2); Chud—247 (0); Estonian—4,723 (536); Lapp—9 (0); Zyryan—6,008 (0); Samoyed—5 (0); Tatar—63 (13); Persian—1 (1); Chinese—1 (1); not ascertained—138 (7).

These are comparatively accurate figures. They show that the national composition of the population is extremely mixed, although they apply to one of the basically Great-

Russian districts of Russia. The extremely mixed national composition of the population of the large city of St. Petersburg is at once evident. This is no accident, but results from a *law* of capitalism that operates in all countries and in all parts of the world. Large cities, factory, metallurgical, railway and commercial and industrial centres generally, are certain, more than any other, to have very mixed populations, and it is precisely these centres that grow faster than all others and constantly attract larger and larger numbers of the inhabitants of the backward rural areas.

Now try to apply to these real-life data the lifeless utopia of the nationalist philistines called "cultural-national autonomy" or (in the language of the Bundists) "taking out of the jurisdiction of the state" questions of national culture, i.e., primarily educational affairs.

Educational affairs "shall be taken out of the jurisdiction of the state" and transferred to 23 (in St. Petersburg) "national associations" each developing "its own" "national culture"!

It would be ridiculous to waste words to prove the absurdity and reactionary nature of a "national programme" of this sort.

It is as clear as daylight that the advocacy of such a plan means, *in fact*, pursuing or supporting the ideas of bourgeois nationalism, chauvinism and clericalism. The interests of democracy in general, and the interests of the working class in particular, demand the very opposite. We must strive to secure the *mixing* of the children of *all* nationalities in *uniform* schools in each locality; the workers of all nationalities must *jointly* pursue the proletarian educational policy which Samoilov, the deputy of the Vladimir workers, so ably formulated on behalf of the Russian Social-Democratic workers' group in the State Duma.[149] We must most emphatically oppose segregating the schools according to nationality, no matter what form it may take.

It is not our business to segregate the nations in matters of education in any way; on the contrary, we must strive to create the fundamental democratic conditions for the peaceful coexistence of the nations on the basis of equal rights. We must not champion "national culture", but expose the clerical and bourgeois character of this slogan in the name of the international culture of the world working-class movement.

But we may be asked whether it is possible to safeguard the interests of the *one* Georgian child among the 48,076 schoolchildren in St. Petersburg on the basis of equal rights. And we should reply that it is impossible to establish a special Georgian school in St. Petersburg on the basis of Georgian "national culture", and that to advocate such a plan means sowing *pernicious* ideas among the masses of the people.

But we shall not be defending anything harmful, or be striving after anything that is impossible, if we demand for this child free government premises for lectures on the Georgian language, Georgian history, etc., the provision of Georgian books from the Central Library for this child, a state contribution towards the fees of the Georgian teacher, and so forth. Under real democracy, when bureaucracy and "Peredonovism"[150] are completely eliminated from the schools, the people can quite easily achieve this. But this real democracy can be achieved *only* when the workers of *all* nationalities are united.

To preach the establishment of special national schools for every "national culture" is reactionary. But under real democracy it is quite possible to ensure instruction in the native language, in native history, and so forth, *without* splitting up the schools according to nationality. And complete local self-government will make it impossible for anything to be forced upon the people, as for example, upon the 713 Karelian children in Kem Uyezd (where there are only 514 Russian children) or upon the 681 Zyryan children in Pechora Uyezd (153 Russian), or upon the 267 Lettish children in Novgorod Uyezd (over 7,000 Russian), and so on and so forth.

Advocacy of impracticable cultural-national autonomy is an absurdity, which now already is only disuniting the workers ideologically. To advocate the amalgamation of the workers of all nationalities means facilitating the success of proletarian class solidarity, which will guarantee equal rights for, and maximum peaceful coexistence of, all nationalities.

Proletarskaya Pravda No. 7,
December 14, 1913

Published according to
the *Proletarskaya Pravda* text

STRIKES IN RUSSIA[151]

In the majority of West-European countries, strike statistics were placed on a proper footing comparatively recently—some ten or twenty years ago. In Russia there are strike statistics dating from 1895 only. The chief defect in our official statistics, apart from understatement concerning the number of participants, is that they cover only workers in enterprises subordinated to the Factory Inspectorate. Railwaymen, metallurgical workers, tramway workers, workers in trades subject to excise, etc., miners, building and rural workers are not included in the statistics.

Here are summarised data for the entire period covered by Russian strike statistics.

Year	Number of strikes		Number of strikers	
	Total	Percentage of all enterprises	Total	Percentage of all workers
1895	68	0.4	31,195	2.0
1896	118	0.6	29,527	1.9
1897	145	0.7	59,870	4.0
1898	215	1.1	43,150	2.9
1899	189	1.0	57,498	3.8
1900	125	0.7	29,389	1.7
1901	164	1.0	32,218	1.9
1902	123	0.7	36,671	2.2
1903	550	3.2	86,832	5.1
1904	68	0.4	24,904	1.5
1905	13,995	93.2	2,863,173	163.8
1906	6,114	42.2	1,108,406	65.8
1907	3,573	23.8	740,074	41.9
1908	892	5.9	176,101	9.7
1909	340	2.3	64,166	3.5
1910	222	1.4	46,623	2.4
1911	466	2.8	105,110	5.1
1912	1,918	?	683,361	?

The extent to which these figures are understated may be judged, for example, from the fact that such a cautious writer as Mr. Prokopovich cites another figure for 1912— *683,000* strikers, but "according to another estimate, 1,248,000 in factories, and in addition a further 215,000 in enterprises not under the Factory Inspectorate", i.e., *1,463,000* or almost a million and a half.

The number of economic strikes (from 1905) is as follows:

Year	Number of strikes	Number of workers	Year	Number of strikes	Number of workers
1905	4,388	1,051,209	1909	290	55,803
1906	2,545	457,721	1910	214	42,846
1907	973	200,004	1911	442	96,730
1908	428	83,407	1912	702	172,052

Thus the history of strikes in Russia may be divided into four clear-cut periods (if we omit the eighties with their famous Morozov strikes[152], noted even by the reactionary publicist Katkov as the emergence of the "labour question" in Russia):

		Average number of strikers per annum
1st period (1895-1904),	pre-revolutionary . .	43,000
2nd period (1905-07),	revolutionary . . .	1,570,000
3rd period (1908-10),	counter-revolutionary	96,000
4th period (1911-12),	present, beginning of revival	394,000

In general, the average number of strikers a year in Russia over the eighteen years was 345,400. In Germany the average for fourteen years (1899-1912) was 229,500, and for Britain the average for twenty years (1893-1912) was 344,200. To give a clear picture of the connection between strikes in Russia and the country's political history, we cite the figures for 1905-07 in three-month periods (*quarters*):

Years		1905				1906		
Quarters	I	II	III	IV	I	II	III	IV
Number of strikers (thousands) per quarter	Beginning of revolution			Revolution		First Duma		
Total	810	481	294	1,277	269	479	296	63
Economic	411	190	143	275	73	222	125	37
Political	399	291	151	1,002	196	257	171	26

Year		1907		
Quarters	I	II	III	IV
Number of strikers (thousands) per quarter		Second Duma		
Total	146	323	77	193
Economic	52	52	66	30
Political	94	271	11	163

The extent to which workers from various parts of Russia participated in strikes may be seen from the following figures:

| Factory disrtict | Number of factory workers (thousands) in 1905 | Number of strikers (thousands) | |
		Total for 10 years (1895-1904)	Number in 1905
St. Petersburg . . .	299	137	1,033
Moscow	567	123	540
Warsaw	252	69	887
3 Southern regions	543	102	403
Totals	1,661	431	2,863

This table shows the relative backwardness of Moscow, and still more of the South, and the outstanding priority of St. Petersburg and its area (including Riga), and also of Poland.

The strikers in the main branches of industry were distributed as follows:

Groups of industries	Total number of factory workers (thousands) in 1904	Number of strikers (thousands)	
		Total for 10 years (1895-1904)	Number in 1905
Metalworking . . .	252	117	811
Textile	708	237	1,296
Printing, woodwork- ing, leather, chem- icals	277	38	471
Ceramics, food . . .	454	39	285
Totals	1,691	431	2,863

This shows that the metalworkers are in the lead and the textile workers are backward, the remaining workers being still more backward.

The strikes are grouped in accordance with their causes in the following way (for 14 years, 1895-1908): political, 59.9 per cent of the strikers; on wage issues, 24.3 per cent; on the issue of the working day, 10.9 per cent; labour conditions, 4.8 per cent.

In respect of the results of the strikes we get the following division (if the number of strikers whose strikes ended in a compromise be divided equally between "won" and "lost"):

Number participating in economic strikes (thousands)

	Total for 10 years (1895-1904)	%	1905	%	1906	%	1907	%	1911	%	1912	%
Won . . .	159	37.5	705	48.9	233	50.9	59	29.5	49	51	55	42
Lost	265	62.5	734	51.1	225	49.1	141	70.5	47	49	77	58
Totals	424	100	1,439	100	458	100	200	100	96	100	132	100

The figures for 1911 and 1912 are incomplete and are not fully comparable with the preceding figures.

In conclusion we give brief data on the distribution of strikes according to the size of the enterprise and according to the location of the enterprise:

Number of strikers per 100 in each category:

Category of enterprise	Total for 10 years— 1895-1904	In 1905
20 workers or less	2.7	47
21 to 50 workers . . .	7.5	89.4
51 to 100 " . . .	9.4	108.9
101 to 500 " . . .	21.5	160.2
501 to 1,000 " . . .	49.9	163.8
Over 1,000 " . . .	89.7	231.9

Percentage of strikes

	in towns	outside towns
1895-1904 . .	75.1	24.9
1905	85	15

The dominance of the workers of big industrial establishments in the strike movement and the relative backwardness of rural factories are quite clear from these figures.

Written in 1913

Published in December 1913
in the pocket calendar
Sputnik Rabochego for 1914
Priboi Publishers, St. Petersburg
Signed: *V. I.*

Published according to
the calendar text

THE NATIONAL PROGRAMME OF THE R.S.D.L.P.

The Conference of the Central Committee has adopted a resolution on the national question,* which has been printed in the "Notification", and has placed the question of a national programme on the agenda of the Congress.

Why and how the national question has, at the present time, been brought to the fore—in the entire policy of the counter-revolution, in the class-consciousness of the bourgeoisie and in the proletarian Social-Democratic Party of Russia—is shown in detail in the resolution itself. There is hardly any need to dwell on this in view of the clarity of the situation. This situation and the fundamentals of a national programme for Social-Democracy have recently been dealt with in Marxist theoretical literature (the most prominent place being taken by Stalin's article [153]). We therefore consider that it will be to the point if, in this article, we confine ourselves to the presentation of the problem from a purely Party standpoint and to explanations that cannot be made in the legal press, crushed as it is by the Stolypin-Maklakov oppression.

Social-Democracy in Russia is taking shape by drawing exclusively on the experience of older countries, i.e., of Europe, and on the theoretical expression of that experience, Marxism. The specific feature of our country and the specific features of the historical period of the establishment of Social-Democracy in our country are: first, in our country, as distinct from Europe, Social-Democracy began to take shape *before* the bourgeois revolution and continued taking shape *during* that revolution. Secondly, in our country

---

* See pp. 427-29 of this volume.—*Ed.*

the inevitable struggle to separate proletarian from general bourgeois and petty-bourgeois democracy—a struggle that is fundamentally the same as that experienced by every country—is being conducted under the conditions of a complete theoretical victory of Marxism in the West and in our country. The form taken by this struggle, therefore, is not so much that of a struggle for Marxism as a struggle for or against petty-bourgeois theories that are hidden behind "almost Marxist" phrases.

That is how the matter stands, beginning with Economism (1895-1901) and "legal Marxism" (1895-1901, 1902). Only those who shrink from historical truth can forget the close, intimate connection and relationship between these trends and Menshevism (1903-07) and liquidationism (1908-13).

In the national question the old *Iskra*, which in 1901-03 worked on and completed a programme for the R.S.D.L.P. as well as laying the first and fundamental basis of Marxism in the theory and practice of the Russian working-class movement, had to struggle, in the same way as on other questions, against petty-bourgeois opportunism. This opportunism was expressed, first and foremost, in the nationalist tendencies and waverings of the Bund. The old *Iskra* conducted a stubborn struggle against Bund nationalism, and to forget this is tantamount to becoming a Forgetful John again, and cutting oneself off from the historical and ideological roots of the whole Social-Democratic workers' movement in Russia.

On the other hand, when the Programme of the R.S.D.L.P. was finally adopted at the Second Congress in August 1903, there was a struggle, unrecorded in the Minutes of the Congress because it took place in the *Programme Commission*, which was visited by almost the entire Congress—a struggle against the clumsy attempts of several Polish Social-Democrats to cast doubts on "the right of nations to self-determination", i.e., attempts to deviate towards opportunism and nationalism from a quite different angle.

And today, ten years later, the struggle goes on along those same two basic *lines*, which shows equally that there is a profound connection between this struggle and all the objective conditions affecting the national question in Russia.

At the Brünn Congress in Austria (1899) the programme of "cultural-national autonomy" (defended by Kristan, Ellenbogen and others and expressed in the draft of the Southern Slavs) was *rejected*. *Territorial* national autonomy was adopted, and Social-Democratic propaganda for the obligatory union of all national regions was only a *compromise* with the idea of "cultural-national autonomy". The chief theoreticians of this unfortunate idea themselves lay particular emphasis on its *inapplicability* to Jewry.

In Russia—*as usual*—people have been found who have made it their business to enlarge on a little opportunist error and develop it into a system of opportunist policy. In the same way as Bernstein in Germany brought into being the Right Constitutional-Democrats in Russia—Struve, Bulgakov, Tugan & Co.—so Otto Bauer's "forgetfulness of internationalism" (as the supercautious Kautsky calls it!) *gave rise* in Russia to the *complete* acceptance of "cultural-national autonomy" *by all* the Jewish bourgeois parties and a large number of petty-bourgeois trends (the Bund and a *conference* of Socialist-Revolutionary national parties in 1907). Backward Russia serves, one might say, as an example of how the microbes of West-European opportunism produce whole *epidemics* on our savage soil.

In Russia people are fond of saying that Bernstein is "tolerated" in Europe, but they forget to add that nowhere in the world, with the exception of "holy" Mother Russia, has Bernsteinism engendered Struvism,[154] or has "Bauerism" led to the justification, by Social-Democrats, of the refined nationalism of the Jewish bourgeoisie.

"Cultural-national autonomy" implies precisely the most refined and, therefore, the most harmful nationalism, it implies the corruption of the workers by means of the slogan of national culture and the propaganda of the profoundly harmful and even anti-democratic segregating of schools according to nationality. In short, this programme undoubtedly contradicts the internationalism of the proletariat and is in accordance only with the ideals of the nationalist petty bourgeoisie.

But there is *one case* in which the Marxists are duty bound, if they do not want to betray democracy and the proletariat, to defend one special demand in the national question;

that is, the *right* of nations to self-determination (§ 9 of the R.S.D.L.P. Programme), i.e., the right to political secession. The Conference resolution explains and motivates this demand in such detail that there is no place left for misunderstanding.

We shall, therefore, give only a brief description of those amazingly ignorant and opportunist objections that have been raised against this section of the Programme. In connection with this let us mention that *in the course of the ten years'* existence of the Programme *not one single unit* of the R.S.D.L.P., not one single national organisation, not one single regional conference, not one local committee and not one delegate to a congress or conference, has attempted to raise the question of changing or annulling § 9!

It is necessary to bear this in mind. It shows us at once whether there is a grain of seriousness or Party spirit in the objections raised to this point.

Take Mr. Semkovsky of the liquidators' newspaper. With the casual air of a man who has liquidated a party, he announces: "For certain reasons we do not share Rosa Luxemburg's proposal to remove § 9 from the Programme altogether" (*Novaya Rabochaya Gazeta* No. 71).

So the reasons are a secret! But then, how can secrecy be avoided in face of such ignorance of the history of our Programme? Or when that same Mr. Semkovsky, incomparably casual (what do the Party and the Programme matter!) makes an exception for Finland?

"What are we to do ... if the Polish proletariat wants to carry on a joint struggle together with the whole proletariat of Russia within the framework of one state, and the reactionary classes of Polish society, on the contrary, want to separate Poland from Russia and, through a referendum, obtain a majority of votes in favour of separation; are we, Russian Social-Democrats, to vote in a central parliament together with our Polish comrades *against* secession, or, in order not to infringe on the 'right to self-determination', vote *in favour* of secession?"

What, indeed, are we to do when such naïve and so hopelessly confused questions are raised?

The *right* to self-determination, my dear Mr. Liquidator, certainly does *not* imply the solution of the problem by a central parliament, but by a parliament, a diet, or a referendum of the *seceding minority*. When Norway seceded from Sweden (1905) it was decided by Norway *alone* (a country half the size of Sweden).

Even a child could see that Mr. Semkovsky is hopelessly mixed up.

"The right to self-determination" implies a democratic system *of a type* in which there is not only democracy in general, but specifically one in which there *could not be an undemocratic* solution of the question of secession. Democracy, speaking generally, is compatible with militant and tyrannical nationalism. The proletariat demands a democracy that *rules out* the forcible retention of any one of the nations within the bounds of the state. "In order not to infringe on the right to self-determination", therefore, we are duty bound *not* "to vote for secession", as the wily Mr. Semkovsky assumes, but to vote for the right of the seceding region to decide the question *itself.*

It would seem that even with Mr. Semkovsky's mental abilities it is not difficult to deduce that "the *right* to divorce" does not require that one should *vote* for divorce! But such is the fate of those who criticise § 9—they forget the ABC of logic.

At the time of Norway's secession from Sweden, the Swedish proletariat, if they did not want to follow the nationalist petty bourgeoisie, were *duty bound to vote* and agitate against the annexation of Norway by force, as the Swedish priesthood and landed proprietors desired. This is obvious and not too difficult to understand. Swedish nationalist democrats could refrain from a type of agitation that the principle of the *right* to self-determination demands of the proletariat of *ruling, oppressor nations.*

"What are we to do if the reactionaries are in the majority?" asks Mr. Semkovsky. This is a question worthy of a third-form schoolboy. What is to be done about the *Russian* constitution if democratic voting gives the reactionaries a majority? Mr. Semkovsky asks idle, empty questions that have nothing to do with the matter in hand— they are the kind of questions that, as it is said, seven fools can ask more of than seventy wise men can answer.

When a democratic vote gives the reactionaries a majority, one of two things may, and usually does occur: either the decision of the reactionaries is implemented and its harmful consequences send the masses more or less speedily over to the side of democracy and against the reactionaries; or the conflict between democracy and reaction is decided by a civil or other war, which is also quite possible (and no doubt even the Semkovskys have heard of this) under a democracy.

The recognition of the right to self-determination is, Mr. Semkovsky assures us, "playing into the hands of the most thorough-paced bourgeois nationalism". This is childish nonsense since the recognition of the *right* does not exclude either propaganda and agitation *against* separation or the exposure of bourgeois nationalism. But it is absolutely indisputable that the denial of the *right* to secede is "playing into the hands" of the *most thorough-paced reactionary Great-Russian* nationalism!

This is the essence of Rosa Luxemburg's amusing error for which she was ridiculed a long time ago by German and Russian (August 1903) Social-Democrats; in their fear of playing into the hands of the bourgeois nationalism of oppressed nations, people play into the hands not merely of the bourgeois but of the reactionary nationalism of the *oppressor* nation.

If Mr. Semkovsky had not been so virginally innocent in matters concerning Party history and the Party Programme he would have understood that it was his duty to refute Plekhanov, who, *eleven years ago*, in defending the draft programme (which became the Programme in 1903) of the R.S.D.L.P. in *Zarya*,[155] made *a special point* (page 38) of the recognition of the right to self-determination and wrote the following about it:

"This demand, which is not obligatory for bourgeois democrats, even in theory, is obligatory for us as Social-Democrats. If we were to forget about it or were afraid to put it forward for fear of impinging on the national prejudices of our compatriots of Great-Russian origin, the battle-cry of world Social-Democracy, 'Workers of all countries, unite!' would be a shameful lie upon our lips."

As long ago as the *Zarya* days, Plekhanov put forward the basic argument which was developed in detail in the conference resolution, an argument to which the Semkovskys have not attempted to draw attention for eleven years. In Russia there are 43 per cent Great Russians, but Great-

Russian nationalism rules over the other 57 per cent of the population and oppresses all nations. The National-Liberals (Struve & Co., the Progressists, etc.) have already joined forces with our national-reactionaries and the "first swallows" of *national* democracy have appeared (remember Mr. Peshekhonov's appeal in August 1906 to be cautious in our attitude to the nationalist prejudices of the muzhik).

In Russia only the liquidators consider the bourgeois-democratic revolution to be over, and the concomitant of *such* a revolution all over the world always has been and still is national movements. In Russia in particular there are oppressed nations in many of the border regions, which in neighbouring states enjoy greater liberty. Tsarism is more reactionary than the neighbouring states, constitutes the *greatest* barrier to free economic development, and does its utmost to foster Great-Russian nationalism. For a Marxist, of course, *all other conditions being equal*, big states are always preferable to small ones. But it would be ridiculous and reactionary even to suppose that conditions under the tsarist monarchy might be equal to those in any European country or any but a minority of Asian countries.

The denial of the right of nations to self-determination in present-day Russia is, therefore, undoubted opportunism and a refusal to fight against the reactionary Great-Russian nationalism that is still all-powerful.

Sotsial-Demokrat No. 32,
December 15 (28), 1913

Published according to
the *Sotsial-Demokrat* text

KAUTSKY'S UNPARDONABLE ERROR

In *Proletarskaya Pravda* No. 6, we commented on the speech Comrade Kautsky delivered* during the discussion of Russian affairs in the International Socialist Bureau, and on the amazing—to the Russian reader—complete and deplorable ignorance of Russian affairs that he then displayed.

In his speech Kautsky said that in Russia "the old Party is dead". In a second speech, replying to the objections that had been raised to this, Kautsky said: "I did not say that Russian Social-Democracy is dead; I merely assert that the old forms are broken and that new forms must be created." This is how *Vorwärts*, the central organ of the German party, whose delegate Kautsky was, reports the matter. *Vorwärts* is published in the city where Kautsky lives, and, of course, if he had found that he had been incorrectly reported he would have hastened to correct the report, as he has done on more than one occasion on questions far less important than the "question of the existence" of an entire Party, and of one affiliated to the International at that.

And now, No. 101 of *Novaya Likvidatorskaya Gazeta* publishes its *own* report of the meeting of the International Bureau, in which Kautsky's second speech is so reported as to make it appear that Kautsky definitely *denied* that he had stated that the "Party is dead".

We would have been the first to rejoice had Kautsky really spoken a second time in order emphatically to withdraw the view which he had expressed, and which was based on his most deplorable ignorance of Russian Party life. But alas! We have no grounds whatever for giving more credence to the report in *Novaya Likvidatorskaya Gazeta* than to the report in the central organ of the German party.

---

* See pp. 528-30 of this volume.—*Ed.*

The liquidators' newspaper is trying to hush up the matter. But it is quite clear. In his statement about the old Party being "dead" Kautsky not only betrayed ignorance of the facts about the Russian working-class movement, but also revealed what sort of influence the liquidator whisperers abroad exercise upon our foreign comrades.

After uttering his monstrous phrase and meeting with objections, Kautsky tried to correct himself. As reported in *Vorwärts*, the central organ of the German Social-Democratic Party, he appears to have corrected himself badly, and as reported by the liquidator correspondent he appears to have corrected himself better, but not very much better, for what does he mean by the "form" of Social-Democracy, if not the Party?

The point, however, is not how Kautsky *corrected* himself, but the unpardonable mistake he *committed* as a result of liquidator efforts abroad. Class-conscious workers in Russia could, of course, easily expose these whisperers abroad if only they wanted to, and it is high time they did want to! They must organise the work of informing our foreign comrades about their movement in such a way as to tear this business out of the hands of irresponsible émigré coteries. They must *counteract* the efforts being made by whisperers to use the ignorance (natural) of foreign parties for their own liquidator ends. That is why we called upon the worker comrades to respond as vigorously as possible to the International Bureau's appeal to clarify the disagreements between the Marxists and the liquidators. Let the foreign comrades at last hear the voices of the workers themselves and not those of the liquidator whisperers. This is important, this is essential if we value the idea of international unity.

We make this appeal for a genuine clarification of disagreements, for keeping our foreign comrades informed by means of resolutions, decisions and voting by the workers themselves in order to counteract the liquidators' attempts to conceal or garble the facts of what took place at the meeting of the Bureau.

Proletarshaya Pravda No. 8,
December 15, 1913

Published according to
the *Proletarshaya Pravda* text

ONCE MORE ON THE SEGREGATION OF THE SCHOOLS ACCORDING TO NATIONALITY

Marxists resolutely oppose nationalism in all its forms, from the crude reactionary nationalism of our ruling circles and of the Right Octobrist parties, down to the more or lees refined and disguised nationalism of the bourgeois and petty-bourgeois parties.

Reactionary, or Black-Hundred, nationalism strives to safeguard the privileges of one nation, condemning all other nations to an inferior status, with fewer rights, or even with no rights at all. Not a single Marxist, and not even a single democrat, can treat this nationalism with anything else but the utmost hostility.

In words, bourgeois and bourgeois-democratic nationalists recognise the equality of nations, but in deeds they (often covertly, behind the backs of the people) stand for certain privileges for one of the nations, and always try to secure greater advantages for "their own" nation (i.e., for the bourgeoisie of their own nation); they strive to separate and segregate nations, to foster national exclusiveness, etc. By talking most of all about "national culture" and emphasising what separates one nation from the other, bourgeois nationalists *divide the workers* of the various nations and fool them with "nationalist slogans".

The class-conscious workers combat *all* national oppression and *all* national privileges, but they do not confine themselves to that. They combat all, even the most refined, nationalism, and advocate not only the unity, but also the *amalgamation* of the workers of *all* nationalities in the struggle against reaction and against bourgeois nationalism in all its forms. Our task is not to segregate nations, but to unite the workers of all nations. Our banner does not carry the slogan "national culture" but *international* culture, which unites all the nations in a higher, socialist unity, and the way to which is already being paved by the international amalgamation of capital.

The influence of petty-bourgeois, philistine nationalism has infected certain "would-be socialists", who advocate what is called "cultural-educational autonomy", i.e., the transfer of educational affairs (and matters of national culture in general) from the state to the individual nations. Naturally, Marxists combat this propaganda for the *segregation of nations*, they combat this refined nationalism, they combat the *segregating of the schools according to nationality*. When our Bundists, and later, the liquidators, wanted to support "cultural-national autonomy" *in direct opposition to* our Programme, they were condemned not only by the Bolsheviks, but also by the pro-Party Mensheviks (Plekhanov).

Now Mr. An, in *Novaya Rabochaya Gazeta* (No. 103) is trying to defend a bad case by subterfuge, and by showering abuse upon us. We calmly ignore the abuse; it is merely a sign of the liquidators' feebleness.

To have schools connected in the native languages— this, Mr. An assures us, is what is meant by segregating the schools according to the nationalities of the pupils; the *Pravda* people, he says, want to deprive the non-Russians of their national schools!

We can afford to laugh at this trick of Mr. An's, for everybody knows that *Pravda* stands for the fullest equality of languages, and even for the abolition of an official language! Mr. An's impotent rage is causing him to lose his head. This is dangerous, dear Mr. An!

The right of a nation to use its native language is explicitly and definitely recognised in § 8 of the Marxist programme.[156]

If Mr. An is right in stating that having schools conducted in the native languages means segregating the schools according to nationality, why did the Bundists in 1906, and the liquidators in 1912, "supplement" (or rather, *distort*) the Programme adopted in 1903—at the very Congress which *rejected* "cultural-national autonomy"—which *fully* recognises the right of a nation to use its *native language*?

Your subterfuge will fail, Mr. An, and you will not succeed in covering up with your noise, clamour and abuse the fact that the liquidators have *violated* this Programme, and that they have "adapted socialism to nationalism", as Comrade Plekhanov expressed it.

We do not want to have the Programme violated. We do not want socialism to be adapted to nationalism. We stand for complete democracy, for the complete freedom and equality of languages, but give no support whatever to the proposal to "transfer educational affairs to the nations" or to "segregate schools according to nationality".

"The question at issue is that of segregating the schools according to nations," writes Mr. An, "hence, these nations must exist in each locality, hindering each other's development; and consequently, *they must be segregated* in the sphere of public education as well."

The words we have emphasised clearly reveal how liquidationism is dragging Mr. An away from socialism towards nationalism. The *segregation* of nations within the limits of a single state is harmful, and we Marxists strive *to bring the nations together and to amalgamate them.* Our object is not to "segregate" nations, but to secure for them, through full democracy, an equality and coexistence as peaceful (relatively) as in Switzerland.*

Proletarskaya Pravda No. 9,
December 17, 1913

Published according to
the *Proletarskaya Pravda* text

---

* Mr. An boldly asserts that "there is no intermixing of nations even in the cantons of Switzerland". Will he not blush if we mention *four* cantons: Berne, Fribourg, Graubünden and Valais?

MR. GORSKY AND A CERTAIN LATIN PROVERB

Mr. Gorsky, in the liquidator newspaper, is continuing to defend the obvious mistake of the seven deputies who adopted the deplorable clause on "criminally-liable actions". Mr. Gorsky, your wriggling is all in vain! It is no use saying that you are not familiar with F. D.'s draft; you can easily obtain it through the editorial office of your newspaper. Don't let F. D. play the part of the witness who is "not to be found". That would be ridiculous.

In vain does Mr. Gorsky assert that Lenin, Zinoviev and Kamenev have "by their silence" accepted responsibility for the draft made by F. D. and his friends. Each of the three writers mentioned would need a staff of ten secretaries and a special newspaper to refute all the nonsense that is uttered in the wide world.

In vain does Mr. Gorsky hide behind the backs of the *worst* (possible) socialists, who would *lessen* the penalties for "criminally-liable actions" if they are not abolished altogether. There is a good Latin proverb which says: "It is natural for all men to err; but only a fool persists in his error."

Remember this proverb, Mr. Gorsky and Mr. F. D., and advise the seven deputies to delete the Octobrist clause on "criminally-liable actions" from their bill!

Proletarskaya Pravda No. 10,
December 18, 1913

Published according to
the *Proletarskaya Pravda* text

THE MARX-ENGELS CORRESPONDENCE[157]

The long-promised edition of the correspondence of the famous founders of scientific socialism has at last been published. Engels bequeathed the work of publishing it to Bebel and Bernstein, and Bebel managed to complete his part of the editorial work shortly before his death.

The Marx-Engels correspondence, published a few weeks ago by Dietz, Stuttgart, consists of four big volumes. They contain in all 1,386 letters by Marx and Engels covering an extensive period, from 1844 to 1883.

The editorial work, i.e., the writing of prefaces to the correspondence of various periods, was done by Eduard Bernstein. As might have been expected, this work is unsatisfactory both from the technical and the ideological standpoint. After his notorious "evolution" to extreme opportunist views, Bernstein should never have undertaken to edit letters which are impregnated through and through with the revolutionary spirit. Bernstein's prefaces are in part meaningless and in part simply false—as, for instance, when, instead of a precise, clear and frank characterisation of the opportunist errors of Lassalle and Schweitzer which Marx and Engels exposed, one meets with eclectic phrases and thrusts, such as that "Marx and Engels were not always right in opposing Lassalle" (Vol. III, p. xviii), or that in their tactics they were "much nearer" to Schweitzer than to Liebknecht (Vol. IV, p. x). These attacks have no purpose except to serve as a screen and embellishment for opportunism. Unfortunately, the eclectic attitude to Marx's ideological struggle against many of his opponents is becoming increasingly widespread among present-day German Social-Democrats.

From the technical standpoint, the index is unsatisfactory—only one for all four volumes (Kautsky and Stirling are omitted, for instance); the notes to individual letters are too scanty and are lost in the editor's prefaces instead of being placed in proximity to the letters they refer to, as they were by Sorge, and so forth.

The price of the publication is unduly high—about 20 rubles for the four volumes. There can be no doubt that the complete correspondence could and should have been published in a less luxurious edition at a more reasonable price, and that, in addition, a selection of passages most important from the standpoint of principle could and should have been published for wide distribution among workers.

All these defects of the edition will, of course, hamper a study of the correspondence. This is a pity, because its scientific and political value is tremendous. Not only do Marx and Engels stand out before the reader in clear relief in all their greatness, but the extremely rich theoretical content of Marxism is graphically revealed, because in their letters Marx and Engels return again and again to the most diverse aspects of their doctrine, emphasising and explaining—at times discussing and debating—what is newest (in relation to earlier views), most important and most difficult.

There unfolds before the reader a strikingly vivid picture of the history of the working-class movement all over the world—at its most important junctures and in its most essential points. Even more valuable is the history of the *politics* of the working class. On the most diverse occasions, in various countries of the Old World and the New, and at different historical moments, Marx and Engels discuss the most important principles of the *presentation* of the *political* tasks of the working class. And the period covered by the correspondence was a period in which the working class separated from bourgeois democracy, a period in which an independent working-class movement arose, a period in which the fundamental principles of proletarian tactics and policy were defined. The more we have occasion in our day to observe how the working-class movement in various countries suffers from opportunism in consequence of the stagnation and decay of the bourgeoisie, in consequence of the attention of the labour leaders being engrossed in the triv-

ialities of the day, and so on—the more valuable becomes
the wealth of material contained in the correspondence,
displaying as it does a most profound comprehension of
the *basic* aims of the proletariat in bringing about change,
and providing an unusually flexible definition of the tasks
of the tactics of the moment from the standpoint of these
revolutionary aims, without making the slightest concession to opportunism or revolutionary phrase-mongering.

If one were to attempt to define in a single word the focus, so to speak, of the whole correspondence, the central
point at which the whole body of ideas expressed and discussed converges—that word would be *dialectics*. The application of materialist dialectics to the reshaping of all political economy from its foundations up, its application to
history, natural science, philosophy and to the policy and
tactics of the working class—that was what interested Marx
and Engels most of all, that was where they contributed
what was most essential and new, and that was what constituted the masterly advance they made in the history of
revolutionary thought.

We intend in the following account, after giving a general
review of the correspondence, to outline the most interesting remarks and arguments of Marx and Engels, without
pretending to give an exhaustive account of the contents
of the letters.

I. GENERAL REVIEW

The correspondence opens with letters written in 1844
by the 24-year-old Engels to Marx. The situation in Germany at that time is brought out in striking relief. The
first letter is dated the end of September 1844 and was sent
from Barmen, where Engels's family lived, and where he
was born. Engels was not quite 24 years old at the time.
He was bored with family life and was anxious to break
away. His father was a despot, a pious manufacturer, who
was outraged at his son's continual running about to political meetings, and at his communist convictions. Engels
wrote that had it not been for his mother, of whom he was

deeply fond, he would not have spent at home even the remaining few days before he was due to leave. "You would never believe," he complained to Marx "what petty reasons, what superstitious fears were put forward by the family against my departure."[158]

While he was still in Barmen—where he was delayed a little longer by a love affair—Engels gave way to his father and worked for about two weeks in the factory office (his father was a manufacturer). "Huckstering is too horrible," he writes to Marx. "Barmen is too horrible, the way they waste their time is too horrible, and above all things it is too horrible to remain, not merely a bourgeois, but a manufacturer, a bourgeois who actively opposes the proletariat." He consoled himself, Engels goes on to say, by working on his book on the condition of the working class (this book appeared, we know, in 1845 and is one of the best works of world socialist literature). "And perhaps one can while being a Communist remain in one's outward status a bourgeois and a huckstering beast as long as one does not write, but to carry on a wide communist propaganda and at the same time engage in huckstering and industry will not work. Enough. At Easter I quit here. Add to this the drowsy life of a thoroughly Christian-Prussian family— I cannot stand it any longer; I might in the end become a German philistine and introduce philistinism into communism."[159] Thus wrote the young Engels. After the Revolution of 1848 the exigencies of life obliged him to return to his father's office and to become a "huckstering beast" for many long years. But he was able to stand firm and to create for himself, not Christian-Prussian surroundings, but entirely different, comradely surroundings, and to become for the rest of his life a relentless foe of the "introduction of philistinism into communism".

Social life in the German provinces in 1844 resembled Russian social life at the beginning of the twentieth century, before the Revolution of 1905. There was a general urge for political life, a general seething indignation in opposition to the government; the clergy fulminated against the youth for their atheism; children in bourgeois families quarrelled with their parents over their "aristocratic treatment of servants or workers".

The general spirit of opposition found expression in the fact that everybody declared himself to be a Communist. "The Police Commissary in Barmen is a Communist," Engels writes to Marx. He was in Cologne, Düsseldorf, Elberfeld—wherever he turned he stumbled upon Communists! "One ardent Communist, a cartoonist ... named Seel, is going to Paris in two months. I shall give him your address; you will all like him for his enthusiastic temperament and his love of music, and he could very well be useful as a cartoonist."[160]

"Miracles are happening here in Elberfeld. Yesterday [this was written on February 22, 1845], we held our third communist meeting in the largest hall and the best restaurant of the city. The first meeting was attended by 40 people, the second by 130 and the third by at least 200. The whole of Elberfeld and Barmen, from the moneyed aristocracy to the small shopkeepers, was represented, all except the proletariat."

This is literally what Engels wrote. Everybody in Germany at that time was a Communist—except the proletariat. Communism was a form of expression of the opposition sentiments of all, and chiefly of the bourgeoisie. "The most stupid, the most lazy and most philistine people, who take no interest in anything in the world, are almost becoming enthusiastic over communism."[161] The chief preachers of communism at that time were people of the type of our Narodniks, "Socialist-Revolutionaries", "Popular Socialists",[162] and so forth, that is to say, well-meaning bourgeois, some to a greater, others to a lesser degree, furious with the government.

And under such conditions, amidst countless pseudo-socialist trends and factions, Engels was able to find his way to *proletarian* socialism, without fearing to break off relations with a mass of well-intentioned people, who were ardent revolutionaries but bad Communists.

In 1846 Engels was in Paris. Paris was then seething with politics and the discussion of various socialist theories. Engels eagerly studied socialism, made the acquaintance of Cabet, Louis Blanc and other prominent socialists, and ran from editorial office to editorial office and from circle to circle.

His attention was chiefly focussed on the most important and most widespread socialist doctrine of the time—Proudhonism. And even *before* the publication of Proudhon's *Philosophy of Poverty* (October 1846; Marx's famous reply, *The Poverty of Philosophy*, appeared in 1847), Engels, with ruthless sarcasm and remarkable profundity, criticised Proudhon's basic ideas, which were then being particularly advocated by the German Socialist Grün. His excellent knowledge of English (which Marx mastered much later) and of English literature enabled Engels at once (letter of September 16, 1846) to point to the example of the bankruptcy of the notorious Proudhonist "labour bazaars" [163] in England. Proudhon *disgraces* socialism, Engels exclaims indignantly—it follows from Proudhon that the workers must *buy out* capital.

The 26-year-old Engels simply annihilates "true socialism". We meet this expression in his letter of October 23, 1846, long before the *Communist Manifesto*, and Grün is mentioned as its chief exponent. An "anti-proletarian, petty-bourgeois, philistine" doctrine, "sheer phrase-mongering", all kinds of "humanitarian" aspirations, "superstitious fear of 'crude' communism" (Löffel-Kommunismus, literally: "spoon communism" or "belly communism"), "peaceful plans to bestow happiness" upon mankind—these are some of Engels's epithets, which apply to *all* species of pre-Marxist socialism.

"The Proudhon plan of association," writes Engels, "was discussed for three evenings. At first I had nearly the whole clique with Grün at their head against me.... The chief point was to prove the necessity for revolution by force." (October 23, 1846). In the end he got furious, he writes, and drove his opponents so hard that they were obliged to make an open attack on communism. He demanded a vote on whether they were Communists or not. This caused great indignation among the Grünites, who began to argue that they had come together to discuss "the good of mankind" and that they must know what communism *really was*. Engels gave them an extremely simple definition so as to permit no opportunity for evasions. "I therefore defined," Engels writes, "the objects of the Communists in this way: (1) to achieve the interests of the proletariat in opposition to those of the bourgeoisie; (2) to do this through the abolition of private property and its replacement by community of goods; (3) to recognise no means of carrying out these objects other than a democratic revolution by force."[164] (Written a year and a half before the 1848 Revolution.)

The discussion ended with the meeting's adopting Engels's definition by thirteen votes against the votes of two Grünites. These meetings were attended by some twenty journeymen carpenters. Thus the foundations of the Social-Democratic Workers' Party of Germany were laid in Paris sixty-seven years ago.

A year later, in his letter of November 23, 1847, Engels informed Marx that he had prepared a draft of the *Communist Manifesto*, incidentally declaring himself opposed to the catechism form originally proposed. "I begin: What is Communism?" writes Engels. "And then straight to the proletariat—history of its origin, difference from former workmen, development of the contradiction between proletariat and bourgeoisie, crises, results.... In conclusion the Party policy of the Communists."

This historical letter of Engels's on the first draft of a work which has travelled all over the world and which to this day is true in all its fundamentals and as actual and topical as though it were written yesterday, clearly proves that Marx and Engels are justly named side by side as the founders of modern socialism.

Written at the end of 1913

First published November 28, 1920
in *Pravda* No. 268
Signed: *N. Lenin*

Published according to
the manuscript

NOTES

[1] *Bundists*—members of the *Bund (General Jewish Workers' Union of Lithuania, Poland, and Russia)*, organised in 1897. It was an association mainly of semi-proletarian Jewish artisans in the Western regions of Russia. The Bund joined the R.S.D.L.P. at the First Congress (March 1898). At the Second Congress of the R.S.D.L.P. (July 17[30]-August 10[23], 1903) the Bundists demanded that the Bund be recognised as the sole representative of the Jewish proletariat. Upon the rejection of this organisational nationalism by the Congress, the Bund left the Party.

In 1906, after the Fourth (Unity) Congress, the Bund re-entered the Party. The Bundists persistently supported the Mensheviks and waged an unremitting struggle against the Bolsheviks. Although formally belonging to the R.S.D.L.P., the Bund was actually a bourgeois-nationalist type of organisation. It opposed the Bolsheviks' programmatic demand for the right of nations to self-determination by a demand for cultural-national autonomy. It played an active role in creating the August anti-Party bloc and was expelled from the Party together with other opportunists by the Prague Conference in January 1912.

During the First World War (1914-18), the Bund adopted a social-chauvinist position and in 1917 supported the counter-revolutionary Provisional Government. It fought on the side of the enemies of the October Socialist Revolution, and later, during the Civil War, leading Bund members joined forces with the counter-revolution. At the same time a change was taking place among the rank and file of the Bund in favour of collaboration with Soviet power. When the victory of the dictatorship of the proletariat over internal counter-revolution and foreign intervention had become obvious, the Bund announced that it had relinquished its struggle against Soviet power; in March 1921 the Bund went into voluntary liquidation and part of the membership entered the Russian Communist Party (Bolsheviks) in accordance with the general rules for admission to the Party.   p. 17

[2] *Socialist-Revolutionaries (S.R.s)*—a petty-bourgeois party that emerged in Russia in 1902 as a union of Narodnik groups and circles. The party programme adopted at the First Congress in 1905 was a hash of old Narodnik ideas and revisionist falsifications of Marxism. The S.R.s failed to see the class difference between the proletariat and petty proprietors; they glossed over the class contradictions within the peasantry, denied the leading role of the

proletariat in the revolution and rejected the idea of the dictatorship of the proletariat. In the sphere of theory the S.R.s were extreme Right-wing revisionists and reformists, having borrowed their theoretical views from Bernstein, Hertz, David and Vandervelde. As a slogan for the peasant movement they put forward the utopian demand for the "socialisation of the land" under capitalist conditions. The S.R.s preached the subjectivist idea of "active heroes" and the "passive mass", and, adopting terrorism as their chief mode of struggle, did considerable harm to the mass revolutionary movement.

During the Revolution of 1905-07, the S.R.s acted as bourgeois democrats. In 1906 the Right-wing S.R.s founded the semi-Cadet Trudovik Popular Socialist Party and formed a bloc with the Cadets. During the First World War the S.R.s adopted a social-chauvinist position.

Following the victory of the February Revolution, the S.R. Party split into three groups—the Rights, headed by E. Breshko-Breshkovskaya and Kerensky, the Lefts, headed by Spiridonova, and the Centrists, headed by Chernov. The Right and Centrist leaders entered the bourgeois Provisional Government, implemented a Cadet policy and took part in organising the Kornilov putsch that aimed at the establishment of a military-monarchist dictatorship in Russia. Spiridonova's group, the Left wing of the party, officially formed itself into the party of Left S.R.s at the end of November 1917. After the victory of the October Socialist Revolution, the S.R.s conducted counter-revolutionary, subversive activities, joined the armies of the intervention and entered the whiteguard governments set up by foreign imperialists. Following the defeat of the intervention they continued their hostile activities against the Soviet state both inside the country and in whiteguard émigré circles. In an effort to maintain their influence among the peasant masses, they entered the first Soviet Government in November 1917. When the Treaty of Brest was ratified they walked out of the Council of People's Commissars and in the summer of 1918 organised a revolt for the purpose of provoking war with Germany and overthrowing the Soviet Government. The party of Left S.R.s began to disintegrate after the defeat of the revolt.   p. 17

[3] This article was published in 1913 in *Prosveshcheniye* No. 3, dedicated to the Thirtieth Anniversary of Marx's death.

Prosveshcheniye (Enlightenment) was a Bolshevik social, political and literary monthly published legally in St. Petersburg from December 1911 onwards. Its inauguration was proposed by Lenin to replace the Bolshevik journal *Mysl (Thought)*, a Moscow publication banned by the tsarist government. Lenin directed the work of the journal from abroad and wrote the following articles for it: "Fundamental Problems of the Election Campaign", "Results of the Election", "Critical Remarks on the National Question", "The Right of Nations to Self-Determination", and others.

The journal was suppressed by the tsarist government in June

1914, on the eve of the First World War. Publication was resumed in the autumn of 1917 but only one double number appeared; this number contained two articles by Lenin: "Can the Bolsheviks Retain State Power?" and "A Review of the Party Programme". p. 23

[4] *Cadets*—members of the *Constitutional-Democratic Party*—the chief party of the liberal-monarchist bourgeoisie in Russia, founded in October 1905. The Cadets called themselves the "party of people's freedom", but in reality strove to come to terms with the autocracy in order to retain tsarism in the form of a constitutional monarchy. At the time of the First World War (1914-18) they demanded "war till victory is won". After the victory of the February Revolution they came to terms with the S.R. and Menshevik leaders of the Petrograd Soviet and as a result acquired a leading position in the bourgeois Provisional Government where they pursued an anti-popular, counter-revolutionary policy. Following the October Socialist Revolution they acted as the agents of foreign imperialism and were the organisers of the internal counter-revolutionary forces. Lenin called the Cadet Party the all-Russian headquarters of the counter-revolution. p. 31

[5] *Octobrists*—members of the *Union of October Seventeenth*—a party that took shape after the publication of the tsar's Manifesto of October 17, 1905. It was a counter-revolutionary party that represented the big bourgeoisie and big capitalist farmers. Its leaders were the well-known industrialist and Moscow house-owner, A. Guchkov, and the big landed proprietor M. Rodzyanko. The Octobrists gave full support to the domestic and foreign policy of the tsarist government. p. 31

[6] *Rech (Speech)*—the central daily newspaper of the Cadet Party that was published in St. Petersburg from February 1906 onwards. It was suppressed by the Military-Revolutionary Committee of the Petrograd Soviet on October 26 (November 8), 1917, but continued to appear under other names until August 1918. p. 31

[7] Lenin here refers to a statement by Marx in his Introduction to *A Critique of the Hegelian Philosophy of Right*: "A school that legitimises the vileness of today by the vileness of yesterday, a school that declares every cry of the serf against the whip to be rebellious since the whip is an ancient, hereditary, historical whip ... that *historical school of law* would have invented German history if it had not itself been invented by German history." (See Karl Marx, Friedrich Engels, *Werke*, Bd. 1, S. 380, Dietz Verlag, Berlin, 1956.) p. 32

[8] The MS. has no heading. This title was provided by the Institute of Marxism-Leninism of the Central Committee of the C.P.S.U. p. 33

[9] *Diehard* was the name given to the extreme Right wing of the reactionary landed proprietors. p. 33

10 *Senate*—one of the highest government bodies in tsarist Russia. It was founded by Peter I in 1711 to replace the Boyars' Council as the supreme administrative and executive body dealing with current governmental questions. The members of the Senate were appointed by the tsar from among the higher civil servants.

Council of State—one of the highest government bodies of tsarist Russia. It was founded in 1810 as a legislative advisory body whose members were appointed or approved by the tsar. The Council of State was a reactionary body that rejected even moderate bills passed by the State Duma.   p. 34

11 See "Material on the Conflict Within the Social-Democratic Duma Group", p. 458 of this volume.   p. 43

12 This is the concluding line of Ivan Krylov's fable "Musicians"; it has become proverbial in Russian. The fable is about a landowner who boasted to his neighbour of the choir that he had formed from his serfs. The singers had no ear for music and no voices, but this did not bother the serf-owner, who valued them mainly for their soberness and exemplary behaviour.   p. 44

13 *Pravda (Truth)*—Bolshevik legal daily published in St. Petersburg. It was founded in April 1912 on the initiative of St. Petersburg workers.

Pravda was a mass working-class newspaper maintained by funds collected by the workers themselves. Articles were contributed by a large group of worker-correspondents and worker-writers—in one year alone the paper published 11,000 items from its worker-correspondents. The average circulation was 40,000, and occasionally it reached 60,000 copies.

Lenin directed the work of the paper from abroad, writing an article almost daily; he gave his advice to the editors and mustered the Party's best literary forces for the paper.

The police persecuted *Pravda* systematically; in the first year of publication 41 issues were confiscated and 36 summonses were made against the editors.

In the course of two years and three months *Pravda* was suppressed eight times but each time it again appeared under a new name—*Rabochaya Pravda (Workers' Truth)*, *Severnaya Pravda (Northern Truth)*, *Pravda Truda (Labour's Truth)*, *Za Pravdu (For Truth)*, *Proletarskaya Pravda (Proletarian Truth)*, *Put Pravdy (The Way of Truth)*, *Rabochy (The Worker)*, *Trudovaya Pravda (Labour Truth)*. The newspaper was finally suppressed on July 8 (21), 1914, on the eve of the First World War, and publication did not begin again until after the February Revolution. From March 5 (18), 1917, *Pravda* was published as the Central Organ of the R.S.D.L.P. Lenin joined the editorial board on April 5 (18), 1917, on his return from abroad and guided the work of the editors. On July 5 (18), 1917, the *Pravda* offices were wrecked by military cadets and Cossacks. From July to October 1917, *Pravda*, persecuted by the Provisional Government, frequently changed its name and appeared as: *Listok Pravdy* (*Pravda's Sheet*), *Proletary* (*The Proletarian*), *Rabochy* (*The Worker*), and *Rabochy Put* (*Workers' Path*). Since October 27 (November 9), 1917, the newspaper has appeared regularly under its original name of *Pravda*.   p. 45

¹⁴ This newspaper report of a lecture delivered by Lenin in Cracow on April 18, 1913 (N.S.) was published in *Naprzód* (*Forward*), the Central Organ of the Polish Social-Democratic Party of Galicia and Silesia, issued in Cracow from 1892 onwards.   p. 47

¹⁵ Lenin is here referring to the reactionary coup d'état of June 3 (16), 1907 when the government dissolved the Second Duma and changed the law regulating elections to the Duma.

The new election law greatly increased the Duma representation of the landed proprietors and the commercial and industrial bourgeoisie and greatly reduced the already tiny number of peasant, worker and non-Russian deputies. The new law allotted one elector to 230 voters in the landowner curia, 1,000 voters in the first urban curia (big bourgeoisie), 15,000 voters in the second urban curia (other urban voters), 60,000 voters in the peasant curia, and 125,000 in the worker curia. As a result of the June Third Election Law, the Third and Fourth Dumas were mainly Black-Hundred and Cadet in composition.   p. 48

¹⁶ The *"patriarchal slogans" of Katkov and Pobedonostsev* was the name Lenin gave to their demand for the "inalienability" of peasant allotments, the preservation of the village commune and other survivals of serfdom. Katkov was the editor of the reactionary *Moskovskiye Vedomosti* (*Moscow Recorder*) and Pobedonostsev was the Procurator General of the Synod; both were ardent advocates of the policy of privileges for the landed nobility, pursued by Alexander III.   p. 49

¹⁷ This refers to a reactionary organisation, the *Council of the United Nobility*, founded in May 1906. The Council exercised considerable influence over the policy of the tsarist government. Lenin called it the "Council of the United Feudalists".   p. 49

¹⁸ *Russkoye Bogatstvo* (*Russian Wealth*)—a monthly magazine published in St. Petersburg from 1876 to the middle of 1918. In the early 1890s it became an organ of the liberal Narodniks. From 1906 onwards the magazine was actually the organ of the Popular Socialist Party, a semi-Cadet organisation. In this period Lenin defined the policy of *Russkoye Bogatstvo* as "Narodnik, Narodnik-Cadet".   p. 50

¹⁹ The law referred to was promulgated on June 23 (July 6), 1912; it provided for insurance against illness and accidents and was adopted by the Third Duma under pressure from the working-class movement. The law covered only 20 per cent of all industrial workers and did not provide benefits in cases of disablement, old age and unemployment.

The Bolshevik Party organised a mass campaign for the expansion of workers' insurance, thereby strengthening its influence among the working-class masses.   p. 50

[20] The struggle within the Austrian Social-Democratic Party resulted in the fragmentation of the united party into six national Social-Democratic parties—German, Czech, Polish, Ruthenian, Italian and South-Slav. There was constant friction between these parties.   p. 51

[21] The Social-Democrat Bolshevik organisations in the Caucasus united the advanced proletarians of many nationalities.   p. 51

[22] The reference is to the shooting of unarmed workers in the Lena Goldfields (Siberia) on April 4 (17), 1912.
News of the bloody drama in the Lena Goldfields aroused the wrath of the working class throughout Russia; there were street demonstrations, meetings and protest strikes all over the country. The Social-Democratic Duma group submitted a question to the tsarist government on the Lena shootings. The insolent answer given by the Tsar's Minister Makarov: "So it has been, and so it will be in the future" served to increase the indignation of the workers. Up to 300,000 workers took part in strikes of protest against the Lena shootings. The strikes merged with the May Day strikes in which 400,000 workers took part.   p. 52

[23] *Promyshlennost i Torgovlya (Industry and Commerce)*—the organ of the council of congresses of industrial and commercial representatives; the journal was published in St. Petersburg from January 1908 to December 1917. It expressed the views of the big industrial and commercial bourgeoisie.   p. 59

[24] *Kit Kitych*—the nickname of Tit Titych (*Kit* in Russian means "whale"), a rich merchant in A. N. Ostrovsky's comedy *Shouldering Another's Troubles*. Lenin applies the epithet to capitalist tycoons.   p. 59

[25] *Zemstvos*—the name by which local self-government bodies in the rural districts were known; they were set up in the central gubernias of tsarist Russia in 1864. The Zemstvos were dominated by the nobility and their competence was limited to purely local economic and welfare matters (hospital and road building, statistics, insurance, etc.). They functioned under the control of the governors of the gubernias and the Ministry of the Interior, which could block any decisions the government found undesirable. p. 59

[26] *F. D.*—F. Dan, one of the leading Menshevik liquidators.   p. 63

[27] *Luch (The Ray)*—legal daily newspaper published in St. Petersburg from September 1912 to July 1913 by the Menshevik liquidators.   p. 63

[28] *Khlestakov*—the hero of Gogol's *Inspector-General*; an inveterate braggart and liar.

Nozdryov—a character from Gogol's *Dead Souls*; a brawling landowner and swindler.   p. 63

[29] As early as the summer of 1912, Lenin had spoken of the need to publish a legal working-class newspaper in Moscow. "Every politically conscious worker realises that St. Petersburg without Moscow is like one hand without the other," he wrote. "... Moscow will of course have to have a workers' daily newspaper of *its own.*" Nevertheless Lenin considered it necessary to consolidate *Pravda* and then start the newspaper in Moscow—*Moscow Pravda*, he called it in a letter to Maxim Gorky. The question of publishing a Party newspaper in Moscow was discussed at the Conference of Central Committee members in Poronin on July 27 (August 9), 1913.

A campaign to collect funds for a Moscow newspaper began in December 1912 after a letter had appeared in *Pravda* (No. 176, November 24, 1912) from a group of Moscow workers pointing out the importance and the feasibility of launching a working-class newspaper in Moscow; the letter also appealed for collections to be made for a newspaper fund. The appeal was taken up energetically by the workers, but the appearance of the paper was delayed by the arrest of a group of Bolsheviks making preparations for its issue. The first issue of the Moscow workers' newspaper appeared on August 25 (September 7), 1913 and was called *Nash Put (Our Path).*   p. 64

[30] *Rus (Russia) (Molva [Tidings], Novaya Rus [New Russia], Oko [The Eye])*—the various names under which a bourgeois-liberal newspaper was published in St. Petersburg from 1903 to 1910. p. 67

[31] *Marshal of the Nobility*—the elected representative of the nobility of a gubernia or uyezd. He was in charge of all the affairs of the nobility, occupied an influential position in the administration and took the chair at meetings of the Zemstvo.   p. 70

[32] *Russkaya Mysl (Russian Thought)*—a monthly bourgeois liberal magazine that began publication in Moscow in 1880. After the 1905 Revolution it became the organ of the Right wing of the Cadet Party. In this period of its existence Lenin referred to it as "Black-Hundred Thought". The magazine was suppressed in mid-1918.
                                                                       p. 72

[33] *Vekhi (Landmarks)*—a symposium issued in Moscow in the spring of 1909 by counter-revolutionary bourgeois liberal journalists. In articles on the Russian intelligentsia, the *Vekhi* writers attempted to denigrate the revolutionary-democratic traditions of the liberation movement in Russia and the views and activities of the prominent revolutionary democrats of the nineteenth century— V. Belinsky, N. Dobrolyubov, N. Chernyshevsky and D. Pisarev. They reviled the revolutionary movement of 1905 and thanked

the tsarist government for having saved the bourgeoisie from "the fury of the people with its bayonets and jails". p. 72

³⁴ *Kievskaya Mysl* (*Kiev Thought*)—a liberal-bourgeois daily published from December 1906 to December 1918. The Menshevik liquidators were closely connected with the paper. p. 74

³⁵ *Zemshchina* (*Land Affairs*)—a Black-Hundred daily published in St. Petersburg from July 1909 to February 1917. It was subsidised by the tsarist government and the Council of the United Nobility. p. 78

³⁶ *Novoye Vremya* (*New Times*)—a daily newspaper published in St. Petersburg from 1868 to October 1917. It was at first a moderately liberal paper but towards the end of the 1870s it became an organ of reactionary nobility and bureaucratic circles. The paper conducted a struggle not only against the revolutionary movement, but also against the liberal-bourgeois movement; from 1905 onwards it was one of the organs of the Black Hundreds. Lenin referred to *Novoye Vremya* as an example of the venal press. p. 78

³⁷ *Derzhimorda*—the name of a policeman in Gogol's *Inspector-General*, a boorish, insolent oppressor, a man of violence. p. 86

³⁸ The decisions here referred to were Draft Terms for the Union of the Bund with the R.S.D.L.P. (adopted at the Fourth [Unity] Congress of the R.S.D.L.P. in 1906) and the resolution on "The Unity of National Organisations in the Localities" (adopted at the Fifth [All-Russian] Conference of the R.S.D.L.P. in 1908). p. 87

³⁹ *Nasha Zarya* (*Our Dawn*)—a Menshevik liquidator monthly published legally in St. Petersburg from 1910 to 1914. It served as a rallying centre for the liquidationist forces in Russia. p. 88

⁴⁰ *Torgovo-Promyshlennaya Gazeta* (*Commercial and Industrial Gazette*)—government daily published in St. Petersburg from 1893 to September 1918. The newspaper carried statistics and economic reviews of industry, trade, agriculture and finance. p. 96

⁴¹ The June Third Law (see Note 15) marked the beginning of the period known as the "Stolypin reaction" (also the June Third system). p. 103

⁴² Lenin here refers to the decisions passed by the Fifth (All-Russian) Conference of tne R.S.D.L.P. held in Paris between December 21 and December 27, 1908 (January 3-9, 1909). The Conference was attended by 16 delegates with full powers: five Bolsheviks, three Mensheviks, five Polish Social-Democrats and three Bundists. Lenin represented the Central Committee of the R.S.D.L.P.; he delivered a report on "The Tasks of the Party in the Present Situation"; he also spoke on the Social-Democratic Duma group and on organisational and other questions. At the Conference the Bolsheviks fought two opportunist trends in the Party—liquidationism

and otzovism. On Lenin's proposal the Conference condemned liquidationism and called upon all Party organisations to struggle resolutely against all attempts to liquidate the Party. Bolshevik resolutions on all questions were adopted.   p. 109

[43] "In 1912" refers to the decisions of the Sixth (Prague) All-Russian Conference of the R.S.D.L.P. held from January 5 (18) to January 17(30), 1912, which actually fulfilled the functions of a Party congress. Lenin guided the work of the Conference.

The important business of the Conference was that of purging the Party of opportunists. The resolutions adopted on "Liquidationism and the Group of Liquidators" and on "The Party Organisation Abroad" were of great importance both from the theoretical and from the practical points of view. The liquidators grouped around two legal publications, *Nasha Zarya* (*Our Dawn*) and *Dyelo Zhizni* (*Life's Cause*). The Conference put on record "that by its conduct the *Nasha Zarya* and *Dyelo Zhizni* group had definitely placed itself outside the Party". The liquidators were expelled from the R.S.D.L.P. The Conference condemned the activities of anti-Party groups abroad—the *Golos* group of Mensheviks, the *Vperyod* group and Trotsky's group. It recognised the absolute necessity for a single Party organisation abroad promoting Party interests under the guidance and control of the Central Committee and resolved that groups abroad "which refuse to submit to the Russian centre of Social-Democratic activity, i.e., to the Central Committee, and which cause disorganisation by communicating with Russia independently and ignoring the Central Committee, have no right to use the name of the R.S.D.L.P." These resolutions played an important part in strengthening the unity of the Marxist party in Russia.

The Prague Conference played an outstanding part in the organisation of the Bolshevik Party, a party of a new type. It summed up a whole historical epoch of the struggle of the Bolsheviks against the Mensheviks and strengthened the victory of the Bolsheviks. Party organisations in all localities were consolidated on the basis of the Conference decisions; the Conference also strengthened the Party as an all-Russian organisation, and outlined the political line and tactics of the Party under conditions of the new revolutionary upsurge. The Bolshevik Party, purged of the opportunists, headed a mighty new upsurgence of the revolutionary mass struggle.

The Prague Conference was of great international significance. It offered revolutionary elements in the parties of the Second International a model of determined struggle against opportunism, pursuing the struggle as far as complete organisational rupture with the opportunists.   p. 109

[44] "In 1913" refers to the Joint Conference of the Central Committee of the R.S.D.L.P. and Party officials held in Cracow from December 26, 1912 to January 1, 1913 (January 8-14, 1913). Underground Party organisations in St. Petersburg, Moscow Region, the South, the Urals and the Caucasus were represented. Lenin presided over

the Conference and spoke on "The Revolutionary Upsurge, Strikes and the Party's Tasks" and on "The Attitude to Liquidationism, and Unity" (the texts of these speeches have been lost); Lenin also compiled or edited all the Conference resolutions and wrote the "Notification" of the Central Committee of the R.S.D.L.P. on the Conference.

The Conference took decisions on the most important questions of the working-class movement—the tasks of the Party in connection with the new revolutionary upsurge and the growth of the strike movement, the building of the underground organisation, the work of the Social-Democratic Duma group, the insurance campaign, the Party press, the national Social-Democratic organisations, the struggle against liquidationism and the unity of the party of the proletariat.

The decisions of the Conference played an important part in strengthening the Party and its unity, in extending and consolidating the Party's contacts with the masses, and in the elaboration of new forms of Party work fitted to the mounting activity of the working-class movement. The Resolutions of the Cracow Conference were confirmed by the Central Committee of the R.S.D.L.P.   p. 109

[45] Lenin wrote this Draft Platform for the Latvian Bolsheviks in May 1913, when preparations were being made to convene the Fourth Congress of the Social-Democrats of the Latvian Area. It was a time when the struggle between the Bolsheviks and Mensheviks in the Latvian Social-Democratic Party had become sharper; all the central positions in the Party had been seized by Menshevik liquidators and conciliators. The Latvian Bolsheviks formed their own group with the support of Bolshevik-minded workers. Lenin helped them in their struggle against the liquidationist leadership.

The Bolshevik leaders of the Latvian Social-Democrats set up their centre abroad—the Bureau of Groups Abroad—and published Lenin's platform as a reprint from No. 8 of their *Bilitens (Bulletin)* under the heading "Our Platform for the Fourth Congress of Social-Democrats of the Latvian Area". The Draft Platform was republished in issue No. 9-10 of the *Bilitens*. The editors of the *Bilitens*, influenced by the conciliatory elements among them, omitted the section of the platform dealing with the national question, and made some alterations and deletions in other sections.   p. 110

[46] *An*—pseudonym of N. N. Jordania, leader of the Caucasian Mensheviks.   p. 110

[47] *Vperyod* group—an anti-Party group consisting of otzovists, ultimatumists, god-builders, empirio-monists (supporters of the reactionary idealist philosophy of Mach and Avenarius); it was organised abroad in December 1909 and was headed by A. Bogdanov and G. Alexinsky; there were several small circles, mainly of intellectuals, in Paris, Geneva and Tiflis. The views of the *Vpe-*

ryod group were, to use Lenin's words, "a caricature of Bolshevism". The group found no support among the workers and disintegrated in 1913.   p. 114

[48] The programme referred to is the Austrian Social-Democratic Party's Programme on the National Question adopted at the Congress in Brünn (Brno) in September 1899.   p. 117

[49] See K. Marx and F. Engels, "Manifesto of the Communist Party", *Selected Works*, Vol. I, Moscow, 1955, p. 42.   p. 121

[50] Until 1954 this article was known under the heading given by the editors "Apropos of Cadet Maklakov's Speech". In 1954 the Institute of Marxism-Leninism of the C.C.,C.P.S.U. received a number of documents from the Cracow-Poronin Lenin archive, among them Lenin's list of articles written for *Pravda*, from which it was established that Lenin had entitled this article "An Incorrect Appraisal (*Luch* on Maklakov)".   p. 132

[51] *Russkiye Vedomosti (Russian Recorder)*—a daily newspaper published in Moscow from 1863 onwards by liberal professors of Moscow University and Zemstvo officials; it expressed the views of the liberal landowners and bourgeoisie. From 1905 onwards it was an organ of the Right Cadets; shortly after the October Revolution in 1917 it was suppressed.   p. 135

[52] Lenin prepared this draft speech for a Bolshevik deputy to the Duma; the speech was delivered on June 4 (17), 1913 by A. E. Badayev during the debate on the Budget Committee's report on estimates of the Ministry of Education for 1913. The greater part of Lenin's draft was read almost word for word by Badayev, but he did not finish the speech. When he read the sentence "Does not this government deserve to be driven out by the people?" he was deprived of the right to speak.   p. 137

[53] The reference is to the Menshevik agrarian municipalisation programme adopted at the Fourth (Unity) Congress of the R.S.D.L.P. Lenin criticised this programme in his "Report on the Unity Congress of the R.S.D.L.P." (see Vol. 10) and "The Agrarian Programme of Social-Democracy in the First Russian Revolution, 1905-07" (see Vol. 13).   p. 152

[54] *Pro-Party Mensheviks*—a small group of Mensheviks led by Plekhanov that broke with the Menshevik liquidators and opposed liquidationism in the 1908-12 period.   p. 152

[55] Lenin quotes from the decision condemning liquidationism and otzovism adopted by the January 1910 Plenary Meeting of the Central Committee of the R.S.D.L.P. on the question: "The State of Affairs in the Party".   p. 154

[56] *Vozrozhdeniye (Regeneration)*—a legal journal published by Menshevik liquidators in Moscow from December 1908 to July 1910.
                                                p. 156

[57] *Nevsky Golos* (*Neva Voice*)—a legal newspaper published by Menshevik liquidators in St. Petersburg from May to August 1912. p. 157

[58] Lenin refers to the *law*, promulgated on *December 11* (*24*), *1905*, on the convening of a "legislative" State Duma; the law was promulgated by the tsarist government when the Moscow insurrection was at its height. The First Duma, elected under this law, had a Cadet majority. p. 162

[59] By "*Sabler's parsons*" Lenin means the orthodox priests who were drawn into active participation in the election to the Fourth Duma on instructions issued by the reactionary Sabler, Procurator General of the Synod, to ensure the election of deputies amenable to the tsarist government. p. 162

[60] *Narodniks*—supporters of Narodism, the petty-bourgeois trend in the Russian revolutionary movement in the sixties in the eighties of the last century. The Narodniks campaigned for the abolition of the autocracy and the transfer of landed estates to the peasants. They denied that in accordance with the regular laws of capitalism, capitalist relations and a proletariat were developing in Russia and, as a consequence of this, considered the peasantry to be the chief revolutionary force; they regarded the village commune as an embryonic form of socialism. The Narodniks, therefore, went out to the villages to arouse the peasants to struggle against the autocracy. The Narodniks proceeded from a false premise on the role of the class struggle in history, believing that history is made by heroes, who are passively followed by the masses. The Narodniks adopted terrorist tactics in their struggle against tsarism.

In the eighties and nineties of the nineteenth century the Narodniks adopted a conciliatory policy towards tsarism, began to fight for the interests of the kulaks and conducted a stubborn struggle against Marxism. p. 162

[61] *Stolypin*—Minister of the Interior and Chairman of the Council of Ministers from 1906 to 1911. With his name are connected the suppression of the First Russian Revolution (1905-07) and the period of brutal political reaction that followed.

Stolypin workers' party—was the name given by the Russian workers to the Menshevik liquidators who adapted themselves to the Stolypin regime and, at the cost of renouncing the programme and tactics of the R.S.D.L.P., attempted to obtain the sanction of the tsarist government to establish an open, legal, allegedly working-class party. p. 166

[62] *L. S.* (*L. Sedov*)—pseudonym of the Menshevik liquidator B. A. Ginsburg. p. 166

[63] The articles referred to were published by M. S. Olminsky (Vitimsky) in *Pravda* No. 106 and No. 123 on May 10 and May 30, 1913 under the heading "Who Is on Whose Side?" and "The Truth". p. 170

[64] This letter to the editors of *Pravda* was evoked by the publication of a declaration by A. Bogdanov in *Pravda* No. 120 on May 26, 1913. Bogdanov tried to deny Lenin's point that the renunciation of work in the Duma and the use of other legal possibilities were connected with the *Vperyod* line (see p. 154 of this volume). In a comment to Bogdanov's letter made by the editors, it was stated that Bogdanov's declaration had been published for "purposes of objectivity"; this Lenin vehemently objected to.

In answer to this comment Lenin sent, together with this letter, an article (unpublished at that time and not found since) against Bogdanov's distortion of Party history. On a number of occasions Lenin warned the editorial board that Bogdanov's collaboration with a Bolshevik newspaper was impermissible. On Lenin's demand Bogdanov was excluded from the list of *Pravda* contributors after he had written an article, "Ideology", which contained open propaganda of Machist views.   p. 173

[65] *Otzovism* (from *otozvat*—to recall)—an opportunist trend that took shape among Bolsheviks after the defeat of the Revolution of 1905-07. The otzovists believed that under the conditions obtaining in the period of reaction the Party should conduct only underground work; they demanded the recall of the Social-Democratic deputies from the Duma and refused to participate in trade unions and other legal and semi-legal working-class organisations. The policy advocated by the otzovists would have alienated the Party from the masses and converted it into an isolated sect.   p. 173

[66] *Domov*—pseudonym of M. N. Pokrovsky.   p. 174

[67] *Volsky, Stanislav*—pseudonym of A. V. Sokolov.   p. 174

[68] *Stepinsky*—pseudonym of V. R. Menzhinsky.   p. 174

[69] The publication referred to is *Der čechoslavische Sozialdemokrat.*   p. 176

[70] By "*Prussian Octobrists and Cadets*" Lenin meant the Progressives, the party of the Prussian liberal bourgeoisie.   p. 178

[71] Lenin prepared this speech for a Bolshevik deputy to the Duma. It was delivered by N. R. Shagov on June 9 (22), 1913, during the debate on the Budget Committee's report on the estimates of the Department of State Lands. The speech aroused shouts from the Right deputies and the speaker was several times warned by the chairman that he would be deprived of the right to speak for breaking the rule prohibiting the reading of speeches. Shagov was forced to leave out a number of passages from Lenin's text; about half the speech was delivered.   p. 180

[72] The *village commune* in Russia was a communal form of peasant land tenure characterised by compulsory crop rotation and undi-

vided woods and pastures. Its principal features were collective liability (compulsory collective responsibility of the peasants for making their payments in full and on time, and the performance of various services to the state and the landowners), the regular reallotment of the land with no right to refuse the allotment given, the prohibition of its purchase and sale.

The Russian village commune dates back to ancient times and in the course of historical development gradually became one of the mainstays of feudalism in Russia. The landowners and the tsarist government used the village commune to intensify feudal oppression and to squeeze redemption payment and taxes out of the people. Lenin pointed out that the village commune "does not save the peasant from turning into a proletarian, yet in practice acts as a medieval barrier dividing the peasants, who are, as it were, chained to small associations and to categories which have lost all 'reason for existence'". (See present edition, Vol. 15, p. 78.)

The problem of the village commune aroused heated arguments and brought an extensive economic literature into existence. Particularly great interest in the commune was displayed by the Narodniks, who saw in it the guarantee of Russia's socialist evolution by a special path. By tendentiously selecting facts and falsifying them and employing so-called "average figures", the Narodniks sought to prove that the commune peasantry in Russia possessed a special sort of "stability", and that the peasant commune protected the peasants against the penetration of capitalist relations into their lives, and saved them from ruin and class differentiation. As early as the 1880s, G. V. Plekhanov had shown that the Narodnik illusions about "commune socialism" were unfounded, and in the 1890s Lenin completely refuted the Narodnik theories. Lenin brought forward a tremendous amount of statistical material and innumerable facts to show how capitalist relations were developing in the Russian village, and how capital, by penetrating the patriarchal village commune, was splitting the peasantry into two antagonistic classes, the kulaks and the poor peasants.

In 1906 the tsarist Minister Stolypin issued a law favouring the kulaks that allowed the peasants to leave the commune and sell their allotments. This law laid the basis for the official abolition of the village commune system and intensified the differentiation among the peasants. In the nine years following the promulgation of the law, over two million peasant families withdrew from the communes.   p. 180

[73] This expression originated during the Russo-Turkish War, 1877-78. There was heavy fighting in the Shipka Pass but the headquarters of the Russian Army issued communiqués stating "All quiet on Shipka". The expression was used ironically in respect of those who tried to hide the true state of affairs.   p. 185

[74] The Stolypin reforms were agrarian laws promulgated in 1906 and 1907. On November 9 (22), 1906 a law was published giving peas-

ants the right to withdraw from the communes and giving them the title to their allotment lands. Before this (on August 12 [25]) a law was passed on the sale of some of the crown lands and (August 27 [September 9]) on the sale of state lands through the Peasant Bank. Later, on November 15 (28), a law was passed permitting loans to peasants from the Peasant Land Bank on the security of peasant allotments.   p. 191

[75] This refers to the Slavophil demonstrations organised by reactionary nationalist elements in St. Petersburg on March 17, 18 and 24 (March 30 and 31 and April 6), 1913 on the occasion of the Serbo-Bulgarian victories over the Turks during the first Balkan War. The reactionaries tried to use the national liberation struggle of the Balkan peoples in the interests of the expansionist, Great-Power politics of Russian tsarism in the Near East.   p. 219

[76] The strike referred to here took place in Belgium from April 14 to April 24 (N. S.), 1913. It was a general strike of the Belgian proletariat demanding a constitutional reform—the introduction of universal suffrage. Of the more than one million Belgian workers, between 400,000 and 500,000 took part in the strike. The development of the strike was regularly reported in *Pravda*, and lists of Russian workers' contributions in aid of the strike were also printed.   p. 221

[77] April 4, 1913 was the first anniversary of the shooting of workers in the Lena Goldfields; it was marked by a one-day strike of St. Petersburg workers in which over 85,000 people participated.   p. 224

[78] The Organising Committee was the Menshevik guiding centre; it was formed at the liquidators' conference in August 1912 and functioned until the election of the Central Committee of the Menshevik Party in August 1917.   p. 229

[79] *The elections to the Executive of the St. Petersburg Metalworkers' Union* took place on April 21 (May 4), 1913. The election meeting was attended by 800 metalworkers and 400 others were unable to crowd into the premises where the meeting was held. The Bolsheviks proposed a list of candidates that had been published in *Pravda* No. 91 and distributed beforehand among those attending the meeting. Despite the insistence on the part of the liquidators that candidates be elected irrespective of political allegiance, the overwhelming majority of those present voted for the *Pravda* list. Ten members out of fourteen were elected to the Executive from the *Pravda* list.   p. 230

[80] *Diskussionny Listok (The Discussion Bulletin)*—supplement to the newspaper *Sotsial-Demokrat*, Central Organ of the R.S.D.L.P., published in accordance with a decision taken by the January (1910) Plenary Meeting of the Central Committee of the R.S.D.L.P. from March 1910 to April 1911 in Paris. There were three issues.

Diskussionny Listok No. 2, published on May 25 (June 7), 1910 contained the final part of Lenin's "Notes of a Publicist". (See Vol. 16, pp. 195-259.) p. 230

[81] *Der Kampf* (*The Struggle*)—a monthly published by the Austrian Social-Democratic Party; it was opportunist, centrist in trend, and concealed its betrayal of the cause of the proletarian revolution and its service to the counter-revolutionary bourgeoisie by Leftist phrases; it was published in Vienna from 1907 to 1938. p. 230

[82] *Russkoye Slovo* (*Russian Word*)—a bourgeois liberal daily published in Moscow from 1895 to November 1917; it appeared again for several months in 1918 under the title *Nashe Slovo* (*Our Word*). p. 235

[83] *Plehve, V. K.* (1846-1904)—a reactionary statesman; from 1867 he served in the Department of Justice; as public prosecutor he conducted the investigation for and took part in the Narodnaya Volya trial. In 1902 he became Minister of the Interior and Chief of the Gendarmerie, in which posts he did everything possible to stifle the growing revolutionary movement, dealing ruthlessly with workers' strikes and demonstrations and with the peasant movement; he tried to break up the working-class movement by means of provocations, etc. In 1904 he was assassinated by the Socialist-Revolutionary Sazonov. p. 238

[84] See K. Marx and F. Engels, "Manifesto of the Communist Party", *Selected Works*, Vol. I, Moscow, 1955, p. 36. p. 241

[85] These theses were written by Lenin for his lectures on the national question delivered on July 9, 10, 11 and 13 (N. S.), 1913 in the Swiss towns of Zurich, Geneva, Lausanne and Berne. p. 243

[86] The decisions of the Prague Conference (1912) called the relations that the national Social-Democratic organisations had with the R.S.D.L.P. from 1907 to 1911 *"federation of the worst type"*. Although the Social-Democratic organisations of Poland, Lithuania and the Latvian Area, and also the Bund, belonged to the R.S.D.L.P., they actually held themselves aloof. Their representatives did not take part in guiding all-Russian Party work; directly or indirectly they promoted the anti-Party activities of the liquidators. (See Vol. 17, pp. 464-65 and Vol. 18, pp. 411-12.) p. 250

[87] *Russkaya Molva* (*Russian Tidings*)—a bourgeois daily, organ of the Progressists, founded in 1912. Lenin called the Progressists a mixture of Octobrists and Cadets. The paper appeared in St. Petersburg in 1912 and 1913. p. 250

[88] *Narodowa Demokracja* (*National Democracy*)—a reactionary, chauvinist party of the Polish bourgeoisie, founded in 1897. Afraid

of the growing revolutionary movement, the party changed its original demand for Polish independence to one for limited autonomy within the framework of the autocracy. During the 1905-07 Revolution, Narodowa Demokracja was the main party of Polish counter-revolution, the Polish Black Hundreds, to use Lenin's expression. They supported the Octobrists in the State Duma.

In 1919 the party changed its name to Zwiazek Ludowo-Narodowy (National-Popular Union) and from 1928 it became the Stronnictwo Narodowe (National Party). After the Second World War, individuals from this party, having no longer any party of their own, attached themselves to Mikolajczyk's reactionary party, the Polske Stronnictwo Ludowe (Polish Popular Party).
p 250

[89] This refers to the segregation of the schools according to nationality, one of the basic demands of the bourgeois-nationalist programme for "cultural-national autonomy"   p. 251

[90] The Fourth Duma adjourned for the summer vacation after the first session. The summer vacation lasted from June 25 to October 15 (July 8 to October 28), 1913.   p 258

[91] *Leipziger Volkszeitung* (*Leipzig People's Newspaper*)—the organ of the Left wing of the German Social-Democratic Party, published daily from 1894 to 1933; for a number of years it was edited by Franz Mehring and Rosa Luxemburg. From 1917 to 1922 it was the organ of the German "Independents", and after 1922 it became the organ of the Right Social-Democrats   p. 260

[92] *Sovremenka* refers to *Sovremennoye Slovo* (*Contemporary Word*)— a Cadet daily published in St. Petersburg from 1907 to 1918. p. 262

[93] *Rossiya* (*Russia*)—a Black-Hundred daily published in St. Petersburg from 1905 to 1914. From 1906 onwards it was the organ of the Ministry of the Interior. Lenin called it "a venal police newspaper"   p. 262

[94] The Bolshevik Deputy, G. I. Petrovsky, spoke at the session of the State Duma on May 20 (June 2), 1913, during the debate on the estimates of the Ministry of the Interior. The speech was drafted by Lenin. In a letter dated April 18 (May 1), 1913, sent by Nadezhda Krupskaya from Cracow to St. Petersburg on Lenin's instructions, she said that every effort must be made to deliver the speech in full on account of its outstanding importance. The manuscript of the draft has not been found   p. 266

[95] *Trudoviks*, *Trudovik group*—also known as the peasant group; a group of petty-bourgeois democrats formed in April 1906 by peasant deputies to the First Duma They demanded the abolition of all social-estate and national restrictions. democratisation of the rural and urban local government bodies. and universal suffrage

in elections to the State Duma. Their agrarian programme was
based on the Narodnik principle of equalitarian land tenure and
envisaged the formation of a national land fund to include state,
crown and monastery lands, as well as private holdings exceeding
the area that could be tilled by the owner's family, with payment of compensation for land alienated from private owners. The
implementation of the land reform was to be entrusted to local
peasant committees.   p. 268

[96] Lenin refers here to an article in the *Neue Rheinische Zeitung* "The
Berlin Debates on the Revolution" ("Die Berliner Debatte über
die Revolution") (Karl Marx, Friedrich Engels, *Werke*, Bd. V,
Dietz Verlag, Berlin, 1959).   p. 271

[97] *Frankfurter Zeitung (Frankfort Newspaper)* —a bourgeois daily
published in Frankfort-on-Main from 1856 to 1943.   p. 275

[98] *L. M.—L. Martov*, one of the Menshevik leaders.   p. 285

[99] *Rural superintendent*—an administrative post introduced by the
tsarist government in 1889 to increase the power of the landowners
over the peasantry. The rural superintendents, appointed from
among the local landed nobility, were granted tremendous powers,
not only administrative, but juridical, which included the right
to arrest peasants and order corporal punishment.   p. 289

[100] *Der Sozialdemokrat (Social-Democrat)*—the illegal organ of
the German Social-Democratic Party published from 1879 to
1890.   p. 299

[101] The speeches referred to are "The Attack on the Fundamental
Views and Tactics of the Party" delivered at the Congress of
the German Social-Democratic Party in Hanover (October 9-14,
1899); "The Tactics of the Party" and "Collaboration with
the Bourgeois Press" delivered at the Dresden Congress (September 13-20, 1903).   p. 300

[102] *Bulygin Duma*—the advisory representative institution that the
tsarist government promised to convene in 1905. The draft of a law
founding an advisory State Duma and the election procedure were
elaborated by a commission under the chairmanship of Minister
of the Interior Bulygin and promulgated on August 6 (19), 1905.
The Bolsheviks declared an active boycott of the Bulygin Duma and
put it into effect; the government was unable to convene the Duma, its attempts to do so being foiled by the political general strike
of October 1905.   p. 304

[103] This refers to Lassalle's well-known thesis that all other classes
constitute one reactionary mass as compared with the working class.
The thesis was included in the programme of the Socialist Workers'
Party of Germany adopted at the Gotha Congress in 1875.

Marx criticised this anti-revolutionary thesis in his "Critique of
the Gotha Programme". (See K. Marx and F. Engels, *Selected
Works*, Vol. II, Moscow, 1958, pp. 25-27).   p. 304

[104] *Saltykova, Darya Ivanovna* (1730-1801)—a serf-owner notorious
for her brutal treatment of her serfs.   p. 310

[105] *Decree allotment*—was fixed by the law of February 19, 1861. In
the black-earth and non-black-earth regions two sizes of allotment
were fixed, a higher and a lower (the latter being one-third of the
former), but for the steppe areas, because of the abundance of land,
only one type of allotment was fixed by special decree and was
known as the "decree allotment".   p. 337

[106] *G. R.* (*G. Rakitin*)—pseudonym of the Menshevik liquidator V. O.
Tsederbaum.   p. 343

[107] Karl Marx, *Theories of Surplus Value* (*Theorien über den Mehr-
wert*. 2. Teil. Dietz Verlag, Berlin, 1959, S. 36).   p. 344

[108] The Executive of the St. Petersburg Metalworkers' Union was re-
elected on August 25 (September 7), 1913. The meeting was attended
by about 3,000 workers. Despite the efforts of the liquidators to
turn the meeting against the Bolshevik Executive of the union, a
resolution of thanks to the Executive for its work was adopted by an
overwhelming majority. The list of candidates, first voted on, put
up by the liquidators obtained about 150 votes; the Bolshevik
list, published in *Severnaya Pravda*, was adopted by a vast
majority.   p. 350

[109] When this article was published in *Nash Put* (*Our Path*) it was accompanied by the following editorial comment: "The editors offer
the author their apologies for the *necessary* deletions and amendments to his article." Exactly what changes were made is not known
since Lenin's manuscript has not been found.   p. 358

[110] *Justice*—a weekly founded in London in 1884 as the central organ
of the Social Democratic Federation of Great Britain; from 1911
onwards it was the organ of the British Socialist Party. When the
party was split in 1916 it became the organ of the minority of social-
chauvinists; it continued publication until 1925.
In 1902 and 1903, Lenin's *Iskra* was printed by the *Justice*
press.   p. 369

[111] *Manilov*—a character from Gogol's *Dead Souls*, a chatterbox and
empty day-dreamer whose name has become a synonym for the
passive, easy-going attitude to reality typical of such charac-
ters.   p. 378

[112] *The Law of March 4 (17), 1906*—temporary rules for associations,
unions and meetings—permitted their organisation but placed so

many obstacles in their way that the law was practically reduced to nought. The law granted the Minister of the Interior the right to suppress associations and unions at his own discretion and also to refuse the registration of new unions.

The Law of December 2 (15), 1905 was the name given to the temporary regulations under which strikers were subject to conviction as criminals.   p. 386

113 *Yeniseiskaya Mysl (Yenisei Thought)*—a daily bourgeois liberal newspaper published in Krasnoyarsk from 1912 to 1915.   p. 391

114 *Grazhdanin (The Citizen)*—a reactionary magazine published in St. Petersburg from 1872 to 1914. From the 1880s it was the organ of the extreme monarchists and was edited by Prince Meshchersky and financed by the government. It had a small circulation but was influential in bureaucratic circles.   p. 392

115 This description of the evolution of tsarism in the period of the Stolypin reaction is quoted from a resolution of the Fifth (All-Russian) Conference of the R.S.D.L.P., held in 1908.   p. 401

116 The *Brest (Tenth) Congress of the French Socialist Party*—was held in the town of Brest, March 23-25, 1913.   p. 406

117 This refers to the Fourth Congress of Commercial and Industrial Employees held in Moscow, June 29-July 3 (July 12-16), 1913. The Congress was attended by 378 delegates. The Bolsheviks, who were supported by almost half the delegates, also had the support of the Left Narodnik section of the Congress, which gave them the majority. The liquidators were represented by an insignificant group. Detailed reports of the Congress were published in *Pravda*. The Congress was closed by order of the Minister of the Interior. p. 410

118 Lenin is here quoting, with some words changed, from Nekrasov's poem "A Man of the Forties":
> *But at times avoids an issue,*
> *That is urgent, that alarms....*   p. 413

119 The *Joint Conference of the Central Committee of the R.S.D.L.P. and Party Officials* (for purposes of secrecy it was known as "the summer" or "August" Conference), was held from September 23 to October 1 (October 6-14), 1913 in the village of Poronin (near Cracow) where Lenin spent the summer months. The Conference was attended by twenty-two delegates (17 with a vote and 5 with voice but no vote). Sixteen delegates represented local Party organisations: St. Petersburg—Inessa Armand, A. Y. Badayev and A. V. Shotman; Moscow and the Central Industrial Area—F. A. Balashov, Y. T. Novozhilov, R. V. Malinovsky and A. I. Lobov (the two last-named were found to be provocateurs); Ekaterinoslav—G. I. Petrovsky; Kharkov—M. K. Muranov; Kostroma—N. R. Shagov; Kiev—Y. F. Rozmirovich ("Galina"); Urals—S. I. Deryabina ("Sima", "Elena"). Lenin, Krupskaya, Troyanovsky and others

represented the Central Committee Bureau Abroad, the Central Organ of the Party *Sotsial-Demokrat* and the magazine *Prosveshcheniye*. The Bolshevik deputies to the Fourth Duma also represented the Party organisations in the constituencies and towns that elected them to the Duma. Representatives of the Left wing of the Polish Social-Democratic Party, J. S. Hanecki, G. Kamenski ("Domski") and others attended; these delegates had a voice but no vote.

The Conference discussed the following questions: (1) reports from the localities, report on the work of the Polish Social-Democrats, report on the work of the Central Committee; (2) the national question; (3) the work of Social-Democrats in the Duma; (4) the situation in the Social-Democratic Duma group; (5) the question of organisation and the Party congress; (6) the strike movement; (7) work in legal associations; (8) the Narodniks; (9) the Party press; (10) the forthcoming International Socialist Congress in Vienna. The first two days were devoted to a private conference of the Duma deputies on questions of practical work in the Duma.

Lenin guided the work of the Conference; he opened the meeting with an introductory speech and delivered reports on the work of the Central Committee, the national question and the International Socialist Congress in Vienna; Lenin also spoke on almost all the points of the agenda, made proposals and compiled or edited the draft resolutions.

Reports from the localities told of the growth of the working-class movement. The Conference decided in favour of united All-Russian Party work to guide the actions of the working class on a country-wide scale.

Lenin's report on the Central Committee activity summarised what had been done since the Prague Conference in 1912. In his report on the Vienna International Socialist Congress Lenin proposed sending as many delegates as possible from both legal and illegal organisations, and suggested the holding of a Party congress at the same time as the International Congress. The Conference ended with Lenin's closing speech.

The minutes of the Conference at Poronin have not been found. The resolutions were published as a separate pamphlet under the title *Notification and Resolutions of the Summer, 1913, Joint Conference of the Central Committee of the R.S.D.L.P. and Party Officials*, issued abroad by the Central Committee. For reasons of secrecy some of the resolutions were not printed in full; omitted were point 6 of the resolution on the strike movement and points 1-5 of the resolution on the Party press. The full texts of the resolutions were published illegally in a mimeographed edition. p. 417

120 It was intended to hold the Party congress at the same time as the International Socialist Congress, which would have made it easier to keep secret the preparations for calling it. Intensive preparations for the congress were made during the spring and summer of 1914, but owing to the outbreak of war the congress was not held.   p. 421

[121] The newspaper referred to was *Nash Put* (*Our Path*) published in Moscow from August 25 to September 12 (September 7-25), 1913. The paper was launched on Lenin's proposal and under his guidance; Lenin sent his articles simultaneously to *Pravda* and to *Nash Put*. Among the contributors to *Nash Put* were Maxim Gorky, the Bolshevik deputies to the Fourth Duma, Demyan Bedny, M. S. Olminsky and I. I. Skvortsov-Stepanov. The newspaper was popular among the workers and received immense help from them; 395 groups of workers supported the paper by monetary collections. Its daily circulation was from 17,000 to 20,000 copies.

The newspaper was persistently persecuted by the police and finally suppressed; only 16 issues appeared. Moscow workers responded to the suppression of *Nash Put* with mass strikes in protest against the persecution of the working-class press. They did not, however, succeed in re-starting the paper.   p. 423

[122] The *Central Organ of the R.S.D.L.P.*, the newspaper *Sotsial-Demokrat*, began appearing illegaly in February 1908. The first issue was printed in Russia but owing to the arrest of the editors and destruction of the printing-press the paper was moved out of the country—first to Paris and then to Geneva. Altogether 58 issues appeared.

In accordance with a decision of the Central Committee of the R.S.D.L.P. the Editorial Board was composed of representatives of the Bolsheviks, Mensheviks and Polish Social-Democrats. The newspaper printed Lenin's articles giving guidance to the Party. On the Editorial Board Lenin conducted a struggle for a consistently Bolshevik line. Some of the editors (Kamenev and Zinoviev) adopted a line of conciliation towards the liquidators and attempted to prevent Lenin's political line from being implemented. The Mensheviks Martov and Dan sabotaged the work of the Central Organ Editorial Board and at the same time openly defended liquidationism in the newspaper *Golos Sotsial-Demokrata* (*Voice of a Social-Democrat*). Lenin's implacable struggle against the liquidators led to Martov and Dan's resigning from the Editorial Board in June 1911. From December 1911 *Sotsial-Demokrat* was edited by Lenin.

In 1912 and 1913 the paper appeared with big intervals between issues, only 6 issues appearing in those years. After the outbreak of the First World War *Sotsial-Demokrat* was published more regularly, the last issue appearing in Geneva on January 18 (31), 1917.   p. 424

[123] The subsection referred to was that of a resolution on "The Social-Democratic Group in the Duma" adopted by the Fifth (All-Russian) Conference of the R.S.D.L.P. in 1908. Lenin's draft for this subsection was adopted by the Conference with some amendments that spoiled the original formulation (the conditions under which voting was permissible for items of expenditure on cultural requirements were less definite in the resolution than in Lenin's draft). This part of the resolution on "Social-Democratic

Activities in the Duma" was confirmed in a new, improved version by the Poronin (Summer) Conference.   p. 424

[124] The congresses referred to are the Fifth (London) Congress of the R.S.D.L.P. in 1907 and the International Social Congress at Stuttgart in the same year; the resolutions were directed against the opportunist principle of trade union "neutrality"   p. 426

[125] The resolution refers here to the decision adopted by the liquidators' August Conference in 1912 to the effect that "cultural-national autonomy" was compatible with the Programme of the R.S.D.L.P.   p. 427

[126] *Zavety* (*Testament*)—a legal Socialist-Revolutionary literary and political monthly published in St. Petersburg from April 1912 to July 1914.   p. 432

[127] *Rodichev, F. M.*—a landowner from Tver Gubernia, one of the organisers and most active members of the Cadet Party.   p. 440

[128] The text of the *"Declaration"* was worked out by Lenin together with the Bolshevik deputies to the Duma at the Poronin (Summer) Conference.

At the first meeting of the Social-Democratic Duma group on October 16 (29), 1913, at the beginning of the second session of the Fourth Duma, the Bolshevik deputies submitted to the Menshevik deputies an ultimatum in which they demanded equal rights for the "six" and the "seven" The Bolshevik deputies left the meeting when no satisfactory answer was forthcoming. On October 18 (31), the "Declaration" was published in *Za Pravdu* over the signatures of the Bolshevik deputies accompanied by an appeal to workers to discuss the demand made by the "six" of the "seven" and give support to the worker-deputies in re-establishing the unity of the Social-Democratic Duma group.   p. 446

[129] In sending this *"Material"* to the newspaper *Za Pravdu*, Lenin proposed that the Sunday issue of the paper contain a separate leaflet dealing exclusively with the campaign to support the Bolshevik "six" When Lenin heard that the issue containing the article had been confiscated he proposed that the editors reprint it in the following issues. The article was not, however, published again in the paper. It was reprinted in 1914 in the symposium *Marxism and Liquidationism* under the heading "Material on the History of the Formation of the Russian Social-Democratic Workers' Group in the Duma", and added to it was a section entitled "Workers' Comment on the Formation of the Russian Social-Democratic Workers' Group in the State Duma"   p. 458

[130] *Zvezda* (*The Star*)—a Bolshevik legal newspaper, the immediate predecessor of *Pravda*; it was published in St. Petersburg from December 16 (29). 1910 to April 22 (May 5), 1912 (it was at first a

weekly but from January 1912 it appeared twice a week and from
March three times a week). On February 26 (March 10), 1912,
Nevskaya Zvezda (The Neva Star) No. 1 appeared simultaneously
with *Zvezda* and when the latter was suppressed became its
successor. The last, twenty-seventh issue of *Nevskaya Zvezda*
appeared on October 5 (18), 1912.

Up to the autumn of 1911 the pro-Party Mensheviks (Plekhanov's
group) contributed to *Zvezda*. Lenin guided the work of the paper
(from abroad) ideologically, about fifty of his articles being published in *Zvezda* and *Nevskaya Zvezda*.

Zvezda contained an extensive section "Correspondence from
Workers" and maintained regular contact with workers. The circulation of some issues reached 50,000-60,000 copies.

The newspaper was constantly subjected to government persecution; of 96 issues (*Zvezda* and *Nevskaya Zvezda*) 39 were confiscated
and fines were imposed on ten others. *Zvezda* prepared the way for
the publication of the Bolshevik daily *Pravda*; *Pravda* No. 1 appeared on the day *Zvezda* was suppressed by the government. p. 463

[131] *Gorodskoye Dyelo (Urban Affairs)*—a Cadet fortnightly devoted to
questions of municipal economy and administration; it was published in St. Petersburg from 1909 to 1918.   p. 475

[132] This article was written in answer to a slanderous version of the
split in the Russian Social-Democratic Duma group that was published unsigned in the German Social-Democratic *Leipziger Volkszeitung* on November 15 (N.S.), 1913.

Lenin tried to acquaint the International Social-Democratic
movement, and especially the German Social-Democrats, with the
true state of affairs in the working-class movement in Russia, but
the opportunist leadership of the German Social-Democratic Party
did not print articles by Bolsheviks in *Vorwärts*, its central organ.
Leipziger Volkszeitung alone published the article after a long
delay, which it explained as due to lack of space and "other reasons".   p. 480

[133] *Volnaya Mysl (Free Thought)*—one of the names under which the
Left-Narodnik (S. R.) legal newspaper *Zhivaya Mysl (Living
Thought)* was published; the paper appeared in St. Petersburg from
August 1913 to July 1914 and frequently changed its name. p. 485

[134] *Royal-Prussian socialism* is the name Marx and Engels gave to the
policy of conciliation with Bismarck's government, a policy pursued by Lassalle and by his successor Schweitzer, editor of the Las-
sallean newspaper *Sozialdemokrat*.   p. 490

[135] The differences of opinion between the Executive Committee
of the Social-Democratic Party of Poland and Lithuania and the
Warsaw organisation, the strongest and most consistently revolutionary Polish Social-Democratic organisation, arose in 1908 at the
Sixth Congress of that party. The line of behaviour of the Executive

Committee headed by Rosa Luxemburg, L. Tyszka and others was
sharply criticised at the Congress; the Board was criticised for its
unprincipled position in the R.S.D.L.P., for not allowing criticism from the local organisations, etc. The Congress passed a vote
of no confidence in the Executive.

The Executive, in 1912, announced the dissolution of the Warsaw Committee on the grounds of its "schismatic" activities, accused
it falsely of connections with the secret police, and established
a new Warsaw Committee from among its own supporters. From
this moment the Social-Democratic Party of Poland and Lithuania
was split into two.

Lenin kept track of the struggle within the Polish Social-Democratic Party. He published a number of articles in both the Russian
and Polish Party press on the split in the Polish Social-Democratic Party and spoke in the International Socialist Bureau
against the attacks of the Executive on the Warsaw organisation.

The "schismatics" agreed with the tactical line of the Bolsheviks
on a number of points and tried to establish organisational ties
with the Bolsheviks despite their differences on the national question (the "schismatics" adopted the semi-Menshevik position of
Rosa Luxemburg and her followers). The "schismatics" took part in
the Poronin Conference (see Note 119). During the First World War
the two divisions of the Polish Social-Democrats formed a single
party with an internationalist platform. In December 1918 the Social-Democratic Party of Poland and Lithuania together with the
Left elements of the Polish Socialist Party established the Communist Workers' Party of Poland.   p. 495

[136] *The International Socialist Bureau* was the executive body of the
Second International established by a decision of the Paris Congress in 1900.   p. 496

[137] Lenin here refers to a passage in Engels's "Critique of the Draft
Social-Democratic Programme of 1891". (Engels, "Zur Kritik des
sozial-demokratischen Programmentwurfes 1891", *Die Neue Zeit*,
1901-02, 20 Jhrg. 1. Band, Stuttgart, 1902.)   p. 500

[138] The lectures here referred to are those Lenin delivered in 1913 in
Switzerland. (See Note 85.)   p. 501

[139] *J. K. (J. Karski)*—pseudonym of J. J. Marchlewski.   p. 509

[140] The *Beilis case*—the trial of the Jew Beilis, organised for provocative
purposes by the tsarist government in 1913 in Kiev. Beilis was
falsely accused of the ritual murder of a Christian boy, Yushchin-
sky (the murder was actually committed by the Black Hundreds).
The tsarist government staged this trial to stir up anti-Semitism and
make use of anti-Jewish pogroms to divert the attention of the
masses from the revolutionary movement that was growing throughout the country. The trial aroused public indignation; in a number
of towns workers' demonstrations of protest were held. Beilis was
acquitted.   p. 512

141 The *Dreyfus case*—the trial in 1894 of Dreyfus, a Jewish General Staff officer who was falsely accused of espionage and high treason; the trial was staged for provocative purposes by French reactionary militarists. A Court Martial sentenced Dreyfus to imprisonment for life. The strong public movement for a review of the case led to a sharp conflict between republican and monarchist forces in France. Dreyfus was acquitted in 1906.

Lenin described the Dreyfus case as "one of the many thousands of fraudulent tricks of the reactionary military caste". p. 513

142 See K. Marx and F. Engels, "Critique of the Gotha Programme", *Selected Works*, Vol. II, Moscow, 1958, p. 33. p. 514

143 This letter was addressed by Lenin to the editors of *Za Pravdu* when he received the first report of the decisions of the December session (1913) of the International Socialist Bureau on the unification of the R.S.D.L.P.

The question was raised by Rosa Luxemburg (member of the Bureau from the Social-Democratic Party of Poland and Lithuania) in support of the Russian liquidators, who had been defeated in their struggle against the Bolsheviks. At the session on December 14 (N.S.), 1913, the resolution proposed by Kautsky was adopted; in this resolution the Executive Committee of the Bureau was instructed, allegedly for the purpose of re-establishing the unity of the R.S.D.L.P., to organise an exchange of opinion "between all factions of the working-class movement in Russia".

At the conference held in July 1914 in Brussels in accordance with the decision of the Bureau, the leaders of the Second International, on the pretext of "reconciling" the Bolsheviks and liquidators, demanded that the Bolsheviks cease their criticism of the liquidators; the Bolsheviks refused, and continued their struggle against the liquidators. p. 516

144 *Burenin, V. P.*—staff employee of the reactionary newspaper *Novoye Vremya (New Times)*; engaged in libelling and besmearing all progressive social and political trends. Lenin uses the name as a synonym for those who conduct polemics by dishonest methods.

Gamma—pseudonym of L. Martov. p. 522

145 *Novaya Likvidatorskaya Gazeta (New Liquidators' Gazette)*— Lenin's ironical appelation for the Menshevik *Novaya Rabochaya Gazeta (New Workers' Newspaper)*. p. 522

146 This refers to a committee to assist the Social-Democratic group in the Third Duma in preparing bills for the Duma; it was set up in Paris in 1909, both Bolsheviks and Mensheviks participating. The committee had subcommittees to elaborate bills on the eight-hour day, on the right to strike and on trade unions. The bill on strikes was drawn up by the Menshevik Dan; it included a point recognising the criminality of participation in strikes. When the bill was discussed by the committee Lenin spoke vehemently against this point. p. 522

[147] *Shlyakhi (Paths)*—nationalist organ of the Ukrainian Students' Union; it was published in Lvov from April 1913 to March 1914. p. 525

[148] *Vorwärts (Forward)*—the central organ of the German Social-Democratic Party; from 1876 onwards it was edited by Wilhelm Liebknecht and others. Engels conducted a struggle in the paper's columns against all manifestations of opportunism. From the middle nineties, after the death of Engels, *Vorwärts* regularly published articles by the opportunists dominant in the German Social-Democratic Party and in the Second International. During the First World War *Vorwärts* adopted a social-chauvinist position. p. 529

[149] Samoilov made his statement at a session of the State Duma on November 26 (December 9), 1913, during the discussion on a bill to increase the salaries of teachers of religion in agrarian schools. p. 532

[150] For Lenin's characterisation of Peredonov see the article "The Question of Ministry of Education Policy". (See p. 143 of this volume.) p. 533

[151] Lenin wrote this article for the pocket calendar *Sputnik Rabochego (Worker's Handbook) for 1914*, issued by the Priboi Party Publishing House in December 1913. It contained essential information on labour legislation in Russia, the Russian and international working-class movement, political parties, associations and unions, the press, etc. The *Worker's Handbook* was sequestered but the issue was sold in one day before the police could confiscate it. When Lenin received a copy of the *Handbook* he wrote in a letter to Inessa Armand that 5,000 copies had already been sold. A second, amended edition was published in February 1914 with deletions and amendments made for purposes of censorship and with a list of books for self-education added. Altogether 20,000 copies of the *Handbook* were sold. p. 534

[152] For details of the strike at the Morozov mills see "Explanation of the Law on Fines Imposed on Factory Workers", V. I. Lenin, *Collected Works*, Vol. 2, pp. 29-72. p. 535

[153] The work referred to is Stalin's *Marxism and the National Question*. p. 539

[154] *Struvism*—a variety of the bourgeois distortion of Marxism.
Struve, P. B.—Russian bourgeois liberal, exponent of legal Marxism in the nineties. He later became one of the leaders of the Cadet Party and after the October Revolution, as a white émigré, was an inveterate enemy of the Soviet Union. p. 541

[155] Lenin here refers to Plekhanov's article "Draft Programme of the Russian Social-Democratic Party" published in *Zarya* No. 4, in August 1902.
Zarya (Dawn)—a Marxist scientific and political journal published in Stuttgart in 1901-02 by the editors of *Iskra*. Four numbers

appeared in three issues. The Lenin writings published in *Zarya* were: "Casual Notes" (Vol. 4), "The Persecutors of the Zemstvo and the Hannibals of Liberalism" (Vol. 5), the first four chapters of "The Agrarian Question and the 'Critics of Marx'" (published under the title "The 'Critics' on the Agrarian Question" [ibid.]), "Review of Home Affairs" (ibid.) and "The Agrarian Programme of Russian Social-Democracy" (Vol. 6).   p. 544

156 This refers to §8 of the Programme of the R.S.D.L.P. adopted at the Second Congress of the Party.   p. 549

157 The article "The Marx-Engels Correspondence" here published was the beginning of an extensive article that Lenin planned at the time of the publication of the German four-volume edition of the Marx-Engels Correspondence in September 1913. Lenin made a deep study of the correspondence; the Institute of Marxism-Leninism has in its possession a thick notebook (76 pages) in which Lenin summarised the letters and copied extracts from them.

Lenin intended to publish "The Marx-Engels Correspondence" in the magazine *Prosveshcheniye* in 1914, and an announcement to that effect was printed in *Proletarskaya Pravda* No. 7 on December 14, 1913; the article, however, remained unfinished and was first published in *Pravda* on November 28, 1920, on the occasion of the hundredth anniversary of Engels's birth. On this occasion Lenin added a subtitle "Engels as One of the Founders of Communism" and provided a footnote to the title: "The beginning of an unfinished article written in 1913 or early 1914".   p. 552

158 Marx-Engels Gesamtausgabe, dritte Abteilung, Band I, Marx-Engels Verlag GmbH, Berlin, 1929, S. 1 u. 20-21.   p. 555

159 Marx-Engels, *Selected Correspondence*, Moscow, 1955, pp. 29-31.   p. 555

160 Marx-Engels Gesamtausgabe, dritte Abteilung, Band I, Marx-Engels Verlag GmbH, Berlin, 1929, S. 3.   p. 556

161 Marx-Engels Gesamtausgabe, dritte Abteilung , Band I, Marx-Engels Verlag GmbH, Berlin, 1929, S. 14.   p. 556

162 *Popular Socialists*—a legal petty-bourgeois party formed in 1906 by the separation of part of the Right wing of the Socialist-Revolutionaries. The demands put forward by the party did not go beyond a constitutional monarchy.   p. 556

163 Engels an das Kommunistische Korrespondenz-Komitee in Brüssel; Paris, 1846, September 16. [Marx-Engels Gesamtausgabe, dritte Abteilung, Band I, Marx-Engels Verlag GmbH, Berlin, 1929, S. 34.]   p. 557

164 See K. Marx and F. Engels, *Selected Correspondence*, Moscow, 1955, pp. 35-36.   p. 558

THE LIFE AND WORK
OF
V. I. LENIN

Outstanding Dates
(March-December 1913)

March-April	Lenin lives in Cracow.
March 22 *(April 4)*	Lenin's "Big Achievement of the Chinese Republic" published in *Pravda* No. 68.
March 23 *(April 5)*	In a letter to *Pravda* editors Lenin indicates how the six Bolshevik deputies to the Fourth State Duma are to be supported in their struggle against the seven Mensheviks, gives instructions on the campaign to gain subscribers for *Pravda* and on expansion of the publication of illegal literature.
March 26 *(April 8)*	"Old Problems and the Senile Decay of Liberalism" published in *Pravda* No. 71.
Not earlier than *March 26* *(April 8)*	Lenin writes "The 'Oil Hunger'" when the question of the oil syndicate is being debated in the Duma.
March 27 *(April 9)*	"The Cadet Assembly Bill" published as the leading article of *Pravda* No. 72.
March 29 *(April 11)*	"The Balkan War and Bourgeois Chauvinism" published in *Pravda* No. 74.
March-April	Lenin writes "Conversation".
April 5 (18)	Lenin lectures in Cracow on "Contemporary Russia and the Working-Class Movement"; a report of the lecture is published in the Polish newspaper *Naprzód* No. 92.
April 6 (19)	Issue No. 3 of the journal *Prosveshcheniye* devoted to Thirtieth Anniversary of the death of Karl Marx carries Lenin's "Three Sources and Three Component Parts of Marxism".
April 11 (24)	"Who Stands to Gain?" published in *Pravda* No. 84.
April 12 (25)	"In Britain" published in *Pravda* No. 85.

April 12 (25)- *June 2 (15)*	Series of articles under the general heading "Controversial Issues" published in *Pravda* Nos. 85, 95, 110, 122, 124 and 126.
April 13 (26)	Lenin lectures in Leipzig on "Social Revival in Russia and the Tasks of the Social-Democrats".
April (later *than 13 [26])*	Lenin writes an article in which he criticises Potresov for his attacks on Plekhanov's anti-liquidationist position.
April 14 (27)	"Civilised Europeans and Savage Asians" published in *Pravda* No. 87.
April (earlier *than 18 [May* *1])*	Lenin sends a draft speech on the national question to G. I. Petrovsky for him to read in the Duma.
	Lenin sends May Day leaflets to *Pravda*.
April 18 *(May 1)*	Lenin attends workers' May Day meeting in Cracow.
April 20 *(May 3)*	"Merchant Accountancy" published in *Pravda* No. 90.
April 21 *(May 4)*	Lenin sends a letter to Bolshevik deputies to the Fourth State Duma asking for new bills and Duma reference material.
	"A Great Technical Achievement" published in *Pravda* No. 91.
April 23 *(May 6)*	"A Few Words on Results and Facts" published in the special issue of *Pravda* (No. 92), devoted to the paper's first anniversary.
April 23-24 *(May 6-7)*	Lenin and Krupskaya move for the summer to the village of Poronin (near Cracow).
Not earlier than *April 26 (May* *9)*	In a letter to Maxim Gorky, Lenin asks him to write an article or story for the May issue of *Prosveshcheniye*.
April 27 and *May 1 (May 10* *and 14)*	"Significance of the Resettlement Scheme" published in *Pravda* Nos. 96 and 99.
April 29 *(May 12)*	Following the victory of the Bolsheviks at the elections to the Executive of the Metalworkers' Union, Lenin writes letter to *Pravda* concerning

the consolidation of the Union in the struggle against liquidationism and on aid for the periodical *Metallist*.

May 4 (17) Issue No. 4 of *Prosveshcheniye* is published carrying Lenin's "*Vekhi* Contributors and Nationalism".

"The Liberals and Freedom for the Unions" appears as the leading article of *Pravda* No. 101.

May 5 (18) *Pravda* No. 102 carries two of Lenin's articles— "For the Attention of *Luch* and *Pravda* Readers" and "Twenty-Fifth Anniversary of the Death of Joseph Dietzgen".

May 7 (20) *Pravda* No. 103 carries two of Lenin's articles— "The Bourgeoisie and Peace" (leading article) and "The Awakening of Asia".

May 8 (21) *Pravda* No. 104 carries the article "Separatists in Russia and Separatists in Austria".

May 9 (22) "The Resettlement Scheme Again" published in *Pravda* No. 105.

Not later than May 10 (23) Lenin sends draft speech to St. Petersburg to be read in State Duma by Bolshevik deputy during 1913 budget discussion.

May 10 (23) "The Working Class and the National Question" published as the leading article of *Pravda* No. 106.

May (not earlier than 13 [26]) and June 3 (16) In letters to *Pravda* editors Lenin congratulates staff on improvements in paper and gives practical advice on how "to obtain hundred-thousand circulation"; he demands correction of mistakes made.

May 14 (27) "British Socialist Party Conference" published in *Pravda* No. 109.

May 16 (29) "Is the Condition of the Peasants Improving or Worsening?" published in *Pravda* No. 111.

May 18 (31) "Backward Europe and Advanced Asia" published in *Pravda* No. 113.

May 19 (June 1) "A Discreditable Role!" published in *Pravda* No. 114.

May 21 (June 3)	*Pravda* No. 115 publishes the articles—"The Land Question Settled—Landowner Fashion" (leading article), "Armaments and Capitalism" and the note "Helplessness and Confusion".
May (before 25 [June 7])	Lenin writes the Draft Platform for the Fourth Congress of Social-Democrats of the Latvian Area. The Draft Platform was published separately in Lettish in November 1913 as a reprint from *Biletens* No. 8 (issued by the Bureau of Groups of Social-Democrats of the Latvian Area Abroad) and in *Biletens* No. 9-10.
May-June	Lenin takes charge of the organisation and enrolment to the Party school at Poronin; draws up the curriculum; writes to Plekhanov and Gorky inviting them to lecture at the school and arrange talks with students. "Factory Owners on Workers' Strikes" published in *Pravda* Nos. 123, 126, 127 and 131 dated May 30, June 2, 5 and 9.
Beginning of June	Lenin writes "An Incorrect Appraisal (*Luch* on Maklakov)".
June 1 (14)	"Frank Speeches by a Liberal" published in *Pravda* No. 125.
Not later than June 2 (15)	Lenin writes draft speech for Duma Deputy A. E. Badayev "The Question of Ministry of Education Policy".
June 3 (16)	Lenin writes letter to M. S. Olminsky (Vitimsky) and a second letter to *Pravda* editors on "The Question of Mr. Bogdanov and the *Vperyod* Group"; sends note for *Pravda* against Bogdanov.
June 5 (18)	"Has *Pravda* Given Proof of Bundist Separatism?" published in *Pravda* No. 127.
June 6 (19)	"Liberals as Defenders of the Fourth Duma" published as the leading article of *Pravda* No. 128.
Not later than June 7 (20)	Lenin writes draft speech for Duma Deputy N. R. Shagov "The Question of the (General) Agrarian Policy of the Present Government".
June 7 (20)	"Capitalism and Taxation" published in *Pravda* No. 129.

June 8 (21)	Issue No. 5 of *Prosveshcheniye* publishes "Liberal and Marxist Conceptions of the Class Struggle".
	"Economic Strikes in 1912 and in 1905" published in *Pravda* No. 130.
June 9 (22)	"The Growth of Capitalist Wealth" published in *Pravda* No. 131.
June 9-11 (22-24)	Lenin takes N. K. Krupskaya to Berne for her to obtain medical treatment; on the way from Poronin to Berne they visit Vienna.
June 11 (24)	"The Peasantry and the Working Class" published in *Pravda* No. 132.
June 12 (25)	The articles "Child Labour in Peasant Farming" and "The Results of Strikes in 1912 as Compared with Those of the Past" published in *Pravda* No. 133.
June 13 (26)	"In Australia" published in *Pravda* No. 134.
June 15 (28)	*Sotsial-Demokrat* No. 31 carries Lenin's "May Day Action by the Revolutionary Proletariat" as leading article and also "Notes of a Publicist".
	"Apropos of One Untruth. Letter to the Editors" published in *Pravda* No. 136.
June 16 (29)	"The Working Class and Neomalthusianism" published in *Pravda* No. 137.
June 17 (30)	In a letter addressed to N. I. Podvoisky in St. Petersburg, Lenin outlines for the Bolshevik Duma deputies their tactics in respect of the Menshevik deputies (in connection with the preparation of the Duma group's report on its activities).
June 20 (July 3)	"Liberal Appeals to Support the Fourth Duma" published in *Pravda* No. 139.
June 23 (July 6)	"Bourgeois Financial Magnates and Politicians" published in *Pravda* No. 142.
June, before 26 (before July 9)	Lenin compiles his "Theses on the National Question" and a plan for a lecture on the subject.
June 26 (July 9)	The St. Petersburg court passes a decision on the destruction of Lenin's pamphlet: "*When You Hear the Judgement of a Fool....* (From the Notes of a Social-Democratic Publicist)", St. Petersburg, 1907.

Lenin delivers a lecture on the national question in Zurich and takes notes of the discussion.

June 27
(July 10)
Lenin lectures in Geneva on "Social-Democracy and the National Question" and takes notes of the discussion.

June 28
(July 11)
Lenin lectures in Lausanne on the national question.

June 30
(July 13)
Lenin lectures in Berne on the national question and takes notes of the discussion.

Beginning of
July
Lenin writes "Instructive Speeches".

July 2 (15)
Pravda No. 149 publishes "Pictures from Life".

July 5 (18)
Pravda No. 151 publishes "The Adjourned Duma and the Embarrassed Liberals" as the leading article. Beginning with this issue *Pravda* is suppressed by the tsarist government.

July 12 (25)
On the suppression of *Pravda*, Lenin writes to Maxim Gorky suggesting a meeting between them on Lenin's return journey from Berne to Poronin to discuss the possibility of Gorky's helping restart the publication of a Bolshevik newspaper.

July 13 (26)
"Fifth International Congress Against Prostitution" published in *Rabochaya Pravda* No. 1.

July 16 (29)
The articles "Word and Deed" (leading article), "Cadets on the Question of the Ukraine", "Fresh Data on German Political Parties", and "Exposure of the British Opportunists" published in *Rabochaya Pravda* No. 3.

July 17 (30)
"The Ideas of an Advanced Capitalist" published in *Rabochaya Pravda* No. 4.

July 18 (31)
"What Can Be Done for Public Education" and "Petty Production in Agriculture" published in *Rabochaya Pravda* No. 5.

July 21
(August 3)
"A 'Fashionable' Branch of Industry" published in *Rabochaya Pravda* No. 8.

Lenin reports on "The State of Affairs in the Party" at the Second Conference of R.S.D.L.P. Organisation Abroad in Berne.

July 22-24 (August 4-6)   Lenin and Krupskaya return to Poronin from Berne.

July 24 (August 6)   "Dead Liquidationism and the Living *Rech*" published in *Rabochaya Pravda* No. 10.

July 26 (August 8)   "Mobilisation of Allotment Lands" published in *Rabochaya Pravda* No. 12.

July 27 (August 9)   Lenin guides the conference in Poronin of members of the Central Committee of the R.S.D.L.P., which discussed the situation in the Party and current tasks, the Duma Social-Democratic group, the Party school and the Party press, in particular the question of publishing a Bolshevik newspaper in Moscow.

Lenin participates in a conference of Central Committee members on the question of co-opting new members to the Central Committee and the selection of "representatives" or "agents" of the Central Committee.

August 3 (16)   "How Can Per Capita Consumption in Russia Be Increased?" published in *Severnaya Pravda* No. 3.

August 4 (17)   Lenin's condolences on the occasion of the death of August Bebel, sent in the name of the Central Committee of the R.S.D.L.P., published in the German newspaper *Vorwärts* No. 211.

August 8 (21)   Lenin's article "August Bebel" published in *Severnaya Pravda* No. 6.

August 11 (24)   "The Separation of Liberalism from Democracy" published in *Severnaya Pravda* No. 9 as the leading article.

In a letter addressed to S.G. Shahumyan Lenin asks for material on the national question and statistics on the Caucasian nationalities.

August 18 (31)   "A Fine Business!" and "The Nationalisation of Jewish Schools" published in *Severnaya Pravda* No. 14.

August 21 (September 3)	The St. Petersburg court passes a decision on the destruction of Lenin's pamphlet: "Martov's and Cherevanin's Pronouncements in the Bourgeois Press", St. Petersburg, 1906.
	"Iron on Peasant Farms" published in *Severnaya Pravda* No. 16.
August 24-October 25 (September 6-November 7)	"Metalworkers' Strikes in 1912" published in the journal *Metallist* Nos. 7, 8, and 10.
August 27 and 28 (September 9 and 10)	"The Russian Bourgeoisie and Russian Reformism" published in *Severnaya Pravda* No. 21 and *Nash Put* No. 3.
August 28 and 29 (September 10 and 11)	"The Role of Social Estates and Classes in the Liberation Movement" published in *Severnaya Pravda* No. 22 and *Nash Put* No. 4.
August 29 and 30 (September 11 and 12)	"Class War in Dublin" and "New Land 'Reform' Measures" published in *Severnaya Pravda* Nos. 23 and 24 and *Nash Put* Nos. 4 and 5.
September 1 (14)	Lenin instructs a representative of the Priboi publishers on arranging the publication of legal Party literature and a journal on questions of insurance; he also conferred with a representative of *Prosveshcheniye* on the further work of that journal.
	"The Merchant Salazkin and the Writer F. D." published in *Severnaya Pravda* No. 26.
September 3 (16)	"The Struggle for Marxism" and "A Week After the Dublin Massacre" published in *Severnaya Pravda* No. 27; the latter article also appeared in *Nash Put* No. 8.
September 4 (17)	"Questions of Principle in Politics" published in *Severnaya Pravda* No. 28 and *Nash Put* No. 9.
September 5 and 7 (18 and 20)	"Liberals and Democrats on the Language Question" published in *Severnaya Pravda* No. 29 and *Nash Put* No. 12.
September 6 (19)	The St. Petersburg court passes a decision on the destruction of Lenin's pamphlet: "The Social-Democrats and the Duma Elections", St. Petersburg, 1907.

September 8 and 10 (21 and 23)	"The Language of Figures" published in *Nash Put* Nos. 13 and 14.
September 11, 12 and 14 (24, 25 and 27)	"Bourgeois Gentlemen on 'Family' Farming" and "Harry Quelch" published in *Nash Put* Nos. 15 and 16, and *Pravda Truda* Nos. 1 and 4.
September 12 (25)	"Marxism and Reformism" published in *Pravda Truda* No. 2.
September 13 (26)	"The Land Question and the Rural Poor", "How Does Bishop Nikon Defend the Ukrainians?", "Notes of a Publicist" published in *Pravda Truda* No. 3.
September 17 (30)	"Civilised Barbarism" published in *Pravda Truda* No. 6.
September 23-October 1 (October 6-14)	Lenin directs the work of the "summer" or "August" Joint Conference of the Central Committee of the R.S.D.L.P. and Party officials at Poronin; writes and edits the draft resolutions adopted by the Conference.
September 23-24 (October 6-7)	Lenin conducts a private meeting with the Bolshevik Duma deputies on questions of work in the Duma.
September 25-October 1 (October 8-14)	Lenin takes the chair at the Poronin Conference; delivers reports on the work of the Central Committee, the national question and the International Socialist Congress; takes part in the discussion on a number of questions.
October 1 (14)	Lenin guides a meeting of the Central Committee which discusses practical steps to be taken by the Bolshevik Duma deputies in respect of the Menshevik deputies.
September 26 (October 9)	"The Black Hundreds" (leading article) and "Russian Government and Russian Reforms" published in *Pravda Truda* No. 14.
September 29 (October 12)	Issue No. 9 of *Prosveshcheniye* carries Lenin's "How Vera Zasulich Demolishes Liquidationism".
October 1 (14)	"There's a Trudovik for You" published in *Pravda Truda* No. 18.

October 4 (17)	"Bewildered Non-Party People" published in *Za Pravdu* No. 3.
October 7 (20)	Lenin and Krupskaya return to Cracow from Poronin.
October 12 (25)	"The Liberals and the Land Problem in Britain" published in *Za Pravdu* No. 8.
October 17 (30)	"A Weak Defence of a Weak Case" published in *Za Pravdu* No. 12.
October 18 (31)	*Za Pravdu* No. 13 publishes the declaration, written by Lenin, which the Bolshevik deputies presented to the Menshevik Duma deputies.
October, not earlier than 20 (November 2)	In a letter to the *Za Pravdu* editors, Lenin tells the Bolshevik Duma deputies how they should act in the event of the Menshevik "seven" announcing that they are the Social-Democratic group in the State Duma.
October 25 (November 7)	"The Duma 'Seven'" published in *Za Pravdu* No. 19.
October 26 (November 8)	"The Liberal Bourgeoisie and the Liquidators" published in *Za Pravdu* No. 20.
October, before 27 (November 9)	Lenin instructs the *Za Pravdu* editors to organise a newspaper campaign in support of the Bolshevik "six".
October 29 (November 11)	"Capitalism and Workers' Immigration" and "Material on the Conflict Within the Social-Democratic Duma Group" published in *Za Pravdu* No. 22.
October 30 (November 12)	"A Cadet Property-Owner Argues 'According to Marx'" published in *Za Pravdu* No. 23.
End of October	In a letter to the *Za Pravdu* editors Lenin offers his congratulations on the victory over the disorganisers of the Party, the Menshevik "seven" and on the formation of the Social-Democratic workers' group in the Duma.
October-December.	Lenin writes his "Critical Remarks on the National Question" published in Nos. 10, 11 and 12 of *Prosveshcheniye.*

Beginning of November	Lenin writes to Gorky criticising his justification of god-building.
	Lenin writes: "The Working-Class Masses and the Working-Class Intelligentsia" and "The Split in the Russian Social-Democratic Duma Group", the latter published in the German newspaper *Leipziger Volkszeitung* No. 298.
November 13 (26)	"The Left Narodniks on the Controversies Among the Marxists" published in *Za Pravdu* No. 34.
November 15 (28)	"The Agrarian Question and the Present Situation in Russia", "Two Methods of Controversy and Struggle", and "Would-Be 'Uniters'" published in *Za Pravdu* No. 36.
Middle of November	In a letter to Maxim Gorky Lenin exposes the reactionary nature of god-building and criticises Gorky's views on that subject.
November 23 (December 6)	Lenin writes to S. G. Shahumyan on the national question.
November 28 (December 11)	"'Cultural-National' Autonomy" and "Coteries Abroad and Russian Liquidators" published in *Za Pravdu* No. 46.
November 29 (December 12)	Lenin sends "Notes for a Report to Local Branches" to St. Petersburg; they dealt with the Poronin (Summer) Conference of the Central Committee of the R.S.D.L.P. and Party Officials.
	"The Cadet Maklakov and the Social-Democrat Petrovsky", and "Zabern" published in *Za Pravdu* No. 47.
December 2 (15)	Lenin writes to the *Za Pravdu* editors on "The Question of Bureau Decisions".
December 3 (16)	"Working-Class Unity" published in *Za Pravdu* No. 50.
December 7 (20)	"A Stubborn Defence of a Bad Case" published in *Proletarskaya Pravda* No. 1.
December 11 (24)	"The Cadets and 'The Right of Nations to Self-Determination'" published in *Proletarskaya Pravda* No. 4.

December 13 (26)	"A Good Resolution and a Bad Speech" published in *Proletarskaya Pravda* No. 6.
December 14 (27)	"The Nationality of Pupils in Russian Schools" published in *Proletarskaya Pravda* No. 7.
	The pocket calendar *Worker's Handbook for 1914* published with Lenin's article "Strikes in Russia".
December 15 (28)	"The National Programme of the R.S.D.L.P." published in *Sotsial-Demokrat* No. 32.
	"Kautsky's Unpardonable Error" published in *Proletarskaya Pravda* No. 8.
December 17 (30)	"Once More on the Segregation of the Schools According to Nationality" published in *Proletarskaya Pravda* No. 9.
December 18 (31)	Lenin's note on "Mr. Gorsky and a Certain Latin Proverb" published in *Proletarskaya Pravda* No. 10.
End of the year	Lenin studies the four-volume edition of the Marx-Engels correspondence in German; makes notes, and copies extracts from the letters.
	Begins his article "The Marx-Engels Correspondence".